Danzón Days

MUSIC IN AMERICAN LIFE

*A list of books in the series appears
at the end of this book.*

Danzón Days

Age, Race, and Romance in Mexico

HETTIE MALCOMSON

Urbana, Chicago, and Springfield

Publication of this book was supported in part by the
University of Illinois Press Fund for Anthropology.

© 2023 by the Board of Trustees
of the University of Illinois
All rights reserved
1 2 3 4 5 C P 5 4 3 2 1
♾ This book is printed on acid-free paper.

Library of Congress Cataloging-in-Publication Data
Names: Malcomson, Hettie, author.
Title: Danzón days: age, race, and romance in Mexico
  / Hettie Malcomson.
Description: Urbana: University of Illinois Press,
  2023. | Series: Music in American life | Includes
  bibliographical references, filmography,
  discography, and index.
Identifiers: LCCN 2022042472 (print) | LCCN
  2022042473 (ebook) | ISBN 9780252045004
  (hardback) | ISBN 9780252087134 (paperback) |
  ISBN 9780252054273 (ebook)
Subjects: LCSH: Danzón (Dance)—Social aspects—
  Mexico—Veracruz (Veracruz-Llave) | Veracruz
  (Veracruz-Llave, Mexico)—Social life and
  customs—21st century | Veracruz (Veracruz-Llave,
  Mexico)—Race relations
Classification: LCC GV1796.D36 M35 2023 (print) |
  LCC GV1796.D36 (ebook) | DDC 792.80972/64—
  dc23/eng/20221116
LC record available at https://lccn.loc.gov/2022042472
LC ebook record available at https://lccn.loc.gov/2022042473

Danzón dedicado a ... Mónica

Contents

Acknowledgments ix

OPENING VIGNETTE. Gerardo, Elena, and Miguel 1

INTRODUCTION. Danzón, Veracruz, and Ambivalence 3

VIGNETTE ONE. Teresita 27

CHAPTER ONE. Racial Ambivalence: Veracruz,
Blackness, and Danzón 29

VIGNETTE TWO. Pancho 57

CHAPTER TWO. Ambivalent Nostalgia: Histories and
Memories of the Port and Its Danzón 59

VIGNETTE THREE. Renata 89

CHAPTER THREE. Elegant Moves: Modernist Aesthetics
and Danzón in Veracruz 91

VIGNETTE FOUR. Lulú and Antonio. 123

CHAPTER FOUR. Moves to Rescue: Reviving the Dance,
State Sponsorship, and Power............................... 125

VIGNETTE FIVE. Hettie and Uriel 161

CHAPTER FIVE. United in a Vipers' Nest: Group Dynamics,
Conviviality, and Rivalry.................................... 163

VIGNETTE SIX. Carmen and Ernesto 183

CHAPTER SIX. Loving Ambivalence: Dance Groups,
Amorous Encounters, and Aging Bodies 185

VIGNETTE SEVEN. Diana 207

Notes 209
Glossary 219
Select Discography 223
Select Filmography 225
Bibliography 227
Index 247

Acknowledgments

This book started life as a project on British new music composers funded by the UK Arts and Humanities Research Council. Then I fell in love. My new partner was about to finish a project in the UK and return to her country, Mexico. A choice was made: we would go there together and I would find an alternative topic. Shortly afterward, I bumped into David Lehmann, who, having seen María Novaro's 1991 film Danzón, suggested I do a project around this genre. Having lived in Ecuador in the 1980s, I spoke Spanish, and with three days to write another proposal, this project emerged. I was mentored by David and guided by my guardian angel, Henry Stobart. The focus was initially on standards and standardization, and I later reframed the material into its current form. This book is based on thousands of conversations I have had with people in Mexico, Cuba, the United Kingdom, and elsewhere; people who have contributed ideas, reflections, critiques, and refinements. I would like to thank everyone who helped with the project.

First, I am extremely grateful to all the people I interviewed, danced and musicked with, chatted to and hung out with in Veracruz, Mexico City, Guadalajara, Havana, and Matanzas, including Adán "El Muerto" Álvarez Garrido, Adolfina de Valdés, Alberto Corrales, Alejandro Aguilar Torres, Alicia Valdés Cantero, Antonia González de la Torre, Armando Valdés Abreu, Armida Applebaum de Nieto, Artemio "El de los Pies Descalzos" Uscanga Dorantes, Arturo "El Capullo" Sánchez Rivera, Arturo Márquez, Arturo Nuñez, Arturo Pitalúa, Arturo Sánchez Rivera, Aurelio Dalí Fernández, Benito Gutiérrez Antonio, Benjamín Bautista, Bernardo López García, Carlos López Contreras, Daniel "El Catrín" Rergis, Daniel Rosas Cruz, Diana Hernández Franco, Diego Pérez y Reyes, Efraín Sierra Hernández, Eliseo "Manzanita"

Matus Melenguez, Eliseo Díaz Vázquez, Eutiquio Madrigal Hernández, Fabiola Juárez Olvera, Felipe Urbán, Félix Rentería Hernández, Fidel Matus Maldonado, Frank Droeshoet Hernández, Gerardo Castro Pacheco, Gilberto Martínez Gallardo, Gonzalo Varela Palmeros, Guillermina Moreno Ruiz, Helio Orovio, Ignacio Durán, John Eichenour, Jesús Flores y Escalante, José "Pepe Luis" Rodríguez Ortega, José Dolores Mártir Velásquez, José Loyola Fernández, Juan Carreto, Juan García Patraca, Juan Medina, Longino Espíndola Jiménez, Lucia Fortuno, Manuel Méndez, María Emilia Pérez, María Novaro, Maru Ayala, Maximiliano Gutiérrez Orozco, Miguel Ángel Cisneros Sosa, Miguel Ángel Zamudio Abdalá, Miguel García Cortés, Mina Arreguín, Natalia Pineda Burgos, Óscar Garrido Pérez, Pablo Dueñas Herrera, Pablo Tapia, Pio Nieto González, Rafael Argumedo, Rafael Figueroa, René Varela Palmeros, Roberto Angoa Huerta, Roberto Romero Pérez, Rosa María Cruz Herrera, Ruby Eichenour, Santiago Cruz Hernández, Simón Jara Gámez, Víctor "El Toby" Escobar Bautista, Víctor Manuel Sánchez Marín, Yvonne Angoa Lara; and Amanda, Araceli, Aurelio, Catita, Cristina, Dionisio, Elsa, Eva, Gabriel, Joaquín, Jorge, Juan, Margarito, Marisela, Marta, Pablo, Pedro, Porfirio, Pilar, Raúl, Rafael, Sara, Susi, Teodora, Tomás, Toño, and Vicky. For support, joy, friendship, and advice, I would particularly like to thank Ciro Carlos Mizuno Guzmán, Margarita Castro, and Ricardo Cañas Montalvo, and also Dora Herrera de Cinta, Gonzalo Hernández Lara, Hipólito "Polo" González Peña, Memo Salamanca, and Silverio López Contreras. Without all of you, this book could not be.

Second, I want to thank my core intellectual support team: David Lehmann for mentoring the project, his careful editing and especially for his encyclopedic knowledge of Latin America; Henry Stobart for being so enormously generous with his rigorous reading, critical comments, fabulous ideas, constant support, and encouragement; Rebecca Ellis for being an incredible inspiration throughout; and Mónica Moreno Figueroa for being my rock, bashing ideas around, calling me out when needed, and encouraging me endlessly.

Third, a massive thanks to my backup team, the people who also read drafts and provided critical and transformative input: Les Back, Rachel Beckles Willson, Anna Bull, James Butterworth, Ella McPherson, Sue Miller, Carolyn Pedwell, Simon Susen, Allison Torres Burtka, Peter Wade, and the two anonymous reviewers.

Fourth, to Jo Browning Wroe, whose creative writing class prompted the vignettes, I am extremely grateful, both for the inspiration and for feedback.

Fifth, a shout-out to other friends and colleagues who have supported me in many, many ways, intellectual and otherwise, through this process:

Abeyamí Ortega Domínguez, Abigail Moreno Figueroa, Aída María Noval, Adriana Welsh, Alejandro Madrid, Alejandro Villanueva, Alison Rooke, Américo Saldívar, Amparo Sevilla, Andrew Green, Andrew Wood, Anna Strahn, Arathi Sriprakash, Ariadna Acevedo, Bernadette O'Brien, Byron Dueck, Carlos López Beltrán, Carlos Ruiz Rodríguez, Cathrine Degnen, Charlotte Faircloth, Chloë Alaghband-Zadeh, Christian Rinaudo, Christina Sue, Christine Carrington, Consuelo Sáizar, Denise Dresser, Dhiraj Murthy, Diana Paton, Elizabeth Cunin, Emiko Saldívar Tanaka, Fergus Earley, Fiorella Montero Diaz, Francesca Hanley, Frank Bock, Fred Moehn, Gail Farrara, Gayle Murchison, Geoff Baker, Geoff Ryman, Georgina Born, Gill Addison, Gisela Carlos Fregoso, Graciela Figueroa, Jan Fairley, Jennifer Jones, Jessica Gottfried Hesketh, Jill Wigle, Judith Bautista Pérez, Julia de la Fuente, K.E. Goldschmitt, Kali Argyriadis, Kate Ahl, Kate Chedgzoy, Katia Chornik, Kel Weinhold, Laudan Nooshin, Laura Lewis, Laurie Stras, Lois Lee, Lorena Zárate, Luke Stoneham, Magali Arce, María Moreno Parra, Maricarmen Rion, Matthew Wood, Megan Rivers-Moore, Miguel Zuñiga, Mónica Benítez Dávila, Monika Gosin, Natasha Tanna, Nick Boston, Nila Ramírez Quintero, Noël Greig, Patricia de los Ríos, Petra Rivera-Rideau, Randall Kohl, Rebecca Coleman, Robert Smith, Robin Moore, Sergio Navarette, Shireen Kanji, Shzr Ee Tan, Sol González Eguía, Spencer Jackson, Steve Kruse, Sue Earley, Susan Drucker Brown, Susan Walker, Susanna Rostas, Tala Jarjour, Thomas Aldridge, Thomas Hilder, Tianna Paschel, Tiffany Page, Tracey Jensen, Vic Seidler, Yuiko Asaba, and Zeynep Gurtin; participants in the NYLON group led by Richard Sennett; and colleagues in Music and Modern Languages at the University of Southampton. To those I have forgotten to mention, my apologies.

Sixth, to my mum, Jane Malcomson, whom I miss inordinately. To my sister, Bim Malcomson, who has been unfailingly supportive and disciplining, as well as teaching me much about dancing bodies. To Chris Malcomson, Virginia Bradley, Nic Malcomson, Richard Bleasdale, and the Moreno Figueroa family for being so supportive. And to Hugo Bleasdale and Jane Bleasdale for bringing me so much joy.

Danzón Days

OPENING VIGNETTE

Gerardo, Elena, and Miguel

(fiction)

Gerardo. 76. Black trousers draped over unpolished black shoes. Beige, short-sleeved guayabera: its bagginess a testimony to a once-fuller body. Clipped gray moustache, curved above receding lips. Brown, unruly eyebrows. Black narrow hatband on perforated Panama. Hands roughened by years of labor: building; distributing gas canisters; dusting streets.

Gerardo parked his bike. Black lettering painted freehand along the crossbar revealed his nickname: Lenin. More dancer than revolutionary, he liked going to the Plazuela de la Campana on Sunday evenings. Its stone floor made dancing smooth. He scanned the plaza. Most of the women he danced with sat on the public cast-iron benches that overlooked the dancing area, rather than the white and red plastic chairs belonging to the bars.

Manzanita's Danzonera piped up, the trumpet raging slightly. Gerardo asked María to dance; she accepted as usual. María didn't like it much that she towered over him, but at least he was a good dancer. Gerardo led her to the dance floor. He enjoyed their movement, even if a little stiff. Then he saw Elena. She was with Miguel. As he turned María, his head kept swinging: he couldn't help himself, he had to see them.

Elena. Red stilettos with narrow ankle straps. Grayish pink tights. Shiny red dress beneath shapeless navy cardigan. Bright gray hair. Piercing eyes, staring ahead. Gerardo knew that stare, that blankness that was so Elena. He would have done anything to be with her again.

Gerardo and Elena had been together for twelve years, on and off. She'd left her husband for him, but her nervous episodes had been too much. She hated being doped up. Reduced her medicines. Gerardo hadn't dealt with that well. They'd danced together in the *Grupo Rojo*. Elena still did. With Miguel.

It hurt Gerardo to go to danzón events. He knew he shouldn't, but he wanted to be close to her, even if she was with Miguel. Slowly he'd tried to come back to the dance. Drinking helped at first. Now he managed going sober. Mostly. He hated seeing Elena dancing with him. Him holding her, steering her, loving her. Gerardo remembered her breath, the faint smell of her perfume, the fragility of her blank stare.

Introduction

Danzón, Veracruz, and Ambivalence

All Is Not As It Seems

Several evenings a week in the main square of Mexico's port city of Veracruz, musicians strike up, and up to two hundred amateur dancers position themselves before tourist cameras and local onlookers to perform danzón, a genre that emanated from Cuba and has been performed in Veracruz for over a century.[1] This book explores how danzón intersects with racialization processes, nostalgia, aging, and romance in Veracruz in the early twenty-first century. Drawing on longitudinal ethnographic research with amateur dancers and semi-professional musicians, the book analyzes how danzón practices embody deep ambivalences that disrupt utopian accounts of music and dance as joyful and community-building. In relation to Veracruz, scholarship and popular discourse have commented on the (racialized) happiness that pervades the city, on the conviviality of danzón practitioners, on the Cuban influences on its people and cultural practices, on the happily married couples dancing together, and on the older age of most danzón practitioners, generating nostalgic concerns that the genre is dying out.

Yet this view is partial, and it obscures significant tensions and ambivalences that are key to understanding the complexities of not only danzón, but also cultural practices more broadly. *Danzón Days* analyzes the social life of a particular dance but is applicable to many dance forms. It focuses above all on interpersonal relationships to interrogate how danzón both *is and is not* linked to joyousness, blackness, cultural identity, conviviality, older age, and romance in Veracruz. This book is an ethnographic exploration of the frictions and opportunities created by such paradoxes and ambivalences, which I understand as tensions between apparently contrary sentiments, ideas, sensations, and/or impulses.

Let me turn to such a story to explicate the ethnographic specificity of Veracruz and the people embroiled in danzón there in the early twenty-first century. This story focuses on one of my closest friends and interlocutors in the Port, Margarita Castro Olvera, a petite woman in her late sixties with light-colored skin and short reddish hair.[2] One Sunday afternoon, in the early 1980s, Margarita walked with her husband, Eligio, a post-office worker, and their youngest daughter past Veracruz's Parque Zamora. They had been on their way to the cathedral for mass but were distracted by hearing danzón. They followed the yearning clarinets, alto saxophone, trumpet, timbales, and güiro blasting from a cassette deck and encountered a group of men and women dancing the slow, stately couple dance.[3] Eligio and Margarita decided to watch, and then rather hesitantly joined in, while their ten-year-old daughter sat with their bags. They danced for an hour or so, before rushing off to catch the final, 9 p.m. mass. Margarita loved dancing, and she particularly liked danzón, as it gave her a sense of pride for being from Veracruz, the city this genre is associated with in Mexico. Although she had never been taught how, she could dance danzón in a free style, and Eligio, her husband, led her: he had learned danzón as a young man in the dance halls of Mexico City.

Danzón emerged in Cuba in the late nineteenth century and soon became popular in the Port of Veracruz. Veracruz had regular maritime links with Havana and was often allied to Cubanness. The popularity of danzón had dwindled somewhat in the 1960s and 1970s, but through the 1980s, it regained popularity, spurred by the formation of dance groups in Mexico City and in Veracruz. Rather than being a music that is sought out to listen to, danzón is what Cubans call a music-dance genre (*música bailable*): it is a participatory practice usually involving both music and dance. Few danzones have lyrics. While the genre plays important roles in habitués' lives, there is no lifestyle associated with danzón. For example, people dress up to dance danzón, but they do not dress as danzoneros at other times during their daily lives (as is the case with hip-hop and heavy metal). While music and dance groups may play important social roles in people's lives and contribute to local identity formation, danzón is something people *do* rather than something people *are* (as is the case with some popular music scenes).

A fortnight after encountering danzón in the park, Margarita and Eligio would return and were invited to join the dance group, *Hoy y Siempre*, that had been set up with a view to rescuing danzón in 1983. The popularity of danzón would blossom over the following decades, further propelled by María Novaro's film, *Danzón*, released in 1991, which featured members of

Hoy y Siempre as extras, including Margarita and Eligio. In the late 1990s, Eligio died of a heart attack. Now Margarita had to rely economically on the widow's pension that he left her, amounting to half of the money they previously lived on. She no longer had a stall selling chickens, as she had had for many years, so was keen to be involved in other activities.

By the time I met her in the mid-2000s, Margarita had learned to dance danzón beautifully and was president of the dance group *Hoy y Siempre*: she organized, both logistically and financially, the danzón events in the Parque Zamora on Sunday evenings, which featured the danzón music ensemble *Danzonera Manzanita y su son 4*. Danzón had become very popular, especially among people aged fifty to eighty-plus from the lower-middle classes. The Parque Zamora was one of two regular danzón venues in the Port. The other was the main square where danzón was performed five evenings a week by the Municipal Band or a danzonera employed by the municipality, and by dozens of amateur dancers.

Local and state governments had promoted danzón as characteristic of Veracruz from the 1990s, as an attraction for the predominantly Mexican tourists to the Port. Miguel Zamudio, a local danzón dancer, teacher, and entrepreneur, started organizing an institutionally supported annual danzón festival that attracted danzón performers from around the country; and danzón increasingly became "culturally expedient" (Yúdice 2003), that is, a resource employed instrumentally for social, economic, or other ends (such as tourism, business integration, and marketing). Margarita's event in the Parque Zamora grew, too, although beyond permission to use the space, it did not receive government funding.

People mostly joined the dance for the love of dancing and/or exhibiting their talents, as a form of therapy, as exercise, as an opportunity to perform something considered local, and in search of conviviality, friendship, and/or amorous encounters. One thing that makes danzón both particularly attractive and intimidating for novices is its difficulty in comparison with other social dances: danzón contains sections where dancers rest, the nondanceable *descanso* (rest) sections of its rondo form (often the first repetition of the A sections of its AABAACAAD structure). Not everyone enjoys dancing (all the time); some struggle with knowing when to dance (and not), and with remembering and managing prescribed steps and routines. Where connoisseurs know when to stop and stand, some facing the musicians or an audience, novices continue dancing alone, and their lack of experience is made particularly public. From the 1980s, new recruits increasingly joined dance groups and attempted to tackle the difficult aspects of this dance, as well as meet dance partners and forge new relationships.

Like Margarita, some of the women lived from widows' pensions inherited from their deceased husbands and/or were supported by their children, and/or continued to work, for example, as cooks, nurses, seamstresses, secretaries, and teachers. Many of the men who danced danzón had retired from working as dockers, shipbuilders, and railway men, for the Tubos de Acero de México (TAMSA) Steel Tubes of Mexico factory, in smaller businesses, or in other manual trades. Some dancers were wealthier than others and identified as middle class, such as graduates and professionals, but most danzoneros described themselves as lower-middle class (rather than the poorest class, a category usually reserved for people living in rural areas). Most of the musicians were men; women musicians were few and far between, young or old. But on the dancing front, women far outnumbered men at danzón events, in part because social dances tend to attract more women than men, but also because women tend to outlive men.

My first encounter with danzón in the Port was a Sunday in the Parque Zamora in 2006. The Sunday danzón events in the Parque Zamora had been organized by Margarita for several years at that point. This was no ordinary Sunday, however. The danzonera musicians had fought with her over money, those present told me, and neither Margarita nor the musicians were anywhere to be seen. People prefer not to dance to recordings in Veracruz, so several dancers sent for a marimba ensemble so that people could dance. Although I did not realize it at the time, the combination of convivialities and animosities that became apparent that Sunday were not uncommon: musicians and dancers repeatedly told me that they were *unidos en un nido de víboras* ("united in a vipers' nest," the "united" punning with "nest"). Margarita concurred, while reassuring me it wasn't that bad. With time, I, too, would become entwined in this nest.

Over the 2000s and 2010s, four dance groups frequented the main square events on Saturdays, and each wore matching outfits, which they called uniforms. Numerous women and men who were group members told me how much they enjoyed the conviviality of being in these groups, the elegance of their uniforms, and the delight of dancing unison group choreographies. While some groups were choreographically prescriptive, others were more fluid. Over time, people told me how they had been ostracized from certain groups, creating tensions and ambivalences around participation at local danzón events. Margarita herself had not been immune to such frictions, and nor had I (see Vignette 5).

Moreover, although not advertised as such, the Port's danzón events provide spaces for people aged fifty and over to meet, to dance, and to find romance. The majority of women who danced were separated, divorced, or widowed and had adult children. Some lived with family members, while others lived alone. Relatively few of these women were remarried. Although some of the men who danced were also widowers, divorced, or separated, a significant number claimed to be but had wives they did not bring to danzón events. Some younger people also danced at these events, but most stopped in their early twenties to focus on their studies, careers, professions, marriages, and child-rearing, as did Margarita's daughter.

Significantly, opportunities to participate in such dances were rare for married women. Margarita and her husband had been unusual, for married couples seldom dance in public spaces in the city. Given the larger number of women and the prevailing logics of romantic love, men dominate this sexual arena, despite many of them being married. Ambivalences around the moral dictates of appropriate behavior, racialized notions of decency, and Catholicism collide with a sexual world that includes post-menopausal women and impotent or Viagra-fueled men in very public contexts. Gossip abounds. As I write this book, I feel ambivalent about danzón: for all the joy and companionship that this genre engenders, particularly for older people, it can also cause enormous heartache and tension. Think back to the opening vignette, to the painful ambivalences Gerardo experienced at danzón events: his desire (and not) to be with Elena, to be near her, to see her with Miguel.

Danzón, Veracruz, and Ambivalence

This book examines tensions, opportunities, and ambivalences in the lives of Mexican danzón practitioners. I explore a place and several objects and subjects: Veracruz (a city steeped in nostalgia, where both notions of blackness and the mestizo (mixed) nation are key to local identity), music and dance (nostalgic sound, newer and older movement styles, and racialized histories of danzón in Mexico and Cuba), an embodied aesthetic (elegance and discipline), and the older women and men who regularly perform danzón (entwined in friendships, romances, and personal and group rivalries).

The markers in this landscape entail different qualities and registers of attachment, including but not limited to individual and collective desire, delight, love, patriotism, paternalism, rivalries, ostracism, and aggression. They also incorporate distinct, but overlapping, ambivalences. For example, Veracruz is loved by many Mexicans for its place in the history of the mestiza nation, its nostalgic atmosphere, and its blackness. Ambivalence is pervasive. Aging, blackness, and nation are embraced and shunned, with varying intensities. Yet hardly anyone wants to be black in Veracruz.[4] Likewise, few people want to be classified as old, even though all those whose lives are not cut short will eventually become old. Blackness is, in this setting, flexible as both an identity and a non-identity. There are parallels here with aging, for relationality and context determine who are judged as black (darker or lighter than others) and old (older or younger than others). Class, privilege, gender, sexuality, and nationalism play into these dynamics and produce assemblages where, despite ambivalences, race and age are mobilized to create imaginaries of this port city and its danzón. In this book, I explore how such ambivalences relate to expediencies (of culture, blackness, and age).

But why pick ambivalence as a thematic tool to think about connecting music, dance, and logics of inclusion and exclusion? This connection is not fortuitous, for to understand danzón in Veracruz, and other social dances in their empirical contexts, we need to move with the flows of ambivalence and contradiction. Much of the literature on ambivalence was written between 1910 and the late 1970s and is concerned with dualisms. And although the concept has since been a trope that many academics have used as a formula to explain outcomes of tensions or particular dynamics (for example Hale 2006; Wade 2009; Hillcoat-Nallétamby and Phillips 2011; Connidis, Borell, and Karlsson 2017, among others), it is rarely defined, and most authors have not clarified their positions in relation to the variety of possibilities that being ambivalent might mean. To apprehend the complexities of ambivalence in greater depth, the next section of this introduction is dedicated to thinking through its logics and workings. This will enable us to navigate the danzón landscape in the chapters that follow, to get closer to the nuances of its textures. I discuss at some length what we can learn from ambivalence as a term, typologies, psychological and more sociologically grounded approaches to its causes, and its relationships to power and temporality, so the discussion may be of interest to a broader readership. I propose three models of ambivalence—static, dialectic, and utopian—based on static dualisms, dynamic dialectics, and idealism. Rather than insisting that one model is better than another, however, I argue that these models provide ethnographic tools that are good to think with and against. These models of ambivalence should be treated as complementary and entangled, rather than as definitive, alternative, theoretical orientations.[5]

On Ambivalence

Ambivalences manifest in distinct forms, and their everyday negotiations can engender different intensities. Etymologically, ambivalence refers to having value or worth on both sides. The term was coined in 1910 by Swiss psychiatrist Eugen Bleuler to describe phenomena where agreeable and disagreeable sentiments were experienced simultaneously. Bleuler and other psychologists (famously Bleuler's contemporary Sigmund Freud) became concerned with the impacts and conflicts created by latent, acknowledged and/or repressed ambivalences at different levels of consciousness. Dualisms—life and death, love and hate, attraction and repulsion, inclusion and exclusion—were understood as polar opposites and as tensions in dynamic processes. Bleuler (1911) identified three types of ambivalence relating to feelings, wishes, and thoughts: *affective*, where the same idea provokes positive and negative feelings (such as a Freudian Oedipal boy loving and hating his father, or Gerardo in the opening vignette loving and hating being with and near Elena); *voluntary*, when someone wants something and does not want it simultaneously (like a sickly sweet cake); and *intellectual*, where opposing sides of an argument or idea are held. George Orwell's "doublethink" in *Nineteen Eighty-Four* provides an insightful example of intellectual ambivalence: doublethink is "to know and not to know, [...] to hold simultaneously two opinions that cancelled out, knowing them to be contradictory and believing in both of them; to use logic against logic" (1949, 40–41). Like affective and voluntary ambivalences, intellectual ambivalences (like doublethink) include diametrical oppositions, rationales, and contradictions that may or may not be acknowledged. Language is key, particularly to intellectual ambivalence, for the very notion of contradiction is the speaking against, requiring speech. Further typologies of ambivalence were suggested by Jan Hajda in 1968: *psychological ambivalence*, akin to Bleuler's affective ambivalence; *social or structural ambivalence*, relating both to individual-social tensions and to the conflicts created by roles and statuses; *cultural ambivalence*, where personal values collide with social norms; and *biological ambivalence*, where opposing tendencies are manifest in the same bodily function (such as wakeful sleepfulness) (Hajda 1968, 22–23). Hajda's notion of biological ambivalence might be extended beyond bodily functions, to what I shall refer to here as *embodied ambivalence*, which includes both functional and non-functional sensations: for instance, the joy and discomfort of dancing awkwardly (or in relation to Argentine tango, for example, of enjoying dancing a genre one associates with a time of dictatorship, see Taylor 1998; or with gender inequalities, as a feminist performer, see Davis 2015). Although such typologies may no longer be fashionable, they provide orientations.

Let us consider an example relating to danzón in Veracruz: an upper-middle-class, discreetly made-up, lighter-skinned woman, older than her seventy-two-year-old, darker-skinned dancing partner, dances elegantly but stiffly, hesitant about the sexual tension she feels between herself and this smiling, gangly man, his face weathered by years of working outside on building sites. Their ambivalences are embodied, felt, willed, thought, dictated by classed and racialized social prescriptions of decent behavior and by their gendered roles as dancers. His role is to lead her in the dance, yet he has little experience; hers is to follow, but she cannot repress a desire to lead and a patronizing tone toward him at times. Their ambivalences would continue, for Carmen and Ernesto would become more than just dance partners (see Vignette 6). These ambivalences were not merely individual but socially produced, and power and violence were inherent in, and between, these dynamics. The ambivalences integral to the logics of love were also at play.

The causes of ambivalence have been central to psychological considerations, which have tended to focus on stimuli specific to the individual, and that person's feelings, desires, thoughts, and sensations. Carolyn Pedwell (2014) analyzes how Melanie Klein, and later Eve Kosofsky Sedgwick, explored love and ambivalence in their discussions of reparation, for example.[6] More sociological approaches have emphasized how ambivalences internal to an individual cannot be separated from those produced by sociological forces. Back in 1986, for example, Robert Merton and Elinor Barber investigated how some roles and statuses produce sociologically ambivalent positions, such as the medical doctor who must respond compassionately to patients while maintaining professional detachment. Merton and Barber (1976) concluded that doctors' professional ambivalences are resolved by temporal displacement, so, for example, the medical doctor oscillates between being compassionate and formal. Temporal disjuncture may ease such ambivalences, but some social positions are less transitory and produce far more intense and violent configurations. A more intense example than the doctors' experience of ambivalence is provided by the flight attendants, analyzed by Arlie Hochschild (2003), who must perform emotional labor, with sometimes unexpected consequences. Moreover, the ambivalences created by being in structurally subaltern positions, for example, be they racialized, classed, gendered, sexualized, aged, and/or otherwise, can be intensely violent and anxiety provoking. We might think of W. E. B. Du Bois's (1897) notion of "double-consciousness," which he famously coined to refer to the experience of Black people in the United States in the late nineteenth century (post-slavery) who measured themselves, and were measured, from the stance of a world filled with white racist laws and ideologies. Du Bois's insights resonate with the racialized power dynamics of early-twenty-first-century Veracruz, where many people live the tension of both being and not being black (see Chapter 1).

Dualisms have been essential to theorizations of ambivalence. However, the dualisms assessed by Bleuler (1911), Hajda (1968), and Merton and Barber (1976) elide the complexities of actors occupying multiple positions (be they racialized, classed, gendered, sexualized, aged, or otherwise). When we think about ambivalence in Veracruz, and elsewhere, we need to attend to its nuances, since many ambivalences are more knotty than mere dichotomies and contradiction; are more enigmatic, inarticulate, and incoherent; and involve multiple elements, be they linguistic, non-linguistic, felt, thought, desired, sensed, or embodied. Several scholars have begun work in this area. Peter Wade (2009) points to the complexities of multiple structural ambivalences by drawing on Lacanian psychoanalysis, particularly the anxieties provoked by the disjuncture between the experience of the self and the ideal image of the self (as portrayed to a child in the mirror, for example, where the awkwardness of his or her movements counter the ideal of embodied independence) (see Lacan 1990). Specifically, Wade analyzes the anxieties produced by the ambivalences inherent in sexualized racial logics in Latin America as they are experienced by both whiter elites and, building on Du Bois (1897), by those labeled indigenous, mestizo, and black. As I explore in Chapter 1, these ambivalences chime with danzón practitioners' experiences of sexualized racial stereotypes. Hillcoat-Nallétamby and Phillips (2011) analyze the complexity of ambivalence in terms of relational interactions that shift over time and include structural, group, and individual dynamics. On a larger temporal scale, scholars such as Zygmunt Bauman (1991) have proposed that whole eras, such as so-called modernity, are characterized by an ambivalence. For Bauman, this ambivalence is a disorder that creates chaos "because of the anxiety that accompanies it and the indecision which follows" (1991, 1).[7]

While anxiety is the main response to ambivalence that Wade (2009), Bauman (1991), and others have identified, further responses can also be elicited when we consider the varied intensities of different forms of ambivalence. Alternative or coexistent responses to anxiety include anger, fear, guilt, shame, fascination, tolerance, indifference, and a desire for ambivalence to be sustained. For example, Gloria Anzaldúa (1987) famously explores tolerance for ambivalence and ambiguity, arguing for a new "mestiza consciousness" that "break[s] down the subject-object duality that keeps her a prisoner" (1987, 80). Ambivalence involves painful work in breaking down unitary elements for Anzaldúa (1987), but it enables the transcendence of binaries and transformation. Ambivalences may also produce resistance, subversion, and/or expediency, as I examine in Chapter 1.

When interrogating intersecting intensities of ambivalences, it is important to consider temporality (as Merton and Barber, 1976, did) and also intentionality, that is, the desire for and/or fear of ambivalences. Where ambivalences are not intended or desired, concurrence may create greater ambivalences than temporally separate or alternating emotions, desires, senses, impulses, or ideas. Moreover, expectations of ambivalences may be greater in certain kinds of relationships: in marriage, for example, a normative expectation of permanence may engender more of a tolerance for ambivalence than may exist in certain friendships. Distinct intensities of, and responses to, ambivalences may accumulate or fold into each other over time, and greater or lesser tolerance may be inherent in certain social positions, roles, or institutions (see Willson et al. 2006 for an analysis of ambivalences between mothers and adult children, for example). Thus, to understand ambivalences, we need to attend to intention, expectation, intensity, and temporality.

So far, I have discussed ambivalences in relation to a model based on static polarities: static ambivalences relating to feelings, thoughts, desires, and sensations inclined toward one thing *or* another, or one thing *and* another. We might also think of a more nebulous concept of ambivalence that is neither *and-or* nor *both-and*, but that is *neither-nor*: a double negative that may provoke uncertainty—the question of "what then?" or a "maybe." Rather than relying on one model of ambivalence based on static polarities, then, let us consider another dualistic approach that is more dynamic.

When the notion of ambivalence was conceived in 1910, concern with dichotomies was far from new. Dualisms had been fundamental to the Socratic dialectic method of reasoning promoted by Plato (around 380 BC), in which contradictions to propositions were sought to ascertain truths. But it was Georg Hegel's dialectical thinking in the first quarter of the nineteenth century that provided a focus on dynamic processes. For Hegel (1874), the notion of *aufhebung* was key to dialectics. *Aufhebung* refers to sublation, to both preserving and transcending, to absorbing and canceling. We might think of a thesis—*being*—and its antithesis–*not being*—as sublated by their synthesis, *becoming* (which is neither being nor not being, but the dynamic between the two). As Hegel wrote: "life, as life, involves the germ of death" (1874, 126). This is well illustrated in an introduction to Hegel's writings by William Wallace in 1874. Wallace explicated Hegel's dialectic as being like a seed that is sublated into the plant that emerges from it: while the seed is destroyed, it is preserved and transcended by the plant that succeeds it. In this process, neither the seed (thesis) nor the plant (antithesis) exists as static essences, but they are parts of a dynamic process of becoming. For Hegel, "wherever there is movement, wherever there is life, wherever anything is carried into effect in the actual world, there Dialectic is at work" (Hegel 1874, 126). Dialectics are essential to the very nature of being, and temporality and movement are central, for everything must be considered as part of a dynamic. (And much post-structuralist thought draws on and writes against Hegel's idea of binaries and dialectics to get at the relationality of being, language, and so forth (for example, Derrida 2001). While static ambivalences include a temporal component, this is likely to be either concurrence or disjuncture, rather than the dynamism of dialectic ambivalences.

Beyond writing, the following representational models may facilitate your understanding of these manifestations of ambivalences. Static ambivalences might be visualized as discrete, unconnected single points with diametrically opposed values (say good and bad): these points are static, and variation is restricted to being one or the other (good or bad), with no in between. Dialectic ambivalences might be imagined as a line within which there is constant movement, constant becoming, but without pure essences: no fixed ends denoting purely good or bad.

So far, then, we might think of two models of ambivalence: static and dialectic. Hegel (1874) juxtaposed his dialectic method with reflection, which merely ponders the thesis and antithesis as isolated forms without considering their dynamic relationship. The analyses of ambivalence provided by Bleuler (1911), Hajda (1968), and Merton and Barber (1976) are akin to such a reflective or static model. Rather than juxtaposing dynamic dialectic and more static reflective models of felt, thought, desired, embodied, and sensed ambivalences as absolute alternatives, however, I propose that dialectic dynamics provide useful tools for thinking about certain ambivalences, while for others, the more reflective, static types of oscillating between a thesis and an antithesis that much of the literature on ambivalence has employed are apposite. For example, both static and dialectic models of ambivalence provide insights into racialization and aging processes in Veracruz (see Chapters 1 and 6). Moreover, ambivalences may cohere into knotty assemblages where multiple sensed, thought, felt, embodied, and desirous ambivalences, with varying levels of intensity, stick together and/or collide. Such is the case with love, which we can think about in relation to another combination of articulations of ambivalence: first, static ambivalence (love juxtaposed with hate), and second, love as actually incorporating ambivalence, which provides a good example of the final type of ambivalence we will consider here, *utopian ambivalence*.

Let us dwell on love, not only because it provides a paradigmatic example of utopian ambivalence, but also because love is relevant in various ways to this ethnography—in relation to dance, music, convivial intimacies, romance, nostalgia, and nationalism. I draw extensively from Lauren Berlant's exploration of how desire engenders a "cluster of promises [that] could be embedded in a person, a thing, an institution, a text, a norm, a bunch of cells, smells, a good idea—whatever" (2006, 20). The object of desire is inevitably disrupted when crises and compromises clash with its promises, with its optimism. So, for example, incompatibilities of everyday life and undisciplined passions can complicate vernacular love's ethics. Rather than static polarities of love and hate, we have here a notion of love that incorporates Berlant's "cruel optimism," that is, "a relation of attachment to compromised conditions of possibility" (2006, 21). In other words, love incorporates ambivalence. Moreover, this cruel optimism is ever present: "its potential failure to stabilize closeness always haunts its persistent activity" (Berlant 1998, 282). Such cruel optimism enables patience and endurance for contradiction, for untangling antagonisms, for love's promises (Berlant 2011). The power of the promises that romantic love engenders is evidenced by the few alternatives to this dominant form of love—in Europe, Mexico, and the United States, at least—whether in heterosexual, homosexual, monogamous, polyamorous, or other configurations (Berlant 2011). The ways in which romantic love is negotiated may shift over the life course: some widows in Veracruz, for example, engage with romantic love in ways distinct from their pre-marriage and marriage days (see Chapter 6), but the logics of romantic love often continue.

So how is tolerance sustained for the ambivalences created by love? In terms of language, Berlant (2011) suggests that the comfort of intimacy depends on unexpressed ambivalences, for love is disrupted by talk, by linguistic precision, causing anxiety, and even forms of violence. Love enables a desire for a thing, a person, a world, together with ambivalence, anxiety, fear, loss, guilt, and grief. Love "holds open the possibility that, beyond all cynical knowledge and wisdom, reason and optimism might not be opposites—that there might be forms of nonviolent intimacy that will structure reliably what a life is, what fulfillment feels like" (Berlant 2001, 439). What we might think of as the *logic of romantic love* dictates that if the promise of love is to be sustained, both this ideal and ambivalences, such as optimism versus reason, must prevail. Such ambivalences are thus utopian, for they are incorporated into an ideal or utopia—an imagined place or state of being where everything is perfect—that is inevitably disrupted. Moreover, while the ambivalences created by love may be utopian, they may also include or combine with static or dialectic models of love and hate, creating complex configurations of ambivalences. And although the logics of romantic love are paradigmatic of utopian ambivalence, these logics are also applicable beyond love.

A second illustration of utopian ambivalence might be elucidated from Josh Kun's (2005) notion of "audiotopia," where "music functions like a possible utopia for the listener, that is experienced not only as sound […] but as a space that we can enter into, encounter, move around in, inhabit" (2005,

2). Kun highlights the ambivalences of audiotopias by drawing on Foucault's (1986) notion of heterotopia: he grounds his audiotopias in "their own auditory somewhere" (2005, 2–3), arguing that they may act as social and sonic "identificatory 'contact zones'" (2005, 23) bringing people and sounds together that are usually kept apart. Kun points to two famous examples of this relating to the United States: the promise, hope, and despair of the "sorrow songs" of black enslaved people analyzed by W. E. B. Du Bois (1994, 162) in *The Souls of Black Folk*, and Graham Lock's "blutopia," that is, "a utopia tinged with the blues, an African American visionary future stained with memories" (Lock 1999, 3). Kun's notion is also developed by Frederick Moehn (2007) in relation to the fragile audiotopia of Brazilian popular music (MPB), which is threatened by violence and inequality.

A third example of utopian ambivalence is political democracy, where frictions are created between ideals and everyday life. For example, we might consider what Charles Hale terms the "racial ambivalence" felt by Guatemalan *ladinos* (non-indigenous people) who "both critique racism and cling to racial privilege as the guarantee that Maya ascendancy will not wreak havoc" (2006, 217). Framed in terms of the logics of utopian ambivalence, the ideal of racial democracy—the promise of racial and cultural equality—includes both racial ambivalences, such as a desire for anti-racism, and the threat of the removal of (*ladino*) privilege. Moreover, these racial ambivalences intersect with political ambivalences, specifically the aspirational, utopian elements of nationalism that were implicit in racial ideologies of mixture (*mestizaje*) in Latin America for much of the twentieth century and into the twenty-first.

Thus, utopian ambivalence is created where an ideal—be it love, racial or political democracy, or a better future—includes both promises and elements that collide with and undermine these same promises and elements, and that themselves may be static, dialectic, or multiple ambivalences. Utopian ambivalences involve at least three elements: static and/or dialectic ambivalences with a reciprocal relationship to an ideal, in that the ambivalence would not exist without the ideal. We have, then, three models of ambivalence—*static* (dualistic, relating to feelings, thoughts, desires, and sensations inclined toward one thing *or* another, or one thing *and* another), *dialectic* (another dualistic mode, but more dynamic than static ambivalences, involving constant becoming, akin to a Hegelian [1874] dialectic), and *utopian*—that may combine, clash, and/or stick. For example, someone may feel a static ambivalence (love or hate) to a utopian ambivalence (democracy, love) precisely because of its ambivalences!

I hope that by creating this typology, I have laid a ground for more work on this concept, offering approaches to thinking through ambivalence that will be useful for other kinds of projects and setting out a typology that may be augmented with further models. It should be noted, however, that I am not proposing that neat models of ambivalence should be advocated without accounting for messiness. Instead, I am putting ambivalence center stage here, as a thinking tool and as a method for analyzing an ethnographic landscape. Ambivalence provides one of the tools in the toolbox with which I approach the ethnography that follows.

Overview of Chapters

Let me turn to the question of how ambivalence sheds light on the everyday lives and performance practices of older danzón dancers and musicians in the specific context of Veracruz, and vice versa, and what the implications and uses of such connections might be. The first ambivalences around danzón emerge from popular renditions of its history, which proclaim it black, then white, then black music in Cuba, and black music in Mexico. The routes and roots of danzón are outlined in Chapter 1, where I interrogate how these popular histories relate to contemporary Veracruz, what purposes such narratives serve, and what imaginaries they allow.[8] I contend that it is enlightening to compare the racial logics at play in racialized stereotypes of people and canonic histories of music-dance forms, specifically how blackness is articulated in relation to danzón and people in Veracruz, and how links are made in both instances to Cuba. The blackness of both the people of Veracruz and their danzón is displaced in time and space, associated with the past and a foreign country (Cuba) rather than the Veracruz of the present. I explore how bodies identified as black are associated with foreignness in Veracruz, and how notions of blackness threaten the sense of national belonging. I propose that static and utopian ambivalences around the blackness of local people and of danzón enable both blackness and danzón to be expedient in Veracruz, while simultaneously making racism invisible. That is, while darker-skinned men and women in Veracruz are subjected to racism, racialized identities may be appropriated expediently by members of the lighter-skinned middle and upper classes.

While Chapter 1 spans from the sixteenth century to the present to interrogate the racial logics of danzón and Veracruz, Chapter 2 brings Boym's (2001) classic work on nostalgia into conversation with my typology of ambivalence to explore the particular history of danzón in the Port of Veracruz from the 1890s until the 1980s. I propose that "restorative nostalgia" (where the past is made solid, preserved in a moment shaped by the present) invokes static ambivalences, while "reflective nostalgia" (a yearning for homecoming) engenders utopian ambivalences. Madrid and Moore (2013) argue that Boym's notion of restorative nostalgia is key to the Mexican danzón revival, as exemplified by pachucos associated with Mexico City's dance halls. I suggest, however, that in the specific case of Veracruz (where pachucos are absent), local people's relationships to the city and its danzón are mostly characterized by reflective nostalgia, the yearning for an age epitomized by creative carnival practices, and workers from the docks performing and dancing to Afro-Cuban music. It is the era of strong dockers' unions and industry before the docks were privatized in the 1990s that is evoked nostalgically, rather than pre-modern times. Despite danzón undergoing a form of national revival in the 1980s, I argue that the restorative nostalgia characteristic of other revivals (see Livingston 1999; Hilder 2012; Bithell and Hill 2014) is not apparent in the practices and discourses around danzón in Veracruz. References to tradition and restorative nostalgia tend to be fleeting in the Port (in contrast to the contemporary zoot-suit-clad, danzón dancing pachucos in and around Mexico City analyzed by Madrid and Moore 2013). I conclude the chapter by arguing that nostalgic representations of the Port and its danzón enable lower-class dockers to be celebrated for their creativity, ingenuity, wit, and homely familiarity, yet such nostalgic representations of lower-class cultural practices reproduce and erase past and present inequalities.

I move away from ambivalence in the next two chapters to focus on everyday socialities and aesthetics. In Chapter 3, I analyze the weekly danzón event in the Port and outline the differences between the older, lírico style of danzón and the disciplined, codified, académico style that became popular from the 1980s and was mostly performed in groups. Group dancers learned académico steps and choreographed sequences, and they danced in unison in uniformed groups. An ideal of elegance stimulated, and became increasingly embodied in, the académico aesthetic, and spectacle akin to nationalist presentations of folkloric dance became highly valued. In this chapter, I argue that the newer académico style assumed a modernist aesthetic linked to elegance, whiteness, elite cosmopolitanism, nationalism, and colonial violence. I interrogate this aesthetic by bringing together scholarship on modern and Latin ballroom dance (Bosse 2007, 2015), European Early Music (Taruskin 1995), cosmopolitanism (Turino 2000), Amalia Hernández's Ballet Folklórico de México (Hutchinson 2009; Shay 2002), and regional folkloric dances, including Veracruz's son jarocho (González 2010).

In Chapter 4, I explore how this modernist aesthetic emerged in relation to danzón, specifically how a non-heritage revival that spread throughout Mexico from the 1980s enabled sufficient consensus to be achieved for the dance's movement aesthetic to become disciplined, schooled, and ritualized in performance spectacles. I also explicate how most newcomers to danzón are over fifty years old: older practitioners form the new generations. The age of newcomers has been generally overlooked in literature on music and dance transmission, rescue, and revival, which tends to focus on transmission to younger generations, as do many cultural practitioners. It should not be assumed, however, that the future of cultural practices is determined by younger people engaging with them. These practices may flourish even when no or few younger people participate. Danzón shares many of the elements present in other music-dance revivals, yet there was strikingly little concern with historical fidelity as a key driver of the danzón revival. In contrast to other revivals, most older performers' practices have been ignored by revivalists when seeking authoritative forms of dancing or playing danzón. Yet the older age of many practitioners is culturally expedient for Veracruz's culture industries that invoke age to authenticate this practice as a local "tradition," to justify its "rescue" and promotion to younger generations. Rather than being a resource for older people's well-being (although it may act as such), this music-dance genre is first and foremost something promoted as a local tradition and a tourist attraction in Veracruz.

In Chapter 5, I contribute to literature on cultural practices by not only proposing that rivalries can be productive in propelling revival movements, but also analyzing how such rivalries operate. While there is a great deal of conviviality, I interrogate the difficult group and personal dynamics that habitués often alluded to, such as the dynamics between Gerardo, Elena, and Miguel depicted in the opening vignette. I analyze the frictions arising from the aesthetic and social changes brought about by the danzón revival, that is, new group dynamics, dancing styles, and forms of transmission. I revisit Kracauer's classic essay on groups (1922), together with ethnographic analyses of Amazonian communities (e.g., Santos-Granero 2000), to examine the quality of group experience. I challenge Iannaccone's influential (1998) rational-choice model of (religious) groups whereby "free-riders" undermine the viability of a group's conviviality and collective aims, instead proposing that it is intimacy that threatens group cohesion. I also consider how group rivalries are key in the reproduction of groups. Throughout, I point to static and utopian ambivalences provoked by conviviality, rivalry, envy, and group ostracisms.

In Chapter 6, I explore what the flexibility of dance groups enables, beyond conviviality and the disciplining of the dance. I examine dancers' motivations for participating in groups, and specifically how aging intersects with romance on the one hand and shifting dance aesthetics and groups on the other. Many studies of popular music, dance, and sexuality have concentrated on younger people (past and present). Where the voices of older people have been considered, the focus has often been retrospective, that is, on older people's experiences when young or their attitudes toward contemporary situations, rather than shifting mores and cultural practices over the life course. Moreover, most studies of music and dance assume that older people are not sexual, particularly older women. I argue that older people's romantic lives have been largely ignored and deserve to be interrogated as much as younger people's: it should not be assumed that people do not form new relationships just because they are older. Likewise, social attempts to harness the reproductive power of younger, elite women underpins moral boundaries in many contexts: older women's sexuality is free from such constraints, and morality around older women's sexuality should not be treated in the same way as that of younger women.

Marriage should not be analyzed as an end point: instead, it may be something that people do for part of their lives. Notably, being married may exclude people from events that others engage in before or after being married. Such is the case for women who dance danzón in Veracruz. Danzón is not accessible to most married women in the Port (unless their husbands also perform it, which is uncommon). Instead, women tend to perform danzón before or after marriage, that is, once they are separated, divorced, or widowed. The married men who dance danzón mostly do so without their wives, and many of them have romantic relationships with women dancers. Older men and women remain constrained by social and religious mores, and morality and gossip continue to act as disciplining forces, but there is space for romantic engagements. In the case of danzón in Veracruz, the apparent joyousness of many dancing couples is best explained by their recent acquaintance, rather than long marriages: most of the women are no longer married, and their dance partners sometimes have wives left at home. Moreover, new generations of older dancers keep flocking to danzón, particularly since the danzón revival of the 1980s, some of whom are only interested in dancing and socializing, and others in romance. As most newcomers to danzón are over fifty years old, I address the relationship of the revived modernist aesthetic of the dance to older people's bodies, particularly in relation to elegance, discipline, and spectacle.

This book complements Alejandro Madrid and Robin Moore's (2013) analysis of historical circulations of danzón in the circum-Caribbean, and contemporary articulations of the genre in Mexico City, Monterrey, and Pachuca, Hidalgo. *Danzón Days* offers a nuanced, longitudinal ethnographic interrogation of danzón practice in the Port of Veracruz, the city famed for danzón in Mexico, drawing on over a decade of fieldwork. While Madrid and Moore emphasize the pleasure and joy of dancing, elucidating tensions between morality, sensuality, and hegemonic gender relations, they present a view of danzón as something people "love" (2013, 18). In contrast, *Danzón Days* highlights how pleasure cannot be assumed, and that non-enjoyment, tensions, and ambivalences also pervade some dancers' experiences of performance. Madrid and Moore explore race and nation broadly in relation to danzón in Mexico and Cuba, yet racial formations in Mexico are regionally specific: *Danzón Days* analyzes the particular processes through which local people and danzón are racialized in Veracruz, an area renowned for its links to Cuba, and the ways these processes enable racism to persist. The particular contribution that *Danzón Days* offers is its being the first full-length ethnographic study of danzón in Veracruz, and crucially its interrogation of intersections of music, dance, racial and national imaginaries, aging, and romance. Moreover, rather than contending that there is one logic at play in understanding ambivalence, it offers a typology as a first step to thinking and analyzing further how ambivalence operates. It points to the reach of the concept of ambivalence for thinking about and illuminating understandings of race, nostalgia, and social life more broadly.

Ethnographic Orientations and Violence

Methodologically, I treat Veracruz's danzón events as a pointer on an ethnographic compass: I followed that pointer wherever it took me for over a decade beginning in 2006, exploring what danzón practitioners in Veracruz thought was important, and trying to understand the nuances of their everyday lives—their experiences, actions, and interactions. The methodological strategy of following a music-dance genre around both provided me a historical object (see Malcomson 2011, 2014a) and took me to various social worlds. I lived in the Port for a year between 2006 and 2007, returning for several months a year thereafter until 2019, and I conducted contextual research in other parts of Mexico and Cuba (including Mexico City, Guadalajara, Havana, and Matanzas).[9] I learned to dance danzón and gained a basic knowledge of congas, timbales, and güiro/clave playing: knowledge of the dance enhanced my knowledge of the music and vice versa. And, crucially, danzón dancers lack respect for experts who cannot dance.

The possibilities, limits, partialities, and power dynamics knotted in this ethnography are implicated by my experience as a middle-aged, middle-class, white British, queer cis woman living and performing with mostly working-class, mestiza/o, Mexican, heterosexual cis women and cis men, old enough to be my parents. Homophobia is rife in Veracruz, and the LGBTQ+ folks I knew (who occasionally frequented danzón events) did not "come out" in this hyper-heteronormative context, and nor did I (following advice from LGBTQ+ friends in Veracruz, a decision that weighed on me throughout the project as I became close to several rather homophobic danzón practitioners). Matt Cook argues that "people's backgrounds, families, and the places they live have made a portable closet a comforting, desirable and even enjoyable queer accessory in the years since gay liberation" (Cook 2020): I was in a "portable closet" in Veracruz, coming up for air with queer, non-danzonerx friends in Mexico City from time to time. Because the context I describe in this book is so cis-binary and heteronormative, I use the term *Veracruzana/ os* because I worked most with cis men and women from Veracruz. However, by this I do not mean to exclude people of other genders.

I spent over a year dancing daily in Veracruz's plazas, and my positioning affected whom I could dance with and what I learned in this highly gendered sphere. I danced with men and spent much of my time in women's company, getting to know women better than men. Many performers foregrounded positive elements of danzón participation in the first months I knew them, only later to reveal the complexities of their entanglements with this world; I too had similar experiences (see Vignette 5, Chapter 5), but I glided through with ease compared with many others, largely due to *malinchismo* (an overvaluing of foreignness, particularly global-northern whiteness, above the national). In what follows, I try to embrace complexity, contradiction, and multiplicity: that many things are and are not. Rather than "to be or not to be," "to be *and* not to be" was more often apposite. Ambivalence emerged as a theme, as did the transformations to the dance and the social worlds of danzón from the 1980s.

Life in Veracruz changed dramatically over the decade that this book spans. The Port of Veracruz is beloved by Mexicans for its hot, humid climate; its sandy beaches overlooking crane-lined docks and container-laden ships; its quayside walkways and cafés; its music and dance (ambulant musicians, marimbas, genres including danzón, son cubano, and son jarocho); its carnival and partying atmosphere; and the sense that locals share a relaxed lifestyle and a collective irreverence for authority. By the late 2000s and through the 2010s, however, like many other parts of Mexico, Veracruz was also a site of huge insecurity and brutal violence.

The danzón practitioners I know did not want me to write about the violence and were keen for me to represent Veracruz as *bello* (beautiful, chiming with the 1949 film *Solo Veracruz es bello*, "only Veracruz is beautiful"), rather than the *feo* (ugliness) of the increasing violence that they would later lament or play down in conversations with me. But even if the violence is downplayed, presenting Veracruz and people's lives as merely beautiful and joyful tells a one-sided story, so I briefly introduce this violence here, and occasionally mention it throughout the rest of this ethnography.

While land routes across Mexico are famed for drug trafficking to the United States, an important means of transporting narcotics globally is via ships, particularly in containers that often include both licit and illicit goods (Griffiths and Jenks 2012; see also Castillo and Murillo 2020). Because Veracruz is Mexico's main port to the Gulf of Mexico and the Atlantic, it remains an important territory for drug traffickers to control (as are the ports of Manzanillo and Lázaro Cárdenas on the Pacific coast). In the mid-2000s, criminality and violence increased in Veracruz, as it did throughout the country. There were officially 269,904 homicides in Mexico between 2008 and 2018, with 10,718 people officially killed in the state of Veracruz. José Manuel Valenzuela Arce has called the disregard for young lives in particular a "*juvenicidio*" (2014, 15), a youth genocide: 53 percent of Mexico's 269,904 official homicides between 2008 and 2018 were people under thirty-five years old, and 81 percent were under fifty (INEGI 2021). Moreover, 1,295 of those killed in Veracruz were women, a slightly higher percentage than the northern border states (Veracruz 12.08 percent women; Chihuahua 8.81 percent; Tamaulipas 11.98 percent; nationally, 28,659 women were killed in this period, which is 10.62 percent of the national total), yet Veracruz was not famed for femicides specifically (INEGI). Although scholarly literature has addressed the impact of drug-related violence on younger people and on the social fabric in Mexico, little has been written about how this violence affects older men and women, and further research is needed in this area.

State policing and judicial mechanisms have failed to protect people of all ages for decades: the national impunity rate was just 69 percent in 2018, and there were states with almost no justice system (Le Clercq Ortega and Sánchez Lara 2018, 7). Reasons for this include: decades of state policies that failed to work against organized crime and corruption (see Astorga 2005); a shift of power away from the Institutional Revolutionary Party (PRI) in 2000, after over four decades of rule; the disruption this shift in power caused to unofficial links between the state and organized criminal groups; and the declaration of a "war on drugs" in 2006, by then-President Felipe Calderón, which was accompanied by militarization and contributed to the splitting of organized criminal factions. It is crucial to understand that the state competes with organized criminal groups for control of violence in early-twenty-first-century Mexico, as Sayak Valencia Triana (2018) propounds.

In the city of Veracruz, violence escalated markedly from 2010: extortion and shoot-outs became more prevalent, and isolated killings increased. Seventeen journalists were assassinated in the state during the 2010–2016 state governorship of Javier Duarte (the names of these journalists are detailed by Ureste 2017). And on September 20, 2011, two trucks were left on the main boulevard, piled high with the bodies of twenty-three men and twelve women who bore the signs of torture (see Redacción Animal Político 2011). Forty-six more bodies were found in local houses in the following days. The danzoneros I knew were horrified. Many were afraid to go out, especially at night. Operation *Veracruz Seguro* (Secure Veracruz) began: the Army, Navy, and Federal Police now patrolled the streets with machine guns and grenades, their faces hidden behind balaclavas and sunglasses (so that they would not be targeted once in civilian clothing). At first, this added to the anxiety, but one dancer, Manuela, told me that once she got used to it, these same soldiers and marines made her feel protected. Esmeralda, a danzón dancer aged sixty-five, explained to me that she stayed at home whenever she heard helicopters overhead, and she did not even go to the market to buy food. When no helicopters were about, however, she felt it was safe enough to carry on her daily business and attend danzón events. For many danzón performers and other locals, anxiety ebbed and flowed, as it did from person to person, as everyday life collided with violence: violence seen, heard, feared, and imagined. Gabriela, a regular danzón dancer aged seventy-one, told me: "Danzón is wholesome because just old people go to danzón. There are a few fights between people at danzón, but there are no stabbings or deaths." Many dancers and musicians continued to perform but left quickly at the end of danzón events. The Municipal Band musicians changed their uniforms so as not to be confused with marines or other military.[10] One musician I knew stopped doing gigs after having a gun held to his head when deputizing for another musician: two years later he died of a heart attack. Violence was both fast and slow.

In keeping with danzón practitioners' wishes not to dwell on the violence, I do not explore the concept of dystopian ambivalence in this book, but for future reference, dystopian ambivalences occur where there is an investment or joy in the horror of a difficult or bad place or situation. In Christian terms, we might think of imaginaries of heaven (in relation to love, egalitarianism, and immortality) as a utopia that is disrupted by earthly pragmatism, and hell (as painful, nightmarish, and eternal damnation) as a dystopia that is disrupted by earthly relish of it. In relation to Veracruz, the salacious consumption of blood-splattered bodies photographed in "red-top" newspapers, like the local *Notiver*, is an example of dystopian ambivalence.

Regarding the Vignettes

To enable people's struggles to be alluded to, intimate feelings to be intimated, stories that pervade the danzón world to be told that would otherwise be absent, I interweave vignettes of experimental ethnographic writing between the more conventionally written chapters of the book. The book is structured akin to a danzón, in rondo form (ABACAD). From Hurston's *Mules and Men* of 1935 to the "writing culture" turn of the 1980s (articulated influentially by Clifford and Marcus 1986), to more recent interventions (e.g., Pandian and McLean 2017), academics have grappled with the difficulties of capturing the complexity of people's lives through creative writing. Experimental academic writing has ranged from authorial reflexivity in the form of what Back (and others) refer to as "me-search" (2014, 767) on the one hand, to examples that capture tensions around translation, translocation, and corporeality (e.g., Savigliano 2003), embodied movement (e.g., Browning 1995; Taylor 1998; Hahn 2007; Bosse 2015), and the textures of people's lives (e.g., Lortat-Jacob 1995; Stewart 2007). My aim is that the vignettes in this book do the latter. Rather than merely ethnographic nonfiction, these vignettes combine fiction and nonfiction to enrich your understanding of danzón practitioners' lives, and to simultaneously make familiar and imply the sentiments and yearnings of people I got to know well. My hope is that they produce a different, more open-ended kind of knowledge, rather than the more formulaic, academic approach where the obvious must be stated. I chose to end the book with a vignette rather than a conclusion so that the proportions of the chapters and interludes mimic the rondo form of a danzón: a short conclusion would have altered the balance of the form. Instead, the key contributions are articulated in this introduction and at the ends of chapters.

The opening vignette elucidates how it pains Gerardo to go to danzón events because he is still in love with his ex, Elena, who now goes to events with her new partner, Miguel. Vignette 1 elucidates Teresita's lived experiences of racism in Veracruz. Vignette 2 relates how Pancho struggles to direct his danzonera because he is not from Veracruz. Vignette 3 documents Renata's relationship to danzón events, her fondness for the people she's fought with over the years, and the painful absence of her ill lover, Óscar. Vignette 4 alludes to the dynamics between a *maestro*, Antonio, and his dance and romantic partner, Lulú. Vignette 5 recounts how Uriel threw me (Hettie) out of his danzón dance group rehearsal because I had been fraternizing with Alejandra's danzón group. Vignette 6 alludes to the awkwardness and violence of Carmen and Ernesto's romance, despite public appearances. Vignette 7 portrays how important danzón is in the lives of Diana and her brain-damaged son, Tito; the losses they have suffered; and how they were ostracized from a dance group. These vignettes not only provide insights into dancers' lives, but they also let threads hang. For example, the domestic violence in Carmen and Ernesto's relationship is made visible in Vignette 6, and although this is not a theme I explore here, I think it is important to highlight that some danzoneras live with domestic violence.

While there is an ethics to laying bare people's intimacies and their vulnerabilities, there is also an ethics in failing to do so. As Les Back has argued, "we have to allow the people about whom we write to be complex, frail, ethically ambiguous, contradictory and damaged" (2007, 157). If we depict people only positively, Back continues, "we make the very people whose humanity one may want to defend less than human. We do not allow them to be as complicated as we are, namely compounds of pride and shame, weakness and strength" (2007, 157–58). Through these vignettes, I am attempting to approximate the "vulnerable ethics" (2017, 13) proposed by Tiffany Page, that is, an ethics that questions how we talk about people's lives when their stories fail them, both in terms of explanation and in terms of communicating struggles and pain. My hope is that the vignettes enrich your understanding of danzón practitioners' lives, of their dance, of their humanity.

VIGNETTE ONE

Teresita

(fiction)

Teresita. 67. Veracruz born and bred. Dark skin. Freckles. Round head. Loose Afro curls. Luscious lashes around wide, chestnut eyes. Petite nose. Discreet gold earrings. Unpainted lips. Short. Wiry thin.

Teresita had been a secretary. Now retired, she had time to run long distance four days a week and dance danzón the other three. She also kept a diary. When she went to danzón on Saturday evenings in the main square, she wore the white uniform of her dance group, the *Grupo Blanco*. She liked that, but preferred to be understated otherwise. Often she sat. Alone. While others danced.

Wednesday 25th May.
Dear Diary, she wrote:
   Yesterday, Emilio asked me to dance. Even though he presses his enormous stomach against mine, I accepted. It was strange. Dancing with him. People say we match because we're both dark skinned. I hate that. Am I really that ugly? Is that why Jorge jilted me at the altar; why no one decent has ever approached me?

Friday 27th May.
   Today I took a taxi. So expensive. The driver asked me where I was from. Can't he see that I'm from Veracruz? Listen to me speak. Puh-lease.

Saturday 28th May.
   Sebastián asked me to dance. I can't quite believe I accepted. He's so pale, so handsome, so flamenco. It was glorious: he turned me, twirled himself, twirled us. All the tourists watched, took photos, clapped. I couldn't wipe the grin off my face.

CHAPTER ONE

Racial Ambivalence

Veracruz, Blackness, and Danzón

While in most parts of Mexico, people negotiate national belonging and *mestizaje* (racial and cultural mixture) in relation to Spanishness and indigeneity, in contexts such as Veracruz, blackness is explicitly thrown into the mix, adding to the complexities of belonging and otherness. This blackness creates daily pain and humiliation for those positioned as darker, yet for some lighter-skinned locals, it is something positive to be harnessed at will. In this chapter, I examine how the Port's blackness is flexible enough for whiter locals (and in particular the Port's cultural, political, and academic elites) to evoke, embody, and strategically employ, while this flexibility is not available to darker locals, and it contributes to rendering racism invisible.
I argue for the methodological move of comparing widely circulated histories of music-dance forms and hegemonic racializations of humans because, as the example of danzón and people in Veracruz illustrates, there are striking parallels in the racial logics at play. I begin by interrogating racial logics in the popular history of danzón reproduced in Mexico and beyond by danzón experts (aficionado-investigators and masters of ceremonies, see Malcomson 2014a for an analysis of danzón aficionados and knowledge production). I then turn to Veracruz to analyze local people's relationships to danzón and to blackness. I propose that the racialization of danzón and Veracruz are displaced in space and time: the blackness of both this music-dance form and local people is associated with the past and a foreign country, Cuba, rather than the Veracruz of the present. Finally, I explore how such spatial and temporal dislocations contribute to enabling and maintaining ambivalences.

Racializing Music: Popular Histories of Danzón

Popular histories of danzón traverse three continents and four centuries and follow a single route. They have a beginning (the English Country Dance), a middle (where *danzón*, our protagonist, appears), and an end (the *cha-cha-chá*). The story goes that the seventeenth-century English Country Dance was taken to France and transformed into the French *contredanse*. With imperial enterprises, the contredanse traveled to "French" Saint Domingue (later Haiti) and then, with the late-eighteenth-century rebellion of enslaved people, the Saint Domingue elites fled, taking some enslaved people and contredanse to "Spanish" Cuba. It was in nineteenth-century Cuba, so the story goes, that African rhythms were added and the *contradanza cubana* emerged (see Malcomson 2014b), followed by the *danza* and the *danzón*. The first official performance of a danzón was in Matanzas, Cuba, in 1879: Afro-Cuban composer Miguel Faílde Perez's *Las Alturas de Simpson*. A final *montuno* section was added to the danzón around 1910 (with rhythmic and harmonic ostinati and call-and-response patterns), and the genre then gave rise to the *danzonete* (in the late 1920s), the *mambo* (around the 1940s), and the *cha-cha-chá* (around 1948). We have here a story where a semi-classical European music-dance form journeys to the Caribbean and is mixed with so-called African rhythmic elements (the tango, cinquillo, and tresillo; see Music Example 1.1), which become defining markers of the danzón, as does the Afro-Cubanness of Miguel Faílde Pérez. Rather than interrogating the accuracy of this history here (as I do elsewhere, 2011), let us consider several issues it raises that relate to the racialization of this music.[1]

First, migratory flows mark this popular history of danzón. Yet, the multiplicities and complexities of music-dance forms, of transnational flows, and of transformations are downplayed. This enables complex articulations of political, economic, religious, reproductive, cultural, and/or violent encounters to be elided. Relatedly, we have here a linear history, a focus on something that appears constant, and that moves and is then transformed. It is akin to what Paul Gilroy, drawing on Leroi Jones (aka Amiri Baraka), calls a "changing same" (1991, 126): something persistently present, but continually hybridized, over long periods of time. Transformations to our changing same are marked, above all, by new generic names: country dance becomes

Music Example 1.1. Tango (a), cinquillo (b), and tresillo (c).

contredanse becomes *contradanza* becomes *danza* becomes *danzón* (see Malcomson 2011).

Second, this "changing same" is portrayed as principally European: an Anglo-French, notated music-dance form that travels to the Caribbean and is augmented by an African-derived rhythm, the cinquillo, in Cuba. African-derived rhythms are depicted as additional and secondary, and crucially as though they *racialize* this dominant European music-dance form. Even though European musics are already racialized within a logic of invisible white privilege, African-derived rhythms make race appear in this story, as does the darker skin of many of the musicians and dancers who performed these musics and their purportedly African-derived movements (see Frankenberg [1993], Nayak [2007], and Ferber [2007] for analyses of white privilege). But as Philip Tagg argued in 1989, the markers that are used to stereotype music as black and African ("blue notes," call and response, syncopation, improvisation) exist in some African musics and not others, as well as in some European musics and not others. There is no evidence to back up assertions that any music is exclusively black or white; thus, music and dance have often been sites of political, social, and economic contestation. The racialization evident in this history of danzón provides a case in point (see García 2006a and Miller 2021 for other examples in relation to the racialization of Cuban music in the United States). The (contra)danza and danzón were the subject of numerous tirades in the nineteenth and twentieth centuries, accused of vulgarity, lasciviousness, and immorality. These critiques were highly racialized, gendered, and political.

As political leanings shifted in Cuba, the contradanza and danzón were defined variously as black, white, African, European, Spanish, or Cuban. Let us consider some examples. In 1809, the contradanza and waltz brought by the Saint Domingue exiles were described as "French libertinism" in the *Aviso de La Habana*, as Alejo Carpentier critiqued in his assertion that this was "colonial 'chauvinism'" (1946, 134). Osvaldo Castillo Faílde (1964) demonstrates how during the nineteenth-century wars of independence, pro-Spain Cuban conservative newspapers denigrated danzón as an immoral African music-dance form. Now danzón was African. Meanwhile, more liberal pro-independence newspapers emphasized the Cuban characteristics of danzón, and the genre was adopted (or coopted; Acosta 2004) by pro-independence Cuban criollo elites in their spontaneous parties (*asaltos*) to which Spaniards were not invited (Chasteen 2004). Now danzón was Cuban. In the meantime, patriotic contradanza lovers were outraged by the new orquestas típicas because of their "louder, livelier instrumentation taken from the Spanish bands" (León 1991, 20). Danzón now sounded Spanish. Yet while these debates raged, racial hierarchies were retained and the enslavement of black people persisted, not to be abolished until 1886.

By the 1920s, conservative columnists "attempted to establish the danzón—rather ironically—as an example of *white* Cuban music, without any African influence," according to Rogelio Martínez Furé (1991, 33). Similarly, nationalists such as Eduardo Sánchez de Fuentes (1928) suggested that danzón had hardly any black influence and was European, unlike rumba, son, and the jazz bands he condemned. Danzón was now white Cuban music. Meanwhile, *afrocubanismo* was in vogue, the cultural movement that was critical of the politics of post-independence Cuba and that promoted African-influenced expression as representative of the Cuban nation, including danzón (Carpentier's work falls into this category): danzón was also Afro-Cuban.[2] Danzón did not become more black or white during this history—for such ideas hold only if essentialist notions of black and white musics are adhered to in the first place. Instead, danzón was variously described as black, white, colonial French, Spanish, or (independent) Cuban according to political leanings. And such ideas about this music were further bolstered by tropes of purity, authenticity, tradition, and hybridity.

The third issue I want to raise here is how, once racialized, music is conceptualized in this history. While the changes to the predecessors to danzón are made explicit by the numerous generic titles (country dance, contredanse, contradanza, danza), the African-derived cinquillo rhythm is rendered homogenous and constant, a rhythmic pattern without historical or geographic variety. There are also parallels here with the way the African subcontinent and blackness are portrayed in these histories. The African subcontinent is mostly treated as a country (even a conceptual nation), a homogenous mass that, like the cinquillo, is constant, unvarying, and without geographic and historical variety. So it is implied that a non-evolving, generically "African" element is added to a dominant, evolving European music-dance form. While the heterogeneity of the African subcontinent is recognized by most Mexican danzón experts, discussion of Africanness tends to gravitate to African groups famed in Cuba (such as Congo, Dahomey, Mandinka, and Yoruba), to notions of an Africa without agency, without input into post-enslavement transatlantic flows (see Matory 1999 for an analysis of Yoruba exchanges). Moreover, while the migratory flows of this changing same may be explicit in this history, the brutal violence and suffering of enslavement, war, and imperialism is not. This is also the case in local accounts of the Port's racial configuration, which tend to focus on Cuba as the point of origin of local blackness, rather than the African subcontinent (as is the case with more politicized Black movements). Rather than excavating accuracies or alternative understandings of these histories further here, however, my primary concern is how these popular narratives relate to contemporary Veracruz, what purposes such histories serve, and what imaginaries they allow.

Veracruz and the Adoption of Danzón 1

Like the other popular music-dance forms that predominate in the Port (such as son cubano and reggaeton), danzón is said to originate from abroad. Specifically, danzón is ascribed foreign nationality: danzón is Cuban. What is of interest here is that danzón is promoted by the municipality as a marker of Veracruz (unlike son and reggaeton, which have not spawned Mexican variants or been institutionalized as much). Danzón is at once local and foreign. It is neither a regional music-dance form like Veracruz's "folkloric" son jarocho, nor national like Mexico's mariachi or the *jarabe tapatío* (the Mexican hat dance). It is quite distinct from these and from Argentine tango (Savigliano 1995), Brazilian samba (Vianna 1999; Hertzman 2013) and Colombian *música tropical* (cumbia, porro, vallenato) (Wade 2000), where the music's place of origin and national association correlate, despite initial marginalization. While Ulloa Anasco (1992) argued that danzón was the "National Dance of Cuba" after the Revolution in 1960 and forty years after the peak of its popularity, by the early twenty-first century, it was not generally considered Cuba's national music (as it was by Carpentier until around 1920); son cubano is a more favored candidate. Danzón remains firmly Cuban, despite its transformations in Mexico (in terms of instrumentation and musical and choreographic performance practice). This music-dance form, originating in Cuba, has come to claim a local attachment and a sense of rootedness because danzón, Cuba, and Veracruz are all linked, to varying degrees, to blackness. It is important to note that Cuba is correlated with blackness in Mexico, rather than a racially mixed population (despite people's awareness that the Cuban population is mixed) or whiteness (as it is in the United States).

Most people in Veracruz identify as Mexican, and if pushed, label themselves as *mestizo* (mixed), occasionally with some blackness, described vaguely. While no group of people in the Port identify as Black (as a politicized identity), many lower-class Veracruzana/os describe themselves as having a distinct mestizaje to the national version (Spanish-indigenous).[3] Mestizaje, a dominant Latin American ideology, refers to racial or cultural intermixture, mainly of Spanish and indigenous peoples, brought about by both sexual and social relations. While the concept of mestizaje has taken different forms historically and geographically throughout Latin America, it has been characterized by its strong association with nation-building projects, particularly in the twentieth century, when it was central to the official homogenizing discourse of several countries, including Mexico.[4] In contrast to European whiteness, mestizaje afforded these nations a singularity, an originality (as Vasconcelos famously argued in relation to Mexico in "The Cosmic Race" back in 1925). Yet the racial configuration of Veracruz is almost always portrayed by locals and other Mexicans as different from the national mestizaje (Spanish-indigenous). Instead, it is a discursive tripartite mestizaje, incorporating stereotypes associated with indigenous, Spanish, and black "blood." Neither Blackness nor Indigeneity is a prominent racial identity in the Port, however, and neither is considered local: indigenous people are mostly said to come from rural areas (in the State of Veracruz and elsewhere), while those considered black are designated as foreign and usually assumed to be Cuban (rather than African or from other parts of the circum-Caribbean). So when considering danzón and blackness in Veracruz, we are interrogating racial logics in a context where the music's origins are considered foreign and the local racial configuration appears at first sight non-national.

Danzón is seldom performed in Cuba (beyond annual festivals) in the early twenty-first century, while in Mexico it is thriving, particularly in Mexico City and in the Port of Veracruz, where it has been performed for over a century. It is disputed when and where danzón arrived in Mexico. Danzón aficionados from Yucatán, such as Civeira Taboada (1978), are prone to promoting Yucatán as the first place danzón was performed in Mexico. Meanwhile, Veracruz-biased danzón aficionados opt for Veracruz, Mexico's principal port and an important hub of socioeconomic and cultural routes with important links with Havana. Historian Bernardo García Díaz, for example, proposes that: "already by Summer 1880, in the Sunday retreat of the Plaza de Armas [Zócalo], that brought together the families and beauties of the languid port, the notes of the danzón *Malaca* could be heard" (1992, 113).[5]

What is striking about disputes regarding where danzón initially arrived in Mexico is the common desire to be the first, to host the "original" Mexican danzón performance. It is as if originality can be acquired, at least to some degree, by being the first place of arrival in another land, an affiliated place that is bestowed some measure of originality, of ownership, of authority. Some of these qualities, however, can also be acquired by being a place where there is sustained danzón performance. By the early twenty-first century, danzón was being performed almost every evening in the Port's main square or nearby smaller plazas. While danzón was practiced arguably more prolifically in Mexico City than in Veracruz (in dance halls and weekend public dance events supported by local councils), its magnitude was diluted by the size of the capital (8,851,080 in the 2010 INEGI census, excluding the greater metropolitan area). Meanwhile, in the smaller Port of Veracruz (552,156 people in the 2010 INEGI census), danzón was danced daily in prominent public spaces and promoted as a tourist attraction.

When I asked local musicians and dancers about danzón, they often began by talking about its history, pointing to Veracruz's place in it. Natalia Pineda Burgos, a seventy-four-year-old who had danced danzón for over sixty years and led a couple of dance groups, told me:

> Hay un dicho, no sé si tú lo sepas: "que es más padre el que cría que el que engendra." [...] Entonces Cuba lo sacó, lo formó, lo parió, pero nosotros lo recogimos y lo hemos alimentado 117 años. [...] Somos más padres nosotros, los veracruzanos, porque lo hemos sostenido tantos años y [las y los cubanos] lo dejaron morir. [...] En Mérida no fue muy bien recibido, pero nosotros, los veracruzanos, todo lo recibimos bien, y más que si se trata de bailar, entonces los veracruzanos lo adoptamos.
>
> There's a saying, I don't know if you know it: "he who raises the child is more of a father than he who conceives it." [...] So Cuba produced it [danzón], formed it, gave birth to it, but us, we gave it shelter and have fed it for 117 years. [...] We are more parents, us, the Veracruzanos, because we have supported it for so many years and [the Cubans] let it die. [...] In Merida, it wasn't very well received, but we, the Veracruzanos, receive everything well, and especially if it's to do with dancing, so the Veracruzanos adopted it.

In this quote, Cuba is the parent that "gave birth" to danzón, but Cuba also let danzón "die"—let it go out of fashion (after the 1950s). Meanwhile, Veracruz "brought it up," "fed it," "adopted it." The reproductive terminology here is striking. Many local dancers and musicians I know shared these views, and it was Veracruz, rather than other parts of Mexico, that was considered the adoptive parent of danzón. Kinship links were not referred to, however, when people discussed the relationship of danzón to Mexico City.

Blackness, Danzón Music, Veracruz, and Mexico City

For readers familiar with music analysis, it is worth dwelling on how danzón is performed in Veracruz and Mexico City, given the commonplace assertion that blackness is apparent in danzón performance practice in Veracruz. Differences include endings, instrumentation, and the ways the unnotated percussion parts are performed. Percussion tends to be racialized and

Music Example 1.2. Transcription of melodic line of "Nereidas" (1932) by Amador "Dimas" Pérez (clarinet or alto sax line). Permission to include Nereidas in this book was granted by Roberto Romero Pérez. All transcriptions are my own unless otherwise stated. The ABCD sections are marked and are performed AABAACAAD, where D is the *montuno*. The A, B, and C sections are in 3–2 clave (with the anacrusis measure being on the 2 side), and the D section is in 2–3 clave. Regarding shifts in clave direction, Sue Miller commented: "Richard Egües told me danzones could be 3–2 baqueteo [see Music Example 1.5] and then have 2–3 son clave *montunos* when I studied La Reina Isabel with him back in 2001—he told me not to fuss about clave direction in this respect! I have found most danzones in the charanga repertoire have 3–2 baqueteo and 2–3 *montunos*." (Email correspondence, 12 January 2022.)

Music Example 1.3. The final measures of danzones are performed as written in Mexico City. For example, Nereidas is performed this way.

Music Example 1.4. A pause is added to the end of danzones in Veracruz, so, for example, Nereidas is performed this way.

is thus my primary focus here. To exemplify similarities and differences in percussion performance practice, I provide an overview of timbales danzón base (or foundational) patterns as performed in these cities as they relate to one danzón: Amador "Dimas" Pérez's (1932) classic *Nereidas* (Music Example 1.2). I draw from conversations with timbaleros from two renowned ensembles about timbales playing generally, as well as observation of their playing *Nereidas* and other pieces: Silverio López Contreras (*Alma de Veracruz*, Veracruz) and Hipólito "Polo" González Peña (*Danzonera Acerina*, Mexico City).[6]

In terms of the endings of danzones, Veracruz's danzoneras usually insert an additional measure's rest before the final cadential chords, while danzoneras in Mexico City perform the final measures as written (see Music Examples 1.3 and 1.4). Veracruz's dancers hold still, like musical statues, during this one-measure pause, often with left leg extended, ready to perform the final step. Sue Miller told me that the renowned Cuban charanga Orquesta Aragón also sometimes insert a pause at the end of danzones (for example, *Naranjo y Lucas*), but in the Aragón case, this is a matter of arrangement choice made in rehearsal, rather than the more generic performance practice found in Veracruz.

In terms of instrumentation, the impact of swing bands can be clearly heard in Mexico City's danzoneras with their fuller, brassier sound: Mexico City's danzoneras often include four or five saxophones, including a baritone, rather than Veracruz's usual lineup of two clarinets or alto plus tenor sax, which is closer to the orquesta típica.[7] Mexico City's *Danzonera Acerina*

Music Example 1.5. Two-measure cinquillo pattern (baqueteo) (in 3–2 clave). The baqueteo is an elaborated clave consisting of a cinquillo measure followed by a measure of straight eighth notes (or vice versa in 2–3 clave).

includes a violin, associated with the Cuban charanga, and its baritone sax might be likened to the ophicleide of the orquesta típica: so overall, while the Veracruz sound is closer to the (originally Cuban) orquesta típica, the danzoneras in Mexico City have also been influenced, albeit slightly differently, by Cuban instrumentation (I am grateful to Sue Miller for this observation.). Percussion-wise, like the Cubans, Veracruz's danzoneras include a congas player and a (mambo) cowbell (*cencerro*) attached between the timbales. While the güiro player often doubles on claves in the C section of danzones in Veracruz, this practice is uncommon in Mexico City. In both cities, güiro patterns are founded on the cinquillo, played as a one- or two-measure unit (Music Example 1.5). Akin to performers in Cuba, güiro performers in Veracruz move the left hand while scraping the instrument with the right, creating a looser, longer-lasting sound than the crisp attack achieved by güiro players in Mexico City, who hold instruments still when playing.

Timbales in Veracruz tend to have goat skin heads (see Figure 1.1), while in Mexico City, synthetic heads are more common. In Mexico City, the instruments sound slightly less boomy and tighter than in Veracruz, yet in both contexts, the timbales are pitched low in comparison with Cuban orquesta típicas and charangas, and with the crisper, higher Tito Puente sounds. Timbaleros in both Mexico City and Veracruz play the drumheads open and dampened (with the hands or fingers), use cross-stick strokes (rim clicks), and hit the rim and shell of the timbales with their timbales sticks (or more often, in Veracruz, reversed drumsticks strengthened with tape). Timbaleros' playing in Mexico City tends to be more energetic, particularly in the A sections, but beyond this, they approach the A section similarly: accompanying the melody in the anacrusis and measure 2; a different figure (akin to sections B and C) in measures 1 and 3; and, as indicated in Music Example 1.6, a marker of the end of the first phrase in measure 4, a cinquillo in measures 5 and 7 (see also Music Example 1.8), and markers denoting the end of the section in measures 6 and 8. In the B and C sections (the

Figure 1.1. Timbales with goatskin heads and cowbell as used in Veracruz.

tangeos), base patterns in each city are distinct. That said, once a pattern or its variation is performed, it is often repeated for four to eight measures in both contexts. In Veracruz, the base pattern is centered on the cinquillo (see Music Examples 1.5 and 1.7), while timbaleros in Mexico City follow the innovations established by the renowned timbalero Consejo "Acerina" Valiente Robert (1899–1987), Polo González Peña told me: employing stick shot strokes (striking a cross stick held in the left hand with the right-hand stick) and playing a son cubano conga base pattern on the timbales (Music Example 1.9). The son cubano pattern is played on the congas in Veracruz (and Cuba) in the *montuno* (Music Example 1.10). In Veracruz, the tempo is increased slightly in the *montuno* (D section) and the A section preceding it, but in Mexico City, the tempo increase is more marked. In both cities, the sonority of the timbales is changed in the *montuno* during some patterns: in Mexico City, the *cáscara* (shell) of the low timbal is struck with the right hand,

Music Example 1.6. Timbales base pattern performed in measures 4–8 of A section of danzones (with Nereidas melody). Note the clear demarcation of phrases with the pattern in measures 4 and 6–8. Timbales are often tuned a fifth apart at the beginning of a set (to A and E, for example), but are not retuned between danzones, so I use older timpani notation with the high timbal as C and the low timbal as G, to indicate that the tuning is not consistent. The gendered terminology for timbales employed in Cuba (hembra and macho) is not used in Mexico: instead, timbales are described as high (agudo) or low (grave).

Music Example 1.7. Timbal cinquillo pattern (in 3–2 clave). This is performed as a one- or two-measure pattern. The left hand plays cross-stick while the right hand strikes the center of the timbales.

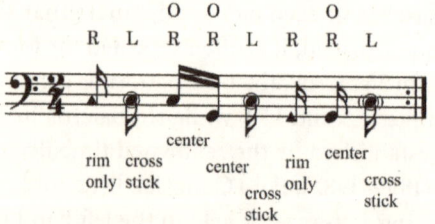

Music Example 1.8. Cinquillo pattern variation as played on timbales in Veracruz. This pattern is performed particularly in the B and C sections.

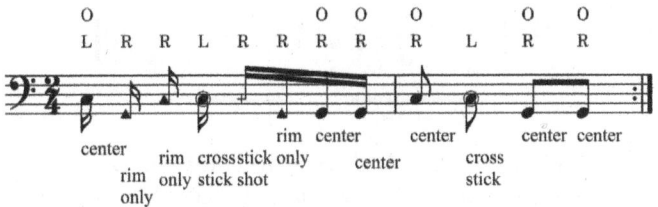

Music Example 1.9. Son cubano conga pattern (in 3–2 clave) as played on timbales in Mexico City. This pattern is performed particularly in the B and C sections.

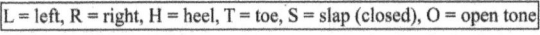

Music Example 1.10. Son cubano pattern (in 3–2 clave) as performed on congas in the *montuno* in Veracruz.

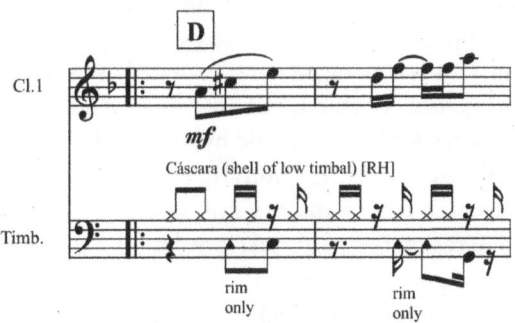

Music Example 1.11. Mexico City timbales *montuno* pattern (in 2–3 clave) with melody of Nereidas.

while the left hand emphasizes the clave (Music Example 1.11); in Veracruz, a cowbell is played more often than the cáscara (as is the case with Cuban charanga and orquesta típica montunos), and the hands are swapped, such that the left hand plays quarter notes on the cowbell that sits between the timbales (Music Example 1.12). In Mexico City, the bass drum is also used to play the clave in the *montuno*. In the danzón *Mi Consuelo es Amarte* by Leopoldo Olivares, the Afro rhythm is played in the *montuno* by timbaleros in both cities (Music Example 1.13), but this rhythm was not allied to blackness in these contexts (it was described as "oriental" by musicians in Veracruz).

cowbell [LH]

Music Example 1.12. Veracruz timbales *montuno* pattern with cowbell (in 3–2 clave).

Music Example 1.13. The Afro rhythm is played on timbales in the *montuno* of "Mi Consuelo es Amarte."

We have seen how there are distinctly Cuban flavors in the instrumentation and sounds of danzoneras in both cities. Yet Veracruz is often described as more black and Cuban than the capital because congas are employed, and goat-skin-headed timbales and the cinquillo provide the rhythmic base of Veracruz's timbales patterns (as it does in Cuban charangas). The son cubano pattern employed in Mexico City's timbales playing could equally be construed as Cuban, however, being first incorporated into danzón performance by Acerina Valiente Robert, who was Afro-Cuban. And it is noteworthy that timbalero Polo González Peña also told me that while Veracruz's musicians are often essentialized as being naturally endowed with rhythmic skills, some güiro players in both Veracruz and Mexico City have little musical knowledge and occasionally confused clave patterns, playing 3 on the 2 side and vice versa.

Notions of music being more black, white, or otherwise are complex and nuanced, as argued above in relation to the history of danzón. And despite the wealth of danzón and other Cuban popular musics in Mexico City (such as being home to Dámaso Pérez Prado's mambo, see Pulido Llano 2017), it is Veracruz that is said to be more Caribbean and to have "adopted" danzón. When I asked "why Veracruz?", it was the Cuban-ness of the region, broadly, that was generally evoked.

Veracruz and the Adoption of Danzón 2

Most danzón practitioners in Veracruz, cultural promoters, and danzón aficionado investigators concurred that Veracruz was an appropriate surrogate parent for danzón because of its Caribbeanness, and in particular its racial configuration. Aficionado-investigator Flores y Escalante, for example, claims that "since its arrival to the port of Veracruz in 1879, danzón started to take on completely 'popular' characteristics thanks to its African-derived rhythm (the cinquillo), that was immediately accepted by jarochos [Veracruzana/os] descended mostly from Mandingo blacks" (1993, 39).[8] This example is unusual in that it refers to people from Veracruz as having ancestry in the African subcontinent, specifically the upper Niger valley, rather than, or as well as, Cuba. Cuba is more usually evoked as the source of Veracruz's blackness, and Cuba is associated with a black population, rather than whiteness or mixture. Havana and Veracruz are famously connected by centuries of sea traffic between their ports, and also by the large wave of Cuban émigrés who arrived at the Port toward the end of the nineteenth century with the Cuban wars of independence (1868–1898) and the increased work opportunities of the Port's modernization (García Díaz 2002). Given this link to the Cuban independence movement, it was the independence supporters and freedom fighters among Veracruz's Cuban population who, García Díaz (2002) propounds, adopted and promoted danzón as a patriotic symbol. It was they who purportedly initially played and danced danzón with Veracruzana/os (Rivera Ávila 1992).

This was an era before widespread commercial air travel, an era when travelers arrived and departed from Mexico via the port, and migrants came in search of work and refuge. Despite the Port's diverse migration history (see Sefchovich et al. 2000 for information on Spanish, Lebanese, German, Japanese, and other migrants), it is the Cuban migration that is highlighted in many local histories of danzón. And it was the bodily visibility of darker-skinned musicians, dancers, and baseball players, Christina Sue (2013) claims, that contributed to the notion that Veracruz's blackness comes from Cuba. Also, many lighter-skinned Cubans visually "blend in" more in Mexico, making darker-skinned Cubans particularly visible.

Crucial to our story is that some academics, musicians, and aficionados go beyond Cuba in their understanding of Veracruz's links to the "Black Atlantic" (Gilroy 1993). Historian García Díaz asserts that the late-nineteenth-century Cuban migration merely reaffirmed "the Mexican-Caribbean soul of the port" (2002, 271), which existed "independently of the presence of the Cuban colony, to welcome and adopt the different rhythms imported from the heart of the Caribbean" (2002, 273). Mexico had had a mixed population for centuries, including an (possibly conservatively) estimated 200,000 enslaved people (Knight 2002) from the sixteenth century until 1829, when slavery was abolished. These people were brought from the African subcontinent and the circum-Caribbean, and they passed through or stayed in the Port (see Gutiérrez 2018). Yet enslavement scarcely features in local histories of danzón or of Veracruz's racial configuration.

Some local musicians and danzón aficionados had much more controversial accounts of Veracruz's blackness, accounts that suggested pre-Hispanic links to the African subcontinent. They alluded to the Africanness of Olmec heads (for more on this, see Van Sertima 1977) and/or pre-Hispanic *teponaztli* slit drums as proof of Veracruz's pre-Hispanic links to Africa. A few local musicians referred to Pangaea, to the African and American continents once being part of a single land mass. Contentiously, some suggested that Veracruz's African presence was linked to experiments by extraterrestrials. Despite these latter claims being more incredible than the former, to varying degrees, they all purport that the Port is unique and original, with an African cultural and racial heritage of its own. Such claims not only transcend links with Cuba and Europe but also make Veracruz potentially African in its own right, potentially original in its creation of an Afro-Caribbean cultural repertoire (including music, dances, instruments, food, and religion), bypassing the history of the Middle Passage and enslavement.

Whether Veracruz is linked to Cuba or has independent connections to the African subcontinent, Veracruz emerges as unique, distinct both from Cuba and from Mexico. While Cuba is more usually ascribed as the primary source of Veracruz's blackness, early-twenty-first-century Veracruz is distanced from Cuba in terms of both time and space: not only was there less traffic between the ports of Havana and Veracruz than there had been in the nineteenth and the first half of the twentieth centuries (due to shifting technological and political circumstances such as passenger air travel and the Cuban Revolution), but also, by the early twenty-first century, Veracruz had several generations separating it from the substantial Cuban migrations to the Port, generations augmenting what was already a very mixed population. What is emphasized is that Veracruz is clearly not Cuban, but unique in its own regard: Veracruz creates its regional and national identity in part through its relationship with Cuba. While Cuba is referred to as the "natural parent" of danzón (as we saw in Natalia's quote above), Veracruz is distanced from Cuba by merely being the appropriate "adoptive parent" of danzón, as if a parent from another family. While Veracruz was capable of adopting and including danzón, this very adoption maintains the exclusivity of its Mexican national family. Veracruz remains clearly Mexican, and its membership in the Mexican national family is reinforced by its adoption of this music-dance form. But Veracruz also emerges as distinct from the rest of Mexico, and its adoption of danzón enriches its regional singularity (which in turn contributes to its national inclusion). The logic goes that danzón was popular in Veracruz because Veracruz is Caribbean, but danzón is also a vehicle for making Veracruz Caribbean. This is (almost) a Caribbean port with a distinct racial configuration, potentially subject to the shifting moralities aligned to stereotypes associated with blood, race, and class. For example, the heat of the Port is often put forward as a rationale for the sexual temperaments of women and men in Veracruz, making them "hot," like their "black blood," chiming with nineteenth-century Spanish (American) notions of territorial and climatic conditions affecting people's minds and bodies (see López Beltrán 2007).

Racial Logics, Expedient Blackness, and Racism

A tension prevails between blackness as being located in Veracruz and as being located somewhere else. There are parallels here with the temporal and geographic distancing highlighted in, on the one hand, Sarah Daynes's (2004) work on reggae lyrics, in which Africa is referred to as the place of a lost past utopia and of future redemption, brutally ruptured by the enslavement of black peoples and colonial oppression, and often including the present; and on the other hand, David García's (2017) analysis of how black music and dance were experienced from the 1920s to the 1950s as spatially and temporally distant from modernity (as linked to the "bush" and the "primitive"). Yet the brutality of the enslavement of black peoples is not evoked by many of Veracruz's musicians and dancers. Instead, danzón practitioners and other locals tend to refer to settlements of runaway enslaved people, such as that famously led by Yanga from around 1580 (Carroll 2001), and to a cultural repertoire (such as food, language, music, and dance) characteristic of the region said to have been brought by enslaved peoples. And blackness tends to be located in Veracruz's historical past, particularly in areas outside the former city walls, such as the poor neighborhood of La Huaca, which housed many late-nineteenth-century Cuban immigrants, as well as famously being the birthplace of Toña La Negra in 1912. Blackness is not something of the here and now. It is neither past nor present, far nor close.

Several scholars, such as anthropologist Flores Martos (2004, 40–41), have commented on the apparent lack of visible blackness in the Port, promoting the idea that Veracruz's tripartite mestizaje is in some sense imaginary and reinforcing the notion that "nobody really looks black." After centuries of mixing with the numerous lighter and darker migrants who have traversed and stayed in this transatlantic Port, the population is diverse in terms of migration histories and visible racial backgrounds. Yet the terms of visibility are not only highly complex but also relative, and they have their own politics

(Phelan 1996). This is particularly the case where mestizaje is concerned. Mestizaje logics are contextual and relative: people might be darker than others in one context (*morena/o, prieta/o*), but lighter than others in another (*güera/o*) (Lancaster 2003; Moreno Figueroa 2012).[9]

According to the ideologies of the colonial *casta* system, the sexual mixing of a Spanish with an indigenous person (usually woman) created a *mestizo*; the mixing of a mestizo and a Spanish created a *castizo*; and a castizo and a Spanish created a Spanish: in three generations, Spanishness/whiteness could theoretically and officially be achieved. Traces of the ideologies of this system prevail to this day. As Moreno Figueroa (2008) has analyzed, there is an underlying pressure to whiten through procreation, to "*mejorar la raza*" (improve the race) by mixing with lighter people, and to continue colonial racial logics. Yet after centuries of mixing, it is not uncommon for siblings with the same parents to be much darker or lighter than each other and/or their parents. The visibility (and/or lack of visibility) of blackness in Veracruz must be understood in relation to the contextual and relative racial logics applicable to individuals, families, and generations, as must the racism.

As is the case with the supposedly African-derived cinquillo rhythm of danzón, only certain markers are employed to denote Veracruz's blackness—markers linked to this colonial past. As Wade elucidates, there were "particular aspects of phenotypical variation that were worked into vital signifiers of difference during European colonial encounters with others" (1997, 15). One such marker used to identify blackness in Veracruz is curly hair ("*pelo chino*").[10] Although skin color and facial features are also referred to, curly hair is alluded to more commonly, at least at the individual level, as Sue (2009) elucidates. It is individuals, in certain contexts, who become bearers of blackness, of racial otherness, rather than the collectivity. While Veracruzana/os en masse are often described, by themselves and other Mexicans, as *more* black than other national subjects (regardless of whether they are), they are not considered to be Black, where Black is understood as a collective, politicized identity.[11]

Sue (2009) has pointed to the complexity of racialization processes in Veracruz. She argues that in this context, "the black category is simultaneously fixed and fluid" (Sue 2013, 116): it is fluid because it is evoked in relation to others, and it is fixed when certain foreigners are described as Black, particularly Afro-Cubans and African Americans. Veracruzana/os need some notion of fixed blackness, she asserts, so that they can distance themselves from it and from their own blackness. She proposes that "at the individual level Veracruzanos of African descent project an unstable black identity, allowing them to maintain some truth to themselves and their histories without challenging the national ideological stance or jeopardizing their identity as Mexican" (Sue 2013, 116). This "truth," for Sue, relates to knowledge of histories of enslavement, African ancestry, and intergenerational knowledge transmission (Sue 2013, 141).

While Sue proposes an analytical model where Veracruzana/os contend *with two contradictory relationships to a single notion of blackness*—the one fixed and stable, the other fluid and unstable—in my view, it is more appropriate to use a distinct model with two notions of blackness. In the Port of Veracruz, *two understandings of blackness* operate, I suggest, both of which are linked to phenotypical and cultural markers: first, Blackness as an identity and a political position linked to the enslavement of black peoples, oppression, and emancipatory struggles; and second, blackness as a non-identity, something rarely linked to enslavement or emancipatory politics, but to vague racialized, bodily characteristics, moralities, and cultural phenomena. Such a distinction is not unique to Veracruz: the logics of the region are reproduced clearly in this context (see, for example, Paschel 2016 regarding Colombia and Brazil). Such a move enables us to understand how blackness can be used expediently: some Veracruzana/os can claim to be "a bit black" (as a marker of African heritage) without being Black (as a politicized identity), and crucially, without this creating a contradiction as such.

Sue addresses the notion of some Veracruzana/os having some blackness by using the analytical tool of color, where color refers to "various phenotypic markers including skin tone, hair texture, eye colour, and facial features" (2013, 6). Sue treats color as fixed, and she classifies people as "light, light-brown, medium-brown, and dark-brown" (2013, 21), although these are not definitive, she contends. Her argument rests on her understanding of the word *morena*, used extensively in this context, as brown or dark in English. For Sue, *morena* is "a term that literally translates as brown but that can function as a euphemism for the term black" (2013, 3). I would argue, however, following Moreno Figueroa (2011), that *morena* is better understood as "brownness," "darker than," or "darkish," and this darkness is almost always used as an adjective in Veracruz, rather than as a noun. Moreno Figueroa found in a focus group on mestizaje and racism in León, Guanajuato (Mexico), that, when looking at a photograph and at themselves, participants had distinct understandings of dark skin: she argued that skin color is visually relational and that it implied a "shared cultural understanding" (2012, 173). Likewise, in Veracruz, people tend to think of themselves as darker or lighter than others, rather than adopting an identity of Brownness or Blackness, or even considering themselves in such stable terms. Moreover, Veracruz's racial logic enables certain people to be "a bit black" and even to flirt with their blackness, while others have less access to such choices.

Of the two understandings of blackness, I am proposing that some Veracruzana/os appropriate and distance themselves from blackness through danzón. When Veracruzana/os make a "positive" appropriation of such blackness (as "authentic"), this appropriation reproduces racial stereotypes based on exoticized, biological notions of race: blackness is equated with being good at dancing, sexually "hot," happy, rhythmically adept, and so forth. This is akin to the "autoexoticization" analyzed by Marta Savigliano (1995, 2) in relation to Argentine tango, whereby former colonies assume neocolonial exoticizing logics allied to national, and in this case regional, identities; and the "tropicalizing" explored by Francis Aparicio and Susana Chávez-Silverman, whereby tropes are created in response to mythic colonial ideas, such as an "idea of *latinidad* based on Anglo (or dominant) projections of fear" (1997, 8). Yet "autoexoticization" or "tropicalization" in relation to blackness is not homogeneous in Veracruz. The anthropologist Flores Martos suggests that middle-class Veracruzana/os internalize the "tropical" stereotypes of the state and reproduce them as their own (2004, 30). But this is something middle-class Veracruzana/os can choose if they are lighter-skinned: blackness becomes something they can use expediently. This is far from Spivak's (1987) "strategic essentialism," where subaltern groups mimic their negative representations as a politically strategic tool. It is the cultural, political, and academic elites, rather than any subaltern group, who strategically essentialize Veracruzana/os' blackness for their own ends: for example, to promote tourism, and in cultural and academic festivals such as the *Afrocaribeño*, celebrated annually since 1997. Politicians, cultural promoters, academics, and other danzón experts proudly announce their African heritage, and most Veracruzana/os are pleased to be stereotyped as happy and hospitable. And although these elites are aware of the relationships of Blackness to enslavement and emancipation, they rarely evoke them. One Veracruzana academic, who started identifying as "Afro-descendent" as an adult, proudly proclaimed at a conference on mestizaje: "*La herencia africana en México es como el azúcar en el café: no se ve, pero hace que todo sepa mejor*" ("The African heritage in Mexico is like sugar in coffee: you can't see it, but it makes everything taste better"). Violent plantation-related sugar histories aside, while within the continuum of physical narrative allowed by mestizaje, her African heritage may not be "visible" to others, it bestows her with positive attributes, a "better flavor."

Let us consider another example relating to danzón. Cubans are racialized as black in the Veracruzana imaginary, while Veracruzana/os are not. In this respect, one sixty-eight-year-old woman, a lower-middle-class, pale-skinned danzón dancer, told me:

> *Las cubanas ya ves que bailan muy, muy erótico. Las cubanas son algo especial. Y entonces, cuando empezaron a sacar el danzón veracruzano, el jarocho es más lento para bailarlo, no es como el cubano: no, no, no! Al danzón empezaron [las y los Veracruzana/os] a darle un ritmo más asentado, más bonito, más decente por decirlo así, y ahí fue como se formó el danzón veracruzano.*
>
> You know Cuban women dance very, very erotically. Cuban women are something else. And when they started to make Veracruzano danzón, the Veracruzana/o dances it more slowly, not like the Cuban: no, no, no! They [the Veracruzana/os] began to give danzón a smoother rhythm, prettier, you could even say more decent, and that's how the Veracruz style of danzón was formed.

Here Cubans and Veracruzana/os are collectively generalized as enacting danzón in a particular way, despite danzón being a mostly lower-middle-class phenomenon in these contexts. It is the Cuban women who are assumed to be black and stereotyped as highly erotic in this quote, and although Veracruzana women are not mentioned, they become invisible "others" and whiter, Mexican points of reference. The Veracruzanas are the ones who are not Cubanas here, who do not dance like them. Women, rather than men, are usually referred to in terms of racialized decency in Veracruz. Veracruzana women are often compared to Cuban women in terms of their propriety: Veracruzanas are less sexually "hot" than Cuban *mulatas* (women of Afro-Caribbean/African and European parentage). Veracruz's danzón is more decent, more dilute than Cuban dancing. It is as if Veracruzana women are at a safe distance from their blackness: they can be decent while reaping the benefits of being "a bit hot" and dancing in a "prettier way." Again there is a flexibility regarding who can choose to benefit from this safe sexuality, who can strategically embody blackness: decency is gendered, racialized, classed, and relative. Class and racial hierarchies often coincide in Veracruz, and Mexico more generally, and it is the lower classes, together with darker-skinned people, who tend to be allied with "indecencies." Black men were stereotyped as more promiscuous than whiter men by many of the danzón dancers I know, but men were rarely referred to in terms of decency.

But some Veracruzana/os cannot choose when to flirt with their blackness. They are *too* visible (too "darker-than" others) not to be racialized, and their experiences are quite distinct. For example, a middle-aged, lower-middle-class, darker-skinned music teacher told me how he was often stopped by porters when walking into his workplace, while his whiter colleagues and other visitors entered unhindered. Like other darker-skinned locals, he could not elect whether to distance his blackness from himself, and stereotypes ascribed to blackness are not always positive.

He told me:

> *Hay tanto racismo; no queremos admitir lo que tenemos en nosotros. Aplastaron al negro y al indígena—nadie quiere ser negro o indígena. La gente dice: "Pobrecitos indios, gallegos orgullosos, negros huácala."* [*Huácala* is a Mexican, onomatopoeic expression of disgust.]
>
> There is so much racism; we don't want to admit what we have in us. Blackness and indigeneity were crushed—no one wants to be Black or Indigenous. The people say: "Poor Indians, arrogant Spaniards; Blacks, yuck."

Darker-skinned, lower-middle-class Veracruzana/os want the positive elements of their tripartite mestizaje, but they do not want to be subjected to the violence of the "omnipresent dimension" of Mexican racism (Knight 1990b, 99), to the pain caused by their sense of national belonging being disrupted (as we saw in Teresita's story in Vignette 1). These Veracruzana/os simultaneously appropriate and distance themselves from the blackness of the Port's mestizaje: They want the positive elements without the racism. They want to be included within the national category of Mexican, without being racialized as Black and thereby excluded. People who look "too black" in Veracruz are ascribed foreign status and often described as Cuban, stripped of their Mexican nationality. Moreover, Cuba as a nation is racialized by Mexicans (as Black), while Mexico as a nation is not. This gives us a clue as to why racial violence is downplayed so much in histories of Veracruz and its danzón. Veracruzana/os' history is Mexican, not Cuban or Black, thus the lack of association with enslavement, and the subsequent drive by academics, notably Gonzalo Aguirre Beltrán (1946) and Luz María Martínez Montiel (1988), to re-inscribe Veracruz's "third root" (its Afro-descendence).

Ambivalences around national belonging and alienation pertain in Veracruz: some locals experience a tension between being black—a racialized position associated with foreignness—and being Mexican (national subjects). The ambivalences of being and/or not being black are intensified by their intersection with the ambivalences of belonging to the nation and/or not, of having a national subjectivity and/or not. These ambivalences are static, in that they relate to being black and/or not, a national subject and/or not. These static ambivalences are entangled with dialectic ambivalences, inherent in logics of mestizaje, around preserving and transcending, absorbing and canceling racial markers in generational becoming. And these static and dialectic ambivalences combine with utopian ambivalences inherent in the ideology of mestizaje. Utopian ambivalences are provoked where an ideal includes elements that undermine it. Utopian ambivalences are evident in Du Bois's analysis of Black subjectivities in the United States, specifically the ideal and promise of being respected as a full-fledged human (the "longing to attain self-conscious manhood" [1897]), which is disrupted by the black body, racism, deprecation, and humiliation. The logics of mestizaje are distinct from the US one-drop model, however. Mestizaje carries a promise of racial democracy for everyone that is constantly disrupted. This disruption takes two distinct forms according to whether people are lighter or darker skinned.

The first form of ambivalence in relation to mestizaje has been elaborated by Peter Wade, and the second has been analyzed by Charles Hale. In the first form, as Wade contends, the concept of mestizaje incorporates both "democratic inclusivity" (everyone's mixture can be improved, can be whitened) and also discriminatory practices "based on the idea of the inferiority of blacks and indigenous peoples" (Wade 2001, 849). So for those too dark in given contexts, the promise of mestizaje (of being a national subject) is often disrupted by racism. And it is not merely the ideal of every individual being able to be a national subject that is at stake here. As Wade explains, racist outbursts are often an attempt by national elites to construct otherness, "remaking difference because it was fundamental to the reproduction of their own position" (2001, 855). So here we have lighter elites disrupting the promise of racial democracy and creating utopian ambivalences for those who are darker skinned, which, crucially, are generally experienced as individualized (see Moreno Figueroa 2008). The second form of utopian ambivalence relates to whiter people. Hale (2006) calls this form of ambivalence "racial ambivalence," and it is exemplified by his analysis of how Guatemalan ladinos (mestizos) want to promote racial equality while also maintaining their positions of privilege. In short, I am arguing for two forms of utopian ambivalence that relate to the promise mestizaje brings of racial democracy and equality: the first, violent and distressing, where the ideological promise of mestizaje engendering equality is disrupted by racism; and the second, where the desire for equality is disrupted by the urge to sustain a position of power and privilege. What is striking about these ambivalences in relation to mestizaje is that because they are contextual and relative, one person can both experience and cause others to experience both forms of utopian ambivalence, as well as the static ambivalences described above, at different times and in different situations.

Race, Nation, and Danzón (or "One Thing Is Added to and Mixed with Another in Unequal Parts")

To further understand racial logics operating in the Port, we need to unpack how Veracruz's blackness relates to understandings of the nation. Despite the estimated 200,000 enslaved people who entered Mexico from the sixteenth century, and despite the inclusion of blackness in the colonial *casta* descriptions, the cultural and racial mixture promoted as Mexico's national mestizaje in post-revolutionary nation-building projects from the 1920s omitted blackness and mestizaje was merely portrayed as an indigenous-Spanish mixture. The concept of this national bipartite (indigenous-Spanish) mestizaje was accompanied by the imaginary that all Mexicans were in part indigenous, including, purportedly, the whiter elites. In this Mexicanness, indigeneity was added to Spanishness and vice versa: one thing was added to and mixed with another. The notion of Veracruz's racial configuration including a "third root" of blackness was promoted nationally from the 1980s, and locally by Veracruz's Cultural Institute (the IVEC) from 1989 in annual Afro-Caribbean festivals (see García Díaz and Guadarrama Olivera 2004; Rinaudo 2010, 2012). It was from this point on that several locals I know, of various ages, became interested in their own African heritage.

What I found particularly striking when talking to local people was that Veracruz's tripartite mestizaje is often described as though blackness is a so-called ingredient added to and mixed with a monolithic, bipartite Mexican mestizaje: a logic that one minor thing is added to and mixed with something dominant. This logic of one thing being added to and mixed with another in unequal parts follows colonial racial descriptions of elements creating mixture, and it shapes understandings of Veracruz's cultural and racial configuration. That is, to the national mestizaje is added a "third root" that is culturally and racially mixed in. In these logics of one thing being added to and mixed with another in unequal parts, the dominant element (Spanishness/national mestizaje) is envisioned as homogenous and neutral, while the minor element (indigeneity/blackness) is described racially, as something doing the racializing. So in Mexico's national mestizaje, whiteness (Spanishness) is racialized by indigeneity; and in Veracruz's post-1980s (discursive) tripartite mestizaje, Mexico's national mestizaje is racialized by blackness. Yet the heterogeneity and dynamism of European cultural and racial whiteness is rarely alluded to. This has consequences for both the continuation of whiteness as a structuring norm and the obscuring of racist practices (as

Moreno Figueroa 2010 explores in her analysis of the workings of mestizaje as a form of whiteness). Parallels exist with popular histories of danzón in which the cinquillo is described as racializing a discursively neutral, autonomous, European semi-classical music.

Understandings of national subjectivities intertwine with racialized identities in Veracruz. Knight (1990b) and Alonso (2004) have traced shifts to Mexican identity during the twentieth century: after the Revolution, the idea that the national subject was mestiza/o (mixed Spanish/indigenous) was promoted by the government, and by the end of the century, the majority thought of themselves as Mexican (national subjects) rather than mestiza/o (racialized as biologically or culturally mixed).[12] That is, the national discourse of mestizaje is such that notions of race (being mestizo/a) were replaced by the idea of being a national subject (being Mexican). In this bipartite national ideology of mestizaje, national subjectivity had eclipsed any form of racial identity (which explains the discomfort I sensed when I heard foreigners asking Veracruzana/os: "What race are you?").[13]

So what happened when a "third root" was added to this mix? We have seen how the logic of one thing being added to and mixed with another was applied in the idea of the "third root" being added to and mixed with Mexico's bipartite mestizaje in Veracruz. But instead of blackness (race) being added to and mixed with mestizaje (race), here we have blackness (race) being added to and mixed with Mexicanness (nation): race is being added to and mixed with nation. But this race ("third root") being added to and mixed with nation (Mexicanness) did not racialize Veracruzana/os en masse. Instead, Veracruzana/os continue to think of themselves as Mexican subjects, and only if pushed, as mestiza/o (that is, as racialized), despite their knowledge of their "third root."(The sugar in the coffee analogy comes to mind, or the "slightly hot" Veracruzana women.) National subjectivity remains stronger than racial identities (although there is a shift to identity politics stimulated by the inclusion of a self-identification question for Black, Afro-Mexican, and Afro-descendent people in the 2015 intercensal survey and 2020 census, their recognition in the Constitution in 2019, and a growing Black mobilization in the country; see Moreno Figueroa 2022).

Veracruz has played an important role in the history of Mexico: Spanish conquistador Hernán Cortés arrived (near) here in 1519; it was the only official port on the east coast of New Spain (Mexico) until the 1760s, controlling most of the viceroyalty's importation and exportation (including sugar, silver, cochineal, textiles, and tobacco); the city is entitled "four times heroic," having defended the nation against the Spanish in 1823–25, the French in 1838, and the United States in 1847 and 1914, as well as housing Júarez's (1858) and

Carranza's (1914) temporary governments at key moments in Mexico's history. There has been no doubt that Veracruz or its people are Mexican at any point since Mexico's independence, let alone in the twentieth or early twenty-first centuries, before or after the "third root" was made explicit again in the 1980s. When the "third root" is added to and mixed with national mestizaje in Veracruz, Mexican national subjectivity is not disturbed. Mexican national mestizaje is flexible enough to include *some* blackness if this blackness is sufficiently mixed. In such a mixture, the national mestizaje predominates and Mexican subjectivity prevails: blackness is latent—something hidden that can be picked up and activated (like a flavor, a curl in the hair), and rather than disturbing the nation, blackness strengthens Veracruz as national. Thus, in the last instance, Veracruz's (discursive) tripartite mestizaje reinforces and homogenizes its Mexican mestizaje; it reinforces the discourse of Mexicanness, of the nation where everyone is mestiza/o. There are parallels here with popular histories of danzón: the hegemonic, autonomous, European semi-classical music that was constantly hybridized as it traveled in the circum-Caribbean with African elements being "added," but remaining a musical "changing same." So, too, Veracruz's mestizaje changed over time, and its relation to nation transformed but was not threatened.

Conclusion

Essentialized ideas about people, music, and dance have enabled blackness (as a non-politicized marker of African heritage) to be flexible and used expediently, especially by Veracruz's lighter-skinned cultural, political, and academic elites. This flexibility provoked utopian ambivalences for darker-skinned locals, however: while they are national subjects, they are also positioned spatially and temporally as other, linked to Cuba and/or Veracruz's historical past. That is, darker-skinned locals' otherness intersects with national racial ideologies to provoke painful static ambivalences (around belonging or not) and utopian ambivalences (linked to the projects of mestizaje and nationalism), as well as racism. The intensities of these ambivalences remain contextual and relative, depending on how light or dark someone is in relation to others.

To reach this argument, I began the chapter by asking what was elucidated by comparing logics of hegemonic racializations of people and their cultural practices. I proposed that the widely disseminated popular history of danzón is a monumental narrative where music-dance forms are racialized and moralized for political ends. The wish to establish originality, to be distinct, characterized relationships to danzón, and specifically the desire of many Veracruzana/os to have their own African heritage, their own popular musics, to be the first place danzón was performed in Mexico. We saw that in the cases of both danzón and racialization processes in Veracruz, a logic pertained whereby something that racializes was added and mixed: in popular histories of danzón, a hegemonic European music-dance form was racialized with the supposedly African cinquillo; and in the case of Veracruz, the national Mexican mestizaje was racialized by a form of cultural and phenotypical blackness allied to Cuba (Mexico's "third root"). There were important differences, however.

In popular histories of danzón, the cinquillo is treated, like a monolithic "Africa," as a homogeneous and constant ingredient that augments and racializes an evolving hegemonic European music-dance form in Cuba. Yet in Veracruz, while danzón and blackness (both purportedly originating from Cuba) racialize imaginaries and bodies, the dynamic is slightly distinct. The "adoption" of danzón is justified by the Port's blackness and simultaneously reinforces Mexican nationalism and its national mestizaje. As we have seen, over the twentieth century, Mexican subjectivities shifted from being racial (mestiza/o) to national (Mexican): mestizaje was subsumed by Mexicanness, race by nation. In Veracruz, blackness was re-added to and mixed with Mexicanness, race was re-added to nation. In relation to this blackness, Mexican bipartite mestizaje became neutral and homogeneous (akin to whiteness in other contexts). Yet Mexican national mestizaje is flexible enough to include some blackness, if this blackness is sufficiently mixed to be dominated, sufficiently apolitical to remain unnoticed. Context and relationality determine where there is flexibility, what is considered fixed and homogeneous, and who and what are construed as black.

As we have seen, the Port's blackness is flexible to those light-skinned enough to choose when to evoke its positive aspects, when to emphasize race over nation, and when to make blackness expedient, together with cultural practices associated with it, like danzón. Blackness is not rescued as something these people want to be, but strategically employed, strategically embodied by those who can. Those who can are, above all, middle- and upper-class Veracruzano men who are proud to have adopted blackness, like danzón. Women must negotiate mores around decency, and this strategically employed, strategically embodied blackness is something that middle- and upper-class Veracruzana women above all can make their own, clean up and make decent, like their danzón. These Veracruzana women and men have "improved" their mestizaje and their danzón. They have disciplined and domesticated them; made them positive, decent, and safe (especially for women). Should these middle- and upper-class Veracruzana/os feel ambivalences, they involve having to negotiate a blackness that goes beyond positive stereotypes, beyond their sense of being Mexican, belonging to the nation, but such circumstances are rare.

In broader local imaginaries, the negative elements of Veracruz's blackness, like those of popular histories of danzón, including the brutality of war and enslavement, are effaced, related to an "other" at a geographic or historic distance, with no relation to the Mexican present. These negative elements relate to Blackness as a politicized identity that is rarely assumed in Veracruz. Instead, it is blackness (as a non-politicized marker) that is the potentially expedient resource, for those able and willing to use it, for those who rarely suffer the intense and painful static and utopian ambivalences provoked by being described as foreign (black) rather than national (mestizo), as other rather than Mexican, as too sexualized to be decent (especially for women), by being subjected to racism. This happens, sometimes on a daily basis, to locals who are too dark in relation to others, too dark to pass as national, too dark to belong.

VIGNETTE TWO

Pancho

(fiction)

Pancho Pérez. Faint breath of tobacco. 47. Tall. Slight. Straight brown hair with middle parting. Ponytail. Freckled, pale skin. Piercing brown eyes. High cheekbones. Square jaw. Stubbly moustache over strong lips. Slender fingers. Director of the renowned *Danzonera Corona de Veracruz* since 2004.

The rehearsal started late, despite all the musicians carefully positioning their hands on time into the municipal government's fingerprint sign-in pad. The wind and brass players took out their instruments slowly, polishing them as they joked. Beto tinkered on his keyboard, pre-set to a sickly sweet, synth sound. A semblance of the piano part emerged: his arthritic fingers tripping over half the notes, hitting others unintentionally. Pancho would ask sound engineers to turn the keyboard part down: he suspected Beto knew. Chucho clasped his cigarette beside his trumpet, puffing mid-tune as he played from distant memory. Congas player Diego muddied a dexterity that he could only aspire to, as he cupped and slapped his palms and fingers against the tightened skins. Danzón was slow, not like salsa. The danzonera usually learned new tunes on the job; at public events. Pancho hated that: the wrong notes, the chaos, the embarrassment. That's why he'd called the rehearsal.

He tried to tell the danzonera members what to do.

"You're not from Veracruz," came the response.

Pancho's provenance walled him out of discussion, out of directing his own band. Just because he was from inland, from Tepehuacan de Guerrero, Hidalgo, from agricultural territory. They said he didn't have the feel, the Afro of Veracruz. It wasn't in his blood. It didn't seem to matter that he'd studied music at an academy, played in Veracruz since his twenties, excelled in the Marine Band, played with the *Sonora Boca del Río*, that his musicianship had earned him the directorship of the danzonera. Pancho yearned for the players to tune up before performances; to stop the whining dissonances as they hacked through tunes. He yearned to play with musicians who cared about the sound, about the music.

In 2016, Pancho died. Car accident. Miguel Jiménez took over the danzonera. Three years later the band sounded tighter, in tune. It had younger players, new repertoire, no salsa rhythms. Jiménez is from Veracruz.

CHAPTER TWO

Ambivalent Nostalgia

Histories and Memories of the Port and Its Danzón

"It's a port, it's a song," affirmed then-PRI presidential candidate Enrique Peña Nieto in a commercial for his 2012 election campaign, with Veracruz's docks and a ship to his rear.[1] With these words, he evoked the imagery and strains of Agustín Lara's (1936) song *Veracruz*, summoning masculinist representations of a circum-Caribbean city where men walk under the palm trees of Veracruz's sun-drenched or starlit beaches singing songs of love and suffering to beautiful women.[2] The commercial continued with Peña Nieto wandering along the quayside, recounting how Veracruz is one of the happiest states in the country, how it pains him that it was been struck by violence in recent years and claiming that, if elected, he would correct government strategy against crime. (Homicides soared nationally under Peña Nieto's presidency (2012–18), with Veracruz being particularly affected.) After watching one of Veracruz's famous *lecheros* (milky coffees) being poured from shiny metal kettles in the Gran Café de la Parroquia, Peña Nieto continued that "the happiness of this state is the happiness of the whole of Mexico," and he is then seen dancing a danzón with a local woman to the *Danzonera Alma de Veracruz*, with Bernardo López on clarinet.

National imaginaries of Veracruz as a place of happiness, nostalgia, and industry are indexed here, a place with a relaxed lifestyle, epitomized by local people playing and dancing to a mid-twentieth-century-sounding Afro-Cuban music, taking breezy quayside strolls to alleviate the humid heat and, when not working in the docks, sitting around in atmospheric cafés chatting and sipping milky coffee. Through these stereotypes, the city's place in the nation is reasserted. And while, as a Cuban music-dance form, danzón is rarely evoked in relation to Mexican nationalism, danzón does contribute to Mexican nationalism in Veracruz by sonically and somatically indexing local identity, national collective memory, and nostalgic longing.

In this chapter, I explore how nostalgia is articulated in relation to Veracruz, to histories and memories of the city, to its homosocial public sphere and its danzón. To do so, I provide a detailed history of Veracruz and its danzón from the 1890s to the 1980s, bringing together accounts from academic texts and danzón practitioners in the Port. From the 1940s on, I interweave broader histories of the Port with narratives of the period as recounted to me by Daniel Rergis Aguiler, a former docker who starred in the 1991 film *Danzón*, and Víctor Manuel Sánchez Marín, a key player in the danzón music ensemble *Danzonera Alma de Veracruz* for many years and a schoolteacher. These academic texts and local accounts focus on men, and rather than excavating a history that includes women here, I recount and analyze the dominant narrative, examining how men's creativity and class are entangled in it, and what nostalgic representations of the Port and its history enable and erase, arguing that nostalgia contributes to reproducing inequalities. First, however, I interrogate relationships between nostalgia and ambivalence in some depth.

Nostalgia and Ambivalence

Drawing from the Greek *nostos* (return home) and *algos* (pain), the term nostalgia was coined in 1688 by Johannes Hofer, a Swiss medical student analyzing homesickness (*Heimweh*) (Starobinski 1966). Over three centuries later, Svetlana Boym famously proposed a typology that encompasses two forms: "restorative" and "reflective" nostalgia (2001, 49–50): restorative nostalgia relates to a desire to return home (*nostos*), while reflective nostalgia is linked to a longing (*algos*), a yearning for another place or time. Boym argued that nostalgia often emerges from the present and projects into the future what a past might have been. Ambivalence pervades nostalgia, Boym proposes: the desire for the old in the new, for continuity in change, for the possibility of the impossible, "the repetition of the unrepeatable, materialization of the immaterial" (Boym 2001, xvii). While their objects and subjects of nostalgia may overlap, Boym contends, restorative and reflective nostalgia have a distinct temporality, the first relating primarily to the present, and the second to a past and present separated by a gulf of ambiguity. I develop Boym's work here to argue that restorative and reflective nostalgia also engender distinct modes of ambivalence.

Restorative nostalgia is concerned with the desire to create "a perfect snapshot" of a lost past, to reconstruct home, to invent truths and traditions

(Boym 2001, 49). The past is made solid, preserved in a moment shaped by the present. Restorative nostalgia is exemplified by nationalist heritage sites and revivalist practices (including monuments, food, rituals, handicrafts, music, and dance). Such newly built pasts are disrupted, however, by the messiness and multiplicity of mundane historical and grounded specificities, by realizations that the traditional and authentic are created by the modern, the past constructed in the present. Restorative nostalgia depends on the past and the present being kept apart, protected by the vagueness of social memory, and nostalgic invented histories are potentially disturbed by historical specificity (the specificity of individual memory is too powerless, too potentially exceptional to carry much weight here). Restorative nostalgia can provoke static ambivalences—representations of the past are positioned as true or false; artifacts and practices as old or new—and where the old is shown to be new, its veracity is quashed. This static ambivalence is not comfortable or easy and must be avoided for restorative nostalgia to be maintained. But if restorative nostalgia is destroyed by ambivalence, reflective nostalgia thrives on it.

Reflective nostalgia delights in the yearning for home where homecoming is elided, aware that this yearning will be disrupted by arrival. Such nostalgia occupies a space between a past that never was and a present that fantasizes about that past. This and other forms of nostalgia do not relate to a specific place between the past and the future, to a moment in a continuum, to a form of becoming. Thus, nostalgia should not be understood as a form of dialectic or as something that provokes dialectic ambivalence. Instead, as Boym contends, Hegelian teleology and linear notions of time are bypassed by most nostalgics, who prefer to look backward and sideways (2001, 13). It is static and utopian ambivalences that are entwined with nostalgia: where restorative nostalgia invokes static ambivalences, reflective nostalgia engenders utopian ambivalences. As a form of long-distance love with the past or with home, reflective nostalgia tolerates and even enjoys the ideal past being disrupted and the reflexivity and irony this entails, as Hutcheon and Valdés (2000) and Boym (2001) argue. Here, ambivalence is something to be relished and cherished, in contrast to the potential anxieties produced by the static ambivalences of restorative nostalgia.

Restorative nostalgia and references to tradition tend to be fleeting in relation to danzón in Veracruz, in contrast to the restorative nostalgia described by Madrid and Moore (2013) in their analysis of contemporary zoot-suit-clad, danzón-dancing pachucos in and around Mexico City.[3] While danzón surged in popularity in the Port, part of a national movement that bears markers of a revival, the discourses and practices around danzón in the city do not share the restorative nostalgia characteristic of certain other revivals (see Livingston 1999; Bithell and Hill 2014; Hilder 2012). Instead, it is reflective nostalgia that mostly characterizes local people's relationships to the city and its danzón, the yearning for a bygone age epitomized by dockers dancing to Afro-Cuban music, humorous carnival comparsas (parade groups), and local "personalities," mostly now dead. Such a yearning for the mid-twentieth-century modern city, linked to music and dance, and coupled with future-oriented optimism and collective amnesia regarding poverty, political violence, and other forms of oppression, is not exclusive to Veracruz and is evident across the Americas (see, for example, Waxer 2002 regarding salsa and cultural memory in Cali, Colombia; Hutchinson's 2016 exploration of the relationship of merengue típico legend Tatico Henríquez to collective nostalgia around Santiago, Dominican Republic; and consider Berlant's 2006 "cruel optimism" and the idealization of the 1950s in US popular culture with its capitalist promise of social mobility and bright futures). The specific articulations of nostalgic representations of Veracruz are marked by the Porfiriato, the Revolution, unionization, and dramatic economic shifts.

The Modernization of the Port, Economic Boom and Bust, and Danzón

It was under the regime of President Porfirio Díaz (1884–1911) that the Port's infrastructure was modernized. The harbor was expanded by the English firm S. Pearson and Son, together with docking areas to cater to larger ships in 1895.[4] New water, sanitation, and drainage systems were installed between 1901 and 1904, improving public health and allaying the Port's reputation for fatal diseases. 1873 had seen the inauguration of the railway, linking Veracruz, Orizaba, and Mexico City, and in 1906, the Veracruz Terminal Company was established, creating 2,000 jobs (García Díaz 1992). Small businesses and related services sprang up and commerce flourished, particularly those based on imports and exports. The main square and quayside were renovated, streets were paved, new public buildings were erected (the Customs House, post office, and train station) and, in 1908, the first electric trams appeared.

This modernization attracted migrants seeking work from other parts of Mexico (especially from other parts of the State of Veracruz, and the states of Puebla and Oaxaca), as well as from Cuba, Spain, Italy, the United States, the Middle East, Germany, Japan, and China. In the first decade of the twentieth century, the Port's population surged from 29,164 to 48,663 inhabitants (García de León Griego 1996). This was an era in which Veracruz is often described as having a "cosmopolitan air" (García Díaz 1999, 236; Guadarrama Olivera 2002, 477), an era before air travel when voyagers arrived and departed from Mexico via the port, and migrants came in search of work and refuge. These migrants included tobacco rollers, tailors, hairdressers, builders, and musicians, many of whom came from Cuba. The brothers who played in the *Danzonera de los Chinos Ramírez*, for example, had a Filipino father and a Cuban mother and came to Veracruz via New Orleans (they were not Chinese as their name suggests) (García Díaz 1992). The Port's first danzón orchestras were formed in the 1880s and mostly consisted of Cuban and Veracruzano men, including those of José "Joseíto Vueltiflor" Vuelta y Flores and Juan "Cumbá" Arredondo (*Juan Cumbá y Joseíto Vueltiflor*), and later *Ochoa, Pachecata y Sonsorico*; *Severiano Pacheco y Albertico Gómez* (formed 1894) and *Los Chinos Ramírez* (formed 1895). These early danzón orchestras included clarinets, trumpet or cornet, trombone, euphonium or ophicleide, bass, timbales, and güiro.[5]

Cuban musicians would continue to migrate to the Port for decades to come, including the timbales player (and tailor) Tiburcio "El Babuco" Hernández, who arrived in Veracruz around 1902 and, according to danzón investigator-aficionado Jesús Flores y Escalante (1993), presented the first orchestra called a danzonera in the Recreo Veracruzano in 1905, playing guarachas, danzas, and danzones, some of which were arranged by another Cuban resident in the Port, the composer Tomás Ponce Reyes (1886–1972).[6] The renowned timbales player Consejo "Acerina" Valiente Robert (1899–1987) also lived and worked in the Port for years before moving to Mexico City and forming his renowned danzonera. By the end of the nineteenth century and throughout the decades that followed, danzón accompanied most significant events in Veracruz, as historian Bernardo García Díaz documents: "It became essential in the docks to celebrate the hundredth arrival of some Norwegian steam ship which was travelling from New Orleans or of some famous traveller or popular sports person. But it was also played, in later years, in the sport fields, in political campaigns, in the cinemas before films, on train trips" (1992, 116). Recordings of danzones also began to circulate in the early twentieth century, with record production beginning in Mexico in the 1930s.[7] While boats had transported scores and musicians between Veracruz, Cuba, and beyond for centuries, they increasingly carried recordings as well.

While the benefits of the Port's modernization were enjoyed by the upper classes who moved to the paved avenues of the southeast of the city, most of the population lived in poorer areas, such as La Huaca, outside the former city walls. Most of the workers and immigrants lived in *patios de vecindad*: usually single-story tenement blocks surrounding shared central open courtyards, with communal taps, washbasins, and toilets (similar in many respects to Cuban *solares*). Men living in these patios found work as dockers, railwaymen, builders, fishermen, and so forth. Although some women managed to work as teachers or secretaries, it was hard for women to find paid work at this time, and most were housewives. Despite the disputes and gossip that coexisted with conviviality and solidarity, these patios were renowned for parties, and it was from here that many of the musicians, dancers, baseball players, and carnival comparsas emerged, for which Veracruz would become renowned. Moreover, it was in these patios that danzón is said to have flourished.

With the onset of the Revolution in 1910, the modernization of Veracruz slowed. Although President Porfirio Díaz went into exile from Veracruz in 1911, the Port did not see military action at first. While there were occasional revolts in the state of Veracruz, these were quickly quashed, and enduring revolutionary movements failed to emerge (see Knight 1990a). Purportedly in response to the Tampico Affair (the clash between some Mexican federal soldiers and US sailors near the oil-rich town of Tampico, Tamaulipas, in April 1914), the United States invaded Veracruz in April 1914. The rationale for this was more probably an attempt by US President Woodrow Wilson (1913–1921) to eliminate his Mexican equivalent, Victoriano Huerta (1913–1914), who had seized power from (and possibly ordered the assassination of) the legally elected President Francisco Madero (1911–1913) (Quirk 1962). A bloody fight ensued, followed by a seven-month US occupation of the city. Emiliano Zapata was outraged; Venustiano Carranza likewise assumed a nationalist stance; but Pancho Villa "gave qualified approval of the Veracruz occupation, in that it acted as an additional squeeze on Huerta" (Knight 1990a, 161). While the invasion of Veracruz created further distance between Carranza and Villa, and Huerta attempted to harness patriotism and anti-US sentiment, Alan Knight (1990a) claims that the invasion had little impact on the outcome of the Revolution, as the turning point had already passed (the desertion of federal troops in the Torreón battles): the Constitutional Army defeated Huerta.[8] From November 1914 until October 1915, Carranza's government was seated in the Port.

Despite and because of the turmoil, recreation flourished. According to Ricardo Pérez Montfort (1999), the US invasion provoked Luis Pazos to compose a danzón entitled *Veracruz Siempre Mexicana* (Veracruz, Always Mexican). And Bertha Ulloa (1986) describes how the Port's elites celebrated the arrivals and departures of military chiefs, as well as victorious military action, in their social clubs, such as the *Regata Club* and the *Casino Veracruzano*. Moreover, it was in these places, Ulloa suggests, that wealthier people

Figure 2.1. Popular Dance (circa 1932). Photograph by Joaquín Santamaria. (Courtesy of Archivo General del Estado, No. de inventario JS/28.702, Fondo Joaquín Santamaria, Tema Baile Popular, Información Circa 1932.)

visiting Veracruz learned danzón. Meanwhile, poorer people danced in patios and other clubs (see Figure 2.1).

The Revolution was a catalyst for the formation of workers' unions: the first National Workers' Congress was held in Veracruz in 1916. Together with the Revolution, the worldwide economic slump following the First World War was also having a major impact on Mexico's economy, and huge discrepancies in wealth remained. The surge in the Port's population in the 1900s had resulted in increased rents, heavily overcrowded living conditions, and health problems (such as the 1919–20 yellow fever outbreak). By 1922, tenants were protesting, and a housing strike, headed by Herón Proal and the Revolutionary Tenant's Syndicate, resulted in general strikes between 1923 and 1925 (see Wood 2001). Antonio García de León Griego has documented how they also prompted the composition of danzones such as *El Desterrado* (The Exile) by Abraham Velasco and *Sueños de Oro* (Golden Dreams). Nationally, major trade unions had already formed: the pro-government Regional Confederation of Mexican Workers (Confederación Regional Obrera Mexicana) in 1919 and the anarcho-syndicalist General Workers' Confederation (Confederación General de Trabajadores) in 1921. And in Veracruz, the Local Workers' Federation of the Port of Veracruz (Federación Local de Trabajadores del Puerto de Veracruz) and the League of Workers of the Maritime Zone (Liga de Trabajadores de la Zona Marítima) were created, and they centered around the Stevedores' Union (Unión de Estibadores). These port workers' unions were to gain substantial power in Veracruz, particularly from the 1930s, when the Stevedores' Union played a key role in forming the national Confederation of Mexican Workers (Confederación de Trabajadores Mexicanos).

By the mid-1920s, Mexico was almost at peace (apart from the bloody Cristero War of 1926–1929, led by Catholics reacting against post-revolutionary anti-clerical laws that had little impact in the Port). Peace, the conquering of epidemics, and the popularization of the concept of sun- and sea-bathing, prompted tourism to start in Veracruz. Soaking up the sun and the sea were considered to bestow health benefits, and bathing spots and swimming clubs sprang up. While trains provided the principal form of transport, roads were beginning to be built in the late 1920s, and by then, around 5,000 visitors per year came to Veracruz (the Port's population in 1930 was around 70,000) (García Díaz 1992). Recreational venues grew for all social classes, providing local bands with more work, as well as the groups of musicians who descended from transatlantic ships and other ensembles visiting the Port. One venue in particular stands out in local discourse: *Villa del Mar*.

Novelist Graham Greene described this dance hall in *The Lawless Roads* as "the shabby Villa del Mar joined by tramway [from 1935] to the town with its big wooden dance hall raised on piles and its little dingy houses smearing out on to the silver sand-hills" (1939, 99). Located on the beach, south of the city center, *Villa del Mar* opened in 1919, initially with a bathing area, gardens, restaurant, bar, shooting range, basketball pitch, and dance hall. But barely seven years later, in 1926, it was destroyed by a cyclone. Although *Villa del Mar*'s popularity never completely recovered, it remained open (on and off) for over ninety years and well into the twenty-first century. What is striking about *Villa del Mar* is that, unlike other venues in the Port, here men and women of higher and lower social classes were reported to gather (albeit, some say, at different times of day). The writer Armando Moreno, who traveled to the Port in the mid-1940s, narrated: "In Villa del Mar, [...] people dance all morning, afternoon and evening. People of all classes gather there, without distinctions nor courtesies. He who pays enters the place. Due to the heat men dance without jackets, in shirt sleeves: they dance and they sweat" (1992, 265). And in his *Mexico South* of 1947, artist and anthropologist Miguel Covarrubias wrote: "Villa del Mar, or rather what the hurricanes have left of it, is a half-ruined boardwalk facing a great dance hall where the whole of young Vera Cruz gathers on Sunday evenings to dance American swing between danzón numbers" (1947, 6).

Older danzón practitioners frequently recall *Villa del Mar* as a hub of danzón in their youth. Some of the Port's best-known musicians found work here (often playing in several ensembles): by 1933, Chato Rojas's *Jazz Montezuma* and Manuel Blanco Cancino's *Jazz Nacional* (for whom Chato Rojas also performed) played there; and from 1938 to 1946, *Chinto Ramos y su Orquesta* had a regular set, being taken over by Manuel Blanco Cancino's *Orquesta Villa del Mar* in 1946 (González García n.d., 56). *Villa del Mar* is most fondly remembered by local danzón practitioners for its two Sunday dances (held until the late 1950s). It was here that many of them learned to dance danzón and other popular dances. I was often told how, from 1 to 4 p.m., Veracruz's young elite women, accompanied by their chaperones, would mingle with cadets from the Naval School (formed in 1897) and dance to mostly US music (such as jazz and swing) played by local bands and groups visiting from the capital and beyond.

Several local danzón dancers told me that after the afternoon dance at *Villa del Mar*, they would sometimes go to the Plaza de Armas, the Port's main square. The Plaza de Armas changed little in the first half of the twentieth century and remained similar to local journalist Francisco Miranda's 1900 description of it as "a small garden with a two-storey bandstand in the middle: on the lower level was a bar/cantina and on Thursday and Sunday nights, the garrison corps band would play from the upper part" (1900, 27). Throughout the century, military and civil bands would play several times a week in the main square, sometimes performing from the Municipal Palace overlooking the plaza. Yet for decades, people rarely danced there. Young people would circulate around the square, often flirting with each other, the men in one direction, the women in another, while their parents watched from the surrounding benches.

On Sundays, some went on or returned to *Villa del Mar*, where, from 7 p.m. to 1 a.m., there was another dance: at one end of the hall, a danzonera such as that of *Los Chinos Ramírez* would sound clarinets, trumpets, trombone, ophicleide, bass, timbales, and güiro (to be replaced decades later by Jacinto "Chinto" Ramos's ensemble), alternating with a big band at the other (such as *Orquesta Villa del Mar*, or *Orquesta de Chato Rojas y sus Lobos Marinos*).[9] These later dances were frequented by men working in the docks, women from the local tortilla factory and others, mostly from the lower classes. While both the elites and lower classes danced and listened to jazz,

Figure 2.2. La Lonja Mercantil (circa 1930). Photograph by Joaquín Santamaria. (Courtesy of *Archivo General del Estado, No. de inventario JS/28.494, Fondo Joaquín Santamaria, Tema* La Lonja Mercantil, *Información Circa 1930.*)

danzón was reserved for the later, lower-class event. Higher-class men were freer than women to frequent whatever venues they wished. As in other contexts (e.g., Wade 2000), it was the reputation of young elite women that was most at stake (to ensure that they reproduced elite families), and it was young women who were accompanied by chaperones at the earlier dances and who could only steal moments alone with the men they were allowed to dance with. Elite women would also go to other venues reserved for the higher classes (where their interactions with men were policed), such as the *Lonja Mercantil* (see Figure 2.2).

Like *Villa del Mar*, carnival was another context where danzón and other genres were performed and that brought men and women of several social classes, both locals and visitors, together in theory, although again, elite women were kept separate in practice. There had been carnival celebrations in Veracruz since the colonial period, initially related to Corpus Christi and later to the pre-Lenten period, despite being in the season of the *nortes* (the strong northerly winds that often pound Mexico's gulf coast in the winter months). By the mid-nineteenth century, carnival celebrations had grown substantially but were curbed, as Wood (2003) describes, first by the French invaders in 1867, and then by the late-nineteenth-century Liberal authorities who saw carnival as a residue of colonialism. After the Revolution, in 1925, the pre-Lenten carnival was reinvented, organized by the Port's elite social clubs, hotels, and businesses, and supported by the local government. Carnival would only slowly become entwined with tourism and attracting visitors to the Port (see Wood 2010). There was a carnival queen from 1925, elected from the upper classes and, from 1926, an "ugly" carnival king (*Rey Feo*), usually an older man from the port, railway, or tram workers' unions. Floats sponsored by local institutions and businesses paraded the streets, and there were masked balls in elite social clubs (such as the *Lonja Mercantil* and the *Casino Español*). According to local politician and writer Anselmo Mancisidor Ortiz, in the early years of carnival, "there were never the characteristics of a general fiesta for all the inhabitants of the Port, and certainly not those that had always been associated with the porteño [Port-dwelling] people: openness, merriment and *organized disorder*" (1971, 150 his emphasis). But, Mancisidor Ortiz claims, the Cuban José "Pepe" Frade Álvarez changed all that.

With a group of others, Pepe Frade coordinated the first *entierro del mal humor* (burial of ill humor) in 1927. This was reminiscent of the Spanish "burial of the sardine" event, which had marked the end of the nineteenth-century Veracruz carnival (Cortés Rodríguez 2000).[10] The *entierro del mal humor* consisted of a funeral cortège, with Frade in the coffin, accompanied by Severiano Pacheco's danzonera and, according to Mancisidor Ortiz: "groups of happy workers from distinct organizations like the railways, stevedores, checkers, cart-pushers, employees from different branches, dockers, openers, and people of all social classes" (1971, 152). Four years later, in 1931, Pepe Frade orchestrated the *carnival de locos* (crazy people's carnival) with not only a "crazy" carnival king and queen but also a "crazy" carnival government (including ministers for tax, foreign affairs, defense, and education).

While carnival had been a festival organized by the elites of the Port in the mid-1920s, by the 1930s, historian García Díaz suggests there was "even greater and more effusive participation of the dockers who joined together with tram and railway men to fill the popular happiness of the fiesta" (1992, 241). While the (purportedly happy) lower classes had been invited to be involved from the outset, it took a few years before there were popular carnival dances and comparsas (parade groups) from poorer neighborhoods and workers' unions, and comparsas with people in fancy dress, hoods, and masks. The Municipal Band, danzoneras, and, from the late 1920s, son cubano ensembles formed part of the carnival parades and began to play on stages on the corners of the Avenida 5 de Mayo. Son cubano had arguably arrived in the Port in the late 1920s, with performances by the Cuban group *Son Cuba de Marianao* causing furor in 1928. Like danzón, son cubano was embraced by the Port, but unlike danzón, people do not speak of its "adoption." The 1920s also saw the rise of a powerful, centralized media industry, and local and international theater, radio, and cinema stars were contracted as attractions in the 1930s (including local celebrities such as Toña "La Negra" and Agustín Lara (see Wood 2014), and others from further afield, like Jorge Negrete and Mario "Cantinflas" Moreno).

Dockers and Danzón:
El Catrín ('The Well-Dressed Man')

One Veracruzano, born in 1929, who would become carnival king and also gain employment and renown related to danzón performance, was Daniel Rergis Aguiler. I conducted several semi-structured interviews with Daniel from 2006, as well as having numerous informal conversations with him before he died in 2014, aged 85. Daniel recounted how he was born in a neighborhood patio in the Port. A wall divided Daniel's patio from the dance hall *Las Delicias* and, he told me, "danzón was on top of you all day there." His parents danced danzón, and he watched and learned from them. By the age of nine, Daniel was following his twenty-one-year-old brother to dances in halls such as the legendary *Villa del Mar*. Daniel told me how he plucked up the courage to ask a thirty-year-old woman to dance, Doña Micaela, and they became dance partners for the next nine years. In 1943, aged thirteen, Daniel left school, having completed just four years of primary level education, for his family needed his financial help. The 1929 stock market crash had had a major impact on trade and on Veracruz's economy, and the Second World War (which Mexico entered in 1942) had reduced traffic to the port. Although President Lázaro Cárdenas (1934–1940) nationalized many industries, including oil (PEMEX), mining, electricity, and the railways, agriculture was neglected and unemployment chronic. In Veracruz, unemployment was eased slightly by the building of a naval base from 1942, and there was still some work in the port for those with the right connections. Since his father worked in the docks, Daniel got a job there, becoming an employee of the customs agency Pasquel Hermanos. He opened boxes so that customs lists could be checked and appropriate tariffs applied. Daniel worked for this company for thirty-three years, taking part in many of the activities for which Veracruz's dockers were renowned.

Music Example 2.1. El Viejo.

For several years, Daniel participated with his fellow union workers in carnival, winning several comparsa prizes, as well as in the New Year *El Viejo* (old man) celebration, where the new year is welcomed in and the old year ushered out with groups of people, particularly those unlikely to earn an *aguinaldo* (a month's bonus salary paid at Christmas) asking for money, sometimes dressed as or carrying a stuffed effigy of an old man, and usually singing the associated song *El Viejo* accompanied by guitar and percussion, such as tin cans and cowbells (see Music Example 2.1). The lyrics of *El Viejo* begin "*Una limosna para este pobre viejo* [repeated]; *que ha dejado hijos* [repeated]; *para el año nuevo*" (A donation for this poor old man [repeated]; who has left children [repeated]; for the New Year). Locally, this practice is said to have emerged from the docks.

In 1955 Daniel, now married, held a party in the patio where he lived to celebrate his first son's baptism. As well as buying ten barrels of dark beer, he contracted the *Danzonera de Camerino Vázquez*, which sounded two clarinets, trumpet, euphonium, (Camerino Vázquez on) bass, and timbales. Daniel invited neighbors, family, work colleagues, and friends. The patios were still renowned for parties at that time, for birthdays and other celebrations, and much of the music was provided by danzoneras (son cubano ensembles also being popular). Famously, on the 3rd of May every year, the Day of the Cross was celebrated in the Patio San Carlos with a party, and danzoneras such as those of *Los Chinos Ramírez* (from the 1890s) and *Alma de Veracruz* (from the 1940s) performed. It was not only the attendance of the dockers at these dances that gave them the reputation of being "the authentic ambassadors of danzón in Veracruz," I was told by danzón dancer Natalia Pineda Burgos, but also their dancing abilities.

The Port had many renowned dancers in the twentieth century, such as El Charecua, Inés La Rompecuero, La Babuca, Pepe Castro, Sigfrido Alcántara, and Miguel "El Venado" *Díaz* Andrade. Many of these dancers carried nick-

Figure 2.3. The band of the Hospicio Manuel Gutiérrez Zamora, directed by Víctor Manuel Sánchez García during Carnival (circa 1942). Sánchez García's son, the clarinettist Víctor Manuel Sánchez Marin, is seated in the front row, fourth from right. The other members of the band were Ramón Barcelata, Pablo Bello, Luis Briseño, Ricardo Cabrera, Tito Cabrera, Manuel Camelo, Manuel Cisneros, Jorge Elizalde, Panchito Espinosa, Bernardo García, Beto García, Marcos García, Ángel Gómez, Abraham González, Manolo Gudiño, Dionisio Jar Jón, Carlos López, Mario Morales, Moreno [sic], Victor Parra, Joel Pichardo, Jacinto Ruiz, Femiche Sandoval, Joel Uscanga, José Valencia, and José Manuel Zamora (see El Dictamen 1983). (Photograph courtesy of Víctor Manuel Sánchez Marin.)

names, as did Daniel, who was known as *"El Catrín."* Anthropologist Juan Antonio Flores Martos analyzes the nicknames of Veracruz's bygone crazy characters (*locos*) thus: "it is as if the name holds the key, or is the epitome, of understanding the principal attributes of the 'character', without which it becomes more difficult to 'sketch' them" (1996, 144). As well as being tall and handsome, Daniel was usually impeccably dressed and elegant, as his name El Catrín (the well-dressed/dapper man) suggests. Having a nickname gives a person a popular status in Veracruz: it contributes to depicting the bearer as distinct, particularly in competitive situations such as when men vied to be considered the best dancer or battled for votes for carnival king. Musicians also competed with each other during this time: to play in the best bands, get the best gigs, and perform the best solos. One danzonera that emerged from such competition was *Alma de Veracruz*.

Alma de Veracruz, Danzón, and Economic Boom

The danzonera *Alma de Veracruz* was first led by Víctor Manuel Sánchez García, a trumpeter in the National Symphony Orchestra who had moved from Mexico City to Veracruz toward the end of the Revolution in the 1920s and who played with various ensembles in the Port (also recording with the *Danzonera Veracruzana "Pazos"*). His son, Víctor Manuel "Manolo" Sánchez Marín (born in 1927), would go on to lead the danzonera from 1970 until 1988.[11] This history of the Sánchez family and the Danzonera Alma de Veracruz is based on interviews in the Port with Manolo and other musicians from 2007, and undated, unreferenced newspaper clippings they gave me. Manolo told me how, in 1941, his father had become a music teacher at the Hospicio Manuel Gutiérrez Zamora orphanage, an institution where both the resident orphans and other poor local children were educated. There he taught around 120 boys and girls solfège and how to play instruments, combining his own knowledge and method books. By 1942, Sánchez senior had created three Hospicio bands, and during the annual carnival procession, the twenty-seven players of the best band (including his son Manolo) proudly paraded for two nights through the city center (see Figure 2.3). Several well-known local men emerged as musicians from the Hospicio, including trumpeter Bernardo García, who would go on to tour Europe and later direct the danzonera *Alma de Veracruz*; some of the Hospicio girls went on to become music teachers, but women would be notably absent as instrumentalists in local adult music ensembles throughout the twentieth century. In July 1943, Sánchez senior was asked to enter a competition to create a new danzonera and get a regular danzón gig at the local XEU radio station: he brought together four young players (including Manolo on clarinet, doubling sax) and four older men (whom he was in another band with), and they won. The audience was asked to name them, and thus the *Danzonera Alma de Veracruz* (Soul of Veracruz) was created.

From 1943 the *Danzonera Alma de Veracruz* played a regular lunchtime spot at XEU, and local dancers would come to listen and dance as they played live on air. The show, *La Media Hora del* Danzón (the Half Hour of Danzón), gained local renown, later running for an hour from 12 to 1 p.m. on weekdays. Together with carnival, dance venues and parties, the local radio had increasing influence as both a source of work for local and visiting musicians in the

Port and a promoter of danzón: Mexican radio broadcasts had begun in the 1920s, with Mexico City's XEW transmitting all over Mexico, Cuba, and the southern United States from 1930, the same year that Veracruz's XEU went on air. XEU was directed by Fernando Pazos Sosa and was inaugurated by the *Danzonera de Cipriano Camerero*, which sounded two clarinets, trumpet, trombone, (Cipriano Camerero on) bass, güiro, and (José Luis Argumedo on) timbales (González García n.d.). Radio was an important means of promoting groups, and the *Danzonera Alma de Veracruz* soon played many one-off gigs and were offered other regular engagements, performing for five months in the cabaret *El Quinto Patio*, for example. There was also work in nearby villages, at least until electricity reached rural areas, powering radios, record players, and cassette decks. In 1951, the danzonera changed its name to *Alma de Sotavento* at the request of XEU's director, Fernando Pazos Sosa, and a year later, Sánchez father and son left the danzonera. The reasons for their departure remain shrouded in silence, as is the case with so many stories of musicians and dancers leaving groups in Veracruz. The danzonera continued without them, playing for the radio under the leadership of pianist Fernando Fonseca (1952–1960), and then bass player and carpenter Moisés Camerero (1960–1970).

The late 1940s until the 1970s saw a national economic boom, primarily based on oil, known as the "Mexican Miracle." The State of Veracruz was rich in oil fields, prompting the expansion of local industry. The steel pipes factory TAMSA was inaugurated in the Port in 1954, and related industries opened up, supplying the oil industry and exporting worldwide. Dockers continued to frequent the porticos around the main square (*los portales*) at midday to drink, commissioning musicians there and at their parties; while dance halls opened and closed. Until the 1950s, danzoneras and big bands performed in Villa del Mar, and they were increasingly joined by ensembles playing *música tropical* (such as son cubano, guaracha, and cumbia), ensembles that eventually took over. In the 1950s, the *Rincón Brujo*, *Salón Bahia*, *Salón Zaragoza*, and the Union of Commercial Workers (*Sindicato de Empleados de Comercio*) were active popular dance venues, but by the early 1960s, these closed or dipped in activity, as Stigberg (1980) describes in his ethnography of music in Veracruz.

In the second half of the twentieth century, the city that historians García Díaz (1999, 236) and Guadarrama Olivera (2002, 477) describe as having a "cosmopolitan air," as the gateway to Mexico for transatlantic travelers and migrants, became a holiday destination for Mexican nationals. Yet this was also an era when air travel was taking off. Mexico City's airport slowly became the point of entry to the country, and transatlantic liners stopped carrying their passengers to the port. Veracruz, as a transnational, "cosmopolitan" city, became more national and more parochial in the second half of the twentieth century; it became post-cosmopolitan. I understand post-cosmopolitanism as a marker of an urban setting where, first, substantial migration and flows of transnational travelers (both elite and working class) entered, and where people mixed (in convivial, oppressive, violent, or other ways), creating a form of cosmopolitanism; second, such cosmopolitanism becomes something of the past; and third, post-cosmopolitanism emerges where cultural memory of cosmopolitanism intersects with a more parochial present. The idea of Veracruz as a cosmopolitan city relates above all to voyagers. Veracruz is rarely portrayed by locals or other Mexicans as a sailor town, despite seafarers' continued presence as visitors. Nor is there often mention of locals working as sailors. The imaginary of the Port is of a gateway or doorway to a fixed home, a space where others depart and arrive, rather than a place from which locals come and go. Those others are now predominantly tourists. While tourism to the Port had initially been more seasonal, peaking at Easter and carnival, it slowly became a non-seasonal and weekend retreat for mostly Mexican visitors.

With the rise in tourism, Veracruz's carnival increased in size and fame, attracting thousands of (mostly Mexican) visitors. It also became more dangerous and in 1965, after several murders, masks and hoods were banned from carnival celebrations. In the 1970s, carnival was televised and moved away from the city center to the broader coastal avenue (the Bulevar Manuel Ávila Camacho), and the influence of Brazil became more apparent. Samba schools and batucadas (percussion-based samba bands) appeared in lower-class neighborhoods like La Huaca, together with comparsas consisting of mostly young men dancing salsa steps in formation. The art historian Ida Rodríguez Prampolini (born 1925, who was not only carnival queen in 1945 but also the first director of the Veracruz Culture Institute, the IVEC, in 1987) has argued that Veracruz's carnival shifted from participatory event to spectacle, as people stopped dressing up and instead sat watching and applauding the commercially backed carnival floats (see Guadarrama Olivera 2002). Yet while spectatorship marked one element of this shift to spectacle, globalized capitalist transformations had a larger part to play. Since 1925, carnival had been sponsored by local businesses, but the scale of commercial support slowly changed. By the turn of the century, exclusive sponsorships were being sold to multinational companies, such as Coca Cola and Cervecería Cuauhtémoc Moctezuma (which produces Sol and Superior beers). These companies gained monopolies both for selling their beverages and for overall advertising at and for the carnival. Meanwhile, the commercialization, consumerism, exhibitionism, and violence of the early twenty-first century was increasingly critiqued by nostalgic references to the Port's past, as if sonic and visual consumption and spectatorship were something new.

If, by the 1970s, the purported golden age of carnival was on the wane, the golden age of the *Danzonera Alma de Sotavento* (formerly *Alma de Veracruz*) still prevailed. By 1971, two danzoneras were active in the Port, Stigberg (1980) documents: *Danzonera Alma de Sotavento*, led once again by Manolo Sánchez Marín (junior), and *Danzonera Modelo*, while Luis Argumedo's *Danzonera Veracruz* occasionally played. It was common at that time for beer companies to own and sponsor venues (like *Villa del Mar*), carnival events, and danzoneras (such as the *Danzonera Modelo*, supported by the Cervecería Modelo, which produces beers including *Modelo* and *Corona*). Manolo Sánchez (junior) had rejoined *Alma de Sotavento* in 1964, and in 1970 took over the lead. The danzonera led by Sánchez junior was hugely successful. On Wednesdays, Sánchez junior told me, the danzonera would sometimes travel to Mexico City to play in its dance halls (including the *Salón Colonia*, *Salón Los Ángeles*, and the *California Dancing Club*). In November 1978, they entered a competition at the *Salón Colonia* commemorating a century of danzón in Mexico and battled against the renowned orchestras of Alejandro Cardona, Arturo Nuñez, Gamboa Ceballos, Felipe Urbán, Danzonera México, José Casquera, Chino Flores, and Pachito Pérez, many of which had bigger bands, more saxophones, more brass, and more mambo in their arrangements. But *Alma de Sotavento*'s playing was incredibly tight during this period, and they won with their two clarinets (doubling alto sax), tenor sax, two trumpets, trombone, bass, timbales, güiro, and—unusually—guitar as well. The prize was to make a recording, one of the five LPs they produced in the twentieth century. Eliseo "Manzanita" (Little Apple) Matus Meléndez, who had played the trumpet in *Alma de Sotavento*, then told me how this was the "golden era" of Veracruz's danzoneras, and other musicians I spoke to concurred.

The late 1970s saw the expansion of Veracruz's shipbuilding industry, the state-owned Astilleros Unidos de Veracruz (United Shipbuilders of Veracruz, AUVER), based in Veracruz, to produce oil tankers, as well as repair ships using the port. The 1970s also saw a worldwide shift in freight-handling with the internationally accepted standard of using containers. Freight was converted to standardized units, and freight-handling speeds increased tenfold with associated transportation also becoming more streamlined. Veracruz's port was expanded not only to manage containers but also with specialist terminals for products such as sugar and oil. But while the volume of containers increased fivefold from 1984 to over a million metric tons by 1990, labor requirements decreased (García Díaz 1999). In 1971, President Echeverría Álvarez (1970–1976) created the National Port Commission (Comisión Nacional Coordinadora de Puertos), bringing together users of the port, customs agencies, shipping companies, and representatives of the unionized workers. And two years later, in 1973, Echeverría's government changed the port's administration, awarding a concession to the Mercantile Society of Port Services of Veracruz (Sociedad Mercantil de Servicios Portuarios de Veracruz, SERPOVER) led by the dockers' unions.

These changes led to unionized port workers like Daniel "El Catrín" Rergis becoming part of the company, and Daniel got work as sub-director of the free-trade zone. The company, like the unions that controlled it, was a closed shop, and many members subcontracted their work in the docks to other men, known locally as *cuijes* (small eagles). Where this subcontracting occurred, union members often paid *cuijes* a lot less than they earned, and they sometimes employed *cuijes* around the clock so they could claim wages for twenty-four hours of work a day. Thus, rather than straightforwardly linking unions to socialist principles, the unionized workforce in Veracruz in this period should be understood in relation to layered labor structures, clientelism, and capitalist principles. With the profits from subcontracting work and often taking on additional jobs, many union members enjoyed substantial incomes. Several people told me how this money fed back into the local economy, how dockers filled the bars and cafés of the Port during those years, drinking, making merry, and paying musicians to play one or numerous numbers. Whether this is a nostalgic recollection is unclear, but what is apparent is that union members had substantial political clout at that time, since the unions not only controlled the docks but also influenced large numbers of voters.

Voters were important not only for politicians but also for carnival monarchs. And in 1981, aged 53, Daniel was nominated as the 1982 carnival king by his union, as several of the carnival kings before him had been. Daniel told me that Veracruz's unions, associations, and clubs all proposed carnival monarch candidates. Voting coupons were published by the local newspaper *El Dictamen*, and these organizations would buy thousands of votes to support their candidates, holding dances to raise money. The candidate who raised the most money won. This voting system was a means to provide funds for the carnival committee. Daniel won with an incredible 1.8 million pesos worth of votes, so he told me (worth about 54,000 US dollars at the time). He had checked with his wife, a school teacher, that she approved before accepting the nomination, and he was crowned "King Catrín." Being carnival king brought him local fame. But more was to come.

In 1990, aged 61, Daniel went to a dance hosted by another dockers' union. The film director María Novaro and actress María Rojo were also at this dance: they had started filming what would become the hugely successful film *Danzón* (released in 1991), where María Rojo's character, Julia, searches in Veracruz for Carmelo, her dance partner. Having failed to find a suitable actor to play the part in Mexico City, María Novaro told me, they were still searching for a man to play Carmelo. They spotted Daniel as he entered the dance, and shortly afterward, María Rojo invited him to dance. The next day, María Novaro asked Daniel to play the older heartthrob Carmelo in the film. At first, Daniel thought they were joking, as he had never heard of them. Eventually he agreed, after checking with his wife and verifying that the film was "decent," that is, he told me, not pornographic nor involving him kissing anyone: he wanted to ensure his children and grandchildren would be proud of him. Daniel had been about to retire when he became involved in the film, but a new order from the Salinas de Gortari administration (1988–1994) changed these retirement plans.

Economic Bust and Danzón Boom

The economic crisis from the 1980s had exacerbated urban poverty and unemployment in the poorer neighborhoods to the northeast and southeast of the city center. President Salinas de Gortari's government responded to the legacy of Mexico's 1980s economic crisis, bankruptcy, and huge foreign debt by curbing public spending and privatizing state-owned companies (only Mexican Petroleum, PEMEX, and the electricity industry remained state-owned). In Veracruz, oil-tanker production declined for the state-run shipbuilding industry, AUVER, and in the late 1980s, it was privatized. Mexico's economic growth became dependent on exports, particularly to the United States, and the port continued to play a key role in this. In 1991, Salinas de Gortari's government agreed with directors of SERPOVER and the freight-handling unions to reorganize the port, but progress was not as the government desired, and later in the year, they decided to intervene on the basis that the port, so crucial to Mexico's exports, was not operating efficiently (Domínguez Pérez and López Galván 1994). SERPOVER's concession was canceled, and the federal government requisitioned the port and took over. The government swiftly privatized the docks and approved a new law permitting further modernization and expansion. In 2000, while the Port of Veracruz was still Mexico's main commercial port, production and efficiency declined (Guerrero C. and Rivera T. 2009), and the port's requisition caused a power shift away from the dockers' unions and contributed

Figure 2.4. Daniel Rergis Aguiler as Carmelo and María Rojo as Julia in the film *Danzón* (1991), directed by María Novaro.

to a temporary collapse in the local economy. This was aggravated further by President Salinas de Gortari's 1994 "December Error," which prompted another economic crisis under President Zedillo Ponce de León (1994–2000) with a massive devaluation of the peso. Several members of the port workers' unions committed suicide, having never saved and being unable to sustain their families. And the port's requisition marked the end of an era not only for the dockers but also for the city more generally and for its musicians.

Daniel's role in the film *Danzón* (see Figure 2.4), and subsequently in advertisements, ensured that he was financially solvent. The film had brought him international fame: national and foreign women, particularly tourists, sought him out and asked him to dance with them; danzón dancers now placed a huge expectation on his dancing abilities (criticizing him if they were disappointed); people called out "Carmelo" in the street; and he danced with the film's lead actress, María Rojo, to promote the PRD (the Party of the Democratic Revolution), for whom she became a politician. After his wife died, Daniel moved to Los Angeles for a while, where he had a new partner, but he returned to Veracruz in 2007, remarried, and continued to live there until his death in 2014.

With the requisition of the port, work dropped substantially for musicians, many performers told me. Manolo Sánchez Marín (junior) had stopped playing just before this: he had had a major operation in 1988, which he linked to his many years spent playing and drinking until the early hours (a habit enjoyed by numerous musicians and other so-called bohemians in the Port, including Pepe Frade). For many years, Manolo would get home around 5 a.m., sleep briefly, and wash before starting his day job as a schoolteacher at 7 a.m. (he did take a siesta later in the day). Manolo passed on the leadership of *Alma de Sotavento*, and, crucially, the archive of scores, to Genaro Barcelata Trujillo. *Alma de Sotavento* continued to play for XEU until around 1991, when, several members of the group told me, they were dismissed for being drunk and not turning up (which they attributed to being very poorly paid). The competitive edge seemed to have gone, but despite their dismissal and the requisition of the port, the group did not disband. The popularity of danzón was gaining pace, and these musicians were increasingly getting more work. The name of the ensemble—*Alma de Sotavento*—belonged to the radio station, so the musicians decided to revert to their original name, *Alma de Veracruz*. The *Danzonera Alma de Veracruz* would soon be given permanent employment with the municipal government and were still performing several evenings a week in the main square through the 2000s and 2010s.

Dancing Dockers, Class, and Creativity

So far, I have mapped some of the broad socioeconomic transformations that occurred in the Port over the course of the twentieth century: Veracruz's modernization not only facilitated the growth of the city and the port but also made it a healthier place suitable for a tourist industry; carnival was reinvented in 1925 and would later come to characterize the city. There was a major shift in economic, political, and cultural power to (and from) the unionized dockers, and the dockers' unions both nominated carnival monarchs and promoted politicians. This began with the post-revolutionary labor struggles of the 1920s and 1930s, peaked in the 1970s, and dramatically ended in 1991.

What is striking about descriptions of this history, both in local discourse and much academic scholarship, is that it focuses on men. At first a founding role is conferred on (purportedly lower-class) Cuban men who played Afro-Cuban popular music with Veracruzano men for couples to dance to in the patios. Slowly the (male) dockers, together with the tram and railway men, became renowned as the heart and soul of this festive town, hosting parties in their patios, frequenting *Villa del Mar* and other dance halls, commissioning (male) musicians, and creating carnival comparsas. Moreover, musicians became increasingly sidelined, even though Veracruzana/os rarely dance in public places to recorded music, at least not danzón and son cubano. Musicians who worked in the docks, railways, TAMSA, and other places are invisible in many local narratives, reinforcing the idea that all Veracruz's musicians are professionals, and the docks (and other workplaces) merely produce dancers (rather than dancers *and* musicians). It is the dancing dockers who became known as "the ambassadors of danzón." They are described as representative and *productive* of Veracruz's popular culture and the history of danzón in the Port, enabling Veracruz to claim danzón as its own at some level.

For example, Natalia Pineda Burgos, a seventy-something-year-old dancer who frequented *Villa del Mar* in the 1940s and later led two dance groups and represented Mexico at danzón events in Cuba, told me: "The dockers are the ones who raised danzón here and no one can take that away from them [...] the dockers were the first ones who arrived with their partners at Villa del Mar." Natalia was personally invested in reproducing hegemonic histories of danzón, as her family had worked in the docks, yet most local women and men I knew recounted similar histories. In their histories of both Veracruz and its danzón practices, the dockers are revered and women are sidelined, as in this account.

Also notable about renditions of this history is that little mention is made of changes to dockers' class positions, despite their accumulating wealth. In his ethnography of the poor neighborhood of Santo Domingo in Mexico City, Gutmann described how men base their "class prejudices on social divisions of labour—mental labour (for the wealthy) and manual labour (for the workers)" (2002, 119). In contrast, in Veracruz, we find, in addition to a notion of working-class men engaged in manual labor, enormous value being placed on these men being involved in mental labor characterized by creativity, ingenuity, and wit. This was enabled in part by dockers employing others (*cuijes*) to do their manual labor. Several "workers" were engaged in highly "mental" labor. For example, unionized docker José Pérez de León "El Popocha" (1925–2013) was also a journalist, writing newspaper articles for *El Dictamen* as well as books (and being carnival king in 1953). And tram-ticket collector Félix Martínez González (born 1936), who learned to read when he was 20, became so renowned locally for writing and reciting decimas (verses of ten octosyllabic lines) that in 2008, he was appointed director of the state-supported Agustín Lara Museum, the Casita Blanca. These working-class men acquired symbolic capital and respect based on their wit, ingenuity, and skills, and also opportunities to acquire at least some social capital (and political connection) and travel.

Richard Sennett has suggested that respect must be contextualized within social relations to appear, and "self-respect founded on craft cannot alone generate mutual respect" (2003, 263). While men who were dancers gained some respect for their abilities, musicianship and poetry (especially the spontaneous creation of decimas) were more highly valued. Women were mostly excluded from these practices. Moreover, the sphere of creative labor was predominantly homosocial, centered around meetings of mostly older men in cafés and bars: men joking, stereotypically employing bad language, and enjoying conviviality and solidarity. These meetings would extend to radio shows with live music, where presenters, such as Bernardo *Nayo* Lorenzo Camacho and Félix Martínez González (and earlier, Francisco Rivera Ávila "Paco Píldora") would show off their wit and spontaneous poetry. In the 2000s, for example, Nayo Lorenzo Camacho's Saturday radio show was broadcast live from the seats outside the Gran Café del Portal (the original setting of the Gran Café de la Parroquia), and local musicians, together with suitably qualified passers-by, would be invited to play instruments, sing, and/or talk. In these contexts, the focus was on performance. Rather than a concept of "the working-class man" merely doing manual labor, we encounter a complex configuration of class, levels and types of education (formal/self-directed), and a variety of social and cultural practices.

In Veracruz, local people often assert that it is carnival all year round. I was often told by higher- and lower-class men and women alike how "*Veracruz es un manicomio con vista al mar*" ("Veracruz is a madhouse with a sea view"). Some people also suggested that as Veracruzana/os, they were "a bit mad." But akin to privileged, whiter Veracruzana/os claiming a bit of blackness (see Chapter 1), only people confident enough to claim a bit of madness did so. And most people exemplified Veracruz's madness with reference to the eccentric "personalities" or *locos* (crazy characters) of the past, the infamous (again mostly masculinist) local humor characterized by bad language and a relish for laughing at the grotesqueness of others and at oneself. There are examples of Veracruzana women "personalities," such as the peanut seller "La Chilorio," who ran for the municipal presidency with a hilarious mock election manifesto (see Mancisidor Ortiz 2007), but overall, eccentricity, bad language, and dirty humor are something lower-class men in particular are able to harness and embody.

While the older, lower-class Veracruzana/os I knew rarely expressed pride in their class positions, they remained nostalgic about the lower-class past, about the era of the dockers, of the glory days of the respectable, lower-class Veracruz of old. And although popular culture was promoted by Veracruz's culture industries, and lower-class figures such as Félix Martínez González were given opportunities to lead local venues, the relationship between higher and lower classes in Veracruz was at times tense. I heard one woman from Veracruz's social elites criticizing Félix for being vulgar and coarse. If the lower and bohemian middle classes celebrated Veracruz's popular past and present, the humor and bad language (and historically the eccentric personalities as well), this jarred with certain higher-class sensibilities. As Flores Martos (2004) explores, Veracruz's classes are separated to some extent spatially—the lower classes frequenting the middle of the city and living in poorer neighborhoods, the dominant classes driving to shopping malls and living in richer areas, although they all tend to frequent cafés such as the Gran Café de la Parroquia. Like the Mexican middle classes discussed by Cahn (2008), distinction is largely marked by many of Veracruz's middle classes by consumption, and appearances are often more important than economic status. Veracruz's lower classes also value consumption, and they are often reluctant to spend the little excess money they might have on cultural events. Cultural events in Veracruz's theaters are often the preserve of the dominant classes, while the lower classes attend free events in public spaces.

On Nostalgia, the Carnivalesque, and Ambivalence in Veracruz

By the early twenty-first century, the golden age of Veracruz was recalled with reflective nostalgia by many older, lower-class locals, together with historians, politicians, and local cultural institutions. As we have seen, there was a sense that the glorious past was separate from the more commercialized, impersonal present. And rather than a time of modernization (as if modernization somehow causes a deterioration of social relations) or rural-urban migration, it was often the era when the unionized dockers had economic and political power that was described nostalgically, especially by locals. Although, at first sight, the moment of disjuncture may appear to be 1991, the year when power moved away from the dockers, nostalgia is disrupted by date specificity. Such accuracy provokes utopian ambivalences, because the idealized past of reflective nostalgia is disrupted by the concrete. Instead of specificity, there was a vaguer, more general sense of loss about the fragmentation of the workers' unions, and the consequent decrease in sociability and economic and political power.

Moreover, reflective nostalgia in Veracruz (Boym's yearning for a bygone age) had been present well before the 1990s: for example, more participatory carnivals were recalled and compared with the commercialized spectacles of the 1970s by, among others, IVEC director Ida Rodríguez Prampolini. Past and present nostalgia was further exacerbated by the violence and insecurity that increasingly plagued the Port from the mid-2000s, intensifying around 2011. "*Que bello es Veracruz*" (how beautiful is Veracruz), danzón practitioners and other Mexicans would often say to me—this beauty being linked to music and dance, to food, to the sea, to ideas about a carefree, happy lifestyle—"but how ugly (*feo*) it has become." It was not that Veracruz had stopped being a party town, however, for its carnival, music, dance, and danzón continued despite the violence. What had changed was that nostalgia had become firmly embedded in the collective imaginary of the Port and its carnival, which was no longer epitomized by the dockers and characterized by creativity, wit, and ingenuity.

Locals and historians often point to the dockers' comparsas and the "crazy" carnival as encapsulating Veracruz's characteristic creativity, wit, and ingenuity. For example, historian Horacio Guadarrama Olivera argues that until the 1950s, "without being lavish or spectacular like other American carnivals—such as those of Rio de Janeiro or Havana—[Veracruz's carnival] was characterized by the extravagent originality and creativity of the majority of its participants, as much in making up their disguises and masks as in the preparation of the carnival floats, which were made from simple and cheap materials" (2002, 482). Guadarrama Olivera continues: "humour and popular ingenuity were essential in these first years of Veracruzano carnival" (2002, 481), akin to Mancisidor Ortiz's proposal stated above that the popular character of carnival was epitomized by "openness, merriment and *organized disorder*" (1971, 150, his emphasis). Such an analysis is akin to Bakhtin's (1965) notion of carnival as a "temporary liberation from the prevailing truth and from the established order; it marked the suspension of all hierarchical rank, privileges, norms and prohibitions" (Bakhtin 1984, 10). These are situations in which power structures are mockingly critiqued in creative performances by the lower classes and also simultaneously reproduced through reference to prevailing power structures (such as a monarchy or the organization of local government).

More generally, nostalgia for Veracruz is often framed with reference to the carnivalesque. Flores Martos argues that as Veracruz is already marked by laughter and parody, here carnival emphasizes contradiction and the juxtaposition of difference (2004, 144). He nods to the ambivalence that we find in Bakhtin's carnival laughter, in Veracruz's carnival, and in narratives about the city more broadly. For Bakhtin, carnival laughter is simultaneously, first, collective; second, directed at both those who laugh and those being laughed at; and third, ambivalent in being "gay, triumphant and at the same time mocking, deriding. It asserts and denies, it buries and revives" (1984, 11–12). The ambivalence in Bakhtin's carnival laughter is well exemplified in an example relating to carnivalesque cross-dressing and Daniel "El Catrín" Rergis.

In 1947, several men from Daniel's union made up a comparsa called "María Quiriñonga's Fifteenth Birthday," and they all dressed up in matching dresses and paraded as young women, with Daniel as the birthday girl.[12] Cross-dressing is very much a part of Veracruz's carnival (as is the case in Spain and other parts of Latin America), and carnivalesque cross-dressers should not be confused with trans women (and less frequently, trans men) in the Port, although the two overlap (see Flores Martos 2004 for further analysis regarding Veracruz; and Hutchinson 2016 for an in-depth interrogation of a not dissimilar case in the Dominican Republic). In this context, as in others, carnivalesque crossdressing both reinforces gender stereotypes and disrupts them (pointing to the constructedness of gender binaries, see Butler 1993). There are parallels with Bakhtin's carnival laughter: the exaggerated cross-dressing of the men in Daniel's comparsa enabled them to laugh at themselves and be laughed at; they mocked and remade clichéd, sexualized stereotypes of women, despite respecting some women (as wives, at least in Daniel's case). Hegemonic gender dualisms were reproduced, creating static ambivalences around being a man and/or a woman, but also subverted by dialectic ambivalences around transformation and becoming.[13] But Veracruz's carnivalesque cross-dressing labors hard to reveal its disguise, to assert hegemonic masculinity, to negate its dialectic ambivalence and prove laughter is an aim. It relishes the ambivalences that it cannot dispel. More broadly, in Veracruz's nostalgia for the carnivalesque of the past, we find a collision of pleasurable ambivalences: the relish of at least the dialectic ambivalence engendered by carnivalesque cross-dressing coincides with pleasures of utopian ambivalence encompassed by reflective nostalgia for the city.

Reflective nostalgia is also evident in official representations of the Port (and its adoption of danzón) and invoked by local cultural institutions when marketing the Port as a tourist destination to the mostly national tourists who have increasingly visited Veracruz since the 1930s. Several municipal presidents have commissioned histories of Veracruz's popular past that include pages of glossy photographs of the lower classes and landmarks of the city (for example, Toral 2012; Sefchovich et al. 2000; Mancisidor Ortiz 2007). It is in books such as these where official nostalgia for Veracruz is embedded, but in contrast to reconstructed monuments that embody restorative nostalgia elsewhere and that can be visited, these photographic reproductions do not make the past solid. They signal moments and create possibilities for imaginaries of the past, for yearning and reflective nostalgia. These representations of the Port's history and the intertwining collective and individual memories contribute to a nostalgic collective imaginary of the past not only as a point from which to critique the present, but also a point from which to justify and recreate Veracruz's continuing party reputation. But if government and cultural institutions promote Veracruz as a party town to attract tourists, locals (including those working in these same institutions) simultaneously lament that the present is at best a diluted version of the Port's former glory.

But not all recollections of the past in Veracruz are nostalgic. The promise of Veracruz's relaxed, laissez-faire atmosphere is far from the realities of state control, and it is also a long way from the moral conservatism shared by many locals, especially in relation to sex and sexuality. Like its blackness, the nostalgia for Veracruz is employed strategically by the academic and political elites, while others can merely access its yearning.

Nostalgia and the Reproduction of Inequalities

We have seen how over the course of the twentieth century, the Port saw massive industrialization, the development of the media, a US occupation in 1914 that local people helped to fight off, post-revolutionary labor movements, the emergence of a tourist industry, the reinvention of carnival, and the rise of corporatism in the docks and its subsequent collapse after the 1980s debt crisis. These broad socioeconomic transformations affected social participation in the Port and its danzón: on the (usually male, income-earning part-time) musicians; on the (male and female amateur) dancers who (directly, or indirectly via dance hall attendance) contracted them; and on the male dockers whose economic and political power rose and fell. These processes contributed to recreating an imaginary of the Port as a carnival town with constant partying and a collective irreverence, both led by men from the popular classes. Lower-class men were celebrated for their *alegría* (gaiety), creativity, wit, homely familiarity, disdain for authority, and ingenuity, particularly workers employed in the docks. As Veracruz's "adopted" music-dance form, the history of danzón in the Port reinforces a nostalgic imaginary, largely dominated by men, in which women are remarkably absent, barring a few named dancers of old. With greater passenger air travel after the Second World War, many travelers bypassed the port, and Veracruz became increasingly post-cosmopolitan. The popularity of danzón waned in the 1960s and 1970s, but it burgeoned in the 1980s. In the early 1990s, following containerization and neoliberal reforms, the docks were privatized, and wealth and power were redistributed away from the dockers, their unions, and the local economy. By the early twenty-first century, Veracruz was still represented in the local and national imaginary as a city where revelries never ceased, yet nostalgia was prevalent. So what has this nostalgia enabled?

Nostalgia creates histories to be proud of, free from guilt and shame, dirt and horror. As Boym (2001) contends, nostalgia erases poverty, pain, and violence, and in nostalgic renditions of Veracruz, the poverty and inequality of the past are both acknowledged and erased, producing momentary utopian ambivalences in the disruption of this reflective nostalgia. Nostalgic imaginaries of Veracruz and its lower classes as happy and partying are mobilized by local culture industries to reproduce ideas about the city and its people, past and present, without acknowledging either the poverty and other aggressions of the past or the contemporary discrimination or inequalities of the present. There are resonances here with culture- and tourist-industry representations across Latin America and the Caribbean of the purportedly happy lower classes, for example, in the carnivals of Rio and elsewhere. In Veracruz, the particular qualities of the city's bygone age are portrayed as creativity, ingenuity, and wit, and also the homely, familial atmosphere of local festivities; yet these depictions are devoid of inequality, as we saw when Mancisidor Ortiz wrote about "that unforgettable era in which the people lived as if they were a single and large family" (1971, 149). Likewise, García Díaz described the initial era of carnival as "a domestic, homely fiesta: essentially Porteña [of the Port]" (1992, 222). And anthropologist and director of the IVEC from 2010–12, Félix Báez-Jorge argued that Veracruz's contemporary and past economic and educational inequalities are transcended by the communal, family-like feeling in the Port (Báez-Jorge 2007). Such nostalgic representations erase and enable the reproduction of discrimination and inequalities, be they gendered, classed, racialized, aged, or otherwise.

The construction of Veracruz's uniqueness, particularly the notion of its happiness, is linked not only to poverty but also to racialized stereotypes grounded in Veracruz's relationship to Cuba, and it is epitomized by the male-dominated public sphere where joking and an irreverence for authority appear to prevail. Yet the familiar embarrassment that Herzfeld (2005) described as "cultural intimacy" pertains in Veracruz. Cultural intimacy, for Herzfeld, is "the recognition of those aspects of a cultural identity that are considered a source of external embarrassment but that nevertheless provide insiders with their assurance of common sociality, the familiarity with the bases of power that may at one moment assure the disenfranchised a degree of creative irreverence and at the next moment reinforce the effectiveness of intimidation" (2005, 3). Herzfeld proposes that nation-states thrive on such cultural intimacy, and we might understand such power as being supported by static ambivalences (between, say, pride and embarrassment, or irreverence and intimidation) that are maintained through temporal disjuncture. Similar entanglements of irreverence, intimidation, and corruption by local political forces are not only pervasive in Veracruz but also provoke ambivalences that have been intensified by the violence of recent years.[14]

In addition to cultural intimacy, another pertinent model relating to power is provided by Orwell (1949), who describes a form of power in *Nineteen Eighty-Four* that is maintained through the reconciliation of contradictions. Rather than, or in addition to, being recreated through unarticulated ambivalences, this power is reproduced through the revelation that inconsistencies are compatible: "if human equality is to be for ever averted," Orwell writes, "then the prevailing mental condition must be controlled insanity" (2009, 246). Instead of temporally separate static ambivalences (either-or), we have here a model of power thriving on concurrent static ambivalences. Such controlled insanity enables an abnegation of responsibility for all parties entwined in power dynamics. The specificity of Veracruz comes to mind, as well as governance more broadly in twentieth- and early-twenty-first-century Mexico, where corruption, intense bureaucratization, and violence are widespread, and impunity is enjoyed by both organized criminal organizations and state institutions. This model is a factor, I propose, that has enabled narcoviolence and what Sayak Valencia terms "gore capitalism" to prevail in certain areas of Mexico, that is, "the undisguised and unjustified bloodshed [...] the many instances of dismembering and disembowelment, often tied up with organized crime, gender and the predatory use of bodies [...] as tools of necroempowerment" (Valencia 2018, 19–20).

VIGNETTE THREE

Renata
(fiction)

Here again. Tights on. Petticoat. Insulin daintily injected. Short red sleeveless dress pulled over head. Hair brushed. Foundation set. Renata holds her face as still as she can. Diagonally cut bristles pencil an eyebrow line. Eye shadow: beige to chocolate. Burgundy lipstick. High-heeled, silver-strapped sandals placed over stockinged toes. Greying handbag. Out we go.

As the bus jangles to a halt, Renata descends the stairs cautiously, her sandals shining against the dull metal steps. She takes my arm as we saunter through the sticky air to the main square. Evening light outlines the yellow globes of lampposts. A maze of tree trunks, painted white, sprout into palms and shorter, flat-topped trees. Smooth stone floor slabs, black, speckled cream, greying, amid stripes of black and rust blocks; the occasional crack. A plywood-topped concrete podium in the middle raises the musicians a meter above the dancers. Camera-ready tourists overlook a ring of chairs demarcating the dance floor. Elegant men and women sit on chairs and stand: some wear matching dance-hall finest, others jarocho whites. Tak, tak, ta-da-dum: the timbales strike up the danzón. Spurting trumpets and finer clarinets beckon. Timbales and güiro crunch beats. Grackles squawk. Chatter. Bustle.

Here again. Without her partner, Óscar, Renata feels alone, exposed. She can't bear it that Óscar's got Parkinson's; that his wife won't let her visit the asylum. She can't even get respite from the Church: they won't let her take communion because Óscar's still married. She knows her God is with her, with him, but it hurts.

Renata recalls being young, coquettish, circling the bandstand: the girls in one direction, the boys in the other. That was before she was married, before the kids, before her husband died. She misses him. And Óscar.

The musicians smile to greet her. She yearns to dance with Óscar again, to feel his touch, his out-of-timeness, his buffoonery.

All these people, these danzón dancers she's known for decades. She's even fond of the ones she's fought with. There's Lucía: Renata likes her, but Lucía moans; Lucía's husband's leaves her to dance with other men while he fucks …

I interject. Attempt to curb the usual homophobia.

Renata tenses, uncomfortable. She watches the dance, knowing no one will invite her to join, that they sense her rejection before asking. She hates going dancing without dancing. What is she doing? Here again.

CHAPTER THREE

Elegant Moves

Modernist Aesthetics and Danzón in Veracruz

Chairs have provoked fights and at least one heart attack in the Port of Veracruz. They form a boundary around the smooth, stone floor on which danzón dancing occurs in the city's main plaza. Mostly occupied by older women, and some men, around eighty chairs separate up to two hundred seasoned participants (and the odd other person lucky enough to have secured a chair) from the several hundred casual onlookers who stand behind them. Chairs surround the dancers, the street vendors, older couples courting, and men discussing their affairs. The distinct colors (red, blue, green, white) and positioning of these chairs reveal the current state of play of the Port's dance groups: their number, their size. Outside and overlooking this chaired perimeter, musicians and a master of ceremonies sit on a stage, accompanied on Saturday evenings by uniformed dancers exhibiting their expertise. Habitués anticipate when the municipal workers will bring out the chairs about an hour or so before the danzón event officially begins: they queue and then secure their established spots, jealously guarding both chair and location.

Framing this scene is the Port's main square, the Plaza de Armas or Zócalo that, like other Mexican plazas, is flanked by a cathedral, a municipal palace, and colonial buildings with porticos (portales). It is the political, administrative, and religious hub of the city: what Veracruz chronicler Leonardo Pasquel described as "the interior patio of the community" (1969, 97). Veracruz's Portales de Lerdo house hotels and bars where evenings bring a rich cacophony of marimba ensembles, Norteño trios, mariachis, ambulant bolero singer-guitarists, and son jarocho groups, some meandering opportunistically among the drinkers (in bars and cafes here and throughout the center) in the hope of money or a song commission. Three streets behind lies the port, with its huge vessels and myriad containers, overshadowing the cafés for which the city is renowned, and the seafront, where visitors and locals alike stroll to feel the breeze on their skin rather than just hot, humid air. Along past the tourist memorabilia, boys fish for coins; trans women sex workers promenade; the aquarium beckons holiday-makers to adorn the Port's beaches; and shopping malls (and cinema multiplexes) lure automobiled locals. Veracruz, Mexico's largest gulf-coast port, is a cheaper holiday destination than Cancún or Acapulco. It mostly attracts lower-class tourists, particularly from Mexico City and Puebla, but also the odd middle-class and foreign tourist; its many hotels host business conferences; its port brings sailors from around the globe who disembark in search of the city's pleasures; and its pre-Lenten carnival attracts over two million visitors. Danzón events appear in visitors' guides as one of the Port's attractions. They usually begin early in the evening, when the humidity of the Port sticks less to the skin.

In this chapter, I provide a detailed account of a Saturday danzón event in the Port of Veracruz's main square and explicate differences among dancing styles. I also consider how the dance form's transformation presented opportunities for creativity, as well as the regulation of generic boundaries. Critically, in the second part of the chapter, I argue that the académico style of dancing that became popular in the 1980s assumed a modernist aesthetic linked to elegance and/as whiteness, an aesthetic evident in numerous genres, including nationalist, folkloric, and ballroom dances.

Danzón Dance Styles, Space, and Institutional Support

In Veracruz, a distinction is made between two intersecting styles of dancing: the older, freer lírico style and the more codified, schooled académico style (sometimes referred to as *técnico* or *clásico*). Additionally, four intersecting ways of dancing are referenced by practitioners: *danzón cerrado* (closed), where couples face inward in a waltz-like embrace; *danzón abierto* (open), where couples open out, facing outward and turning, usually holding one hand; *danzón de fantasía* (fantasy danzón), which involves steps from other dances, such as tango and paso doble; and *danzón acrobático* (acrobatic danzón), involving gymnastic feats, such as the son cubano plancha and tornillo steps. Danzón de fantasía and danzón acrobático are rare, while académico style proliferates. Neither danzón académico nor danzón lírico is racialized as distinct to the other: a racialized distinction is instead made between dancers from Veracruz and from Mexico City.

Danzón académico emerged in the 1980s when groups of couples started performing dance routines, moving in choreographed unison to set pieces of music. While people told me that in the lírico style, dancers "just follow the music" to dictate their actions, danzón académico has a strict aesthetic, including a more upright posture and choreographed poses.[1] The académico style involves learning—and creating within rigid parameters—hundreds of codified, geometric, named steps: *caja* (box) / *cuadro* (square), *puente* (bridge) / *columpio* (swing), *paseos* (walks), *laterales* (sideways), and steps named after people (Fredy, Jorge, Lucy). While some of these steps have been around for decades and are performed in the lírico style, the way they are performed became more codified, disciplined, and geometric in the académico style. For example, the basic danzón step, the *cuadro* (square) or *caja* (box) is performed in the académico style by tracing the slightly extended leg and gliding foot as a square on the ground. In the académico style, dancers talk about steps in terms of beats of the bar. Although danzones are sometimes notated in 2/4, they are usually in 4/4, and dancers tend to speak about them in terms of four beats per bar. One whole danzón step is four bars long, with most steps (slow, quick, quick) consisting of the feet moving on beats one (slow), three (quick), and four (quick) for three bars, and beats one (slow) and three (slow) of the fourth bar (see Tables 3.1 and 3.2). The feet should be together in closed position at the beginning and end of each musical phrase (usually a whole step), and at the end of each section (whether couples remain in open or closed position at section endings). When performing the basic *caja* (box) / *cuadro* (square) step, dancers move backward or forward on the slow count and sideways on the quick-quick counts. In the académico style, people learn to count the four-bar phrases of each step, often confusingly, in eleven counts (see Table 3.2), although some dancers count in eight with "ands" added (as is common among choreographers and dance teachers whatever the time signature): in relation to danzón steps, four beat bars are then counted ||:1-2&|3-4&|5-6&|7-8-:|| (where dancers rest on the dash and move on the counts and the ampersands). It is not uncommon to see people's lips move as they dance. Where people count rather than listening to musical phrases, sound becomes numerical knowledge that is then translated into movement. Thus, in the more codified académico style, mathematical concepts are applied; steps become geometrical, sound becomes numbered, and principles of strict rights and wrongs operate. However, the distinction between danzón académico and lírico is not always clear, despite some dancers' insistence that it is. Moreover, differences are also foregrounded between the showier, Mexico City style of dancing, which involves more turns, more separation between couples, and flashier ornamentation than

Table 3.1: Danzón académico step—beats usually moved on (1).

	ONE WHOLE STEP (11 moves) This four-bar pattern is often repeated until the final phrase.	FINAL STEP OF SECTION "REMATE" ("ending") (10 moves). Danced at section endings, that is, going into descansos and at the end of a piece.
Steps (beats usually moved on):	Feet usually move on beats 1, 3, and 4 of the first three bars, then 1 and 3 of the fourth bar (slow, quick, quick | slow, quick, quick | slow, quick, quick | slow, slow).	Feet usually move on beats 1, 3, and 4 of the first three bars, ending on the first beat of the fourth bar (slow, quick, quick | slow, quick, quick | slow, quick, quick | slow).

the Veracruz style.[2] In practice, all these styles operate as a continuum, and in Veracruz, many dancers perform something in between the académico and lírico styles (despite claims to the contrary). Groups usually dance in the académico style, and differences between académico and lírico dancing are as much between (ex-)group (académico) and non-group (lírico) dancers, as between dancing styles.

In Veracruz, there are marked differences between the amount of institutional support group and non-group danzón dancers receive. With local government funding, attendance at danzón events in the Zócalo (principal plaza) is gratis: the local government, and in particular its tourism division, employs the musicians; supplies sound equipment, some instruments, music stands, and chairs (for musicians and dancers); and provides the space (which is policed by municipal officials). Through most of the 2000s and 2010s, danzón was performed several evenings a week in the Zócalo, on Wednesdays in the Plazuela de la Campana, and on Sundays in the Plazuela de la Campana and the Parque Zamora, with the Parque Zamora danzón stopping in the 2010s, and later the Plazuela de la Campana events ceasing by 2020. At the Sunday events in both the Plazuela de la Campana and the Parque Zamora, there was little institutional support: while the authorities licensed the use of these public spaces on Sundays, it was the performers in the Parque Zamora, together with bars in the Plazuela de la Campana, who financed the musicians, sound equipment, and chairs. At Sunday events, men paid around four times the local bus fare to dance, and chairs were rented out at twice the bus fare each. Several women policed these spaces, checking whether men had paid to dance, asking them for their contributions,

Table 3.2: Danzón académico step—beats usually moved on (2).

Bar	1				2				3				4		
Music: beat feet move on	1		3	4	1		3	4	1		3	4	1		3
Dance count (if using 11 count)	1		2	3	4		5	6	7		8	9	10		11
Dance count (if using "ands")	1		2	&	3		4	&	5		6	&	7		8

and, once paid, attaching a colored ribbon to the man's lapel. Groups met to dance together in public only in the Zócalo, which had the highest density of académico performers, although académico dancers also went to dance without their groups in the other spaces. Lírico dancers frequented all these spaces, although this style predominated in Plazuela de la Campana and the Parque Zamora. Some dancers traveled to perform danzón lírico exclusively on Sundays in the Campana or the Parque Zamora.

In terms of representing the Port to spectating tourists, the Zócalo provided the primary arena, followed by the Campana and the Parque Zamora. This was reflected in the institutional support gained by performers in these spaces. Although danzón was already a spectacle in Veracruz's public plazas, danzón groups perform staged exhibition pieces in the Zócalo: groups of uniformed couples, often dancing choreographed routines in formation, exhibit their shows on the stage of Veracruz's Zócalo on Saturdays, rotating so that each group exhibits about once a month. They also do exhibitions in hotels, at danzón festivals, and at special events: I traveled to danzón exhibitions to commemorate the Day of the Grandparent organized by the municipality of Villa Azueta; an IVEC event to commemorate the Day of the Witches (the first Friday of March) in Santiago Tuxtla; and danzón events and festivals in Veracruz and Mexico City convened by the IVEC, Mexico's National Council for Culture and the Arts (CONACULTA), and private individuals. These exhibitions are often patronized and legitimated by local and state government departments and cultural institutions. Moreover, the semi-public spaces (courtyards and palapas) in which groups rehearse their dance shows two or three times a week are provided by the municipality and by the state-funded Veracruz Cultural Institute (IVEC). In sum, group dancers received substantial institutional support in comparison with non-group dancers, and more often than not, it was the newer danzón académico that was performed in groups. An overview of how, when, where, and by whom

Table 3.3: Comparison of danzón académico and lírico in the Port of Veracruz (early twenty-first century)

Danzón	Académico	Lírico
What is danced? What are the markers?	Modernist aesthetic. Hundreds of formalized steps; specific phrase and section ends (the feet coming together on the fourth beat of the last bar of a phrase); upright posture.	Freer steps; looser endings (often ending before or after the fourth beat of the last bar of a phrase). More relaxed posture.
Relationship to music:	Sound conceptualized as numerical knowledge.	"Just follow the music."
Transmission:	Learned in groups, by watching, and/or with friends and family.	Learned by watching and/or with friends and family.
Age of dancers:	Older and younger people, and occasionally children.	Mostly older people.
What dancers wear:	Uniforms on Saturdays and when exhibiting; own dancing clothes on other occasions.	Own dancing clothes.
Primary day (both performed daily):	Saturday.	Sunday.
Where primarily danced in the Port and how spaces funded:	Zócalo. Municipality provides performance space and pays for musicians, sound equipment, and chairs; regional government, IVEC, CONACULTA and Municipality fund festivals.	Zócalo, Plazuela de la Campana, Parque Zamora events. Margarita Castro, president of the *Club de Bailadores de Hoy y Siempre*, organized the Parque Zamora event on Sundays through the 2000s; *Danzonera Manzanita y su son 4* and *Pardiñolas* restaurant organized the Plazuela de la Campana event on Sundays through the 2010s. Municipality provides performance space; musicians, sound equipment, and chairs financed by dancers at Plazuela de la Campana and Parque Zamora events.
Where else danced in Mexico:	Mexico City and nationwide. Characteristic of the danzón revival that emerged from the 1980s.	Mexico City (although not named as such and involves more turns and separation of couple).

the académico and lírico styles of danzón were danced, and who funded what, is detailed in Table 3.3.

A Danzón Event:
Saturday in Veracruz's Zócalo

At the start of this chapter, I began to describe a Saturday danzón event in the Zócalo where chairs demarcate the dance floor, separating habitués and tourists, and uniformed groups perform their académico routines (see also Figure 3.1). Let me now turn to a more detailed account of this event, pointing to some threads that I pursue in other chapters (to group and non-group dancers; histories of the Port and its danzón; musicians; gender dynamics; and older people's sexuality).[3] I begin by giving you a flavor of some of the regulars.

There's eighty-five-year-old Tania, retired from cooking in people's houses, who was financially supported by her son. Tania once danced, but she stopped some years ago and now religiously attends Veracruz's daily danzón events as an onlooker and fervent gossiper. She usually arrives in the Zócalo about two hours before the events begin there, sitting on benches around the sides of the plaza and chatting with other regulars. The Zócalo's evening events (mostly danzón, sometimes son jarocho) provide an opportunity for women to go out alone and sit in this public plaza, usually a more male prerogative. These women are mostly fifty-plus-year-old regulars, assured they will meet people they know. Some habitués, including Tania, told me it was the highlight and focal point of their day. As she arrived so early to danzón events, Tania usually got a seat in the center of the row facing the stage, musicians, and dancers.

Beside her would sit seventy-four-year-old Don Carlos, a retired railway worker and former danzón group leader who had once been married but did not speak of a wife. Don Carlos only danced with sixty-six-year-old Julieta, a widowed secretary: they had recently become romantically entwined and met here every evening. Beside them sat Silvina, a sixty-two-year-old housewife, married to an accountant. Silvina dances in the older, freer lírico style and has several regular dance partners, including Gilberto, a sixty-year-old retired docker who was newly widowed and sought a wife. Silvina's husband, who did not attend, was unusually relaxed about her dancing with other men, leading to gossip that he was gay. Gossip blossomed in this arena, where regulars sometimes knew each other of old in this small city, but many did not. Such gossip created a policing mechanism whereby women in particular strove to maintain their reputations, but men were not exempt. Silvina would

Figure 3.1. Saturday danzón event in the Zócalo, Veracruz.

dance with Gilberto for several months, until he left the dance, having found new romance with a woman who did not care for dance. There were other men she enjoyed dancing with, and she seldom sat while the music played. Danzón was her therapy, she told me, more psychological than physical, for it made her less anxious (see Sevilla 2003 for an exploration of danzón as mental and physical therapy in relation to Mexico City's dance halls). This cluster of regulars perched precariously between the Port's largest danzón dance groups: the Grupo Rojo and the Grupo Verde.[4]

The Grupo Rojo was led by fifty-five-year-old Julio, who worked for the local government and often proudly proclaimed that he had formerly migrated without documents to the United States. Many people admired his dancing, and several of his group's members had joined for that very reason, but Tania complained to me that he thought too much of himself. She bemoaned everyone dancing the same nowadays, the golden days of great danzón dancing in Veracruz being gone, in her opinion. Whereas Tania complained about the disciplining that had occurred to the dance, sixty-two-year-old

Valeria, who walked the chaired perimeter selling fans, extolled the elegant aesthetic of the dance groups dancing their routines. While four groups frequented the Zócalo, Valeria dismissed two of them: the Grupo Amarillo, led by Raquel, was too small to count in her reckoning, with its dozen or so regulars; and the Grupo Blanco, led by Doña Violeta, which was more ad hoc, with couples performing independently, rather than dance routines in unison. Grupo Blanco dancers were generally older than the other groups, and many had already been in several groups. They dressed in white, with the men wearing straw hats. As a group, they provided more space for creativity and individuality. For example, Gerardo, a seventy-six-year-old gardener, always teetered on the edge of being ostracized from this group, as he had been from several others, for he sometimes arrived inebriated and refused to dance with certain group members. But dance was not the only reason that Gerardo went to the Zócalo. He also liked to be near his ex-girlfriend Elena, who now danced with her new partner, Miguel, in the Grupo Rojo (see the opening vignette).

Many danzón habitués had histories with each other, histories in groups, friendships, or work or romantic relationships, but most of these remained shrouded in silence or whispered about in gossip. The violence perpetrated by organized criminals exacerbated this silence. Several danzón practitioners told me that they had family members who have been touched by the violence: the cousin of one musician was decapitated; the nephews of another dancer disappeared, their mutilated bodies found a fortnight later in a ditch; the son of yet another dancer died suddenly, purportedly due to illness. Victims tend to be stigmatized and inculcated in their own deaths, Mariana Berlanga Gayón (2015) argues. But while danzón events had previously been a focal point for gossip, this ceased to some extent. There was little gossip about the parents or grandparents of younger people who had been killed. Anxiety reigned, and while people might talk about where and when incidents have occurred, most discussions of violence and insecurity were rather nebulous. The why and how were rarely speculated, for local people became cautious about whom they could trust. Moreover, they did not want to say what they had seen or heard, or what they knew, for fear of their lives or those of their loved ones. And for many danzón dancers, especially those retired from their jobs, danzón events were still a focal point in their lives, even if, for several months at a time, fewer dancers attended danzón events, because they occurred in public plazas. When the violence was more intense, the events started at 6 or 7 p.m. so that people could get home sooner. This happened a few times during the length of my fieldwork, as the violence brutally ebbed and flowed.

When things were calmer, the cathedral clock chimed the beginning of the Saturday danzón event in the Zócalo at 7 p.m. The portales musicians would quiet, and the master of ceremonies and güiro (doubling claves) player of the *Danzonera Alma de Veracruz*, Eliseo Díaz Vázquez, would officially open the event.[5] A retired TAMSA factory worker—although reluctant to say so, as he enjoyed the prestige of being a public speaker—Eliseo had developed a passion for public speaking over several years and was knowledgeable not only about danzón but also about the history of the Port in general. Eliseo's gratification came from having introduced famous dignitaries and even presidents at public events. He was less interested in acquiring unique expertise, but he prided himself on having superior knowledge to that of the majority of his audiences.

Eliseo speaks of being committed to educating people, particularly danzón dancers. A stout man in his sixties, Eliseo talks for several minutes via a microphone before and in the five-minute intervals between the danzones: he is the voice of the event, punctuating and framing the danzones. He recounts histories of danzón and Veracruz, introducing danzones, greeting people (individually and in their dance groups), and demanding applause. Eliseo relays his historical knowledge to those who pay attention to his sermons. He reiterates details about the origins of danzón, how the seventeenth-century English Country Dance, adopted in France as the *contredanse*, was taken to Haiti and Cuba; how in the 1870s, what was by then called the *contradanza cubana* was transformed into the *danzón*; how danzón traveled to and in Mexico, and its adoption by Veracruzana/os who nurtured it as their own. He speaks about the local pre-Hispanic civilizations, the Totonacs and the Olmecs; of the importance of Veracruz in the colonial period, being the only official port on the east coast of New Spain (Mexico) until the 1760s, and controlling most of the viceroyalty's importation and exportation (including silver, cochineal, sugar, textiles, and tobacco); the people who arrived in (or near) the port—conquistador Hernán Cortés in 1519, pirate Lorencillo in 1683, Emperor Maximilian in 1864 (who left dead in 1867); of Veracruz's title as "four times heroic," having defended the nation against Spain, France, and the United States; its fortress San Juan de Ulúa made of the *múcara* (marine coral) stone for which Veracruz is renowned; Júarez's 1858 temporary government in Veracruz, and Carranza's in 1914; Veracruz's dance halls (particularly *Villa del Mar*); local stars such as Agustín Lara (1897–1970) and Toña la Negra (1912–1982), and local eccentrics such as the chewing-gum seller Rosario González Mendoza, known as Doña Charito and "La Reina del Danzón" (the Queen of Danzón) who, even in her nineties, would leave her wares to dance to the danzón *El Paso del Elefante* (the Elephant's Walk) whenever it was played and who would feature in the Parque Zamora scene in María Novaro's film *Danzón*. While often telling me how unhappy he was, Eliseo, the master of ceremonies, constantly referred to the happiness that prevailed in Veracruz due to its Afro-Caribbean heritage, its location on the Gulf of Mexico, and its tropical weather. Yet many people paid little attention to his interjections: before and during the intervals between danzones, dancers, musicians, and spectators mostly chatted, gossiped, and flirted, although some heeded his words.

The *Danzonera Alma de Veracruz*, to which Eliseo belonged, was the most active danzonera in the Port in the 2000s and 2010s, usually performing four evenings a week. Despite personnel changes, the eleven musicians of this danzonera mostly identified, like the dancers, as lower-middle class. Most had day jobs, while some had retired: electrician, schoolteacher, instrument repairer, builder. Several of these musicians also played with other ensembles, particularly son cubano and salsa. The band was (mostly) made up of two clarinets, a tenor saxophone, two trumpets, a keyboard, electric bass, congas, Eliseo on güiro and claves, and timbales. Through the 2000s, the other instruments that were supposed to sound in the *Danzonera Alma de Veracruz* included a tiny güiro played by Antonio, the band's porter (who was not considered a good enough player by the group's leader to perform on an audible instrument); a third trumpet whose player had been ill for over a year and never turned up; and a trombone, the unfilled vacancy in the ensemble. Over the next decade, these positions would be filled and personnel would change. Danzones may be executed by all manner of instrumentation and in Veracruz are sometimes performed by marimba ensembles and the Naval Band, but it is the danzonera and the Municipal Band (usually combining flutes, clarinets, saxophones, trumpets, trombones, sousaphone, güiro, clash cymbals, bass drum, and timbales) that regularly play at the Port's danzón events. Danzón is demarcated from other genres in terms of instrumentation, repertoire, performance practice, and when and where it has been performed at various points in its history. Veracruz's Municipal Band is exceptional in performing sets of just danzones: elsewhere in Mexico, such bands play a mixed repertoire. Moreover, usually it is only the restrictively denominated danzoneras that play almost exclusively danzón.

Once Eliseo, *Alma de Veracruz*'s master of ceremonies, introduces the first danzón, the timbales player, Silverio López Contreras, sharply hits the shell of his instrument twice (tak-tak), then strikes his preambular pattern, cueing both musicians and dancers to perform (Music Example 3.1). For the musicians in the danzonera, the final stroke marks the beginning of the piece's anacrusis bar: they enter loudly, the güiro cutting through with the two-bar

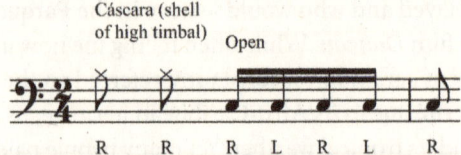

Music Example 3.1. Preambular timbales pattern introducing danzones in Veracruz. This pattern ends on beat 1 of the anacrusis measure.

cinquillo pattern. The danzonera provokes sonic and embodied nostalgia for some, familiarity for others, and trepidation for still others. Potential dancers in the Port's main square stop chatting. The first eight bars are not danced to, so there is a still time to negotiate who will dance with whom and where on the dance floor.[6]

Initiating the dance involves a complex set of interactions. Like other couple dances, danzón involves a leader and follower, usually gendered as a man and a woman. Couples relate to each other as if entwined in hegemonic, heteronormative gender dynamics: it is men who dominate, for it is they who mostly lead (or who think they do), who conventionally invite (the mostly seated) women to dance during these first bars, and who return them to their seats (or other initial location) at the end of each danzón. His invitation may come in the form of catching a woman's eyes, raising his eyebrows and gently nodding, or it may be an outstretched hand or a direct verbal request. Whom will a man ask to dance? Someone he assumes will accept: his partner in the dance and/or otherwise, a friend, neighbor, or fellow group member? Will he traverse the dance floor in search of, or avoiding, particular women? Will he risk rejection and ask a woman he has not danced with before or who has previously rejected him (a woman like Renata in Vignette 3)? Will a woman intimate her inclination to dance before the timbales call? Whose invitation will she accept, if any? How does she deal with multiple offers? Whom and how does she decline? Will she hold a man's hand as they walk onto the dance floor? Whose? Where and how will they position themselves?

Some men who were danzón regulars ventured to dance with new partners, but most had one or several women that they regularly danced with and who they knew were amenable. Group members usually danced exclusively with each other, sometimes being allocated partners by the group leader. Occasionally women explicitly asked a man to dance, but this was unusual unless the woman was a group leader herself. Many danzón dancers told me that they had an obligation as Veracruzana/os to welcome and include tourists in their activities, to offer them chairs and dance with them, but few did so apart from a couple of older men who would seek out young, amenable female tourists (and, if they agreed, stand with them on the dance floor between danzones). Regulars gossiped disdainfully about these men. Local women almost never danced with strangers, despite there generally being more women at danzón events than men, unless a man was an incredible dancer, in which case their reputation might be put on the line slightly in return for a good dance. Even regular, experienced women dancers were sometimes left "wall-flowering" (Savigliano 1998), remaining seated in their dancing clothes, having not been invited to dance.

Once partnered, couples head to their preferred positions on the chair-encircled dance floor and then stand side by side, holding hands. The uniformed groups create blocks of color toward the edges of the dance floor. Most dancers face the musicians at the start and end of the dance, but some dancers in groups face the tourists and other onlookers, making the dancers, rather than the musicians, the focus of attention, and making the dance a form of spectacle. (These dancers were thus accused of being exhibitionists by a well-known danzón aficionado.) Only the Blanco group, in which dancing couples performed more independently (in both the académico and lírico styles) consistently faces the musicians, beneath whom they station their chairs. Non-group dancers carefully position themselves apart from the groups' territorial blocks, in the center of the dance floor or near other edges. Some people remain seated, but most onlookers stand behind the chairs that separate them from the dancers. Often the only non-dancers standing within this chaired boundary are street vendors, who face outward, attempting to sell spectators their wares: danzón CDs, sweets and other food, fans, and photography.

While the musicians play the first section of the danzón, the dancers do not move. They wait for the eight-bar A section to end before the man (usually) directs the woman to face him, either by turning the woman ornately, or by turning in to face her and leading her to do likewise. He places his right hand on her back at waist level, while she rests her left hand on his shoulder, and their other hands hold together in the space between their shoulders, creating the loose embrace of the closed position. Even when they are romantically entwined, dancers rarely look into each other's eyes—a very intimate act—but instead, most hold their heads up high, observing other dancers or onlookers. Novices sometimes stare at their feet, as did a woman who told me that her looking up prompted jealous outbursts from her partner. Couples usually dance "five fingers" apart, considered a "decent" distance, although men sometimes try to hold the woman closer, which she may or may not resist, and Cuban dancers tend to perform closer together.[7] But this does not mean that there is no space for flirting.

Dancers often start the dance with their feet together, an act accentuated by (group-based) académico dancers, while practitioners of the older lírico style may be more relaxed about beginnings, endings, and the dance more generally. In both styles, the man usually takes a step forward while the woman moves backward, landing on the downbeat of the first bar of a phrase. Dancers continue, usually marking the first, third, and fourth beats at a slow walking pace. Some lírico dancers move their feet side to side, and backward and forward, turning as they go, while others use more codified, but still fairly loose, steps. In the académico style, dancers move with varying degrees of control, precision, smoothness, and rhythmic acuity sideways, forward, or backward on beats one, three, and four, until they bring their feet firmly together on the third beat of the fourth bar to mark the end of a phrase (as per Tables 3.1–3.2). In this slow, sensual dance, the upper body remains fairly still, and movement is mostly propelled by the feet and softly held knees, creating subtle hip movements, with the feet moving little more than a foot-length away. The posture of dancers performing in the académico style is, however, more upright, extended, and stretched than the more relaxed lírico style, where shoulders may remain rounded and elbows kept lower and closer to the body, and hips may be moved slightly more. Most couples take little space in their dance, one square meter at most, although occasionally, flamboyant dancers demand more. Where this does occur, it is in the final *montuno* section of the dance when couples usually move into an open position (*danzón abierto*) and, with one or both hands, the man guides the woman into turns, both around his body and, more rarely, inside their former embrace, as their bodies counterbalance each other to both propel and contain motion.

Dancing and non-dancing demarcate the sections of danzón's rondo form (for example, AABAACAAD), interlocking the music-dance relationship and creating boundaries around and within the dance in a particular way. The first performance of each eight-bar A section of danzones structure is considered non-danceable, differentiating danzón from other local music-dance forms. Most dancers start dancing on the repetition of the non-danceable A section. In other words, when the same piece of music is repeated, it becomes danceable (see Table 3.4). While connoisseurs can hear when these non-danceable sections—the *descansos* or rests—occur and do not dance in these sections, novices continue alone. These non-danceable moments

Table 3.4: Outline of dance moves in relation to structure of danzón (as danced in Veracruz)

Section	Length	Dance moves
A	8 bars	Non-danceable
A1 (A repeated)	8 bars (2 steps)	Dance usually begins with a *caja/cuadro* (box/square), and then other steps in closed position
B (1st melody)	Typically 16 bars (4 steps)	Dance continues in closed position
A	8 bars	Non-danceable
A1	8 bars (2 steps)	Dance usually begins with a *caja/cuadro* (box/square), and then other steps in closed position
C (2nd melody)	Typically 16 bars (4 steps)	Dance continues in closed position
A	8 bars	Non-danceable
A1	8 bars (2 steps)	Dance usually begins with a *caja/cuadro* (box/square), and then other steps in closed position
Bridge passage (in some danzones only)	2 bars (half step)	Dance usually begins with a *caja/cuadro* (box/square)—only half the step is danced, and inexperienced dancers are often caught up in danzones with bridge passages
D (montuno)	Typically 32 bars (8 steps)	If no bridge passage, the dance usually begins with a *caja/cuadro* (box/square), and then other steps in open position: *paseos* and turns (*floreando*: flowering). More *cadencia* (cadence/rhythmic movement). Livelier (*movido*).

make dancers' choreo-musical knowledge particularly visible, often deterring those without this knowledge from entering the dance. For example, I was told that in rural areas outside Veracruz, people used to dance for the length of a danzón, bobbing up and down as they moved. But such dancing declined, and with the danzón revival of the 1980s, knowledge that some parts of the dance are non-danceable (emphasized in the académico style) has made such dancing supposedly incorrect. And in the académico style, a controlled, smooth, gliding movement (the feet just above the ground) and a lack of motion in the shoulders is valued as elegant, in contrast to the bobbing up down for the length of a danzón as was previously practiced in rural areas, further highlighting distinctions. It is worth spending some time understanding descansos, the technicalities of how these non-danceable sections work, and how they have been affected by the dance revival that occurred from the 1980s.

During descansos, while Mexican dancers mostly stand hand in hand, Cuban dancers walk in their couples and greet each other. Descansos also occur in other music-dance forms, such as the nineteenth-century *bolero español* (see Galán 1983), and various reasons are given as to why descansos emerged in danzón: that dancers needed to rest and cool off after moving in the sultry heat of Cuba, danzón's "birthplace," and of Veracruz, or more plausibly the dictate of convention. In Mexico City, for example, dancers stop for descansos when danzones are played by danzoneras, but not when they are played by other ensembles such as dance bands or *sonoras*. In Veracruz, in both indoor and outdoor settings and in both académico and lírico styles, couples stop dancing during descansos. Many women open their fans during descansos, moving them slowly to display their elegance, rather than more quickly to cool themselves. At the end of the descanso, they close their fans, moving the fan to their left hand and holding it against the shoulder of their dancing partner. While in the lírico style, the beginning and ending of sections are fairly relaxed and fluid, in the académico style, what is and is not considered danceable becomes clearly demarcated with specific entry and exit steps, which have ten moves instead of eleven (see Table 3.1). The stylization of section endings by académico dancers is sometimes a particularly choreographed feature when groups exhibit routines, particularly at festivals, for example, when dancers may hold completely still, or extend their spines further, hold their heads high, and outstretch their arms and hands to mark the end of the section (see Figure 3.2).

As well as choreographic knowledge, listening knowledge is required to dance danzón: dancers must learn to hear downbeats and musical phrases so that their steps fit to the music. They must hear the push and pull of subtle tempo variation, particularly to listen for the formulaic cadential patterns (*remates*, marking a return to the tonic) that mark the penultimate bar of musical sections (see Music Example 1.6), so that they can adjust their penultimate sub-step to end with their feet together (see Table 3.1). If danzones have completely regular four-bar phrases, this will correspond with the ending of a number of whole steps (if dancers began at what dancers consider the right time). However, when danzones have two-bar bridge passages or irregular phrases (known by some dancers as *falsos* or false ones), the usual four-bar whole steps do not fit with the music's phrasing. Steps must then be modified, since what is considered good dancing, by académico dancers at least, demands alignment with the musical phrasing (see Table 3.4). Dancers

Figure 3.2. Grupo Bello Veracruz at the Forum Danzón Veracruz performing danzón académico in a dance routine.

often get caught up, starting steps mid-phrase and/or finishing steps after section endings.

The onus is on men to hear section starts and endings, as men are supposed to lead and women follow. A woman who has the somatic experience to respond to a leader and does not know danzón may be led by an experienced dancer and dance "well." Very occasionally, women lead, but when they do, often the only visible sign is a tension in the woman's left arm, allowing the man to otherwise appear to lead, a man's prerogative. If a man does not (appear to) lead a woman in a way académico dancers consider correct, especially through descansos, or a woman does not follow, embarrassment is likely to ensue (for both parties), for dancers in Veracruz are on public display, not only to each other, to habitués, to musicians, but also to the scores of national (and occasional foreign) tourists who film and photograph them daily (in contrast to Mexico City's dance halls, where photography is often banned). When things work well, a dancing pair will *acoplarse*—they will fit together and become encoupled in the dance, ideally moving with *cadencia* (rhythmic cadence articulated through subtle hip movement), smooth elegance, and a hint of sexual sensuality (*jícamo*).

Elegant Moves 107

Bodily pleasure cannot be assumed, however, and awkwardness and joy are often combined, for part or all of a dance. When things go badly, there will be an awkwardness between the dancers: they may be out of sync, he may push her or be too close, she may not respond to his intended instruction, or they may bump into other dancers. Tensions often arise when dancing partners make so-called mistakes. Dancing may be embodied and experienced ambivalently, contrary to descriptions of dancing as merely joyous in much literature. One dancer told me how she sometimes welcomed the break that descansos provided from the intensity of the closed-position B and C sections; and that whoever she danced with, she relished the final *montuno* sections where the man moved them into open position and she could dictate her own movement a little more and have a little more space.

Some dancers may bring different expectations to the dance. For example, group dancer Sandra told me how she preferred to dance only to music used in group routine sequences, since this was the only time her dance partner, Jésus, would stop trying to lead her in the dance, which she experienced as being pushed around (there are parallels here with the ballroom and social dance contexts in the United States, analyzed by Bosse 2015). Yet, while dance routines may change a couple's interactions when dancing, they can bring other difficulties. In dance routines, dozens of danzón académico steps must be physically achieved, and sequences of twenty-eight-plus steps per routine must also be remembered. These routines often involve months of preparation and can provoke tensions between couples when dancers forget the sequences and/or make other so-called mistakes.

Descansos, Flirting, and Clothes

The descanso is not only a key moment where choreo-musical knowledge is displayed and a welcome break for some, but it is also a moment to show off one's clothes. Norma, a former dance group leader and docker's widow in her mid-seventies, told me that she loved descansos. When I asked her why, she stated:

Porque yo creo que desde que estaba en la panza de mi mamá soy coqueta. Siempre he sido una mujer coqueta: me gusta mucho sobresalir. Soy leo, entonces siempre he sido coqueta y yo el descanso lo ocupo para abanicarme y lucir mis abanicos. [...] En el buen sentido de la palabra, me gusta que me chuleen. [...] Dicen, esa señora es muy coqueta: coqueta ... que le coqueteas a los varones, que le sonríes y todo, le coqueteas para que se te arrimen y te hablen. Esa coqueta no soy yo. Yo soy coqueta de mí misma. Yo coqueteo mucho conmigo. Me halaga cuando me echan piropos de que... como ahorita mi amiga, "ay qué bonito te queda este color, este color te queda muy bien," eso me fascina, "ay qué bonita te ves." Eso es mi coqueteo. Y cuando bailo soy coqueta porque no bailo acá así …yo bailo acá estiradita. Me gusta lucir la ropa, ese es mi coqueteo. A pesar de que ya estoy vieja, pero ese es mi coqueteo.

Because I think I've been a flirt ever since I was in my mother's tummy. I've always been a flirtatious woman: I like standing out. I'm a Leo, so I've always been a flirt, and I use the descanso to fan myself and make my fans shine (show them off). […] In the good meaning of the word, I like it when people compliment me. […] People say: "that woman is very flirtatious", they mean flirtatious in that she flirts *with* and *for* men, smiles at them and everything, that she flirts so that they approach her and talk to her. I'm not that kind of flirt. I'm a flirt with myself. I flirt a lot with myself. I feel pleased when I'm given compliments, like just now my friend said: "how pretty you look in that color, that color really suits you"; I love that, "oh, how pretty you look." That's my kind of flirtatiousness. And when I dance, I'm a flirt, but I don't really dance *like that* [too close to men], I dance upright. I like to show off my clothes, that's my flirtatiousness. Even though I'm old now, that's my flirtatiousness.

Norma loves dressing up, showing off, being admired. She was a full, pale-skinned woman, with brown curly hair with flecks of gray. The day she said this, she was wearing high-heeled sandals, a beautiful, shiny white short-sleeved dress with a slit up the side ending midway between her knee and her hip, and matching pearl earrings, necklace, and bracelet. Her nails and makeup were, as ever, understated and immaculate, with a muted pink lipstick providing a splash of color. Like other women dancers of a range of ages, Norma enjoys "elegant" clothes and the accoutrements of danzón, fanning herself slowly with aplomb, and she also enjoys flirting. Norma was careful not to flirt with men in the "wrong" way, so she said, not to give the wrong impression and lead them on to approach her or talk to her. She also had to balance the choreographic demands of moving sensually and the potential accusations of flirtatiousness ("of the wrong kind"). Norma was careful to present herself in such a way that she could flirt a bit but maintain modesty. We are reminded of the racialized imaginary of Veracruzanas discussed in Chapter 1, where lighter-skinned women reaped the benefits of being "a bit hot" and dancing a bit sexily while retaining their decency. Darker women must work harder to maintain a decent reputation, to appear "elegant," for racist stereotypes mark them as looser than lighter-skinned counterparts. Although darker men must also work harder to be deemed elegant, I never heard stereotypes about men's sexual prowess mentioned in Veracruz in relation to blackness (it was merely being supposedly "hot" that was an issue).

Unlike music scenes where adherents wear specific clothes most of the time (such as hip-hop), danzón is more of a leisure activity, and practitioners dress up to perform. Elegant clothing often distinguishes danzón performers from non-performers, bestowing them some "distinction" (Bourdieu 1984). Many danzón musicians and dancers humbly apologized to me for living in the poorer neighborhoods of the Port. It was as if the impression they gave betrayed their circumstances. For example, forty-eight-year-old Adriana was poorer than most dancers I knew. When I first met her, she had long, dark, straight hair and lived with her mother and teenage children in a corrugated iron shack with cardboard walls. Adriana recounted how she went to the Zócalo, saw danzón and wanted to look and "shine" (*lucir*) like those dancers. She told me that she now wears her clothes with "the elegance of a proud Veracruzana," and she also dances beautifully. Like other danzón dancers, she dressed extremely smartly, particularly on Saturdays, the highlight of Veracruz's danzón week, when men don beautifully ironed white trousers and guayabera shirts, and sometimes straw hats and two-toned shoes; women wear skirts, usually below the knee, rather than trousers, with high-heeled sandals, jewelry, makeup, and ornate fans. The fan has become an important accoutrement for women, and it is often moved gracefully during the descanso rests to pose and look elegant. Men too enjoyed dressing up in elegant clothes (especially in arenas where they did not have to spend any money), and some men sought to distinguish themselves, especially lírico dancers such as airport porter Pablo Mora, who wore a bowler hat and colorful patterned shirts, and painted elaborate brogue-style patterns on his shoes. Musicians also were usually well dressed, wearing the uniforms of their ensembles: smart dark trousers and guayaberas or classic, open-necked shirts for both men and the Port's few women players.

Attendees who do not dress up at danzón events stand out, particularly women who do not wear skirts and heels, and men who wear jeans. Valeria, a street vendor, told me that, like everyone who goes there, I, too, eventually became smarter, after pressure to adhere to the clothing standards thought appropriate for the dance and begrudgingly pushing aside my privileged desire to wear my everyday clothes. While it is not unusual for people to dress up to perform at dances in Mexico, where danzón events occur outside in public plazas, the difference between performers' clothing and those of casual onlookers is accentuated. Moreover, a distinction between Veracruz and Mexico City danzoneros' clothing is often clear, with men dancing and playing music in the capital wearing double-breasted suits, wide-lapeled shirts, and sometimes pachuco-esque suspenders, long-fob watch chains, and shiny monochrome or two-toned shoes. Acclaimed women dancers from

Mexico City wear flashier dresses, often silky, and sometimes with a ruffled slit revealing their upper thighs (Sevilla 2003; see Madrid and Moore 2013; and Tamariz Estrada 2014 for analyses of danzón practices in Mexico City).

With the move to groups, the clothing dancers wore began to change. When performing on Saturdays in the Zócalo or exhibiting, group members would wear matching outfits, the so-called uniforms. While some groups may have uniforms of several colors, most have only one or two in use and, given the costs involved, create a new uniform only every couple of years. Uniforms are worn by lower-class Mexicans from school age and later in many work-related activities. Several people told me they enjoyed wearing them. Danzón dance group uniforms consist of men sporting the same-colored shirt, trousers, and shoes; and women wearing matching dresses or blouses and skirts. Sometimes particular fabrics and shoes are chosen to make outfits for the women of a dance group. Men in groups continued to wear guayaberas, but women's dresses were increasingly made of shinier synthetic fabrics. The height and elegance of women's shoes also increased. Also, the fan became an obligatory prop rather than an occasional accessory. Group members wear uniforms of a set color to exhibit and to distinguish themselves, to look elegant, and to mark who is and who is not a group member. On Saturdays, groups become blocks of colors. While non-group dancers continued to wear white or pastel shades, group members also wore deeper colors: burgundy, mustard, dark blue. Dancers in their groups not only carve geometric steps in space but also carve larger spaces—they create spaces of color, making space visible with their dance routines and with their uniforms. And, to some extent, uniforms diminish visible differences in wealth among performers. Anyone who can afford to buy smart clothes can join the dance and don the clothes, like Adriana mentioned above.

So what else attracts people to join these groups, and what motivates them to stay? Many people told me that they first went to danzón events to watch, listen, dance, socialize, get out of the house, find (long- or short-term) romantic partners, perform with others, wear elegant clothes, do something characteristic of the Port, and forget their troubles. Women often went with friends or family; men mostly went alone at first. Not only do non-regulars often stand out because their clothing is not as smart as habitués, but also, the pressure to dance "correctly" in public can be overwhelming for novices. Many novice dancers now join groups, learning and reproducing the académico style of danzón. Federico, a recently widowed truck mechanic in his mid-forties, proudly told me how he had gone to the Zócalo and been invited to join a dance group. He was flattered, and this also made finding dance partners easier: he had found it terrifying not knowing how to dance and being expected to lead. He was not aware that men are particularly encouraged to join groups, given the abundance of women (in groups and otherwise) who want men to dance with. With the revival, transmission processes changed: the dance became disciplined and mostly learned within groups, rather than (and as well as) informally by watching and/or with friends and family. Moreover, by joining groups, women learn to dance but also are provided with what dancer Teresa described to me as "safe" men to dance with, men who theoretically "will not try to take advantage."

Groups provide a formal structure in which to find dance and romantic partners, and friends to attend danzón events with—a structure for the intimacy of this couple dance, in which "good" impressions can be managed. But danzón groups in Veracruz operate with norms of exclusivity. Group members are encouraged to dance only with people within their group and to socialize only within the group during danzón events. Members of a group meet several times per week, dance together, and enjoy conviviality (joking and teasing often being employed to create a familial atmosphere), but this can be all too short-lived: people are often chucked out of groups, and infighting is rife. So while groups are exclusive in terms of whom members are encouraged to dance and interact with in dance spaces, they also make the dance more inclusive by welcoming new members.

Creativity and Revival

The danzón revival opened up and repressed possibilities for both choreographic and sartorial creativity. While the lírico style's "just following the music" is quashed in the académico style, the creation of new steps and routines is encouraged. New académico steps are usually created by taking parts of other steps and juxtaposing them. Similarly, on a larger scale, new routines usually consist of new sequences of existing steps. However, danzón aficionados frown on borrowing moves from other genres (such as waltz, tango, paso doble, blues, foxtrot, swing, and mambo), so the parameters within which innovation occurs are fairly narrow. Like the Aymara musicians analyzed by Thomas Turino back in 1989, most of Veracruz's danzón académico dancers "consider a piece to be new and original even if it is the result of only slight alterations of a pre-existing composition" (1989, 23–24). Small differences are sufficient to assert uniqueness, and new routines often consist of a new ordering of standardized steps. Groups in Veracruz create a new dance routine about once a year, often for exhibition at danzón festivals. Two of Veracruz's danzón group leaders told me that they choreograph danzón routines using the following technique: a piece of music is chosen (usually a danzón in the repertoire of *Danzonera Alma de Veracruz*); the number of steps in each section of the danzón is calculated; steps are chosen (from a fairly standard repertoire) or, more rarely, invented specially; the routine is tested by the choreographer with a dance partner; amendments are made (if appropriate); and the group is taught the routine. Spatially, dancing couples are usually positioned on a grid, around one and a half meters apart, not unlike a military display. Very occasionally, routines are created where more complex spatial patterns are employed, couples do not perform in unison, and theatricality is incorporated (as Madrid and Moore 2013, 178, document in relation to zoot-suit-clad men in a group from Pachuca, Hidalgo). Danzón groups often spend months rehearsing the planned routines.

It is interesting to consider the (choreographic) composition of routines, as opposed to the improvisational nature of non-routine dancing in this context. Nettl suggests a continuum between improvisation and composition that distinguishes "improvisatory decision-making and planning [from] preparation, execution and revision" (1983, 30). Danzón groups rehearse the "composed" routines, but most académico dancing is not performed as a choreographed spectacle: distinctions between the choreographic composition of routines and the more improvisational non-routine dancing of danzón académico are blurred. In non-routine dancing, the sequence of steps danced theoretically remains the improvised decision of the partner leading the couple (usually the man). But couples often opt to dance set patterns when supposedly dancing freely, patterns from routines they have learned in groups or created themselves. Parts of routines will fit several danzones if section lengths are similar (usually sixteen or thirty-two bars), and sometimes a whole routine will work for several pieces of music, such as the danzones *Mata Majá* and *Cecilia*. There are resonances here with Titon's analysis of blues improvisation, where "preforms" (1978, 91), blocks of pre-formulated patterns, are juxtaposed in performance but leave space for some flexibility, as well as with the North Indian semi-classical *ṭhumrī* genre (see Zadeh 2012) and Iranian classical music (see Nooshin 2015). Although some dancers consider that some steps fit particular music better than others, many adhere to formulaic patterns. Thus the shift from couple to unison group dancing, from danzón lírico to académico, has influenced the way people conceive of and perform improvised dancing. This has also affected the music repertoire, since académico dancers often request pieces with regular four-bar phrases so that difficulty is reduced and only minor adjustments are required to dance "correctly."

The standardization of danzón the dance has also afforded opportunities for some creativity with clothing: group members may be involved in acquiring and making new uniforms (or shops may be designated where parts for group uniforms are to be purchased). But again, clothing choices are carefully controlled: *maestros* have the final say on who wears what, sometimes sharing responsibility for this with the women (in particular) in the group directorate. But several of Veracruz's groups wear almost identical outfits, with shirt and dress color being the only markers of difference.

Despite the emphasis on innovation, danzón clothing and choreographic boundaries were policed by verbal criticism and praise (akin to the Foucauldian disciplinary techniques at play in new British art music networks, see Malcomson 2013). Creativity was regulated in the académico style: if danzoneros were disciplined and learned to master the dance practice according to its logics, then they were able to express themselves creatively, but only according to those same logics. Too much creativity and over-flashiness in clothing and dancing was considered buffoonish. People have to gauge the boundaries of creativity, acceptability, and spectacle in terms of both their dance and their dress. Should they transcend these boundaries, they are liable to critique, such as that applied to Tomás and Amanda, self-proclaimed founders of *danzón de fantasía*. Tomás (an extremely camp seventy-year-old) and Amanda (a retired school teacher) invariably wore matching clothing: the fabric used to make Amanda's dress often adorned Tomás's shirt collar and hatband.[8] (Their danzón de fantasía was a flamboyant version of danzón académico involving showy hand movements and steps from other dances, including tango). Tomás and Amanda partook in the rotation of groups exhibiting on the main stage of the Zócalo on Saturdays with their own slot through the 2000s (until Amanda became ill). They also often danced danzón immediately after the Saturday danzón event outside the Gran Café del Portal, and beside the tourist tram, the Tranvía del Recuerdo, to the strains of the *Marimba Orquesta La Costeñita*. Crowds of tourists would surround them, responding to their camp, spectacular danzón with a mixture of delight, disdain, and disbelief. In spite of consistently being accused of showing off, Tomás and Amanda relished the attention they gained, and it was Tomás in particular who predominated.

I was told that men should make women *lucir*, a term I translate as "shine," rather than the English equivalent "show off," which includes a deliberateness and pretentiousness absent from *lucir*. Certain steps are considered to make one partner shine more, yet many dancers consider it a man's role to make a woman shine. One man told me: "A gentleman should never use a woman to make himself shine when dancing danzón, even if she is his romantic partner"; a man who attempts to shine too much is considered egocentric. Likewise, a woman who appears to laud the limelight is frowned upon. Académico dancers are more likely to be accused of crossing the fine line between shining and being haughty. And Tomás and Amanda surpassed all levels of acceptability and were often criticized. The two of them, and later Teodora, who became Tomás's partner, were exceptions that proved the rule, the referents for regulating everyone else's exhibitionism, sartorially and choreographically. That is, criticisms of them reinforced the aesthetics admired in both danzón lírico and académico—elegance, restraint, and well-accented musical dancing.

The Modernist Aesthetic of Danzón Académico

To think through the values and aesthetics apparent in danzón académico, it is pertinent to explore the links between elegance, disciplined control, class, and race. I draw extensively from Joanna Bosse's work on ballroom dance here to propose that the elegance, spectacle, and difficulty valued in danzón académico are articulations of a modernist aesthetic, an aesthetic linked to whiteness. I argue that in the 1980s, danzón dancing became entwined with a modernist aesthetic that had been circulating in and beyond Mexico for numerous decades in performances, images, film, and sound recordings, and that is present in historically informed performance of European Early Music, in modern and Latin ballroom dance, and in nationalist folkloric dances (including Amalia Hernández's Ballet Folklórico de México and the Soviet Union's Moiseyev Dance Company). That is, the aesthetic of danzón académico is in many respects akin to the modernism of Early Music, akin to the balletic classicism of modern ballroom and folkloric dance: all these practices share this modernist aesthetic. And while postmodern and post-postmodern ideas and aesthetics circulated in literary and artistic circles in the second half of the twentieth century, their impact has been negligible on these particular practices. Instead, modernist aesthetics have predominated, I propose.

To begin to unpack this modernist aesthetic, let us consider its links to elite, Eurocentric cosmopolitanism. Rather than worldliness or familiarity with other countries and peoples, Turino (2000) uses the term "cosmopolitan" to refer to ideas, formations, and positionalities diffused among economic and educated elites (and others) transnationally. Turino argues that the entanglements of cosmopolitanism, nationalism, and colonialism "underwrite the accelerated neocolonial expansion of modernist-capitalist economics and ethics—what is euphemistically referred to as 'global culture'" (2000, 4). Yet the term "global" is totalizing, Turino suggests, and he proposes cosmopolitan as an alternative. Through his study of popular music performance in twentieth-century Zimbabwe, Turino points to the "greater prestige of modernist cosmopolitan aesthetics, practices, and forms among the more politically powerful cosmopolitans" (2000, 12). Developing Turino's work on cosmopolitanism, Bosse (2007) argues that in many art forms, cosmopolitanism is marked by "'a preference for complexity, virtuosity, and restraint within linear, goal-oriented forms, as well as aesthetic distance, control, and discipline, all couched in the discourse of sophistication" (2007, 27). Bosse (2007) makes explicit that this is an aesthetic with a promise: that with practice and discipline, mental and physical difficulty can be overcome, and controlled action, elegance, and sophistication will be achievable. She argues that "the aesthetic discourse of refinement and control, which posits the overwhelming difficulty of even seemingly simple expressive conventions, is similar [in US ballroom dancing] to that found in other genres associated with Western European upper-class societies, especially classical music" (2007, 43). And as is the case with danzón, it is worth noting that this difficulty is often overcome, Bosse suggests, through disciplined learning in institutional frameworks with resources beyond the institution to support this (resources to acquire requisite accoutrements and to facilitate the desire, time, and ability to practice). In specifying that cosmopolitanism often has "a preference for complexity, virtuosity, and restraint within linear, goal-oriented forms" (2007, 43), Bosse is also making clear that this aesthetic is modernist.

To pinpoint this modernist aesthetic in relation to danzón more specifically, let me compare danzón académico dancing to historically informed performances of European Early Music, which Richard Taruskin (1995) and others have suggested are symptomatic of twentieth-century modernism. The novel, modern style of historically informed performances earned Early Music wide popularity and commerciality that accord with contemporary tastes, argues Taruskin (1995, 102). There are resonances here with danzón académico, although danzón académico is merely a national phenomenon in Mexico and has not achieved wide international popularity (beyond Cuba and Mexico). Akin to the modernist aesthetic of Early Music (Taruskin 1995, 10), danzón académico places certain demands on the performer: restraint, logical consistency, and fidelity to prescribed steps that regulate practice. Dance steps now dictate action, demanding step-fidelity. Taruskin argues that in Early Music, there is an ideal of correct performance (*Werktreue*) that "inflicts a truly stifling regimen by radically hardening and patrolling what had formerly been a fluid, easily crossed boundary" (1995, 10). While the boundaries of danzón performance are not as rigid as those of European heritage classical forms (broadly understood here to include both Early Music and ballet), in relation to the more unrestricted lírico dancing, the newer académico style of danzón became "radically hardened." And, like danzón académico, historically informed performances of European Early Music remain predominantly unracialized, unmarked, and without mention of whiteness.

This modernist aesthetic is intrinsically linked to elegance and whiteness, however. Bosse proposes that cosmopolitan values and aesthetics are explicitly lauded by modern ballroom dancers: grace, classicism, beauty, sophistication, and, above all, elegance, values "deeply encoded in whiteness, dominant culture, and European conventions" (2007, 39). Elegance was constantly referred to as an aesthetic that Veracruz's danzón dancers aspire to: in clothing, dancing, and particularly the académico style, unison group choreographies, and the uniforms donned by group members. Heteronormative, gendered aesthetics based on the idea of elegance, and thus consumption, are key to danzón. Central to the notion of elegance is refinement and appropriateness—of appearance, movement, language, comportment, and conduct—together with freedom from clumsiness, from awkwardness and coarseness.

Bosse contends that assuming the posture of modern ballroom—"elongated spine, locked torso"—and taking up more space in the dance was both a theatrical and a political gesture: "commanding space and attention as one traverses the entire floor" (2007, 30). While danzón as a genre requires little more than a square meter of space for a couple to perform, some dancers relished "commanding space and attention" from musicians, audiences, and other dancers, while others tried to hide more in the middle of the dance floor. Bosse proposes that ballroom dancers felt elevated, both in terms of floating when performing modern genres, and also class-wise. This is also the case with danzón dancers, as we saw with Adriana, described above, who felt she achieved elegance by donning appropriate clothes and dancing danzón.

Yet in Veracruz, as in other contexts, elegance was associated not only with controlled, disciplined movement and clothing, but also with comportment and classed tastefulness (Bourdieu's "distinction," 1984). Elegance is a highly racialized and gendered concept: it appears most easily in those people who embody privileged whiteness, quintessentially upper-class, middle-aged, slender, white women and men. As Ruth Frankenberg (1993) and other critical whiteness scholars have taught us, whiteness is a social and political construction linked to privilege, racial domination, and universality that is often, but not exclusively, attached to the white body. It is important to note that I am not proposing that danzón académico is whiter than danzón lírico or its practitioners, but that its modernist aesthetic is rarely fully achievable by those without white privilege.

Elegance as an ideal engenders embodied power structures and reproduces a classed, racialized system where only certain people can access and mobilize economic, symbolic, and cultural capital. As an ideal, elegance may incorporate ambivalences for those racialized, gendered, or classed in ways that do not fulfil its demands, specifically utopian ambivalences (ambivalences that are incorporated into an ideal or utopia—an imagined place or state of being where everything is perfect—which is inevitably disrupted). Shorter, fatter, brown men and women were rarely referred to as elegant in Veracruz, while lighter-skinned, slimmer dancers achieved this accolade more easily. Younger people were often congratulated for dancing prettily, while "elegance" was a term bestowed more on middle-aged dancers. I was told by a member of the *Tres Generaciones* group of younger dancers that couples should be paired according to gender, height, and skin color to look elegant: it looked "right" if people "matched" (and two trousered dancers performing together did not match in her estimation, as they were inappropriately gendered). That is, whether people matched was determined by heterosexist, classist, racist, and other oppressive logics. Moreover, classed differences (which are predominantly racialized) played out at danzón events in Veracruz and beyond: only practitioners who extolled educational, economic, and symbolic capital could have a variety of expensive outfits and go for coffee regularly after events. While the epitome of elegance was available only to a very few danzoneros in Veracruz, this did not stop the majority from enjoying being more elegant than usual when dressed up and dancing (like Adriana, above). As an ideal, elegance was relative.

In her ethnography of modern and Latin ballroom dancers in Savoy, Illinois, in the United States, Bosse (2007, 2015) explores how modern ballroom remains unmarked, deracialized without reference to its whiteness. In contrast, and in some ways akin to danzón lírico, Latin ballroom dancers were explicitly racialized, essentialized as more natural and sexual: these dancers were said to be able to learn Latin dance without tuition, akin to danzón lírico in Veracruz. Bosse argues that Cartesian mind-body, rational-irrational dichotomies were recreated through the eroticization and othering of Latin ballroom, and through its juxtaposition with modern ballroom, thereby reproducing hegemonic colonialist paradigms. Such dichotomies and paradigms also operate in Veracruz, where danzón académico is considered both more elegant and more difficult than danzón lírico: danzón lírico is not discursively othered and eroticized, but it is often dismissed as less elegant than danzón académico. Moreover, the required aesthetic of elegance in danzón académico is slightly interrupted by the choreographic demand for the subtle hip movements and sensuality associated with both sexual experience and blackness. The more absolute dichotómies available to most modern and Latin ballroom dancers in Savoy, Illinois, were complicated in Veracruz's danzón.

So far, I have argued that danzón académico became entangled with a modernist aesthetic where disciplined, controlled movement, restraint, logical consistency, fidelity to prescribed steps, an ideal of correct performance, creative boundaries, and elegance were extolled. In contexts such as Mexico, such a movement aesthetic, an aesthetic marked by cosmopolitanism, modernism, and whiteness, has political reverberations permeated by colonial violence. The violence inherent in this aesthetic is revealed in Sydney Hutchinson's (2009) interrogation of the politics of Amalia Hernández's Ballet Folklórico de México, and her analysis is particularly pertinent here because of the impact that the Ballet Folklórico de México had on the aesthetics of the regional Mexican folkloric dances practiced by schoolchildren for generations, including middle-aged and younger danzón practitioners, as well as by adults in cultural institutions. To further understand the aesthetics of danzón, we need to understand the aesthetics of these nationalist, folkloric dances.

From the 1950s, Amalia Hernández's Ballet Folklórico de México maintained a prominent role in representing the Mexican nation, touring internationally with presidents, featuring in television shows, and performing for decades at the Palace of Fine Arts (Bellas Artes) as a major attraction for national elites and tourists. Post-revolutionary Mexico had seen cultural nationalism flourish, with intellectuals such as José Vasconcelos and Manuel Gamio and muralists Diego Rivera, José Clemente Orozco, and David Alfaro Siqueiros working toward a national identity based on mestizaje, *indigenismo*, and anti-imperialism (Yúdice 2003).[9] Amalia Hernández was both a product and a producer of Mexican cultural nationalism: she did extensive research to create her pre-Hispanic and regional dances. As the name suggests, the Ballet Folklórico de México combines what the Italian press described in 1964 as "something between folk dance and first-class artistic ballet" (Aguirre Cristiani 1994, 58). Anthony Shay (2002) proposes that Hernández homogenized Mexican regional dances into a balletic, theatricalized aesthetic, an aesthetic steeped in a classicism based on ballet and modern dance that was circulating transnationally. This aesthetic was a dance version of the modernist, cosmopolitan aesthetic I have been describing: an aesthetic linked to elegance, spectacle, and whiteness.[10]

Shay contends that the two most successful folkloric ballets in the world, the Soviet Union's Moiseyev Dance Company and Hernández's Ballet Folklórico de México, converged not only in terms of aesthetic classicism, but also in "the relentless pursuit of spectacle through fast pacing, polished dance techniques, and dazzling primary colors" (Shay 2002, 85). The techniques Hernández applied to create spectacle included choreographed sequences of grinning dancers, often dancing in unison; couples dancing together in brightly colored, visually brilliant costumes, such as voluminous skirts giving dancers "winged flight" (Segura Escalona 1994, 164), headdresses, sumptuous ornamentation and bountiful makeup; raised theatrical stages separating performers and audience members; sets and lighting; short, dynamic scenes with smooth transitions; contrasting scenes and pacing of choreographies in an attempt to avoid repetition; large casts; and exuberant finales. Both Hernández and the Russian Igor Moiseyev professed to have "the ability to distill the 'national' or the 'regional' character of the peoples that they represented through the essentialization found in their choreographies" (Shay 2002, 229). Yet, as Hutchinson poignantly argues, in the process of promoting the logics of both indigenismo and mestizaje, Hernández's Ballet Folklórico de México erases indigenous people's histories and aesthetics. Crucially, Hutchinson states, "the company's repertoire underhandedly promotes particular racial ideologies and replicates a colonialist gaze" (2009, 222). The colonialist gaze inherent in the aesthetic that Hernández promoted became cemented in presentations of folkloric dances throughout Mexico.

Amalia Hernández's Ballet Folklórico de México created stereotyped dances that were then adopted as regional forms, transforming local aesthetics, Segura Escalona (1994, 168) suggests. Regional Mexican folkloric music-dance forms were performed in schools, by folkloric dance companies in urban areas housed by newly formed cultural institutions, on stages, and in the media, forming a canon, Turino (2003) propounds, where each regional music-dance form came to index the nation. Anita González (2010) explores how the aesthetic promoted by Hernández's company affected folkloric dances, including Veracruz's so-called typical regional dance, son jarocho. González argues that "folkloric art forms galvanized the tattered threads of nationalist sentiment into a popular statement of 'Mexicanness'" (2010, 111). González interrogates how what I am calling a cosmopolitan, modernist aesthetic was incorporated into son jarocho. González argues that the embodiment of folkloric aesthetics in son jarocho was a bringing together of what she considers to be an African "polycentric, torso movement with the extended lines and stretched limbs characteristic of ballet, concert modern dance" (2010, 115). González continues: "deemphasizing the hips and maintaining an upright posture also assure that the chorus of dancers have a more uniform look—one of the qualities of folkloric dance that allows multiple communities to assimilate its aesthetic" (2010, 116). González rightly suggests that the aesthetic of folkloric dance embraced dances including danzón, but does not analyze danzón performance further.

Danzón académico became entangled in the aesthetic of Mexican nationalist dance, I propose, despite danzón not being ascribed national status in Mexico. As we have seen, danzón académico assumed the extended postures and lines associated with ballet and modern dance, that is, a cosmopolitan, modernist aesthetic. Moreover, danzón académico routines exhibit the uniformity identified by González (2010) and Shay (2002) in the chorus performances of nationalist folkloric dances. This uniformity is particularly evident at danzón festivals and in mass danzón events, and it was spectacular, unison dance routines, above all, that influenced the development of the danzón académico aesthetic.

In his exploration of folk song in Edwardian England and specifically the British folk music collector Cecil J. Sharp, Ross Cole (2019) highlights the links between fascist ideology and revival movements. Cole argues, building on the work of Zeev Sternhell, that late-nineteenth-century cultural fascism involved "a political outlook revolving around a strong nation-state; a glorification of organic communality; warfare; a denigration of liberal democracy; and a rejection of individualism, philosophical materialism, and capitalism (but not of private property or profit)" (2019, 33). While I would not assert that danzón practice in Mexico is politically fascist, I do contend that further research is required to compare and, if appropriate, establish specific links that might be made between nineteenth-century and/or twentieth-century cultural fascism, revivalist projects such as Amalia Hernández's Ballet Folklórico de México, and danzón académico. In all three, nationalism, a modernist aesthetic, and nostalgia have critical roles to play, as does the rejection of individualism and an emphasis on community, elements that we see became important in the ethos of the danzón dance groups that emerged from the 1980s. Links to military display might also prove fruitful.

Conclusion

In the 1980s, danzón dancing became entangled with a modernist aesthetic, overshadowed by nationalism, an aesthetic considered at once more elegant and more difficult than the older lírico dancing style: torsos were extended, feet slid across the ground, geometric patterns were carved in space. Hundreds of prescribed steps were now danced with more controlled movement and with principles of right and wrong, either by pairs of dancers or by groups performing dance routines in unison. While some dancers continued to perform the older, freer, lírico style of danzón dancing, the majority, including new practitioners, adhered to the schooled, codified académico style. The shift from lírico to académico also transformed the way sound was conceptualized, as musical phrases and sections had to be more precisely identified to determine how and when dancers moved (or not): music became beats to be counted, numbers to be rendered into steps.

To interrogate this aesthetic, I brought together and built on work on cosmopolitanism (Turino 2000), European Early Music (Taruskin 1995), modern and Latin ballroom dance (Bosse 2007, 2015), Amalia Hernández's Ballet Folklórico de México (Hutchinson 2009; Shay 2002), and Veracruz's regional dance, son jarocho (González 2010). I argued that the modernist aesthetic assumed by danzón académico dancers had been circulating transnationally for much of the twentieth and early twenty-first centuries in photographs and recordings, on screens and stages. This cosmopolitan, nationalist aesthetic is associated with both elegance and white privilege, I contended. In the context of Mexico, this aesthetic is steeped in colonial violence. It is an aesthetic that permeated Amalia Hernández's Ballet Folklórico de México and regional folkloric dances throughout the country from the 1950s, as they became spectacles to be consumed by locals and tourists alike. Akin to regional folkloric dances, danzón would become a tourist attraction in the Port of Veracruz from the early 1990s, an attraction involving participation and spectacle where groups exhibit on the stage of the main square on Saturdays, provoking a pride in the local, the region, and the nation.

VIGNETTE FOUR

Lulú and Antonio

(fiction)

Lulú. 53. Paper-straight mid-brown hair: blow-dried. Pale skin. Hazel eyes. Snub nose. Freckles. Strap-shouldered, knee-length maroon dress; maroon like the other dancers in the Lila group. Silver, mid-heeled sandals.

Slide. Back. Lulú's foot scrapes across the dimpled ground, pushing a little too hard to achieve the grace her partner, Antonio, likes. He doesn't notice: too busy grinning at the tourists.

Turn.

Antonio. 62. Leader of the Lila group. Thick brown hair; eyebrows; lashes. Dark skin. Once-broken nose. Bushy moustache. Taut, fleshy lips. Over-white teeth. Maroon, long-sleeved guayabera. Slightly hunched shoulders. White, polyester trousers. Fake leather white shoes. Brown soles.

"I'm fantastic at dancing," Antonio gloats to himself.

Turn.

Lulú knows the dance routine and needs no direction. Antonio pushes her a bit too forcefully. Her muscles tense. They stumble.

Turn.

Antonio grimaces.

"How can Lulú do that? In front of the others, the tourists?"

Turn.

Lulú shoots Antonio a humiliated stare. His cheeks redden; hers remain steely pale. She's had enough: of the dance; of him.

Turn.

Too many steps. Out of time. Glares.

Turn.

The music frees into the *montuno* section. Now she can move: move her hips, dictate her steps. A bit. She holds his left hand, not his whole body; his belly no longer presses against hers. She extends her free hand to shoulder height, mirroring his, turning for the tourists, for herself. She tries to squeeze a grin. His teeth sparkle. Her eyes narrow, jaw locking into fury.

Turn.

CHAPTER FOUR

Moves to Rescue

Reviving the Dance,
State Sponsorship, and Power

Why was it the 1980s when danzón changed so radically? How did differences between lírico and académico dancing materialize? In this chapter, I consider the processes that contributed to danzón dancing assuming a modernist aesthetic, that is, for sufficient consensus to be achieved for danzón académico to be danced in urban centers across Mexico. I draw from interviews with dozens of dance champions, aficionados, and long-standing musicians and dancers in Mexico City and Veracruz.

Together with other fashionable genres, danzón had been performed throughout Mexico in the first half of the twentieth century, but its wide-ranging popularity declined somewhat in the 1960s and 1970s. Danzón performance had continued, however, in the two cities that were particularly associated with the genre: Veracruz and Mexico City. Mexico City's dance halls were renowned for their danzón, as depicted in 1940s and 1950s golden-age films, such as *Aventurera*, starring Ninón Sevilla, and *Salón México*, starring Marga López (see García 2018 regarding *Salón México*). And Veracruz was considered the "adoptive" parent of danzón: here, danzón was linked to local identity. Veracruz, I was told by dancers and aficionados alike, was famed nationally as well as internationally for having the best danzón dancers. That said, Mexico City's champions told me that it was they who claimed choreographic superiority. Despite these assertions, and the constant interactions of musicians and dancers between the two cities (particularly during Veracruz's annual carnival and in Mexico City's dance halls), there was little competition between them, and rivalry between so-called dance champions (a term ascribed to men, mostly) was fairly local in Mexico City's and Veracruz's danzón scenes. Dancers acquired "symbolic capital" (Bourdieu 1993, 75) through their ability to dance, accumulating prestige by winning competitions, which gave them legitimacy to teach and judge others. The "field" in which they operated was fairly local, limited to Mexico City and Veracruz, with little competitive interaction between the two. Mexico City's champions operated in the capital's dance halls, and Veracruz's "best" dancers reigned over the Port's dance halls and *patios de vecindad* (tenement block patios).

From the 1980s, dancers from both cities would come together more, and the field in which they acted was transformed, becoming more institutionally based and opening up to the rest of the country. The emphasis on individual champions shifted to groups (and group leaders) legitimized by broader power structures. This was coupled with the decentralization of cultural institutions, which occurred in conjunction with the political changes that had led to the port's privatization in 1991. It was often with the support of local cultural institutions that new danzón dance groups formed, each incorporating bureaucratic hierarchies with presidents, treasurers, and secretaries. Dancers from such groups began traveling to newly established danzón festivals throughout Mexico, many of which included national demonstrations where dance groups began to represent their states and locales with choreographic displays, reproducing cultural nationalist logics. Numerous festivals expanded with sponsorship from municipal governments and state cultural institutions (such as CONACULTA, the National Council for Culture and the Arts) that were keen to promote local consumption and regional development. María Novaro's acclaimed and widely disseminated film *Danzón* (1991) contributed to attracting new people to the dance. In the Port, tourism increased, and the municipality programmed and funded danzón events, employing a new danzón music ensemble and providing space for danzón dance groups to rehearse and perform. The dance would undergo dramatic aesthetic transformations. Veracruz's dance group, *Tres Generaciones*, and in particular its leader, Rosa Abdala Gómez, were key to the local and national revival. Abdala Gómez's son, Miguel Zamudio Abdala, would go on to create an institutionally supported danzón empire, including an annual danzón festival and a national danzón network, strengthening Veracruz as a hub of danzón.

So, danzón emerged in the late nineteenth century and peaked in popularity in the first half of the twentieth century, and its movement aesthetic became more disciplined, schooled, and modernist in the 1980s, when it was taken up by thousands of mostly older people and staged and supported by cultural institutions and the tourist industry. Despite continuities that evidence that danzón never "died" as such, danzón underwent a revival in many ways. Hill and Bithell define music revival as "an effort to perform and promote music that is valued as old or historical and is usually perceived to be threatened or moribund" (2014, 3). In the 1980s, groups of danzón practitioners framed the genre as old and threatened. Moreover, the transformations to danzón practice have much in common with music-dance revivals elsewhere: specifically, the strategic harnessing of ideas of rescue, the formation of groups, changing transmission processes, aesthetic transformation, cultural promoters organizing events and festivals, and entrepreneurs accruing economic gain from providing services for practitioners (see Livingston 1999; Ochoa Gautier 2006; Bithell and Hill 2014).

Yet the age of the newcomers has been overlooked by scholarship on cultural practices, and the focus has tended to be on transmission to younger generations, based on an assumption that younger people hold the key to securing the future of cultural practices. I argue that we need to interrogate the contributions of older newcomers, and not assume that older people ensure a continuity of the past into the present because they do the same things throughout the life course. In the case of danzón, many older people are new to danzón, and older people form the majority of those involved in the danzón revival, often spending several decades dancing after they begin in midlife. This case study reinforces the point that stereotypes that older people are resistant to novelty, creativity, change, and possibility are ill-founded. Crucially, the age of most danzón performers does not make this a "fragile" or "dying" practice, but older people reinvigorate it, enabling it to expand. Moreover, where age is used to justify rescuing "cultural traditions," caution may be called for and analysis may be required to assess what lies behind such claims and why.

In this chapter, I argue that danzón underwent a non-heritage revival—a revival that was not moderated by strong values of tradition and authentic restoration. I assert that although danzón shares many of the elements present in other music-dance revivals (particularly those proposed by Livingston 1999 and subsequently Hill and Bithell 2014), there are significant differences. First, this was a revival joined predominantly by people aged fifty-plus, rather than younger people attempting to reconstruct the past. Second, while the notion of rescuing performance practices was important in this revival, there was little concern with authenticity or historical fidelity. Third, although core-revivalists were drivers of transformations, I suggest, drawing on classic texts from science and technology studies, that this was not merely top-down, and that more horizontal rivalries were also key to this revival. Fourth, this revival was not evenly spread: shifts to the musical practices of danzón were distinct from changes to the dance and social practices, and the relationship between the dance and the music also changed. In response to the scale and networked complexity of this revival, I interrogate the wide range of enabling factors here.

The Local Field: A Very Brief History of Mexico City's Dance Halls

The twentieth century saw the rise and fall of Mexico City's dance halls, with their businesses being supported and later stifled via licenses from the local government. Danzón had arrived in Mexico City, arguably around the same time it was enjoyed in Veracruz, possibly with the Cuban *bufos* (blackface minstrels) or other performers.[1] Danzón aficionado investigator Flores y Escalante (1993) and academics Madrid and Moore (2013) claim that danzón was first performed in Mexico by the bourgeoisie and was later taken up by the lower classes. I propose that such an oscillation between classes seems unlikely given that in Veracruz, at least, it was being enjoyed by all classes from the 1880s, and this enjoyment was highly gendered, since men could move among classed spaces while elite women could not. Moreover, social dance was changing in urban settings throughout the Americas and Europe (see Malnig 2009). Mexico City's first popular dance hall, *Quinta Corona*, was launched in 1905, with three more opening shortly afterward. During the Revolution, eight more dance halls were established in the capital, and in 1920, the legendary *Salón México* opened its doors, attracting people from distinct social classes. Artists and muralists, musicians, filmmakers, and even politicians frequented the *Salón México*, as well as Aaron Copland (1900–1990), who composed the eponymous dance suite (1933–36).

By the 1950s, big band sounds were permeating Mexico's dance halls with genres including danzón, cha-cha-chá, mambo, swing, and rock and roll. It should be noted, however, that unlike in the United States, rock and roll was associated with neither youth nor "cultural miscegenation" in Mexico (Zolov 1999, 17–18). These new genres were absorbed into the sounds of danzones, with mambo-influenced arrangements appearing from composers such as Veracruz's Alejandro Cardona and Guillermo "Memo" Salamanca, who wrote for Carlos Campos's and Arturo Nuñez's orquestas. While the danzones that preceded them were marked by tonic-dominant harmonies (such as I-V7-I and I-VI-II-VI-I-V-I), mambos were characterized by more chromatic and extended harmonies, including pentatonism, whole-tone and diminished scales, and syncopated motifs, typical of son cubano, in the *montuno* section (Torres 1995).[2]

Dance-wise, *danzón abierto* (open danzón) had emerged by this time, involving a couple moving from the waltz-like closed position (facing inward) into the open dance position (facing outward and holding one or both hands), and from there, *floreando* (flowering). The term *florear* (to flower) is employed to denote ornamentation, especially turns, which are usually enacted by the woman (turns in the closed position are rarer). There were complaints then, as now, that steps were being incorporated from other genres (such as tango, paso doble, and foxtrot), but dancers continued to turn, and turns would come to be characteristic of Mexico City's danzón-dancing aesthetic. Jara Gámez et al. (1994) state that the dancer Enrique Tapia claims to have invented *danzón abierto*, while the Cubans René and Estela Pérez are also attributed to have brought it from Cuba. Danzón champion Arturo "El Capullo" Sánchez Rivera told me that the Mexico City dancers Carlos "El Calcetín" (the Sock) Berriel and Ema (Manuela) "La Negra Palomares" (Black Woman Palomares) may have initiated this change in Mexico, having copied some Cuban dancers around 1935. Turns would become a feature of casino and salsa dancing, which later fed into danzón practice.

While danzón changed and new genres emerged, dancers still considered it to be "king of the dance halls"—the most difficult dance hall dance to perform, with its requirement for both choreographic knowledge and musical awareness, and the worthy subject of the largest prizes in dance hall competitions. Moreover, time was reserved especially for danzón in Mexico City's dance halls, unlike other genres: sets of pure danzón amid sets of mixed genres. By the early twenty-first century, danzón nights in Mexico City's *Salón Los Ángeles, California Dancing Club*, and venues such as *La Maraka, Centro Convenciones Tlatelolco*, and the *Salón Atzin* (a sports-cum-dance hall) usually consisted of hour-long sets of a danzonera (playing just danzones), an orquesta, such as *La Orquesta Universitaria de Pepe Luis* (combining mambos with swing, blues, cha-cha-chá, cumbia, tango, paso doble, Charleston, and the odd danzón), and sometimes a sonora performing son cubano, boleros, guarachas, and so forth. These venues provided regular employment for numerous music ensembles.

In the late 1950s, Mexico City's legendary mayor, Ernesto P. Uruchurtu (1952–1966), nicknamed "the Iron Regent," decreed that "all establishments should shut at 1 a.m., to ensure that workers' families get their salaries and the family inheritance is not squandered in centres of vice" (Jara Gámez, Rodriguez, and Zedillo Castillo 1994, 180).[3] Pedelty (1999) implies that this was linked to the 1950s moralist conservative turn epitomized by the League of Decency, yet several aficionado investigators who frequented Mexico City's dance halls and cabarets at that time told me that it was a response to the fatal shooting of Uruchurtu's brother outside a cabaret. Cabarets were shut down, although several moved to the outskirts of the city. Dance halls had, until this point, stayed open until around 5 a.m., and with business severely reduced, many closed, including the *Salón México* in 1962. By 1963, only four dance halls remained in Mexico City: the *Salón Colonia*, the *Salón Los Ángeles*, the *Salón Riviera*, and the *California Dancing Club*. These four establishments would stay open for decades to come, but by the mid-2000s, there remained only two: the *Salón Los Ángeles* and the *California Dancing Club*. With the dance halls dwindling, some danzoneras vanished. For a while, only a handful of danzoneras were active in the city, until the 1980s saw the emergence of danzón dances in new venues, including public spaces sponsored by local councils (called *delegaciones* until 2016, and then *alcaldías*).

The Local Field: Mexico City's Danzón Champions, Competition, and Reputation

Mexico City's dance halls had been spaces where people from distinct social spheres met, where lower-class urban migrants played music, dressed up, danced, formed communities, climbed social ladders, and engaged in sexual and amorous encounters. Patriarchal values were omnipresent, and in this couple dance where men mostly led, it was the men who were considered champions, who acted as teachers, and who reigned over these spheres. Danzón aficionado investigator Ciro Carlos Mizuno Guzmán told me that there were "power groups who controlled everything."[4] These dancers would position themselves in front of the usually staged musicians, attracting attention when people clustered around to watch them dance or when fellow performers danced in lines, copying their moves (as still occurs in some dance halls, particularly with mambos). They were winners and judges of the sporadic competitions in danzón, tango, foxtrot, and other genres at the dance halls (see Sevilla 2003).

Competition produced (and was produced by) champions, regional styles, and norms. These norms tended to emphasize choreographic and sartorial aesthetics, musical phrasing, rhythm, comportment, knowledge of danzón repertoire, and creativity. Dancers would not know (theoretically at least) what danzones the musicians, organizers, or judges might decide to play during competitions, so musicality and knowledge of danzones was key. A good ear was needed for danzones with irregular phrases and difficult endings (such as *Confesión*, by Laureano Benítez). Individual creativity was encouraged within the boundaries of what was considered danzón: parts of different steps could be recombined, but moves from other genres were less welcome. Such boundaries were determined by competition organizers and judges, but there was no central body that sanctioned them.

Winning competitions not only legitimated particular men as champions but also provided some with teaching opportunities. Competitions produce more losers than winners and create the desire to triumph. These champions taught others to dance and attempt to succeed. Yet these same teacher-champions often judged the competitions for which they trained people. Given the status and economic gains to be had from being a champion and respected dance teacher, unsurprisingly, lots of rivalries developed for power and acclaim. For example, there were often polemics around disagreements between competition judges and audiences, which included other dancers and champions. And, while some champions earned money from danzón, it provided a sole income only for very few. Several of these champions worked for the police and the national electricity company, and as tradesmen and manual workers. Others were renowned as *vagos* (loafers) or *padrotes* (men who live from women's incomes, whether these women did sex work or otherwise), a stereotype resonating with that of the *malandros* (badmen) renowned throughout the region, as well as Dominican *tígueres* (see Hutchinson 2016), and the Argentine *compadritos* (little godfathers) described by Archetti who dance tango, play the guitar, have been to prison, and are irresistible to women (1999, 152). Despite the rivalries and competitiveness among them, many of these champions were also friends, for they depended on some form of mutual appreciation, even if that took the form of others merely caring to denigrate them. They grouped together to gain more power.

When the *Smyrna Club* closed in 1953, several of its habitués, again mostly men, formed Mexico's first danzón group, *Club Inspiración*. *Club Inspiración* facilitated social gathering and, crucially, created a unit of authority presiding over Mexico City's danzón scene.[5] They organized private dances and more competitions, occasionally appearing with danzoneras in theaters and on television. Several of these men created allegiances with danzoneras so that they as dancers and the musicians reciprocated in gaining employment for each other. These teacher-champions not only had the power to judge but also became role models, setting standards of excellence and (mostly unwritten) competition rules, which they then taught other people to satisfy. They were leaders within the capital's danzón scene, who gained both choreographic legitimacy and economically from competitions. While some women were considered great dancers, such as Ema "La Negra" Palomores (Ventura Miranda's wife), Chavela "La Cuata" (the Mate), Elvira Martínez "La Boogie," and Dellanira Gordillo, they were not considered pivotal in terms of power. Status could be gained from these women agreeing to dance with a man, yet ultimately, women's abilities were mostly attributed to the men who led them.

The Local Field: Veracruz's Danzón Champions, Competition, and Reputation

Dancers in Veracruz also vied to be known as the best dancer, and it was again men who generally wielded power. Eliseo "Manzanita" Matus Meléndez, founder of the *Danzonera Manzanita y su son 4*, told me:

> Around 1980, there were many danzón dancers and there was lots of rivalry [*pique*]: "I know how to dance better than you" and "No!" and so there were contests. From there came the man [sic] who was best at dancing danzón. Alcántara, Firpo [Espinoza], Andrés Cazas were around at that time. There were many dancers. Gerardo Pacheco was there too: he is one of the newer ones. But of the old ones there was another man known as El Venado [the Deer, aka Miguel Díaz Andrade] from Boca del Río. They [the older ones] have all died now. And there were danzoneras, and there was rivalry [*pique*] between danzoneras, too. A trumpeter would play some pieces well. Then a trombonist, clarinettist, saxophonist would have to do what they could to match it … but now all that's stopped.

Manzanita nostalgically bemoans the loss of the era of rivalry, as though rivalry was more productive than the current state of play, both of musical and choreographic performance. Manzanita played the trumpet in Veracruz's Municipal Band for most of his career, as well as in the *Danzonera Alma de Sotavento* in 1978 during the period considered the danzonera's golden age, when they won the competition at the *Salón Colonia* against Mexico City's danzón orchestras, and went on to set up his own danzonera, *Manzanita y su son 4* (Little Apple and his four players) around 1980. *Manzanita y su son 4* consisted of trumpet, alto sax, timbales, and guiro/claves and was originally a *piquete* (squad), a small group of musicians assembled for one-off gigs. It soon became more established, however, and a tenor sax, keyboard, and electric bass were later added. In 1991, Manzanita's danzonera performed in María Novaro's widely applauded film *Danzón*, with Manzanita featured playing the trumpet part in Aniceto Díaz's *Teléfono a Larga Distancia*.

While there may have been less competitiveness among danzón musicians when I conducted fieldwork in the 2000s and 2010s, at least those in the Port, there was still plenty among dancers. Sigfrido Alcántara and the other older dancers Manzanita mentions had died before I came to Veracruz, and whether their stories would have made it easier to understand what happened from the 1980s is hard to tell. The dancers and champions I consulted in both Veracruz and Mexico City often claimed sole responsibility for initiating changes; they denigrated others and tried to convince me of the veracity of their version of events. Thus, what follows is a story that seemed most plausible.

Sigfrido Alcántara was renowned as much for his dancing as his height and weight (190 cm, 128 kilos, according to journalist Ángel Trejo 1992). He had worked on the railways, then as a chauffeur, before becoming a tour guide at Veracruz's fort, San Juan de Ulúa. Several dancers I knew had learned danzón from Alcántara in the 1980s, for he was not only a champion, having won five competitions (Trejo 1992), but he also taught extensively in the Port. Alcántara promoted danzón, gathered historical information about it and, he claimed, attempted to "organize the basic rules for dancing it according to the Cuban and Veracruzano choreography" (Trejo 1992, 47). Alcántara was committed to establishing and disseminating not only his rules of dancing but also those of competitions. Trejo states that "the rules of dancing competition danzón are very rigorous and, according to Alcántara, were slowly developed, over the years, by the dancers of the docks, the railways, the Customs House themselves" (Trejo 1992, 47–48).

Developing ideas produced by Veracruz's dockers et al., Alcántara's competition rules (as notated by Trejo 1992) stipulated, for example, that dancers should dress smartly; not drink alcohol; and, in response to stereotypes that danzón was linked to brothels and sex work, Alcántara stressed that couples should perform danzón decently (a continuing concern for many dancers). For example, dancers' bodies should be five fingers apart, and dancers should never put their knees between each other's legs (Trejo 1992, 48). Alcántara also specified that dancers should maintain a straight position and never look down. The woman's right hand should rest in the man's left hand; her left hand on his right shoulder. His right hand should lightly touch above her hip. "The movement of the hips should never be exaggerated," Alcántara warned (Trejo 1992, 49). "The feet should not be lifted more than 2 or 3 cm from the ground and should slide from the toe and end with the heel" (Trejo 1992, 49). Dancers should perform in a space of no more than one square meter. They should begin dancing on the first beat of the repeat of the A section (the ninth bar), respecting the rondo structure of danzón (usually ABACAD), its non-danceable A sections (descansos, where dancers rest while the music continues), and turn (*florear*) only in the final *montuno* section. Dancing couples in Veracruz still performed danzón predominantly in a closed position, in contrast with the more open Mexico City style of dancing. Turning, for Veracruzano Alcántara, was "strict: he lets her go towards the left (with only one hand); then he takes her by the right; turns the woman and, now in the left position, retakes her in the normal position" (Trejo 1992, 48). For Alcántara, the aim of turning was for men to enable the woman to *lucir* (shine), echoing discourses about shining and danzón performance that I often heard in the 2000s and 2010s (see Chapter 2). Overall, Alcántara's stipulations suggest a concern to establish very specific aesthetics and norms for danzón performance, with an emphasis on "decency" (sobriety and sexual propriety, particularly in relation to women), "elegance," and projecting in an understated manner; patriarchal and racialized logics of elegance and decency were clearly at play.

In sum, while Mexico City's champions battled to establish their own rules for the competitions they judged (in the twentieth-century dance halls) and for which they prepared dancers, so too Veracruz's dockers and railwaymen vied to construct their own variants, as did Alcántara. Overall, sufficient consensus was created for competition to occur, but no more. Further consensus would only be achieved as transmission processes began to change and dancers began to perform in groups. These changes were largely justified by rescue rhetoric, but notions of decency and elegance would also remain key.

A Danzón Revival? Rivalry, Rescue, and Officially Sanctioned Dance Groups (in Veracruz and Mexico City)

Tamara Livingston (1999) famously suggested that revivals often include six key elements: "1. an individual or small group of 'core revivalists'; 2. revival informants and/or original sources (e.g. historical sound recordings); 3. a revivalist ideology and discourse; 4. a group of followers which form the basis of a revivalist community; 5. revivalist activities (organizations, festivals, competitions); 6. non-profit and/or commercial enterprises catering to the revivalist market" (1999, 69). Building on Livingston's work, Hill and Bithell (2014) argue that six themes are common in revivals, specifically: "activism and the desire for change, the valuation and reinterpretation of history, recontextualization and transformation, legitimacy and authenticity, transmission and dissemination, and post-revival outgrowths and ramifications" (2014, 4). So in what ways do transformations to danzón practice constitute a revival?

The danzón revival appears to include a core group of revivalists motivated by rescue, but a desire for change driven by power and rivalries also had important parts to play. Before the 1980s, rescue rhetoric had been largely absent in Veracruz, distinct from the nostalgic laments ("it's not what it was") that were being voiced by, among others, the local poet and chronicler Francisco Rivera Ávila "Paco Píldora" (1908–1994). The emergence of rescue rhetoric in relation to danzón (in both Mexico and Cuba) was possibly spurred by the 1979 centenary of the first official performance of a danzón: *Las Alturas de Simpson,* composed by the Cuban Miguel Faílde Pérez. 1979 saw various celebrations not only in Cuba (see Madrid and Moore 2013) but also in Mexico City and Veracruz: competitions, a festival in the *California Dancing Club,* dinner dances, new compositions such as Acerina's Centenary LP, radio shows, and newspaper articles (such as those by Ángel Trejo, which formed the basis of his 1992 book). This centenary reinforced concern about the survival of danzón, given the aging of both danzón dancers and musicians, the lack of interest from younger people, and the reduced number of Mexico City's dance halls. This rescue rhetoric was new, and the concern to revive danzón would be heard for decades to come. More often than not, however, the concept of rescue was invoked instrumentally.

For example, the *Club de Bailadores de Danzón de Hoy y Siempre del Puerto de Veracruz, Asociacion Civil* (Club of Danzón Dancers of Today and Always of the Port of Veracruz, Civil Association, henceforth *Hoy y Siempre*) was established in July 1982 and, according to *Hoy y Siempre*'s statute, their purpose was to rescue danzón, encourage young people to participate, elevate danzón in the Port, and provide a platform for sociability.[6] Initially, *Hoy y Siempre* met weekly by the Alaska ice cream parlor in the Parque Zamora to dance danzón to recorded music. Several years later, after the Parque Zamora was remodeled, the bandstand provided the focal point for this danzón event, and live music was performed by the *Danzonera Manzanita y su son 4*. There had already been a more informal danzón dance group in Boca del Río, the conurbation adjoining the Port of Veracruz, in the 1970s, which gathered on Sundays at the *Salón Copacabana* (members included Miguel "El Venado" (the Deer) Díaz Andrade, Paco Diez, and Antonio River). But the formalized creation of a danzón dance group with a proactive purpose was something new, distinct from a mere social club. Moreover, *Hoy y Siempre* was Veracruz's first danzón group to be legally constituted with a notary as a civil association, a non-profit-making, hierarchically structured group registered with and legitimated by the Ministry of Foreign Affairs (*Secretaria de Relaciones Exteriores*) that included a president, Secretary, and treasurer.

The members of *Hoy y Siempre* were not champions like Alcántara, who was teaching and putting on danzón exhibitions in hotels throughout the Port and charging for his services. They sought the authority to teach and put on shows themselves, and they achieved this by becoming an official body. The rescue rhetoric used to justify the group's formation masked rivalries that pertained at the time. Messy, human, emotional factors in provoking revival movements are highlighted by Hill and Bithell (2014) in the introduction to their handbook of revivals, yet Hill and Bithell point to dissatisfaction and activist desires for change as factors in revivals, rather than a desire for accolade and applause. Hill and Bithell do point to the need to establish legitimacy to justify aesthetic changes as key drivers, yet *Hoy y Siempre* were initially less interested in change, and more concerned with obtaining legitimacy as a group eligible to publicly present their dancing skills. Economic concerns also had a part to play, but as a non-profit-making civil association, *Hoy y Siempre* could only charge expenses for their activities, officially at least. Being a group enabled them to approach state authorities to request resources more easily, however. For example, *Hoy y Siempre* worked to increase opportunities to dance danzón, succeeding in 1986 in persuading the Port's then-Mayor Gerardo Poo Ulibarri to institute a *Noche de Danzón* (Danzón Night) in the main square on Friday nights from 8 to 10 p.m., with the aim that tourists and locals alike could enjoy the Port's adopted music-dance form (El Dictamen 1986). But given the financial restrictions, most of the danzón dance groups that were to follow did not opt for civil association status, and those that did often needed legitimation at the time of their establishment.

In 1984, two years after *Hoy y Siempre*'s formation, a new group was created in Mexico City to rescue danzón: *Pro-Rescate y Difusión de Danzón Clásico* (Pro-Rescue and Dissemination of Classical Danzón). This was not a civil association but a younger generation of champions seeking control of Mexico City's danzón scene.[7] As well as giving exhibitions in theaters and on various television channels, members of *Pro-Rescate* also offered training workshops throughout Mexico City. Until that point, danzón had been concentrated in Veracruz and Mexico City, and *Pro-Rescate* began sowing the seeds of what was to become a national danzón scene by also leading workshops farther afield: in Guadalajara, Queretaro, and beyond. Rivalries were productive in this group, as they would be in those that followed, prompting the group to split and a separate group to be formed: the *Fraternidad del Danzón Clásico* (Fraternity of Classical Danzón).[8] Like Alcántara in Veracruz, the aim of Mexico City's *Fraternidad* was not only to disseminate danzón but also to establish the basis, norms, and structure for dancing and teaching it. These dancers had learned from copying the generation of champions that preceded them, making some changes, but the transmission of the dance was about to be transformed, as was danzón as a business.

Around 1987, a member of the *Fraternidad*, Víctor "El Toby" Escobar Bautista, set up the first dance school dedicated purely to danzón (as opposed to a series of dances): the *Escuela de la Fraternidad del Danzón* (the Fraternity of Danzón School). Although Escobar told me that he did not consider himself a great dancer, he brought to the school over thirty years of experience as a sports teacher. Employing his sports pedagogies, Escobar taught a geometricized version of the dance, stiffer than its Mexico City dance hall prototype, with classified steps and specific moves marking section beginnings and endings. Didactic reference was made to tracing squares, circles, and angles on the floor; to moving a whole or half foot length; to maintaining an upright posture and flexibility in the knees; to counting beats and bars, rather than listening to the music and its phrasing; to smiling to demonstrate enjoyment; to so-called right and wrong practice. While named danzón moves had existed throughout its history, steps acquired pedagogic precision and came to be given esoteric names by Escobar and other members of the *Fraternidad* (such as *cuadro al frente*—forward square). As well as a more disciplined and codified style of dancing, a canon of steps was emerging, although these moves were named differently by different teachers—for example, the *cuadro al frente*, *columpio* (swing), and *puente* (bridge) involve the same movements (for example, feet forward, forward, together; back, back, together [twice]).

Through the 1980s, dancers in Veracruz, including members of *Hoy y Siempre*, continued to perform danzón in the closed embrace (*danzón cerrado*), the style considered characteristic of the Port's danzón into the twenty-first century. This contrasted with the open-position style (*danzón abierto*) associated with Mexico City until the 1980s, involving the couple opening out to hold just one hand and turning in the final *montuno* section. *Hoy y Siempre* exhibited their closed-embrace dancing with couples performing independently during their dance shows in Veracruz and on one-off trips to nearby cities such as Tierra Blanca, Xalapa, and Puebla. There were as yet no coordinated collective danzón choreographies. Some members of *Hoy y Siempre* were eager to learn to turn in the Mexico City style, for they thought opening out and turning was more elegant. From the mid-1980s, these members of *Hoy y Siempre* took classes with dancers from Mexico City's groups, in particular El Toby Escobar Bautista, and also Arturo "El Capullo" Sánchez, Miguel Ángel Cisneros, and Pedro "El Abuelo" Velázquez. Arguments ensued among members of *Hoy y Siempre*, who considered turning to be an elegant innovation, and those who thought turning countered the characteristic closed style of Veracruz's danzón, which was characterized as more authentic. A classic opposition between tradition and innovation (or evolution, as some danzón dancers called it) was evoked, articulated in terms of authenticity and tradition versus added elegance. This was linked to questions of local identity and condescension in terms depicting lírico dancing as non-elegant, causing friction within *Hoy y Siempre*, but for now, the group held together.

From the 1980s, danzón took on many of the characteristics of what Hobsbawm and Ranger coined an "invented tradition" (1983), an idea well-worn within scholarship. Usually linked to a historic past, an invented tradition is a practice, governed by rules, that "is essentially a process of formalization and ritualization" (Hobsbawm 1983, 4). Danzón dancing in particular was formalized in terms of transmission (in schools and groups), practice (a more codified dance, although no one managed to cement rules), and ritualized in terms of creating spectacle. Yet the choreographic transformations that occurred were not "characterized by reference to the past" (Hobsbawm 1983, 4) in terms of that past being something to be mined and preserved, as are Hobsbawm and Ranger's invented traditions and many revivals. Livingston (1999) proposes that key figures of revivals often seek out "informants" and original sources to recreate so-called authentic traditions, while Hill and Bithell frame similar practices as "the valuation and reinterpretation of history" (2014, 4). Yet original sources and authoritative past forms of dancing or playing danzón were rarely sought out by practitioners attempting historical fidelity.

While Mexico City's champions were consulted on forms of dancing considered elegant, older performers (from Veracruz, Mexico City, or elsewhere) were seldom referred to as sources of a more authentic past to be emulated in the present. The dockers et al. might be portrayed as "the authentic ambassadors of danzón" in Veracruz, but no performance practice is mentioned in relation to them. Even in twenty-first-century Veracruz, the older, freer style of dancing (danzón lírico) was not considered more authentic than the transformed (académico) style. Likewise, Cuban dancers were rarely consulted as a reference source in terms of a more authentic past. Into the twenty-first century, the older age of several members of the *Danzonera Alma de Veracruz* provided a form of authentication for this music, and most older musicians and dancers who performed well were respected for their abilities and knowledge, particularly those who had done so for many decades, but they were not considered repositories of so-called traditional knowledge. Some dancers recalled nostalgically how their parents and grandparents had performed danzón, but there was no sense that they were attempting to create a continuity to that past in terms of performance practice.

Transformations to danzón conform to some degree to Livingston's (1999) and Hill and Bithell's (2014) first four revival elements: a group of core revivalists emerged, were keen to revive danzón and change practice, transformed and recontextualized the genre, and created groups to legitimize their practice. Yet danzón is not mediated by key values of authenticity and tradition. That said, the past is clearly important to danzón practitioners: this is a nineteenth-century music-dance form with historical narratives of origin going back to the seventeenth century, associated nostalgically, sonically, and choreographically with mid-twentieth-century Veracruz, and

Mexico City's dance halls. Rather than being brought into the present as something that many practitioners want to reconstruct or restore (as is the case with Boym's "restorative nostalgia," 2001, 49), ideas about the past are articulated by Veracruz's danzón practitioners in ways akin to Boym's "reflective nostalgia" (2001, 50) where historical manifestations of danzón are sensed from afar.

State Involvement in Danzón Sponsorship (Especially in Veracruz): Institutions, Festivals, Tourism

The timing of the danzón revival, the urge for rescue, was partly due to broader socioeconomic changes: Mexico's debt crisis of the 1980s; moves to privatize the state-run shipbuilding industry (completed in the late 1980s) and the port (in 1991) when power was shifting away from working-class men in Veracruz; a burgeoning of cultural institutions in the late 1980s, which provided local people and danzoneros with new forms of institutional support and legitimation; and neoliberal concerns that enabled culture to be harnessed as a resource to be rescued. As Yúdice (2003) famously argued, the neoliberal turn of the 1980s saw the emergence of the concept of culture as a resource that could promote well-being and also solve so-called social problems. Culture became something to be managed by administrators, whether for the purposes of tourism or social amelioration.

The state had been involved in danzón performance throughout the twentieth century: licensing the use of public space in Veracruz, dance halls in the Port and Mexico City; paying Veracruz's Municipal Band (which sometimes played danzones); and, since the 1980s, legitimizing the dance groups that registered as civil associations. Although centralized national cultural institutions such as the National Institute of Fine Arts (INBA) had been created since 1947, danzoneros had little involvement in these institutions. During the 1950s, a small number of regional cultural centers were set up in cities including Veracruz and, in 1954, Mexico's first *casa de cultura* (culture house) was inaugurated. Although publicly accessible, community-oriented, and government-backed, these cultural centers initially catered to the cultural, academic, and political elites. From the mid-1960s, however, they included music, dance, and visual arts workshops aimed at broader audiences of all age groups. The economic crisis of the 1980s and subsequent drive to privatization and foreign investment influenced not only the running of Veracruz's port but also Mexico's cultural institutions. The federal government slowly withdrew its direct involvement in cultural management, transferring power to state and local governments (see Jiménez 2006). In 1988, instead of creating a central ministry of culture to distribute funds, the federal government created an umbrella council, the National Council for Culture and the Arts (CONACULTA), to oversee the organizations that had previously pertained to the cultural secretariat of the Ministry of Education (SEP).[9] Casas de Cultura and cultural centers burgeoned, and by 2003, fifty years after the first Casa de Cultura, there were 1,592 throughout the country (Sandoval 2003).

In 1987, the state-funded Veracruz Culture Institute (IVEC) opened and was to play a key role in danzón's development in the Port. Local academics and intellectuals were involved in establishing the vision of the IVEC (as had occurred with other cultural institutions in Mexico). The institute's first director (1987–1992), art historian Ida Rodríguez Prampolini, argued for an emphasis on popular culture (see Prampolini 2017), as did anthropologist Aguirre Beltrán (a member of the directive council), in keeping with his research (e.g., 1972), which describes Veracruz's popular culture as a mixture of Spanish, indigenous, and black elements. Three core functions for the IVEC were proposed by its founders: "investigation, training and dissemination" (Galindo Valencia 1988, 62). This vision for the Port's new cultural institution would nurture interest in Veracruz's so-called "third root" (its blackness) through research, music and dance training, exhibitions, conferences, and festivals such as the annual Afro-Caribbean festival (*Festival Internacional Afrocaribeño*) (see Rinaudo 2012). Danzón fit neatly into this scheme, and from its outset, the IVEC provided a space for the civil association *Hoy y Siempre* to gather weekly, teach new recruits, and rehearse for exhibitions. Although *Hoy y Siempre* had a president, the role was not conflated with that of teacher, so several members were involved in instructing new arrivals. The new institutional setting attracted many new members, and *Hoy y Siempre* grew: children and young people joined, as did many older people. By 1987, *Hoy y Siempre* had around 150 members.

In 1988, Veracruz's first danzón festival, *danzón dedicado a … Veracruz, Mexico y Cuba,* was held at the IVEC and was funded by the Veracruz state government, the Ministry of Education and Culture (SEC), the Mexican Institute of Social Security (IMSS) and the Cuban Ministry of Culture. Each event would charge admission, making danzón festivals profitable. Like the danzón festivals that were to follow—in Mexico City, Ciudad Mendoza, Puebla, Queretaro, and beyond—danzón as institutional big business had begun. The genre would go on to attract significant numbers of visitors to cities, filling hotels and restaurants, and providing opportunities for entrepreneurs to create and profit from danzón events and package holidays. Like later danzón festivals, Veracruz's first danzón festival included several danzoneras, dinner dances, workshops, conference-type roundtables of experts discussing histories of danzón, and groups of dancers exhibiting their talents. Dance groups were distinguished by region, akin to regional dances making up the nation, and groups were presented as if danzón from regions beyond Veracruz and Mexico City were stylistically distinct (despite remarkable similarities).

Hoy y Siempre had performed at Veracruz's first danzón festival, and the children and youngsters in the group had received considerable praise for their dancing. A marvel at children's ability to perform music and dance is not uncommon in Mexico, and such children often attract considerable attention. Some older members of *Hoy y Siempre* begrudged the attention the youngsters were getting, including the then-president, who expelled the children from the group. The president's argument was framed in classic tradition-evolution terms: the older dancers were said to perform danzón authentically in a closed position, whereas the younger dancers, performing what were considered more elegant turns, were positioned as desiring evolution. Envy was not mentioned. And the expulsion of the children caused outrage, provoking the formation of a splinter group in 1989 consisting of the children and a few adults: a new civil association entitled *Tres Generaciones del Danzón Veracruzano A.C.* (Three Generations of Veracruzano Danzón), whose statutes emphasized "transmission [...] to future generations" (Figueroa Hernández 2007, 25).[10] Like some of the dancers who had preceded them, *Tres Generaciones* were interested in creating pedagogies for transmitting danzón, especially to children and adolescents. They sought advice and tuition from Mexico City's champions and aficionado investigators, and they would become one of the country's most important danzón groups.

Gerardo Pacheco, a founding member of *Tres Generaciones*, told me: "We began to realize that the people from Mexico City were developing a technique, and we began to take things from various teachers [...] to take the best, and we began to develop our own technique." Like dance champions and other groups, *Tres Generaciones* claimed to have developed their own technique. Pacheco said that with this technique, *Tres Generaciones* "respect Veracruzanos' very particular *cadencia* [cadence/rhythmic movement] without too much opening out or adorning turns [...] or the speed or rigidity of Mexico City. [...] Fortunately on the coast there is a naturalness in movement that is very different, probably because of the black Afro-Caribbean influence." *Tres Generaciones* continued to dance danzón mostly in the closed position characteristic of the Port until the final *montuno* section of the dance, but they did this with their own technique. They claimed their technique was specifically Veracruzana/o and combined with a distinctive rhythmic movement and slower feel attributed to the racialized bodies of people from the coast. Not only are Veracruzana/os' bodies elevated here to a capacity beyond the reach of non-Veracruzana/os, with an ability to achieve *cadencia* naturally, but the notion that danzón is a marker of Veracruzana/o identity is also reproduced. (This discourse is also applied to musicians, as we saw with Pancho in Vignette 2.)

Claims of Veracruzano danzón's uniqueness were used not only in justifying institutional support for the music-dance form but also for promoting its performance before tourists in the Port's main square. The Municipal Band still performed once or twice a week in the Port's main square, as it had throughout the twentieth century, and now people danced when they played. During the 1980s, dancers had increasingly approached both the band leader and local officials asking that the Municipal Band play more danzones. Trejo recounts how: "Manuel Díaz Irigoyen, who inherited the baton from Don Camerino Vázquez in the Marine Band says: 'Here people want just danzón! Even the gringos [US/foreign men] ask for it while their gringas [US/foreign women] learn to dance with our *costeños* [men from the coast]!'" (1992, 46). Tourists enjoyed watching and occasionally dancing danzón in the main square. A former mayor of Veracruz told me that with the arrival of the faster motorway to Veracruz in 1990, weekend tourism grew, particularly from Puebla and Mexico City. In 1991, the same year that the port was privatized, the *Danzonera Alma de Sotavento* had stopped playing for the radio station XEU. The danzonera was still the most active in the Port at this time, but demand for musicians was lower than it had been in previous decades. Within months, however, the danzonera became permanent employees of the municipality and were renamed *Alma de Veracruz*. It was difficult to ascertain when and why the danzonera was municipalized, but it was implied to me that Genaro Barcelata Trujillo, the danzonera's director, was the son-in-law of the state governor, Dante Delgado Rannauro (1988–1992). Nepotism aside, the danzonera was already contracted regularly by the municipality to play in the Port's main square and elsewhere, and the danzonera probably was municipalized mainly because it was cheaper to employ them than contract them piecemeal: the musicians in the danzonera earned around three times the national monthly minimum wage for performing three evenings a week. Moreover, the danzonera rather than the Municipal Band was discursively associated with danzón and with local identity.

The *Danzonera Alma de Veracruz* was initially contracted under the auspices of the Fourth Division of the local government, and later the Tourism Division. With the danzonera employed by the municipality, it was up to the municipal president and director of tourism to name the next director when Genaro Barcelata became ill. Municipal President Roberto Bueno

(1995–1997), who also directed and played bass with the *chunchaca* (Mexican cumbia) group *Los Flamers*, nominated trumpeter Bernardo García. Bernardo García was by then an old man. He had been taught by Sánchez senior in the Hospicio Manuel Gutiérrez Zamora orphanage (see Figure 2.3) and had gone on to play with *Chato Rojas y sus Lobos Marinos* and Arturo Nuñez's orquesta, as well as traveling to Europe with *Los Matecocos*. But García's directorship of the danzonera was short-lived, as he soon became ill and left the danzonera's archive of scores to clarinettist Bernardo López. While several of the older players in the danzonera hinted to me that they had been solicited by the then-director of tourism to become directors, without an archive of scores, this option was not available to them. The role was assigned to López, as an esteemed musician in the Port.

With sustained local government support for regular danzón events in Veracruz from the 1990s, danzón became a resource for cultural tourism in the Port (although usually an added value for tourists, Piedras Feria 2006, rather an incentive to visit the city). In return for paying the musicians and providing chairs and space, the authorities got a ready-made tourist spectacle, with dancers avid to perform. It is tourism that distinguishes Veracruz from other danzón towns in terms of space, provision of musicians, and audience. The concept of local identity continues to play a role in terms of gaining institutional and financial support for danzón: the notion of rescuing a local tradition is often evoked to fund its promotion to younger people (particularly in the IVEC). But, although a few young people have joined the dance, most newcomers since the 1980s have been between fifty and eighty years old.

Danzón, Age, and "Cultural Rescue"

Participants' older age is used to justify the notion that danzón should be rescued and promoted to the young. Danzón schools and groups were set up from the 1980s for young people and children, considered the hopes for the future of danzón. Many of these young danzón dancers stop dancing in their twenties, leaving the groups to marry, study, and/or work. Yet far from dying out, danzón has proliferated throughout Mexico, and while some of its older practitioners have danced danzón all their lives, new recruits are mostly older people: a new generation of fifty-plus-year-olds. People rarely do the same thing all their lives, contrary to stereotypes that deny older people temporality and possibility. Although a few older people danced danzón along with other genres in dance halls when they were young, most (re)joined the dance once they were retired, widowed, separated, or divorced, and once their children were adults. Danzón is something that these newly recruited older people now do, and sometimes did when they were young (especially those over seventy), rather than the frequently heard myth that it is something people have done all their lives.

For example, one seventy-four-year-old woman was just ten years old when she started dancing danzón with her parents at *Villa del Mar*, a renowned local dance hall; she stopped dancing when she married and moved away from the city but resumed upon separating from her husband and returning to Veracruz in the 1980s. The dancing lifespan of older people often outstretches that of the young. For example, someone joining the dance as early as five years old may dance for twenty years, leaving the dance aged twenty-five to marry, while a fifty-year-old newcomer may dance for thirty-plus years, surpassing the younger dancer by a decade. In the early twenty-first century, no children danced danzón in Veracruz, and very few young people did. Meanwhile, fifty-plus-year-olds continued to join the ranks of danzón dancers, particularly danzón groups, far outnumbering other age groups.

When a rhetoric of "rescue" is invoked—in justifications for funding, to promote tourism, or to legitimize or critique the formation of groups—it relates more to continuity into the future than to the conservation of the past, or of the past in the present. This is partly why young people are still seen as the next danzón generation, rather than the fifty-plus-year-olds who actually form these new generations. Most of Veracruz's danzón practitioners consider older people as pertaining to the past, and the fact that they are new to the dance and often join dance groups to learn to perform it is rarely acknowledged. What is more, older participants create a continuity to the past (which may or may not be imagined), contributing to nostalgic renditions of the Port as a town where local people party throughout their lives, a town with a long heritage of *alegría* (happiness).

Danzón events in Veracruz are not aimed at older people, however. Instead, these events provide a space for people of all ages to meet, dance, listen, and watch a phenomenon associated with the city. Danzón is linked to cultural identity and tourism rather than older age or health care in Veracruz, both institutionally and in terms of aficionados' practice and discourse. Moreover, tourism underpins the institutional support of danzón in the Port: it is culturally expedient. The well-being of even the oldest dancers is rarely mentioned in official discourses as a rationale for danzón events (in terms of danzón being a form of either sport or therapy). Nor is danzón included in municipal events targeted at older people. INAPAM, the National Institute of Senior Citizens, supports danzón events in towns throughout Mexico (including Xalapa, the capital of the State of Veracruz). The predecessor to

INAPAM, the INSEN (National Institute of Older Age), promoted a danzón group in the Port of Veracruz in the 1990s (the *Bailadores de Danzón del INSEN de Veracruz*, led by Quinto Longino Espíndola Jiménez), but this was short lived. While older people make up the majority of danzón dancers in Veracruz, they perform in the Port's plazas rather than at institutions aimed at older people such as the INAPAM. Some women who are danzón habitués participate in other activities at the INAPAM, but other older danzón regulars, particularly men, steer clear of "older people's" events, preferring events (such as danzón) that are not age specific, and where age is not foregrounded. Men's sexual, emotional, choreographic, and social power in the danzón arena was lost, to a large extent, in the institutionalized settings of old people's centers in the Port.

State Sponsorship and the Rise of Groups

In the 1980s, as the culture sector expanded, *casas de cultura* became available for danzón workshops and festivals throughout the country. Danzón experts emerged in greater numbers, including aficionado investigators, masters of ceremonies, and academics. They talked at mostly government-sponsored conferences and festivals, legitimating and being legitimated by powerful groups, champions and institutions. Danzón expert Jesús Flores y Escalante told me that it was at his suggestion that members of Mexico City's *Fraternidad* and the earlier *Pro-Rescate* group decided to form a civil association in Mexico City in 1993: *La Academia Nacional de Danzón A.C.* (the National Academy of Danzón).[11] What distinguished this group was a new emphasis on research: while members of this association were mostly champions who had their own dance schools, the academy aimed to create a central body to both research danzón and define its technique. The academy created links with other groups, including Veracruz's *Tres Generaciones* and in particular its leader, Rosa Abdala Gómez. While dancers still vied for prominence with rival techniques, a new kind of group dance was about to emerge that would transform danzón performance dramatically.

In 1988, Víctor "El Toby" Escobar created one of the first danzón routines, involving dancers performing in choreographed unison to a set piece of music (in this case the danzón *Mata Majá*). In contrast to individual couples exhibiting their talents in competitions and in theatrical dance performances, these performances involved large groups of couples in matching outfits dancing series of codified steps in unison. Inspired by these routines, *Tres Generaciones* created the first routines for children dancing danzón in unison, dressed immaculately in matching outfits: wonderment at children's abilities and awe at their choreographies and elegant attire coalesced. Here and more broadly, danzón was becoming disciplined and a new kind of spectacle, a pedagogic display.[12]

Another factor contributing to changes to the dance was María Novaro's 1991 film *Danzón,* which was shot in Mexico City's dance halls and in Veracruz. María Rojo starred in the film, together with Veracruzano docker Daniel "El Catrín" Rergis Aguiler (portrayed in Chapter 2). Mexico City dance groups, the Port's dance groups *Hoy y Siempre* and *Tres Generaciones,* and Veracruz's danzoneras *Manzanita y su son 4* and *Alma de Sotavento* also appear. The shifting institutional landscape and the rise of groups and interest provoked by the film attracted thousands of lower- and middle-class fifty-plus-year-olds to danzón, as well as some groups of children. It solidified the imaginary of the Port as a wellspring of danzón. And actress María Rojo would go on to set up a dance hall with Miguel Nieto (owner of the *Salón Los Ángeles*) named after the legendary *Salón México,* and act in a 1996 remake of the 1949 *Salón México* film.

When CONACULTA sponsored a danzón festival, the *Encuentro Internacional de Danzón* (the International Danzón Meeting), in 1994, dancers, champions, dance groups, musicians, and experts from around the country were brought together to participate in workshops, dance exhibitions, dances, concerts, and conferences. There, the young members of *Tres Generaciones* exhibited their routines. The response was jubilant and prompted requests for Rosa Abdala Gómez and *Tres Generaciones* to give workshops throughout Mexico. They traveled around the country teaching danzón in casas de cultura, universities, and other venues, often being contracted by local and state governments. People gain kudos from being invited to travel to teach and perform, especially where they are supported by local government or public institutions. Musicians, dancers, and experts alike boasted to me about how far they had been: the farther the better, foreign travel being considered especially prestigious, and Cuba holding a particular status as the so-called birthplace of danzón. Like Mexico City's champions, Rosa Abdala Gómez and *Tres Generaciones* traveled widely, teaching their own pedagogic version of the dance, and supporting the formation of groups in cities throughout Mexico.

Danzón dance competitions became rarer, and spectacle came to the fore as groups, and the odd individual couple, exhibited their routines wearing matching outfits en masse. Some people told me that they frowned on competitions (as opposed to exhibitions), as they create tensions between winners and losers and are divisive of groups. There was an onus on groups to exhibit collectively. Yet groups did not reproduce a canon of danzón choreographies established by a well-known group (as Heidi Feldman argues was the case with the choreographies and music created by "Perú Negro" in the 1970s, which would be emulated in the subsequent Afro-Peruvian revival, 2006). Instead, an emphasis was placed on groups creating new routines, new sequences of the increasingly codified steps. Well-known steps were juxtaposed, mostly by group leaders, to create group routines that were posited as unique. A canon of steps was emerging, rather than a canon of choreographies. Some groups began to vie with each other to create the best routines, both at a local level and at festivals, but there were no group competitions as such. They competed for applause, congratulation, and to recruit new members. Since there were no winners, they could all claim superiority. In Veracruz, *Hoy y Siempre* created their own group of children who exhibited and competed with *Tres Generaciones* for attention in the main square. Nationally, festivals began to play a key role in publicizing and standardizing the transformed dance, for they gathered people from across Mexico and encouraged them to copy and learn from the dancers who were promoted as admirable.

With the changing choreographic and economic arena, some dancers began to jostle to lead groups, rather than vying to be champions. Beyond the ability to dance well, the credit for which had previously been almost solely attributed to men as leaders in the couple dance, different qualities began to be valued: pedagogic, choreographic, social, and leadership skills increased in importance. Although a few men would continue to hold most economic power, women entered the fray as group leaders. Groups began to multiply and, with them, the number of group leaders. By 1994, twelve years after *Hoy y Siempre* was formed, around thirty danzón groups were in Mexico City, and three were in Veracruz (all led by women).[13] And as more groups spawned, so others disappeared. Akin to other revivals (Livingston 1999; Hill and Bithell 2014), modes of transmission changed. The transmission of the dance shifted from learning individually, in familial contexts or by observing others, to being taught in groups and in the newly founded danzón academies; from listening to the music and learning a few related moves to mastering a series of codified, formalized steps to be danced with others in a group spectacle, with or without instruction on dance technique. In the early twenty-first century, most groups continue to be less interested in pedagogies and more interested in spectacle, and group meetings predominantly consist of rehearsals for dance routines.

Empire-Builders

The proliferation of cultural institutions opened greater possibilities for individual economic gain and the chance for very few dancers to create institutionally backed empires. I found tracing how money moved in the danzón scene incredibly difficult, given prevalent discourses that because danzón was culture, only expenses should be charged for its transmission and exhibition. This was clearly not the case. While mass commercialization did not occur, "even local music is big business," as Ruth Finnegan (1989, 273) reminded in her study of music-making in Milton Keynes, in the United Kingdom. The production and consumption of music and dance contributes to the broader political economy, and several danzón champions, group leaders, and teachers found ways of profiting from the genre explicitly by selling dance lessons, shoes, dance hall space in Mexico City or at one-off events in Veracruz, books, audio and video recordings, and fans, or by running danzoneras. Those dancers who built danzón empires tended to do so formally via institutions (charging for access to competitions, demonstrations, dinner dances, tours, workshops, and conferences), with institutions supplying space, personnel, musical equipment, transport, and publicity at subsidized rates, as well as validation and an institutional base from which to apply for grants.

After his mother, Rosa Abdala Gómez, died in 1996, twenty-two-year-old Miguel Zamudio Abdala took over *Tres Generaciones* and later built Mexico's largest danzón empire, although others had substantial influence and large, esteemed groups in the 2000s and 2010s, including Fredy Salazar and Maru (María Eugenia) Mosqueda in Coyoacán (together with Fredy's mother, Teresa, and brother Jacobo), and Miguel Ángel Vázquez in Tezozomoc (State of Mexico). The generation of the Academia Nacional de Danzón continued to be respected and powerful, but these dancers had mostly operated at a local level. In contrast, Zamudio created a national hub serving over half of Mexico's thirty-two states, as well as the capital. He was not completely alone, however, for Mexico City's El Toby Escobar also created an empire, but his realm was based in sport and focused on ballroom dance more generally, rather than danzón specifically.

Miguel Zamudio started working for Veracruz's cultural institution, the IVEC, as a cultural promoter in 1996, the same year he took over *Tres Generaciones*. From his base at the IVEC, Zamudio set up danzón and salsa courses for the public, established the IVEC's Atarazanas building as a home for *Tres Generaciones*, and took the group to give workshops and demonstrations nationally and internationally (including Argentina, Canada, Cuba, France, Germany, and Japan). In 1997, Zamudio created a series of prizes in his mother's honor, supported by CONACULTA, the IVEC, the local government, and the University of Veracruz: the Rosa Abdala Gómez National Prize for the Preservation and Dissemination of Danzón (*El Premio Nacional a la*

Preservación y Difusión del Danzón "Rosa Abdala Gómez"), with categories including research, dance, music, promotion, preservation, and dissemination. Zamudio bestows these prizes at *Tres Generaciones*'s annual birthday celebration on those he deems appropriate, thereby reinforcing his ties with the great and the good of the danzón scene. In 1997, Zamudio himself was awarded the State Prize for the Preservation of Veracruzano Traditions (*Premio Estatal a la Preservación de las Tradiciones Veracruzanas*).

While Zamudio's Veracruz-based empire focused on danzón, Escobar's concern was sport. In 1998, under the auspices of the Mexican Sport Confederation (and later the National Commission of Physical Cultural and Sport, CONADE), Escobar created the Mexican Federation of Dance (*Federación Mexicana de Baile y Danza Deportiva A.C.*) in Mexico City, incorporating competitive ballroom dance-sport genres and later becoming linked to the International DanceSport Federation. Escobar created affiliate associations in five states throughout the Republic of Mexico, ran workshops for dance teachers, and organized dance-sport competitions in which he included danzón. Yet danzón is rarely referred to as a sport, by Escobar or others, and is not officially a dance-sport genre. Although Escobar continued to teach danzón weekly to a group of older people, he was more interested in setting up a national dance-sport federation than an exclusively danzón-based operation. He was a man with several businesses who organized package holidays to events such as danzón festivals in Mexico and Cuba, and Veracruz's carnival, where he coordinated an annual danzón dinner dance for decades. Rather than expressing a real satisfaction and pride in dancing and being admired by others, either individually or in terms of a group, both Escobar and Zamudio seemed more interested in establishing business and institutional empires. They enacted Livingston's (1999) and Hill and Bithell's (2014) key revival elements of forming organizations, putting on festivals and competitions, and leading businesses that would be characterized by Livingston and Hill and Bithell as post-revivalist given their establishment of mainstream groups and lack of rescue rhetoric.

In 1998, the same year that Escobar set up the Mexican Federation of Dance, Zamudio created an umbrella civil association specifically to coordinate danzón groups nationally: the National Center for the Research and Dissemination of Danzón (CNIDDAC), funded by CONACULTA, the IVEC, and the State of Veracruz. He also instigated the National Danzón Demonstration (*Muestra Nacional de Danzón*), bringing together groups from throughout Mexico to demonstrate their routines to each other at the group's annual birthday celebration. Zamudio also set up two danzón ensembles (the *Orquesta Danzonera Tres Generaciones* in 1999 and *La Charanga del Puerto* in 2004) to play at his and other people's events. In 2003, Zamudio incorporated *Tres Generaciones*'s annual anniversary celebration into his annual festival (*Forum Danzones en el Puerto*: Danzón in the Port Forum), including a "national" demonstration (groups from around Mexico performing a danzón each, to live or recorded music, interrupted occasionally by individual couples and special guest shows), dinner-dances (with danzoneras from Mexico City and Veracruz), book launches, and workshops. The charge for entering the national demonstration tended to be around ten times the price of a local bus journey, and each dinner dance ticket and workshop cost around eight times the national demonstration entrance fee, so with over 2,000 people registered (most of whom came from Mexico City), this was a profitable event. I did not manage to ascertain which elements of the forum came under the institutional auspices of the IVEC or otherwise, but in 2017, while state funding for Zamudio's festival was withdrawn (for one year only), the events went ahead at alternative venues with only around seventy of the usual 140-plus dance groups in attendance.

Many local Veracruzana/os were excluded from participation in Zamudio's events because they could not afford to attend. In some parts of Mexico, such as Coyoacán (Mexico City), Monterrey, and Puebla, more professional and middle-class people have joined danzón groups, and these groups are relatively wealthy. It is these people who can afford to travel to festivals nationally and internationally. Danzoneros in Veracruz tend to be lower-middle and lower class and merely perform at Zamudio's National Danzón Demonstration, rather than participating in the more expensive activities of Zamudio's forum (such as workshops and dinner dances). Despite their financial inability to attend certain events, many locals commended Zamudio for his successful career. At the national level, Zamudio was the institutional king of danzón: by 2004, his National Danzón Demonstration had been included in CONACULTA's Catalogue of Mexican Art and Culture Festivals; and through the 2000s and 2010s, Zamudio controlled Mexico's main danzón social media groups. So while Escobar had a national organization and business for ballroom dance (and danzón) based in sport, Zamudio had another located in so-called culture, promoting and preserving what was framed as a local tradition.

The combination of preserving a local tradition and contributing to the local economy may underpin Zamudio's success, a success dependent on local and national politics. Zamudio has withstood several changes of government and leadership of the IVEC, and risen through its ranks since 1996, serving as IVEC's Subdirector of Regional Cultural Development in 2007, and beginning in 2010, director of Veracruz's main theater, the Teatro Reforma, and then director of the Agustín Lara Museum (Casita Blanca). This is no mean feat, given that Mexican cultural politics remains dependent on the often personal interests of administrations, politicians, and functionaries, as Jiménez (2006) demonstrates. But through his network and events, Zamudio has contributed to the expediency of danzón in the Port, consistently attracting thousands of danzón dancers to attend his danzón festival, providing substantial income for hotels, restaurants, bars, and other local businesses and institutions.

While CNIDDAC and Zamudio's annual festival were thriving, on a daily level, *Tres Generaciones* as a group was fairly inactive in the Port in the 2000s and 2010s: it consisted merely of a few dancers who had participated in the group since their teens. Several people told me that *Tres Generaciones* was not performing to the standards achieved in their heyday in the early 1990s. But *Tres Generaciones* was vital to Zamudio's enterprise and always performed extremely slick choreographies at the Danzón in the Port Forum demonstrations, dinner dances, and other events (often bringing back several dancers of old). The core of *Tres Generaciones*'s performance excellence was maintained by people in their twenties and thirties, rather than the teenagers and younger children for whom this group was renowned. Meanwhile, everyday danzón activities in the Port's main square and smaller plazas, such as the Plazuela de la Campana and the Parque Zamora, were spaces dominated by people over fifty.

Standardization and Attempts to Achieve Consensus

There is no fixed, definitive standard for danzón, the dance, but several people have attempted to become standard-bearers with the ability to enforce a standard and thereby demand, for example, that all students and teachers pay to take exams and become accredited. It is common for standard-bearers to seek national approval. Several dancers told me that they had approached the National Institute of Fine Arts (INBA), but to no avail. What distinguishes Mexican danzón from other revivals and "invented traditions" (Hobsbawm and Ranger 1983) is its disjuncture with the nation. Madrid and Moore suggest that the association of danzón to sex work in the mid-twentieth century made it impossible for danzón to "express Mexican pride" (2013, 174), but that after the 1990s, danzón was reinvented to become "a symbol of nostalgic national culture" (2013, 174). A connection between danzón and sex work was extolled by danzón expert Jesús Flores y Escalante (1993), among others, referencing Mexico City's dance halls and cabarets and 1940s and 1950s Mexican films (see Gutiérrez 2019; Avila 2019 for an analysis of these films), but this connection was repudiated by the majority of people I interviewed, who had decades of experience with Mexico City's dance halls. Nevertheless, such a historic connection is often referenced by practitioners who joined danzón after the 1980s and were concerned with establishing that danzón is a "decent" practice. While concerns about decency might have played a part in danzón not becoming a national symbol, and despite its adoption by Veracruzana/os, danzón remains Cuban (and was designated intangible national heritage in Cuba in 2013) and is ideologically weaker than alternatives such as Veracruz's son jarocho and other regional dances which Mexican states have promoted to be named as Intangible Cultural Heritage by UNESCO. (Parallels exist between danzón's failure to achieve UNESCO recognition and that of the baile de artesa of Mexico's Costa Chica, see Ruiz Rodríguez 2019.) Ultimately, danzón's relationship to the nation was too weak to sustain forms of state support where standards are set or heritage status designated (in contrast to tango, see Luker 2016). Nevertheless, several dancers, notably Zamudio and Escobar, have gained support from cultural and sports associations, respectively, labeling their events "national" and thereby providing kudos and legitimacy.

Despite the existence of festivals and prizes, there is no national regulator of danzón, no regulating body or examination board, no coordinated written code of practice that sets standards of danzón aesthetics and quality. Zamudio's CNIDDAC and Escobar's Mexican Federation of Dance issue certificates to individuals and groups for participation in their workshops, competitions, and group exhibitions, as do local and state governments (often via *casas de cultura*) and dance groups themselves. These certificates often adorn the walls of danzoneros' houses and are both proof of their actions and a great source of pride. They bestow prestige and legitimate not only the recipient but also the bestower. They mark achievement rather than a form of assessment. Some certificates detail prizes and competition victories, rather than mere participation, and some prize-givers are more highly valued than others, especially those with government and institutional backing.

Competitions and festivals provide a means of setting and regulating standards of performance, especially those officially sanctioned and certificated, thereby preventing alternatives from entering the market. Moreover, embodied and discursive aesthetic values, including those around elegance and decency, are recreated at festivals both by exhibiting groups and by competing couples. For example, at festivals, and the now rarer competitions, certain groups or couples are sometimes given additional performance opportunities and implicitly set up as exemplars, such as former champions or *Tres Generaciones* during CNIDDAC's annual forum dinner-dances. Exemplary dancers are selected by event organizers who set and reinforce their own aesthetic agendas and alliances. Many group leaders claim they or their group is different, but non-group members often comment that "everyone dances the same nowadays." While consensus for standardization may not have been explicitly imposed by any one standard-bearer, a repertoire of steps and similar dance routines circulates nationally, and dance practices have become more homogenous. While groups are theoretically distinct, their similarities are striking, not only in the dance steps and choreographies they perform, but also in the matching outfits donned. Zamudio held competition heats in 2009, for example, to amass the best dancers "distinguished by their singularity" to create a National Danzón Company (*Compañía Nacional de Danzón*). His aesthetic choices determined his national standard. Moreover, Zamudio tried to no avail to establish his version of danzón as cultural patrimony of the State of Veracruz in 2010, and meanwhile, he and others in the Port promote a more closed-embrace version of danzón as a marker of the Port's identity to attract tourism and funds.

There were no standard-bearers in Mexico's danzón revival akin to protagonists in standardizing ballroom dance in the United States and the United Kingdom, but comparison is enlightening, despite there being varying degrees of economic motivation and official support in these countries. In the 1920s, with the emergent free-form dances, British dance teachers were afraid that they were about to lose their work and income. So members of the Imperial Society of Teachers of Dancing came together and agreed on a written codification of ballroom dance steps, syllabus, and examination structure, resulting in a national standard that they later promoted as universal (Richardson 1946; McMains 2006). Mexico's dancers have never agreed on a written code of conduct, despite attempts by empire-builders to create national standards; there is no syllabus or examinations; and each has their own pedagogy. In the United States, ballroom dancers built empires around dance schools, such as Arthur Murray's mail-order dance classes and television shows (*the Arthur Murray Dance Party*) (see Malnig 2006; McMains 2006). Yet danzón has received little media coverage in Mexico, and no network of dance schools exists. Danzón empire-builders were simply not able to create national standards, possibly because danzón was not important enough, ideologically (as a Cuban music-dance form) or commercially. Although economics are important in understanding the danzón revival, and institutions are crucial, commercialization was not such a key process at work in the standardization of the dance as it was in Arthur Murray's venture. And despite attempts to make danzón a form of cultural heritage in Veracruz, it is not mediated by strong values of authenticity and tradition.

So how was consensus achieved? To think this through, it is helpful to consider insights from science and technology studies, however far away from dance they at first appear: research in this area has explored how consensus is required for standardization to occur. Latour (1987) argues that the laboratory standards required for Pasteur's anthrax vaccine to work universally were accomplished by building up networks: networks admitted universality, and they were the condition of possibility. Networks have certainly been key to attempts to universalize danzón the dance. As Timmermans and Berg (1997) suggest, however, Latour's analysis gives powerful actors too much weight on two counts. First, Pasteur's efforts should have been located within the broader historical context of attempts to thwart the anthrax disease. Timmermans and Berg assert that "one of the central tensions in creating and achieving universalization is the relationship with past infrastructures, procedures, and practices. Standards will attempt to change and replace those practices but [...] the same standards need, to a certain degree, to incorporate and extend those routines (1997, 274)." More standardized articulations of danzón the dance (the académico style) built on the older, freer lírico style, and on the urge to compete, to publicly perform, and to achieve elegance and accolade.

In their second critique of Latour, Timmermans and Berg (1997) propose that further importance should have been given to the people who were enrolled into, excluded from, uninterested in, or resisted Pasteur's efforts. Moreover, "standardization efforts do not require a central actor—in fact, they often do without it. Achieving universality should be seen as a distributed activity" (1997, 275). Despite attempts to the contrary by Zamudio, Escobar, and others, the danzón revival is best understood as a "distributed activity," rather than merely a top-down process, imposed by a few individuals, institutions, or government.

Mexico's danzón revival has centered primarily around the formation of groups dancing routines of codified steps in unison. These groups learned and developed their steps, directly or indirectly, via Mexico City's champions and *Tres Generaciones*, hubs of power in the emergent national danzón scene. Standards were set and contested at festivals and competitions, and emulated in groups nationwide. Yet danzón groups, founded on both conviviality and rivalry, were created by individuals who, with guile and ingenuity, solicited institutional support (to varying degrees); and cultural and local government institutions that legitimated and supported this practice, and who took advantage of dancers willing to perform for tourists for free, in the Port of Veracruz, at least. And while the opportunities the multiple organized groups and small number of danzón empire-builders gained (in terms of accessing government officials and potential resources) might be construed as generating subaltern empowerment, such claims would be diluted by the clear benefits that danzón practices provided to state institutions in Veracruz (in providing a tourist spectacle).

Revival, Music, and Musicians

In his analysis of the folklorization of Nicaragua's baile de marimba, T.M. Scruggs (1998) argues that critiques of transformations to the genre focused on dancers' movements and clothing, rather than musicians and sound. The same can be said for danzón: dancers and aficionado investigators rarely comment on shifts to the music or impact on musicians. The surge in danzón's popularity, formation of dance groups, and codification of the dance influenced danzón music and musicians in three main ways. First, the number of danzoneras grew to fill the surge in demand, particularly in Mexico City, with the *Danzonera Alma de Veracruz* being municipalized in Veracruz in 1991. But, while there was lots more danzón music work in the early twenty-first century, there was also considerable half-heartedness among the danzón musicians of the Port (see Vignette 2). This related in part to job security (given that the *Danzonera Alma de Veracruz*'s finances were institutionally organized by the municipal council) and the little competition for work, but the lack of interest in performing danzón as a genre by several musicians and the internal dynamics of *Danzonera Alma de Veracruz* and *Manzanita y su son 4* had a greater role to play. The leaders of these groups did not have the willingness of musicians in their ensembles to match the musical, economic, or political ambition of directors like the *Danzonera La Playa*'s Gonzalo Varela (from the village of Paso de Ovejas in rural Veracruz), who gained affiliation to the Xalapa-based Universidad Veracruzana, as well as a national reputation and many one-off gigs (until La Playa split in two in the mid-2010s). While *Danzonera Alma de Veracruz* sounded slightly tighter in the mid-2010s, it remained an institutionally grounded ensemble and rarely sought further commercial work.

Second, the dancers' relationship to the music changed with the revival. In their analysis of translocal music-dance practices, Kendra Stepputat and Elina Djebbari argue that the shift from "'learning by doing' to formalised dance or music classes tends to loosen the structural relation between music and dance" (2020, 14), particularly when recorded music is danced to. While the separation of danzón dancing from live music is mostly limited to group rehearsals in Veracruz, music and dance have become conceptually separated for some académico dancers, particularly novices, with the shift in focus to set steps and routines, rather than merely dancing to the music (danzón lírico). As Scruggs (1998) observed with the folklorization of baile de marimba in Nicaragua, some extant danzoneras began to emphasize musical cues marking phrases and sections in response to the codification of the dance. The *Danzonera La Playa*, for example, began to articulate the beginnings of phrases and sections more clearly so that dancers did not get "lost." Their popularity soared, particularly with dancers of the transformed (académico) style of danzón, who often prefer pieces that their four-bar steps fit neatly into. That is, danzones have eight-, sixteen-, and thirty-two bar patterns without bridge passages, given that bridge passages often de-synchronize dancers' steps from the music if they are not accounted for. *Danzonera La Playa* also released several recordings that were very similar to their live performances, so that if dancers practiced to these recordings, they would not be confounded when dancing to *La Playa* playing live. Older recordings of danzones often omitted all but the first A section of their rondo structure, becoming ABCD, for example, to fit more tracks on records. After the advent of CDs, recordings tended to include the A sections of danzones throughout tracks (such as ABACAD), but Veracruz's *Danzonera La Playa* often repeated these A sections on recordings (for example, AABAACAAD) to align their recordings and live performances for dancers. Meanwhile, other extant danzoneras, such as the *Danzonera Acerina*, continued to focus on musicality, rather than merely dancers' ease in their interpretations of danzones.

Third, most new and extant danzoneras play a core repertoire (at least they did until 2020) that is reminiscent of the 1950s. Pieces in the core *danzón* repertoire still performed in Mexico at the beginning of the twenty-first century include *Almendra,* composed by Abelardo Valdés; *Cecilia,* by Gilberto Guzmán Concha; *Isora Club,* by Coralia López; Mozart's *La Flauta Mágica,* arranged by Antonio María Romeu with Alfredo Brito; *Masacre,* by Silvio Contreras Fernández; *Mi Consuelo es Amarte,* by Leopoldo Olivares; *Mocambo,* by Emilio Renté; *Nereidas,* by Amador "Dimas" Pérez Torres; *Pulque para Dos,* by Gustavo Moreno; and *Teléfono de Larga Distancia,* by Aniceto Díaz, and many more.[14] Although some danzoneras incorporated mambo into their sound in the 1950s and 1960s, notably Carlos Campos's orquesta, danzones in the core repertoire in the late twentieth and early twenty-first centuries did not include mambo-esque danzones.[15] This is partly due to demand: dancers in groups became the main customers of danzoneras and requested a particular canon of danzones that they found easier to perform and that were used for group dance routines.

However, another reason for the continued prevalence of 1950s repertoire was that danzonera directors were rarely composers in the early twenty-first century, as they had been until the 1950s. Instead, anyone with the resources to contract musicians and acquire an archive of scores (not an easy feat, as these are generally unavailable in shops and must be obtained from other musicians or transcribed from recordings), a pair of timbales (small timpani), sound equipment, transport, and ideally promotional recordings, could set up a danzonera and try to obtain gigs. Several dancers have done this, including Miguel Zamudio in Veracruz (with his *Danzonera Tres Generaciones*), and Pablo Tapia, who formed the *Danzonera Yucatán* in Mexico City in 2000. The stasis of the repertoire frustrates some musicians who seek breadth and innovation. The director of a well-known Mexico-City-based danzonera complained to me that it was "boring" playing the same pieces all the time, especially when he had such a large repertoire to draw from. Many older danzoneras have repertoires penned by former directors (or frequently commissioned composers), but there is neither an urge to update these with new compositions and arrangements, nor a sense that certain compositions and arrangements are valued for being "old" or "authentic." Authenticity tropes, when they emerged, related to movement, not to sound (as Scruggs 1998 encountered with the Nicaraguan baile de marimba). Only occasionally are new danzones created, but these rarely update earlier compositional practices and sometimes even take older pieces as their theme (such as Aguilar Alcántara's arrangement of Lennon and McCartney's *Yesterday*). While danzoneras endeavor to create a musical identity for themselves as ensembles in terms of performance practice, and may re-arrange pieces to do this, notions of evolution and modernity are not factors in this process. However, if the repertoire played by danzoneras has changed little in the last few decades, musicians' transmission processes have shifted considerably.

Most musicians play in municipal, naval, or other military bands before joining, and while playing in, danzoneras. Older musicians often learned their instruments through method books and advice from other players, while younger musicians mostly learn to play in music schools (such as the Escuela de Bellas Artes and the IVEC), as well as informally. Rafael Figueroa Hernández implies that band musicians must be taught to play danzones in a way that is not "four-square and articulated like a march" (2007, 78). However, many of the musicians I know who play in danzoneras in Veracruz and Mexico City have a history with these bands, and these institutions are better understood as a vital training ground and source of employment for danzón musicians. In sum, while the dance and social practices of danzón changed substantially from the 1980s, musical practices and repertoires remained remarkably static, despite and because musicians were catering to revivalist audiences.

Conclusion:
Danzón, Revival, and Standardization

I have traced the shifts in power that occurred in Mexico's danzón scene, focusing particularly on Veracruz. In the 1980s, danzón did not re-emerge, for it had persisted, with varying degrees of popularity, throughout the twentieth century, particularly in Mexico City and Veracruz. Until the 1980s, the field was dominated by individual men who gained prestige from being considered the best dancers: they won and judged competitions and taught others. From the 1980s, rescue rhetoric was evoked in Veracruz, Mexico City, and Cuba as a justification for danzón dancers to form officially legitimated dance groups, as well as to fund the promotion and dissemination of danzón to new generations of younger people. Cultural institutions were increasingly decentralized, bringing new opportunities for institutional support and, for very few, a chance to create institutionally backed empires. New pedagogies emerged, and the dance became more codified and standardized. Elegance became increasingly valued, prompting dancers in Veracruz to open out and turn more. The film *Danzón* propelled the popularity of the genre nationally. Tourism to Veracruz was also expanding, and the local government paid for musicians and provided space for dancers to perform. Danzón entrepreneur Miguel Zamudio's activities further contributed to the cultural image of the Port (employed in tourist propaganda). In Mexico City, the national sports federation (CONADE) backed Victor Escobar's Mexican Federation of Dance, a ballroom dance empire (and business) incorporating danzón. Large groups were also set up in and around Mexico City (Xochimilco, Tezozomoc) and in other cities. Empire-builders and institutions facilitated rather than enforced the danzón revival, however. In Veracruz, for example, danzón is sponsored by local government in terms of provision of space, musicians, and other resources, but it is not governed by regulation or even systematic commercialization. More broadly, there was no body or institution that set standards of danzón dancing, despite various empire-builders' attempts to create them: no examinations or examination boards, and few competitions and regulated events. It was groups, transmission processes, and the creativity, stealth, guile, and ingenuity of practitioners that contributed to danzón's surge in popularity and the codification and standardization of the dance—that is, to the danzón dance revival.

In Veracruz, at least, this revival was marked by "reflective nostalgia" (Boym 2001, 50), by a yearning for a past sensed from afar, rather than an attempt to recreate the past in the present in terms of authentic traditions or restorative reconstruction. Elegance was valued more than authenticity by the vast majority of dancers. Danzón thus underwent a non-heritage revival. The formation of groups was prompted largely by rivalries and a desire for accolade: messy, human factors were as much motivations for this revival as the rescue of authentic traditions. Yet rescue and power were not the whole story. People's motivations to dance danzón are myriad, and it was not group leaders and empire-builders alone who effected the codification of the dance and performative innovation; this was not just a top-down affair. Instead, globally circulating aesthetics, individuals' multiple motivations, and groups' flexibility also had important parts to play.

VIGNETTE FIVE

Hettie and Uriel

Hettie was a foreigner. They'd thought it'd be different with her. English. Tall. Pale white skin. Salt-and-pepper hair scraped back into a tight ponytail. Furrowed brow. Jagged scar carved into thick left brow. Gray-blue sparky eyes. Intense stare. No makeup. Slender hoop earrings. Bulbous nose. Full lips. Pink T-shirt. Stubbornly trousered. Cowboy booted. No one could convince her to wear a skirt or heels. Still a student in her mid-forties. Everyone sucked up to her because they want to be in her book. Except Uriel. He'd had enough. Hettie didn't seriously think that she could get away with being in his group and Alejandra's. She even asked Uriel if she could film his rehearsal: "Who does she think Uriel Mendoza is? A chump?"

Uriel. Travolta-like. Hook-nosed. Dark brown, handle-bar moustache over fake grin. Edging on chunky, like his bracelet and fingers. Almost charismatic. Nearly embarrassment-proof. Desperately seeking approval, recognition, respect. Likes women to like him. Hettie doesn't.

When Uriel saw Hettie, she'd already started filming the rehearsal. Uriel pursed his lips: scrunching them forward, making room for his tongue to move, pondering what he should do; how much support he could muster; how his decision would be taken. Up flung his hand like a traffic policeman, palm pushing towards her.

"You're not welcome here, Hettie. You can't film our dance routines. You can't steal our steps. Go!"

Hettie reddened. Bemused. He'd said she could film.

Dropping the camera to her side, Hettie walked out across the courtyard.

The thirty-odd dancers rehearsing halted their practice. Cheeks blushed. Eyes empathized. Backs turned. Uriel continued the rehearsal. Anxiously. It'd worked: the group still responded to him as their leader.

Hettie couldn't afford to be blanked. She came to the danzón event in the main square the next day wearing deep-burgundy lipstick. She walked directly toward Uriel's group, shaking hands with every member, except for him. They all sat on their chairs, some squirming, some delighting in her bravado. She tossed her head, piercing him with her stare. Some smiled. They knew Uriel's antics: being rude to people, lying about them, shouting at them. He'd done it before: to Yolanda, Emilio, and even Gloria when she had cancer, when he was supposed to be looking after her, when they were supposed to be a couple. Hettie was a foreigner. They'd thought it'd be different with her.

CHAPTER FIVE

United in a Vipers' Nest
Group Dynamics, Conviviality, and Rivalry

After I had lived in Veracruz for several months, a seasoned danzón dancer told me: "Almost all of them [dancers] are very conflictive because it's a struggle of all against all, both individually and in groups. It's a war, it's a war of all against all. Danzón dancers are the most conflictive." So what happens in the danzón groups that emerged from the 1980s? By analyzing the quality of group experience, and in particular conviviality, rivalry, gender, and "ability," we gain a greater understanding of the attraction that danzón generates, as well as the tensions groups produce—the forces that keep them together and prompt them to divide.

As we saw in the last chapter, the danzón dance group *Hoy y Siempre* was created as a legitimate structure that could compete with the danzón champion Sigfrido Alcántara. The key dynamic in *Hoy y Siempre* was a collective ethos founded on rivalry, and this dynamic was to be replicated in various forms in the groups that followed. Not all of the Port's subsequent danzón groups were the same, but they all emerged from *Hoy y Siempre,* and in the 2000s and 2010s, danzón groups in Veracruz (and beyond) were organized according to a similar ethos and structure, whether legally constituted as civil associations or otherwise. Groups vary according to the individuals who participate in them at any point in time, but based on interviews and oral histories, certain dynamics have permeated Veracruz's danzón groups since the outset.

In this chapter, I analyze these group dynamics, drawing on Kracauer and studies of Amazonian conviviality. I interrogate the attraction that groups generate, the ambivalences they produce, and the forces that keep them together and that prompt them to divide. I examine group structures, formation, and fissioning; group leadership and how it is achieved, maintained, and destroyed; how hostilities and convivialities regulate groups; the ostracism of group members; and how choreographic knowledge is transmitted and restricted.

Group Structures

When the founders of *Hoy y Siempre* legally constituted their group as a civil association in 1982, they registered not only the club's objectives but also its power structure. Like other clubs in Mexico (and beyond), this Veracruzano dance group was to be run by a directorate, which, according to their statute, consisted of "an honorary president, an acting president, a vice-president, a secretary, a treasurer, a sub-treasurer, a secretary of public relations, a cultural secretary, a coordinator, an advisor; an honour and justice commission consisting of a president, a secretary and a speaker; a fiscal and tax commission consisting of a president, a secretary and a speaker; and finally three speakers who nominate the Assembly."[1]

Of the thirty-one club members listed in this statute, half were on the directorate, together with honorary associates. Like Mexican governmental posts, there would be no re-election to the same post in subsequent terms of office (two years for *Hoy y Siempre*; six for the federal government), and new appointees would be voted in. This one-term rule was adhered to for around six years, but then it lapsed when *Hoy y Siempre* split. All the groups that were to follow created permanent directorates, albeit with only three or four positions, and group leaders became indefinitely installed, theoretically at least. The presidency of groups would usually be assigned to a *maestro*, a man or woman who was "master" or teacher of the group (although not certified as such). Of Veracruz's active danzón groups in the early twenty-first century, the maestro was the president in all cases, and there was a core group close to the maestro who held the other positions in the directorate. *Hoy y Siempre*'s ethos of collective decision-making has endured, and contemporary group leaders take care not to (appear to) be too dictatorial. The directorate, rather than a single person, takes responsibility for ensuring the group's usually unwritten rules are followed.

The ambiguity of these group rules has enabled them to be evoked to both include and exclude group members, and to justify the creation of new groups. *Hoy y Siempre*'s statute includes the following rules: to join, a potential member should be recommended by letter by an existing member and accepted by the directorate and the general assembly; to exclude members, the directorate should have good reason, such as the failure of a member to attend regularly, to pay their monthly subscription, or to abide by the club's "established requirements."[2] Although I never heard of anyone writing letters to enable others to join groups, members are encouraged to attend all group events: the twice- (or thrice-) weekly group rehearsals are considered key; and the Saturday event where groups don their uniforms and show off their dance routines in the Zócalo, obligatory. So too is the payment of subscription charges (around five times the local bus fare per month) and adherence to the group's unwritten established requirements. More specific requirements are not usually clear, and Magdalena, leader and maestra of the Verde group, asserted that her group operated with two maxims: "respect and discipline." Discipline was both social, linked to constant attendance, and physical, in terms of achieving embodied practice, steps, routines. While these are maxims and not rules per se, people constantly told me that danzón should be respected: that dancers should follow the norms of danzón, its structure and moves; they should not be rude to others; and they should dress smartly and be decent. Additional requirements in relation to groups included that people should dance exclusively with other group members (when with the group) and should not interact publicly with former group members who had been ostracized. Some of these requirements were rather vague and involved contradictory principles, for example, being respectful, not being rude, while simultaneously ignoring people when required. The unwritten group rules were summoned only when group leaders or others required them, and they were subject to (mis)interpretation.

The Multiplication of Groups

Let me turn to an incident that exemplifies the effectiveness of the unwritten group rules, both as a regulator of behavior and as a basis for group fission. Angela, a member of the Rojo group, got drunk at a private party hosted by a rare, rich danzón dancer from the state capital, Xalapa. Parties of this kind are rare in Veracruz, and this was a danzón party par excellence, with *Danzonera La Playa* playing and several of Mexico City's danzón champions and groups from other cities as guests. For the Rojo group leader, Magdalena, the presentation of her group was important at this event. Women rarely consume alcohol at Veracruz's danzón events, and when Angela became tipsy, Magdalena reprimanded her for her drunken behavior, stating that it contravened group rules. While Angela apologized and remains in the group, the event prompted the group to break apart, and about ten members left. Whether these members actually agreed with Angela or Magdalena is unclear, for their disgruntlement at Magdalena's invocation of group rules in this context seems to have been more of an opportunity to justify their departure than the actual cause of it. Their departure had been brewing for some time. It centered around Julio, a municipal council officer in his mid-fifties who would become the maestro of the new group, and a character I will refer to throughout this chapter. Julio had already clashed with Magdalena's dance partner, Flavio, claiming that he was a better dancer than Flavio. It is noteworthy that Julio chose to clash with another man, rather than with Magdalena, the group leader. Flavio had suggested that Julio leave and set up a group on his own, unintentionally sowing the seeds for the fission that was to follow. While Flavio had intended Julio to set up with new people, Julio sought allies from within the group.

It is worth considering this story and group fission in relation to Kracauer's essay on "The Group as a Bearer of Ideas," which, although over eighty years old, does provide poignant insights. Kracauer discusses two forms in which groups split, the first grounded in ideological differences, the second more pragmatic. The first form (which chiefly concerned Kracauer) occurs after a group is set up to champion an (often political or religious) idea; the idea is subsequently partly achieved; and the group divides into two (one more moderate, the other "radical," adhering to a utopian vision of the original idea). But the splitting up and re-forming of groups does not provide a solution: groups continue to feud with each other, particularly if they are what Kracauer calls "sibling groups" (1995a, 163), with common origins in a single idea, rather than merely two different groups with ideological differences. While Kracauer suggests that his first form of group splitting is more prevalent (and I discuss it further below), his second form is also common with danzón groups, applying when a group dissolves and new groups immediately are created. Here, "various opinions regarding the group's practical influence on reality had already developed secretly, while the old group existed. The group entity breaks apart because of tactical considerations, but the members adhere steadfastly to the idea itself" (1995a, 161). This is what appears to have happened with the Rojo group: a "sibling group" (1995a, 163) developed secretly from within.

When the Rojo splinter group detached itself from Magdalena's main group, they chose to take the group's name with them, since it had not been legally registered. The splinter group consulted a lawyer and created a civil association, Grupo Rojo A.C. (the A.C. denoting civil association), registering the group's name as their own. They then took a copy of their statutes to the IVEC (Veracruz's cultural institute) and the municipal tourist department, possibly in the hope that they could replace the original group in their rehearsal space at the IVEC and their slot in the rota for groups that exhibit in

Veracruz's main square. Miguel Zamudio of *Tres Generaciones*/CNIDDAC was also informed, for he invites local groups to participate in his annual danzón forum. Yet the splinter group did not inform the original group of their actions. In the end, the splinter group did not manage to replace the original group's activities, but they did take the group name. So Magdalena had to find a new name for her group, which became the Grupo Verde. Magdalena continued as maestro of this now smaller group, and slowly, new people joined. Julio's new Rojo group had to find a rehearsal space for themselves, buy chairs, and create new routines. Since Julio, the new maestro, worked for the municipality, he used his contacts to secure them a rehearsal space in a municipal building patio and a slot on the rota of dancers who perform on the stage of the main square on Saturdays. Julio's group slowly built up a set of routines and bought chairs using money from the group's monthly subscriptions fund. Of all the group fissions I heard about, this was the only case of a name being stolen. This might have been partly the idea of Eduardo, who became president of the new Rojo group (with Julio as maestro), for Eduardo had previous experience setting up groups. Eduardo had been president of an early Veracruz danzón group, formed part of a subsequent early splinter group, and been the romantic partner of the first president of the Rojo group in the early 1990s. It is striking that Eduardo rather than Julio, the new maestro, became president of the splinter group. With Eduardo as president, the new group asserted its collectivity, rather than their simply following Julio as an individual. They thereby maintained the ethos of rivalry and collectivity established by *Hoy y Siempre*, from which the original Rojo group had spawned in the early 1990s.

So far we have seen that rules were evoked by both Magdalena and the splinter group to justify their actions. Magdalena wanted to maintain the reputation of her group, while the splinter group had been secretly plotting. The desire for legitimation of the splinter group prompted their registering the group, and its name, as a legal civil association. The "theft" of the original group's name was probably an attempted coup by the splinter group, trying to replace the original group and claim it as their own, thereby displacing Magdalena as leader. This coup failed, however, and from one group, two spawned. Name theft is unusual, but from what I could glean, the other elements seemed to be fairly common in the formation of Veracruz's danzón groups. While people were happy to talk about leading large groups and exhibiting, they were less keen to discuss why groups had disintegrated. For example, the new Rojo group was fairly stable for a couple of years and grew, but then broke apart. The dancers who followed Julio and Eduardo to form the new Rojo group were their romantic partners, and people who admired Julio's dancing. Several of these people secured roles in the new group's directorate. Raquel, Julio's romantic and dance partner, discovered she had stomach cancer two years later, and Julio promptly finished their relationship. Raquel remained in the group at first, but she left after Julio became romantically entwined with another group member. Several group members, including Eduardo, left, purportedly in disgust at Julio's behavior, and a few months later, these dancers created a new group, Grupo Amarillo, with Raquel as maestra.

Transmission and Restriction of Knowledge

The transmission of music and dance is often gendered, such as when men or women learn to play certain instruments and/or sing and/or have different dances. For example, transmission can be restricted to certain families, as it is in North Indian *gharanas* (musical houses) (Neuman 1990); or it can be reserved for those considered sufficiently "talented" to perform it, as in European heritage classical music (Kingsbury 1988; Nettl 1995; Bull 2019) and ballet (Wainwright, Williams, and Turner 2006). The transmission of danzón the dance in Veracruz includes several of these elements. It is gendered, as are most Latin American couple dances, and while danzón the dance is not restricted to families, maestros' romantic partners often excel (and occasionally, so too do their children, such as Miguel Zamudio, who eventually took over the group *Tres Generaciones* from his mother, Rosa Abdala Gómez, when she died); and although, theoretically, anyone can learn danzón, and many older people told me they joined the dance precisely because it is slow enough to dance with ease, not everyone achieves (or aims to achieve) a sufficiently "good" level of performance to become a maestro. There is usually a division between maestros and the rest: the often-charismatic maestros are expected to excel choreographically; they are supposedly the "best" dancer, the exemplar of the group, setting standards and teaching them to the rest of the group. But there is always the threat that some group members might be plotting, attempting to break away from or dethrone the maestro.

So how do maestros manage choreographic knowledge? Literature on apprenticeship provides insights to help us understand how choreographic knowledge is both transmitted and restricted. Like apprentices (see Coy 1989b; Herzfeld 2004), dancers in the Rojo group, for example, were not usually formally taught by the maestro (Julio) but learned by watching and by doing. Julio led the rehearsals and focused on routines, dictating sequences of steps, rather than how to perfect these steps. Some danzón maestros proactively taught more than Julio, but in his group, novices were taught the basic steps by other group members at the back or side of rehearsal spaces, and then they were encouraged to try to dance the group's routines in the central area with the rest of the group. Most Rojo group members (like the Cretan artisanal apprentices described by Herzfeld, 2004) then turned to other more experienced members (apprentices) for help if they required explanation or were confused, rather than to Julio, the maestro. Group members also taught each other in their homes, and even when maestros, such as Julio, gave individual lessons to people, the focus was on learning routines rather than perfecting steps. Completion of learning was marked by performance of routines and seldom continued from there. Once in the performative spaces of danzón events in plazas, group members would either dance the routines they knew (if the appropriate piece of music was played), or would dance freely, combining académico steps in known or invented sequences. Teaching seldom took place at danzón events (although people continued to learn from dancing with and watching others), and people were not instructed as to how to dance freely.

Dancers and musicians rarely suggested to others how they might improve unless asked. Rodolfo, a percussionist, explained this to me. He asserted that he had refrained from informing another player, who played danzón in a salsa style, how to perform "correctly" because "you have to appear humble, able to appreciate everybody else and respect authority." There are resonances here with the Aymara music groups, analyzed by Turino back in the 1980s, where confrontation is avoided and "equality of opportunity is given precedence" (1989, 4). But unlike Aymara musical logics, where any man in the community can perform with a music group at any time, particularly during important public performances at fiestas, such a communal ethos does not apply to Veracruz's danzón groups and music-making: who may or may not publicly perform with Veracruz's music and dance groups is more limited. Whether Rodolfo's silence was an attempt to appear humble or protect his own knowledge (and surreptitiously boast about it) was unclear, but the point is that such reticence reinforces and perpetuates differences in performance ability.

Several scholars (such as essays in Coy 1989a) suggest that apprenticeships ensure continuity of knowledge, yet they simultaneously provide the greatest threat to controlling that knowledge, for they create competitors. While danzón maestros want their groups to perform to the best possible standard, this creates a tension with the maintenance of their power (and thus, potentially, static ambivalences). How do they teach others while ensuring that they remain the best dancer? Maestros need good dancers to perform as a group with, but seldom do they try to teach more advanced dance movement.

Thus, few dancers end up knowing how to dance as well as the maestros, who thereby preserve their positions. The exceptions are maestros' dance partners, with whom they must excel, and whom they make a special effort to coach. Julio told me: "*Me gusta lucirme y me gusta lucirlas para ser una buena pareja*" (I like to shine and I like to make women shine to be a good partner). It is maestros' partners (men or women) who mostly end up taking over or creating new groups (when the often romantically entwined couple splits up or the maestro dies), but given the small number of groups, there are only a handful of maestros' partners. Danzón transmission has parallels with apprenticeship, which, Marchand argued in rather functionalist terms, "acts as a valve to regulate the numbers permitted access to this realm of specialized knowledge" (Marchand 2001, 136). Some dancers, such as Julio, mastered dancing well despite the regulatory "valve" (Marchand 2001, 136), but access to group leadership is limited.

Buechler (1989) describes how Bolivian apprentices need to acquire their own tools and clients to break away. Similarly, dancers need a network of potential group members, and they have to foster relationships with the local authorities (for example, with the director of tourism to allow them to enter the exhibition rota and store chairs). Attempts at creating new groups sometimes founder, such as when new leaders emerge but are not followed by sufficient numbers of others to create a group. Moreover, new maestros need to create routines, and while creativity is encouraged among group members, dancers are not instructed as to how to create steps, and innovations are often disparaged for incorporating moves from other genres. It is maestros who (supposedly) maintain a creative role, "inventing" new steps and routines. That said, small differences are sufficient to assert uniqueness, and new routines often consist of a new ordering of standardized steps (as we saw in Chapter 3). Copying is disparaged, but I heard of several maestros copying steps and routines from videos they acquired from Mexico City. Guile and artfulness also have roles to play.

Apprenticeships teach people how to learn, as well as specific skills, Esther Goody (1989) proposes. In his study of Cretan artisans, Herzfeld (2004) suggests that apprentices learn by craftiness and guile: their indifferent body language masks their intense interest and engagement with the activity they are observing. I discerned similar behavior from Julio when several of Mexico City's champions came to Veracruz for carnival. For once, he did not dance but walked around, watching their every move with apparent disinterest. Overall, his artfulness has rewarded him, for he has had his own (Rojo) group for years, which he acquired by secretly plotting from within and gaining support. But success is rare, and only a handful of dancers have achieved the status of group leader. Of those that have since lost their groups, most are extremely quiet about it. As *Tres Generaciones*'s first leader, Rosa Abdala Gómez, is renowned to have said: "*Lo difícil no es hacer un grupo sino mantenerlo*" (what is difficult is not making a group but maintaining it) (Figueroa Hernández 2007, 65).

Envy and Power

A word commonly bandied around in Veracruz's danzón arena is "envy." While this envy often related theoretically to knowledge of steps and routines, in practice, people rarely invent new steps, and it was the ability to dance and to gather others to create a potential group that might dethrone that mattered. Ex-group leader Norma told me:

Hay muchas envidias, mucha discolería, todo mundo se siente superior a todos. "No, yo soy más que ella." "No, yo soy campeona." "No, porque yo esto." "No, porque yo lo otro."

There is lots of envy, lots of waywardness, everyone feels above the rest. "No, I am better than her." "No, I am a champion." "Because I this." "Because I that."

Envidia (envy) and *soberbia* (arrogance/pride), the feeling of being above others, were often evoked together, as we see in this quote. Arrogance involves both gloating about oneself and feeling lesser in relation to others one is comparing oneself with: it involves the static ambivalences of combining both high and low self-esteem. Envy combines not only discontent at one's own situation, but also a longing to have what another person has (such as possessions or an ability to dance). It may seem less surprising that arrogance and envy are brought together if we consider Sianne Ngai's argument that "it is through envy that a subject asserts the goodness and desirability of precisely that which he or she does not have, and explicitly at the cost of surrendering any claim to moral high-mindedness or superiority" (Ngai 2005, 21). It is as if arrogance may serve as both an antidote to and provoker of envy. Moreover, envy is thus inherently ambivalent in that it combines the desire for what another has with feeling bad about feeling envious. This is static ambivalence around feeling bad and not, and a utopian ambivalence around a longing disrupted by possession (here, parallels exist with the utopian ambivalences of reflective nostalgia discussed in Chapter 2). As Ngai contends, "envy is, in a sense, an intentional feeling that paradoxically undermines its own intentionality" (2005, 21). Moreover, danzón dancers' narratives implied that the act of provoking envy made people more likely to be described as envious. Unsurprisingly, no one I spoke to claimed to feel envious themselves, and instead it was something others were accused of. People constantly gave me examples of other people who were envious. They pointed to rivalries between dance groups and between individual dancers, to people's ability to dance, as well as to love interests.

I was often told how, for example, Julio was *envidioso* (envious) and excessively *soberbia* (arrogant/proud). Although for many people, Julio transcended acceptable levels of behavior, others admired him, including those in his group, as he was happy to tell me:

> *No es porque yo me quiera alabar, pero la verdad yo he sido uno de los mejores bailadores de aquí, lo mejor. No lo digo yo, lo dice mucha gente, y turismo que llega a filmarme.*
>
> It's not that I want to praise myself, but I have been one of the best dancers from here, the best. It's not just me who says it, many people do, and tourists come and film me.

Julio points to his fans and tourists to corroborate his boasting about the image he wishes to create of himself. Moreover, his status as one of the best dancers and as group leader gains him applause; makes him attractive to women; bestows him with respect; and legitimates him to dictate what "good" dancing consists of, to earn money from teaching (routines) and putting on shows, to social climb, and to access local functionaries in government and cultural institutions. Julio always grinned as he danced, seeking attention from other dancers and facing the tourists rather than the musicians, creating a spectacle of himself and his group, but rarely making his dance partner *lucir* (shine). Julio's critics accused him of dancing like a *payaso* (clown), overly inflating his sense of self and the worth of his performance. Here, the accusation of being envious was applied to someone in (or seeking) power, to a group leader. More generally, such accusations applied to those who were involved in past or present intrigues, relating to groups, sex, or money. People were usually accused behind their backs. They were accused of being envious of potential equals who might encroach on their territory; access something they (might) have (their reputation, success, happiness); threaten their position (as group leader); or be considered a better dancer. But envy was also applied more generically, and I was warned that anyone might be involved in hostilities. Several times it was alluded to me that envious people were engaged in witchcraft, and I accompanied a danzón practitioner to a Catholic healer to dispel the curses they thought had been placed on them. Given their request for confidentiality, I have not written about this (but see Flores Martos 2000; 2004; and Argyriadis 2013 regarding witchcraft and santería in Veracruz).

It is insightful to consider these envies and hostilities among danzón dancers in the context of the poet Octavio Paz's famous (1963) essay, in which he argues that Mexicans are the offspring of the *chingón* (literally "the male fucker"; a term epitomized by Hernán Cortés and the conquistadors) and the *chingada* (a passive female who is "fucked," like the indigenous woman named Malinali, fucked by Cortés, who became known as "La Malinche") (see Franco 1999 for a historical analysis of the story of La Malinche). Rowe and Schelling (1991) propose that Paz attempts to create a psychology of the nation, adopting "a style of decontextualized universality, common until [the 1990s] among Mexican intellectuals" (1991, 66). But as Gutmann propounds, "self-fulfilling interpretation is an issue not to be overlooked" (1996, 269): it is hard to tell to what extent Paz's essay was descriptive and to what extent it has been prescriptive of how some Mexicans would come to see themselves. The choice between "*chingas o te chingan*" (fucking over or being fucked over) was often repeated to me in Veracruz (renowned for its "bad" language), particularly in relation to leading groups. Paz's essay only touches on the surface of the richness of the contemporary usage of the multivalent verb *chingar*, currently applied to both men and women, and applied both negatively and positively (to someone or something very successful).

Veracruz's dance-group maestros (and band leaders) have to be alert not "to be fucked over." They must be aware of potential plotting and of potential competitors (*chingones*) and dispel problems before they escalate. If leaders themselves become arrogant or authoritarian, group members may think that they are *chingones*, wanting "'to fuck them over." Leaders must manage potential *chingones* but also not appear to be *chingones* themselves for, ultimately, groups are founded on the premise that the collective ethos must (appear to) override rivalry. Again there are resonances with Aymara music groups, where the group leader (*guia* or "guide") "must deserve respect because of his ability, but he himself can not publicly stress or emphasize his abilities. [...] The moral authority granted the *guia* is dependent upon an implicit consensus among the musicians rather than on any basis of actual independent power" (Turino 1989, 16, 17). As we saw above with Julio, danzón group leaders can stress their own abilities to some extent, but this must be corroborated by other group members. If danzón leaders are unable to fulfil their role appropriately, or become excessively arrogant, their leadership may be challenged by a new rival who, together with other group members, will "fuck them over," splitting away to create another group. That said, groups tend to last for years rather than months, and people endure substantial authoritarianism before they snap: over the first two years I was in Veracruz, only a single new group was formed (Raquel's Amarillo group, which had split away from Julio's Rojo group), and there was one failed attempt at creating a fission (also in Julio's group). But why will people put up with so much? To grasp this, we have to understand why people who are *not* interested in being "the best" dancers join and stay in groups; we must turn to the collective ethos that prompted the formation of *Hoy y Siempre*, an ethos founded on conviviality.

Conviviality, Hostility, and Ostracism

Danzón groups primarily met to dance, but they also came together for other social events: they marked members' birthdays by bringing food and cake to the danzón event in the Plazuela de la Campana; the members of the Verde danzón group who could afford it met regularly for coffee after danzón events; and more generally, group members often developed friendships beyond the danzón scene, visiting each other's homes, meeting for breakfast, and developing work relationships (such as doing odd jobs, building work, or sewing for each other). It is insightful to consider danzón groups in relation to Goffman's "teams": "Among team-mates, the privilege of familiarity—*which may constitute a kind of intimacy without warmth*—need not be something of an organic kind, slowly developing with the passage of time spent together, but rather a formal relationship that is automatically extended and received as soon as the individual takes a place on the team" (1959, 88, my emphasis). Goffman exemplifies this familiarity by referring to business associates who act as a "performance team" in a sales pitch. This form of intimacy is particularly appropriate to the way newcomers are welcomed into danzón groups, instantly being treated with familiarity. Yet the conviviality encountered in Veracruz's danzón groups also often involves warmth, between some members at least, and is a prime motivation for membership for many dancers. This convivial familiarity has greater social significance than the mere symbolic performance effected before an audience that Goffman describes, but this too can be important (as we saw with Magdalena's response to Angela's drinking above).

While the intensity of conviviality varies within (and among different) danzón groups in Veracruz, it is often the most intimate relationships that provoke hostilities. The English use of the term "conviviality" denotes joviality, feasting, and festivities, or "cohabitation and interaction," as Gilroy (2004, xi) employs it in relation to multicultural, postcolonial Britain, where "the strangeness of strangers goes out of focus and other dimensions of a basic sameness can be acknowledged and made significant" (2004, 3). The (Mexican) Spanish verb *convivir* (which, like the English, has the Latin etymology "to live with") incorporates these English usages and a potential intimacy: for example, *conviviendo*, spending time (sharing life) with one's children. Overing and Passes's (2000a) anthology concerning conviviality in Amazonia contains insights for understanding danzón groups in Veracruz. In Amazonia, they argue, conviviality encompasses humor, banter, bawdiness, friendship, care, compassion, generosity, harmony, and the sharing of affective, intimate relationships (Overing and Passes 2000b, 15). Santos-Granero argues that in what he refers to as "our society" (2000, 283), quarrels with colleagues and neighbors may result in interactions ceasing, but they do not routinely prompt people to leave their house, job, and friends. However, ceasing to interact is impossible in the Amazonian Yanesha communities that Santos-Granero analyzes, where "conviviality also entails strong feelings of love, friendliness, trust and generosity" (2000, 283). A rupture of such intense feelings motivates people to move away. It is kin, rather than outsiders, that pose the biggest threat to conviviality, for here, the level of intensity is greatest. I would add that when romantic partnerships split up in the United Kingdom (and beyond), similarly intense feelings often prompt people to leave their house, job, and friends.

The point is that, as Santos-Granero argues, *intense conviviality may generate equally intense discord* (anger, hatred, guilt, and shame), qualities that disrupt conviviality. This principle holds the key to understanding the ebb and flow of Veracruz's danzón groups. Santos-Granero proposes that there is an optimum point for conviviality when Amazonian Yanesha communities are growing, with intimacy "and commonly held ideals still very much alive" (2000, 283). But, he suggests, ideals of "the perfect conviviality carry the seeds of their own destruction" (2000, 283), since population growth usually increases competition, triggering frictions and eventually unresolved conflicts and settlement fissioning. Likewise, smaller danzón groups are often fractured by growth and the associated potential of subgroups and increased competition. Santos-Granero concludes that in Yanesha communities, "it is a doomed struggle from the beginning for conviviality begins to wear out as soon as it is achieved" (2000, 284). In these contexts, conviviality is an ideal that both incorporates the promise of love and is disrupted by everyday discord. Utopian ambivalence is inherent in such intense conviviality.

In Veracruz, conviviality is productive in both a positive and negative sense, encouraging members to join danzón groups and prompting fission and ostracism. This conclusion is quite distinct to the rational-choice model of (religious) group behavior proposed by Iannaccone (1998) with regard to ostracism of members from religious sects (see also Lehmann 2010). While in both danzón groups and Iannaccone's club-like sects, enthusiastic participation by all members is actively encouraged and inputs into the pleasure and edification of other members, Iannaccone argues that "free-riders" (1998, 1483) undermine the viability of a club's conviviality and collective aims. He suggests that: "apparently gratuitous sacrifices can function to mitigate a religion's free-rider problems by screening out half-hearted members and inducing higher levels of participation among those who remain" (Iannaccone 1998, 1483). Even if we ignore the rather functionalist overtones of Iannaccone's argument in suggesting that ostracism contributes to group cohesion, it is rarely "free riders" who are excluded from danzón groups. If people can dance well and contribute to the group's public exhibitions, they are often encouraged to participate, even if only sporadically. Meanwhile, those who are ostracized tend to be the people most actively involved in group activities, the people most intensively convivial with the group leader, for intense intimacy is potentially volatile.

Let me turn to an example. The first ostracism I encountered was Gonzalo's. A retired public accountant in his early sixties, Gonzalo always went to danzón events with his wife, Marcelina, who had mild learning difficulties and could be a little brusque. Gonzalo and Marcelina attended all the Rojo group's danzón events, arriving at least an hour early at the Zócalo events, where they guarded the group's chairs. On one occasion, Marcelina had a contretemps with Valeria, a street vendor, over a chair, and on hearing about this, Julio, the maestro, took umbrage. Julio was concerned about the impact Marcelina was having on the group's appearance. When Julio was asked to take a subgroup on a trip to another town to do an exhibition, he asked Gonzalo to come without his wife. Gonzalo objected and told Julio that he was leaving the group. With the support of his closest allies in the directorate, Julio subsequently summoned all the group members during a rehearsal to inform them that Gonzalo had chosen to leave the group without giving a reason and was rudely ignoring them. Julio, in his role as maestro, instructed the rest of the group not to talk to Gonzalo or dance with him anymore (since Gonzalo was supposedly not acting convivially). Those present who did not know Gonzalo well (like me at the time) had no reason to doubt the maestro's version of events. And to those who were close to Gonzalo, or with more experience of Veracruz's danzón group dynamics, the maestro was, in Goffman's terms, "staging a definition of the situation […] so that [a teammate] can play his part on the team and feel part of it" (1959, 93). Julio could be charming when he chose, but lying was not that out of character. Even if certain group members did not believe the maestro's version of events and the reasons given for Gonzalo's expulsion, the fear of their own ostracism deterred them from acting independently, so they went along with the group line. A static ambivalence was provoked between staying quiet and standing up for Gonzalo, and potentially being ostracized from the group themselves. On this occasion, all the members of the group chose the former option and behaved as instructed by Julio: they stopped speaking to Gonzalo, ostracizing their former friend.

The British term "blanking" refers to the act of deliberately ignoring someone and not looking them in the eye. Danzón events in Veracruz's Zócalo are rife with acts of blanking, as well as warmth and conviviality. It was not until I experienced blanking firsthand, several months after Gonzalo's ostracism from the Rojo group, that I got a deeper understanding of the process. For my first few months in Veracruz, I focused on the one group, but as I began to give more attention to other groups, their maestro became increasingly disgruntled (see Vignette 5). After a month's absence, I asked permission to film a rehearsal. Although I had been told by the group's treasurer and secretary that the maestro had approved this, when I arrived, the maestro sent another member to ask me to leave, as I might steal some of the group's steps with my camera (despite my having filmed in the past and their not actually inventing any new steps). I was then blanked by the thirty members of the group: they turned their faces and carried on rehearsing. The next day, furious, I dressed particularly smartly, applied some lipstick, and went to the Saturday danzón event in the Zócalo. Rather than choosing to ignore this group, I approached them and greeted every member with a handshake—all, that is, except the maestro. It took several months before he and I would acknowledge each other's presence again. But it was enormously insightful, if unpleasant, to experience blanking at firsthand. From then on, outside of group situations, some members would individually approach and talk to me, but others would not look me in the eye for some time to come.

Until that point, people had been reticent to talk to me about themselves or others being blanked or ostracized from groups, but after I was blanked myself, several dancers (including Gonzalo) opened up about partaking in both sides of the process. The blanking pattern is usually: The blanked is accused (generally falsely) of being rude, disrespectful, or undisciplined, and a web of untruths is then created to back up the accusation (by the maestro and directorate). The blanked leaves the group, with or without a struggle, and may (or may not) persist in the danzón scene, where they will have to endure (re)occurrences of the blanking process by a (sometimes uniformed) group of thirty or more former companions. The blanked can no longer participate in the group's conviviality and routines and is unlikely to wear the group's uniform again. Moreover, the dance routine becomes a hostile act in these circumstances: thirty or so uniformed people performing a dance in unison, in which the blanked knows all the moves but can no longer participate.

While danzón groups provide a wonderful opportunity for conviviality, fear of ostracism and blanking operate as powerful regulating forces, often bestowing the group's leader (and theoretically the directorate) with substantial power. Moreover, it is at times of crisis that the rather vague, unwritten group rules are invoked by group leaders (and directorates) to assert power. The existence of group committees is used to depersonalize decision-making, shifting responsibility away from the individual (maestro or president) to the directorate (and thus the collective) to expel members. It is fairly common for Veracruz's danzón groups to exclude members and to fission.

Kracauer (1995a) and psychoanalysts who studied groups, such as Wilfred Bion (1961), following Melanie Klein (1975; see also Hinshelwood 1989), imply that a third party is involved in group dynamics. For Kracauer, the "original idea" acquires agency: "if a group entity cannot bear to live constantly under the sign of the idea, then the latter, betrayed," becomes attractive to others who form new groups (1995a, 167). For psychoanalysts such as Bion (1961), it is unconscious psychic processes pertaining to the group as a whole, rather than individual members, that acquire (usually destructive) agency. Bion gives agency to the group, bestowing it with a psychology as if it were an individual. However, as Georgina Born (1995) points out, psychoanalytical interpretations of group behavior often fail to account for broader socio-historical processes. Instead, if we assign conviviality as Kracauer's "original idea" and contextualize group dynamics within broader ideological frameworks (as Berlant 2006; and Illouz 2012 do in relation to love), we can see that at both the individual and the group level, it is *the intensity of conviviality* (and thus potential hostility) that is key to danzón dance group dynamics, and that potentially makes these groups doomed from the outset (as Santos-Granero, 2000, suggests in relation to Yanesha communities). An ideal of conviviality, a collective ethos and rivalry, were inherent in the very structure of Veracruz's danzón groups from the outset, and they continue to produce utopian ambivalences and the seeds for potential fission.

I hope it is now clear that Veracruz's danzón groups must be understood within the context of rivalries, conviviality, and the wish for legitimacy, the motivations that prompted the formation of Veracruz's first group, *Hoy y Siempre*. These desires have been translated into group maxims, "respect and discipline," for a disciplined, académico style of danzón is what is considered most elegant in group contexts, and social disciplining within groups is epitomized by the notion of respect. Moreover, if we recall the curbs on creativity and innovation discussed in Chapter 3 and combine these with the notions of respect of discipline—which were sometimes used by group leaders to control group members—we begin to get a picture of how aesthetic and social policing (through the threat of ostracism) feed into reproducing the standardized dance, where innovation is encouraged within narrow parameters.

Yet there is a further tension between competition and other motivations, such as conviviality, that attract the (mostly older) dancers to groups. After several people had been ostracized from the Rojo group, it was hinted to me that Julio, the maestro, did not want older people in his group: those excluded, for example, Ramiro, who had a bad leg, and octogenarian Patricia, did not dance to the standard Julio desired. But they were also very close to Julio: he visited Patricia's house on a daily basis, and Ramiro was the group secretary. Their conviviality was intense, and humiliation signaled betrayal. Other group members would have considered it completely unacceptable for Julio to ostracize these members on the grounds of their age and dancing abilities, going against the maxim of respect, of conviviality. So Julio provoked situations where these members left for other reasons: he humiliated them and they left, betrayed. Patricia, a retired accountant aged eighty-three, spoke to some former members of the group (including Gonzalo) during a Saturday Zócalo danzón event and was chastised by Julio for "not setting a good example." She felt humiliated and stopped attending danzón events, despite the pleas of several group members. Patricia would not tell the other group members what had happened, fearing she would be blanked, and instead claimed that she had stopped dancing due to ill health. Despite being scolded by Julio, she was concerned about speaking badly of him to other group members, since she might then be accused of being rude and disrespectful. Notions of respect acted as a regulating, disciplining force in this context, for Patricia preferred not to dance (or speak out) than risk being blanked and blemishing her reputation within and beyond the danzón sphere.

Patricia's response (and Veracruz's blanking, conviviality, and envies more generally) chimes with research on Mediterranean "honor" and "shame" from the 1980s and 1990s. Michael Herzfeld argued that the notions of shame and honor relate to social rejection and inclusion, self-concealment, and self-protection: "'Shame' centers on the revelation of matters considered as unfit for wider consumption [...]; 'honor' has to do with the aggressive presentation of an idealized self" (1987, 64). While earlier studies (such as Peristiany 1966) had tended to align honor with men's public personae and shame with women's sexuality, Lila Abu-Lughod (1986) proposed that such dichotomies were idealized constructs that were both respected and resisted in practice by women and men. And Jane Sugarman (1997) argued that for

Prespa Albanians, honor "may be thought of as a person's sense of self that develops largely through one's perception of how one's actions are received by others. [...] a person becomes 'honorable' by acquiring a practical, lived mastery of the Prespa *sistem*" (1997, 187, 88). While the term "honor" is rarely used in Veracruz, "decency" is often alluded to in ways that chime with some of this literature on the Mediterranean. Patricia's decision not to reveal her humiliation revolved around her managing a tension between honor and shame, between decency and humiliation, so as to deflect stigma and hurtful gossip. Herzfeld propounded that "the contrast between display and fear of exposure undergirds both 'honour' and 'shame'" (1987, 65), which suggests that the tension between honor and shame can provoke static ambivalences, as can the dynamics of envy. For example, Julio's presentation of himself as one of the best dancers produces such a tension, for dancers know they risk humiliation should they set themselves up as something they are not, but if others believe them, they achieve "the aggressive presentation of an idealized self" (1987, 64). Moreover, I was told by an older woman with regard to her sexuality: "It's not what you do that matters, but what you appear to do." Richard Sennett argues in regard to respect that "self-respect founded on craft cannot alone generate mutual respect" (2003, 263) but must be contextualized within social relations to appear. Likewise, decency in Veracruz is not founded solely on personal behavior but is materialized in social contexts. In Goffman's (1959) terms, it is presenting a performance of the self (and the group) that manages to convince that is pivotal.

Conclusion

In this chapter, I explored how groups facilitate things for older women in particular: leadership in groups (and occasionally in the dance); a space of empowerment in a public place, even if constrained to some extent by appearances and reputation. For most of the fifty-plus-year-old newcomers to danzón (men and women), groups provide a legitimate structure in which to meet and learn to dance with several others at a prescribed distance and with prescribed physical contact, but still enjoy the tactile nature of the dance, being touched and touching other human beings (with or without sexual overtones). Groups enable members to get out of the house (daily), socialize and find conviviality, to wear elegant uniforms, to learn steps and (potentially challenging) routines, to perform these with others in public and on a stage, and perhaps become a part of the directorate or occasionally travel to dance in exhibitions beyond the Port. Surprisingly few people in Veracruz referred to danzón, or the faster son cubano, as a form of exercise.

Not all danzón dancers are interested in competing, in becoming champions or group leaders. Only slowly do they become aware of the vipers' nest I have described, slowly becoming enmeshed.

Group dynamics added a new kind of competitiveness to danzón in Veracruz from the 1980s: there was no longer just "presentation of the self" (Goffman 1959) but also presentation of the group. Most of Veracruz's danzón groups are highly competitive, in part because they are all "sibling groups" (Kracauer 1995a, 163), breakaways from each other often founded on envies and each defining themselves in relation to the others. Members of several groups told me that their group had better dancers, better technique, more steps, better dance routines, more elegant "uniforms," and more "educated" (and thus prestigious) members than other groups. Size matters, and group leaders like to have large groups elegantly dancing their routines in unison. While some of the groups contain the odd graduate (*licenciado*) and engineer, they also all have members who are fairly poor. Unlike the "third age" clubs in Normandy analyzed by Okely (1990), where animosities were based on class "distinctions" (Bourdieu 1984), class is not an obvious marker of difference in Veracruz's danzón groups, and such claims often say more about the snobbery of the contender than the makeup of groups.

But Veracruz's danzón groups must be understood within the context of rivalries, a collective ethos, conviviality, and the desire for legitimacy. The ambiguity of the mostly unwritten group rules enables them to be evoked to recruit and ostracize group members, to justify the creation and fission of groups. Decision-making is depersonalized through group structures. And the threat of exclusion operates as a powerful regulating force, empowering the group leader, and potentially also the directorate. The desire to be in a group, to enjoy conviviality, is a strong motivating force for many group members, and I proposed that in Veracruz's danzón groups, conviviality is productive in both a positive and negative sense, welcoming and embracing new members into danzón groups and also prompting ostracism and group fission. While, as the saying goes, intimacy breeds contempt, intimacy also involves love: intimacy is inherently ambivalent. And here it is group members who become entangled in the utopian ambivalences of intimacy, for the ideal of conviviality is disrupted by envies and rivalries, prompting volatility, ostracism, and occasionally groups to split and new groups to form.

But what of the dancers who choose not to (re)join groups? Since the 1980s, many dancers who at first danced danzón lírico turned to the académico style, so that they could participate in groups, and because they considered académico to be more elegant. But I would estimate that around a quarter of dancers perform some kind of danzón lírico. Some have always danced danzón lírico and others have returned to it, having spent time in groups dancing académico, and later leaving to dance independently with or without regular dance partners. Most of the oldest dancers were not in groups, although many had passed through them. Yet some people who had been ostracized from one group insisted on joining another, as I explicate in the next chapter.

VIGNETTE SIX

Carmen and Ernesto

(fiction)

Carmen: tall, thin, muscular, despite her seventy-four years. Dyed brown, finely bouffant hair, the odd curl escaping. Elegant, closely fitted red dress, patterned with marigolds; scarlet sleeves cut from shoulder to elbows, revealing well-formed biceps and lightly wrinkled arms. Delicate wedge-heeled sandals with thin, red, fabric straps. Pale face smoothed with foundation. Piercing brown eyes, underlined black. Red lipstick. Overlapping teeth. Oyster-white cascading earrings with matching necklace and bracelet. Pink manicured nails clutching a fan of undulating white lace feathers and hard plastic base.

Ernesto. A gawky seventy-two. Wrinkle-carved, light brown face. Too thin for his carefully pressed guayabera and white trousers. Graying, badly cut hair brushed around protruding rounded ears. Narrowed eyes: left side wandering. Bitty, gray, mean moustache under strong nose. Tight lips over veneered teeth. Big smile. Gnarled, sun-soaked hands crusted from decades on building sites. Short, clean nails. Rarely worn, white lace-up shoes.

After six years of romance, Carmen and Ernesto were still an uncomfortable pair. They feigned happiness in public. She dictated their moves, trying to control appearances: what if people knew, of his drinking, his violence. But if she left him, they might think she was loose, available.

When her husband Diego died, Carmen couldn't wait to get out. Out of the house, out of his world, away from those people. She'd married him for his looks and money, and forty-seven years later, she was free. Free to drink coffee with girlfriends, travel. Her best friend, Jazmin, had started dancing danzón. She urged Carmen to join her dance group. Carmen was hesitant: the workers in her husbands' business had performed danzón; they might even see her. But Carmen was also excited. She longed to be touched. So she went to the danzón class with Jazmin. There she danced with a stranger who pushed her around, making her trip clumsily, off the beat: she longed for the music hissing from the ghetto blaster to end, to go back home. Then Jazmin insisted they go to the Parque Zamora.

Eucalyptus. Green. Brown. Dusty gray. Trees and dancers encircled the bandstand, a trumpeter wailing out of tune lead the danzonera. People dressed in their finest. Carmen approached. Yearning sonorities filled her every cell, urging her to dance. Exhilaration! Then she saw him: Ernesto. Drunk, with stale clothes and stench. She never understood what it was that attracted her so much: the music, the potential for movement bristling through her limbs, his smile. He'd staggered toward her carefully, asked her to dance, and she'd surprised herself by accepting. She blocked her nostrils and tried to focus on other bodily sensations: his hand cupping the small of her back, gently guiding her with thumb and mid fingers; his sand-blasted hand against hers; the tension in the fifteen centimeters that separated their torsos; their legs as one. They danced. Slightly awkwardly. She tried to guide him and he followed. Willingly. Fluently. The next day, she bought him new clothes.

CHAPTER SIX

Loving Ambivalence

Dance Groups, Amorous Encounters, and Aging Bodies

In this chapter, I explore perceptions of danzón as an older people's music-dance form, denials of this, and of older age; the tensions that the emergence of the more disciplined style of dancing created when performed by older bodies; what groups enable in terms of amorous encounters; and women's romantic lives beyond marriage, men's potency, and shifting mores over the life course. I interrogate how older danzón practitioners negotiate intimacy, notions of decency, and gossip both at and beyond danzón events. Ambivalences pervade these relationships, and I point to some of them explicitly. Finally, I reflect on gender in Veracruz's danzón scene in relation to María Novaro's film *Danzón*.

Denying Old Age? *Un Baile de Viejitos?* (An Old People's Dance?)

Beyond Veracruz's culture industries, danzón is envisioned as an older people's dance in the broader Mexican popular imaginary. This imaginary is sustained by the large number of older dancers, but it is not a view shared by performers. Some younger dancers asserted that danzón was *un baile de viejitos* (an old people's dance), before promptly denying it and pointing to the number of younger practitioners. A first reason why performers do not associate danzón with old age is that danzón is and has been performed by people of various ages throughout its history, despite the preponderance of older practitioners in the last few decades. As we have seen, in Veracruz, Mexico City, and other urban centers, younger people perform danzón, and there are a few danzón groups dedicated to young people (and occasionally children). Besides these groups, however, younger danzón dancers tend to be few and far between.

A second explanation as to why performers do not portray danzón as an age-related phenomenon is that danzón has never been a genre marketed solely toward particular age groups or youth cultures. Danzón was initially popular before the mid-twentieth century, when genres associated with youth cultures gathered global momentum. The idea of youth is a culturally specific and relational category, often allied to generation rather than being determined by biological age, and thus, it can be prolonged into mid-life and beyond (as Hodkinson and Bennett 2012; and Bennett 2013 explore). Moreover, numerous music genres have acted as markers separating generations. Unlike the United Kingdom and the United States, where mid-twentieth-century youth cultures tended to be associated with the lower classes, Zolov demonstrates how, in Mexico, it was the middle classes that initially took on the often-defiant mores associated with youth. For example, rock and roll (youth music par excellence in the United States) was merely another dance genre consumed by lower- and middle-class adults in Mexico City's dance halls, initially at least, only later becoming associated with urban youth (Zolov 1997, 201).

One reason why Veracruz's practitioners are unwilling to categorize danzón by age, I suggest, is that this music has no history of being a genre ranked in a hierarchy of generations. In Veracruz (as elsewhere), music-dance forms were separated to some extent by age in the early twenty-first century: beyond family parties, reggaeton, for example, was associated with younger people, while danzón was linked to an older public. These age-related associations were often mapped onto venues (younger people tended to go clubbing, while older people danced in public open spaces); times of day (danzón events occurred in the early evening, while younger clubbers went out much later); and, more broadly, understandings of older and younger people's amorous lives (see Aguirre Aguilar 2008 regarding young people and love in Veracruz). Danzón events are not aimed at older people. They provide a space for people of all ages to meet, dance, listen, and watch a phenomenon associated with the Port of Veracruz, albeit mostly dancers under twenty-five and over fifty. The conspicuous lack of people aged twenty-five to fifty exacerbates the notion that some dancers are "younger" and others "older," creating a clear-cut generational divide, even where several generations are represented.

A third reason for negating the association of danzón with older people, I propose, is that few dancers in Veracruz relish or aspire to being "old." Understandings of oldness are key here and have also contributed to danzón not being considered an older person's music-dance form by habitués.

To group people with ages spanning almost half a century into *viejitos* (old people) creates a dilemma: age differences are not clearly defined in discourse or practice, and the relative and contextual nature of age (Kaufman 1986; Thompson, Itzin, and Abendstern 1990, 127) is particularly brought to the fore. Few of the dancers I know aspired to or relished becoming (or being) "old." The notion of being "of the third age" circulated in Veracruz (as it does beyond), and some older dancers used this terminology. The idea that "aging equals decline" (Gullette 2004, 7), as opposed to progress, was hegemonic in Veracruz (as it is in the United Kingdom, the United States, and more globally). Akin to Degnen's (2007) findings in the United Kingdom, in intragenerational settings, few people described themselves as old (given its negative connotations), instead ascribing the term to others, either in jest or when someone's social comportment and mental acuity were open to question. Intergenerational ascriptions were more common: younger people joked that danzón was *un baile de viejitos* (an old people's dance), a joke sometimes shared with and told by older people. Younger dancers, such as those in *Tres Generaciones*, expressed surprise that they had become interested in danzón, having stumbled across the group, and commented on having to explain themselves to their peers at school and university. Rather than being biologically determined, or applied to the self, oldness was predominantly a (social) quality ascribed to others. And as Esposito (1987) has argued, ageism is distinct from (US one-drop rule) racism and sexism in that, if the perpetrator lives long enough, they will become the subject of discrimination. People may be ageist to themselves and/or others, even if they are older, in the same way that Mexicans may be racist and subjected to racism, as Moreno Figueroa (2011) has argued. Thus, a potential fluidity exists between perpetrators and victims of ageism, racism, and other forms of discrimination, where people may occupy both positions in distinct contexts and internalize discriminatory practices (Pyke and Dang 2003). Ultimately, aging creates dialectic ambivalences around becoming old (being neither young nor old, or being contextually one and/or the other), akin to the racial ambivalences discussed in Chapter 1. And, like the utopian ambivalences of love, the dialectic ambivalences of aging reproduce gendered inequalities where men tend to be bestowed more status than women and to maintain more prestige in the public sphere (carrying over from their working lives, if retired).

Despite negations that danzón was an older people's dance, danzón does enable things for older dancers that other genres do not. Danzón is a fairly slow dance that can be achieved even when performers have slightly restricted movement. One seventy-four-year-old man commented that he enjoyed danzón as he was no longer nimble enough to dance the mambo he had in his twenties. That said, many older dancers recounted how their favorite part of danzones was the slightly faster final *montuno* section (taken from son cubano). Some dancers were frustrated, however, that they could not do things the way they had when they were younger. Ramiro, for example, found it frustrating that he could not turn as he would have liked because of the pain in his legs. And Marianita, his partner, bemoaned finding it difficult to remember the large numbers of steps in group dance routines. Other new dancers, however, were proud to learn large numbers of new steps at a time in their lives when they might be thought to be less mentally adroit than they had been in their youth. In a phenomenological exploration of learning to hand drum, Shawn Lindsay (1996) has argued that one becomes particularly aware of one's body as one attempts to learn something new and difficult (like hand-drumming), only for such bodily awareness to disappear once the skill has been acquired and as new senses are foregrounded. But, while this may apply to an able, younger body, awareness of the body increases with age, as Jean Améry argued back in the late 1960s, until one is "only body and nothing else" (Améry 1994, 41). While such awareness limited and frustrated some of the dancers aged seventy-plus (like Ramiro), others opted to risk their bodies for the sake of the dance in their negotiations of their changing bodies. Gabriela, aged eighty-two, was so thin she was almost skeletal and came to danzón events only occasionally with her seventy-six-year-old partner, Martín. She had danced tango as a young woman and always donned her faded red tango dress, the loose threads of its tassels often accentuated by the breeze. Gabriela had a bad heart and had been told by her doctor that she should not turn when she danced for fear of death. Yet she did. She wanted to dance and to live, and she preferred to risk dying dancing rather than not to dance at all. But Gabriela's and Ramiro's difficulties dancing were not shared by everyone their age, and some people their age excelled on the dance floor.

New Generations, Danzón Académico, and Older Bodies

While some older dance champions from Mexico City are revered, their dancing is idiosyncratic, and there is tension between the demands of the newer, more disciplined, danzón académico and the older bodies of the majority of its performers (who have not danced danzón their entire lives). Since most danzón dancers are under twenty-five or over fifty, with almost no participants in the age range between, many people made generalizations about younger and older dancers, without making clear distinctions between people grouped into these huge age categorizations. Many people told me it was easier for younger people to learn danzón and routines, as they are "young sponges," unlike older people (and it was particular people over seventy who were imagined in such descriptions). The notion of the body as a sponge, as something that can absorb and be manipulated, chimes with the late-eighteenth-century notion of the soldier's body described by Foucault: in the early seventeenth century, a soldier was expected to already have an appropriate "bodily rhetoric of honour," but by the late eighteenth century, the soldier's body became something that could be disciplined "out of a formless clay," something "docile," skillful, and technically equipped for any demand (1977, 135). The bodies of all those who performed military service were collectively coerced.

Similar ideas can be applied to contemporary ballet dancers: Wainwright and Turner (2006) draw on Bourdieu's notions of "habitus" (1977, 82)—the internalized social structures that determine individual action—and of history being incorporated into the body, to argue that "ballet training produces a 'ballet habitus'" (Wainwright and Turner 2006, 241). The notion that danzón académico training produces a danzón habitus might be applied to younger dancers in Veracruz, particularly those in the group specifically for young people, *Tres Generaciones*, whose pedagogy is much more didactic (and geometric) than that of other groups. While younger danzón dancers' bodies were described as potentially malleable, capable of easily absorbing the technical demands of danzón académico, there was a sense that older bodies no longer had sponge-like capacities. There is no notion of older people being unable to dance danzón, however, or of necessarily dancing "worse," as there is in ballet.

Age does not theoretically determine whether danzón dancers are considered better or worse, but the exemplars of the more standardized danzón in Veracruz are Miguel Zamudio's group of younger dancers, *Tres Generaciones*. It is generally easier for younger people to dance in the more codified, disciplined académico style, and members of *Tres Generaciones* usually achieve a collective standard of performance considered extremely "elegant" (an important marker of "good" dancing). The excellence of this group gives Zamudio and Veracruz a national reputation for danzón performance. That said, *Tres Generaciones* rarely frequented Veracruz's regular danzón events and merely represented the Port at danzón festivals. Many members of *Tres Generaciones* stopped dancing danzón when they went to university, got married, or moved away, but they return to represent the group by dancing routines in the annual danzón forum. I was told that some members of *Tres Generaciones* had tried to set up groups in the past but failed because they did not have the networks of potential dancers who might join them, or access to the institutional backing achieved by Zamudio (who frequently gives the young members of his group opportunities to work with him for the IVEC). *Tres Generaciones* was both exemplary and exceptional, due to the young age of its dancers, their highly disciplined danzón performance, the group's institutional grounding, and their national profile.

Danzón performance requires not only musical and choreographic knowledge but also *cadencia* (cadence/rhythmic movement). Cadencia involves the subtle movement of the hips, a movement particularly associated with Veracruz and the circum-Caribbean, and Veracruzana/o danzón dancers are quick to remark that "the movement of the hips should never be exaggerated" (Alcántara in interview with Trejo 1992, 49). I was told that Veracruzana/os had cadencia, but other Mexicans did not, because Veracruz and its people were Caribbean (a notion that has been particularly promoted by Veracruz's cultural institutions since the 1980s). Women from Veracruz were referred to in terms of racialized "decency," reaping the benefits of being "a bit hot," purportedly due to having some "black blood" (as discussed in Chapter 1). A certain amount of sensuality and sexiness is valued in danzón performance, and it is older people in particular whose bodies tend to bear incorporated sexual histories (both personal and social). As Bourdieu points out, different generations have different forms of habitus, such that one generational group may "experience as natural or reasonable practices or aspirations which another group finds unthinkable or scandalous" (Bourdieu 1977, 78).

What is important here is that a theoretically level playing field is set up for dancers of all ages in which an aesthetic of disciplined danzón académico is valued, and promoted by empire builders such as Zamudio, and in which younger dancers are emerging as "better" dancers. But, although younger people dance "elegantly," they do not exude sexual experience and cadencia: they have a distinct, more standardized aesthetic. If *Tres Generaciones*'s younger, more disciplined académico style is one representation of the Port and its danzón (to the national danzón scene in particular), then the image of older people dancing provides another. It is the predominantly older people who dance (in groups or independent couples) in Veracruz's main square, in the académico and lírico styles, and who are the focus of Veracruz's tourist gaze.

Amorous Encounters and Dance Groups

I have already touched on some of the factors that attract dancers to danzón: the wish to dance, watch, listen, and meet others, including romantic partners. So how do older men and women's sexuality and notions of decency operate in this context? I focus here on heterosexuals, as no danzón performers came out to me. It was several months into this research before I realized that hardly any married women regularly attended danzón events. Despite initial claims by various couples that they were married, I later discovered that most were not. But rather than creating a transgressive, non-reproductive sexual arena, social mores were generally reproduced and reinforced by such pretences of marriage. Moreover, most women do not dance publicly during their married lives (except with family members at parties), instead performing before they marry and after. Married couples were equally scarce. Most of the lower-middle-class women who attended Veracruz's danzón events were widowed, separated, or divorced, and few of these women had married more than once, mostly bringing up their children during this period. Although appearing open to all, the arena of danzón was not accessible to most of the Port's married women. Thus, the Port's danzón events are spaces where women who are newcomers tend to be single, creating a highly sexually charged context and hugely affecting how this genre is gendered. And while many men who join danzón were also widowers, divorced, or separated, a significant number claimed to be but were not.

Let us consider the example of Ramiro, a confident, quiet, portly man, with pale skin, thinning hair, and a well-kept moustache, who usually wore a panama hat, a beautifully pressed white guayabera shirt, dark trousers, and comfortable shoes to danzón events. Born in Guanajuato in 1935, Ramiro moved to Veracruz in 1964 (aged 29) to work on the railways and started a family. Once he retired in 1996 (aged 61), he took up temporary work in a hat shop and decided to take a course in "folkloric" regional dances, learning to *zapatear* as well as to dance salsa.[1] In 2003, one of Ramiro's hat-shop customers suggested that he also learn danzón. So Ramiro joined a dance group and began to perform danzón regularly. A year later, in 2004 (aged seventy-one), he went to a birthday party where he met Marianita, a fifty-four-year-old nurse with short, dyed-blond hair and bright makeup: they fell in love. Ramiro told me (and Marianita, who was sitting with us as we spoke) that he regarded himself as being very constant: with his work, his family, his children, and with Marianita. Although Ramiro did not mention being married, I discovered later that he lived with his wife but did not bring her to danzón events. I had been frequently advised, particularly by women, that it was common for Veracruz's men to have affairs and leave their wives at home: "Veracruzanos have a wife, a *querida* [female lover] and also a *querido* [male lover]."[2]

This setup might at first appear like a version of the *casa chica* (little house) described famously by Oscar Lewis in *The Children of Sánchez* (1961), where a man provides (housing) for his wife *and* his mistress (and their children). However, as Gutmann (1996) points out, the *casa chica* is more of a myth than a reality (in the lower-class Mexico City colonia of Santo Domingo he writes about, at least), arising from Catholic marriage laws that bar divorce. While couples married by the Church may separate, Catholicism dictates that as far as God is concerned, they are still married, so subsequent relationships are often defined as extramarital affairs. Thus if a man leaves his first wife and moves in with a second "wife" (even marrying her legally), this may be dubbed a *casa chica*. Gutmann argues that the *casa chica* "frequently refers to serial monogamy, and if adultery occasionally occurs, it does so within *this* context" (1996, 140, his emphasis). In Veracruz and its danzón scene, the principle of serial monogamy certainly had a part to play. Several men (and their lovers) justified their extramarital relationships by suggesting (to me at least) that since they did not have sexual relations with their wives, they were not being unfaithful: serial monogamy remained the central moral force, but it was premised on sexual activity. Where serial monogamy was not practiced, "adulterers" were frowned upon. For example, one danzonero was criticized when he argued that he provided for his wife economically so could do as he chose.

Ramiro and Marianita's relationship proved an interesting gauge of morality. Dolores, a widowed danzón dancer in her eighties (and an ex-member of the Rojo group), intimated to me that Ramiro's wife was very ill and maltreated him, which was why he was with Marianita. Dolores felt ambivalent about this but decided to befriend Ramiro and Marianita. She recounted disapprovingly, however, that Marianita was having an affair with a taxi driver, and she expressed sympathy for poor Ramiro. But when, several months later, Dolores met Ramiro's wife at a breakfast and discovered she was extremely pleasant (and not that ill), she changed her tune, condemning both Ramiro's depiction of his wife and his infidelity. Whatever the realities of this situation, the point I want to make is that infidelity was condemned within the constraints of a notion of serial monogamy premised on sexual activity and reputation. To maintain a decent reputation, people have to appear monogamous, and their decency must be contextualized and constantly (re)created within social relations to be sustained. If not, they may be considered a *cabrón* (or a *cabrona*, a more recent version of the term applying to women). The multivalent term *cabrón* literally refers to a he-goat, but it is commonly used to denote someone savvy, good at misbehaving, at cheating (on) others, likely to *chingar* ("to fuck others over"). A close friend and dancer warned me: "*No te confías de nadie hija. Acuerdate que aquí son bien cabrones, son unas hipócritas, cuidate.*" (Don't confide in anyone. Remember that here people are very *cabrones*, they are hypocrites, be careful.) There was a sense that all social relationships, and particularly amorous encounters, were potentially volatile.

So how do these amorous encounters relate to danzón groups? Groups provide legitimate structures, supported by government institutions, in which to perform danzón; they provide structures in which group members are encouraged to dance and practice routines with each other. Ramiro and Marianita, for example, had been through several groups, and I was unclear why. Ramiro joined a danzón group as a novice in 2003. But he clashed with the maestro, so he left a few years later and immediately joined the Rojo group. He proudly told me that he has participated in both state and national events (such as Zamudio's annual Danzón in the Port Forum) and traveled with the group. He liked the Rojo group, the learning, the conviviality, the music. Danzón was also a therapy, he suggested, for his bad knees. By 2006, Ramiro was secretary of the Rojo group, supporting Julio, who was by then president. Ramiro and his partner, Marianita, were among the core members, religiously attending the rehearsals and all the danzón events in the Zócalo, and also the monthly celebrations of group members' birthdays and trips to exhibit. But in 2007, Ramiro and Marianita left the group after Julio, maestro of the Rojo group, teased Ramiro about not being able to turn properly (because of his bad leg). Ramiro took offense and left the group, but Ramiro and Marianita immediately positioned themselves with another group, (Raquel's) Amarillo group, and subsequently joined (Magdalena's) Verde group (which they had not previously been members of). I was perplexed for a long time as to why Ramiro and Marianita (and others) joined new groups, especially after being blanked, rather than dancing independently, like other non-group dancers, for they continued to dance together at every event in the Zócalo. Were they seeking the solace of other former members of their group by moving to a recent sibling group? Although Ramiro and Marianita shared with me their anger and pain at leaving Julio's group and their ambivalence about group dynamics, they told me they sought conviviality and really wanted to be in a group. It transpired, however, that they also had other more compelling reasons. As well as being settings for dancing and conviviality, groups also provide a formal setting in which sentimentally entwined couples can be together without too much explanation (I use the term "sentimental partners," rather than romantic partners or lovers, as this was the preferred term by various locals).

Drawing on Star and Griesemer's (1989) analysis of how standardization is produced where distinct motivations are at play, I propose that Veracruz's danzón dance groups act as "boundary objects": "objects [that] are both adaptable to different viewpoints and robust enough to maintain identity across them" (Star and Griesemer 1989, 387). It should be noted, however, that while the notion of a boundary object is useful to think about in this analysis of danzón dance groups, this concept has been critiqued for eliding cultural, classed, and linguistic differences and power (see, for example, Dar 2018). In Star and Griesemer's example, the boundary object was a method: natural history museum scientists sought to co-opt amateur naturalists to collect animal specimens in a way that was standardized and disciplined, yet not so detailed or "overly-disciplined" (1989, 407) as to interfere with their camping trips or discourage them.

In the case of danzón, the group forms the "boundary object": the object that encompasses the motivations of competitive empire-builders, group leaders, younger dancers (under twenty-five), and older people (over fifty) seeking conviviality, love, dance partners, staged performance opportunities, and elegance. It is groups that transmit the more standardized danzón, but danzón pedagogies have not become "over-disciplined", deterring people less interested in or able to perform high standards of danzón académico from participation. Instead, groups have encouraged thousands of fifty-plus-year-olds to join the dance and perform choreographed dance routines of standardized steps in unison. Groups have also deterred others from dancing in this style—people who no longer wish to deal with group politics. And still others, like Ramiro and Marianita, have chosen to tolerate the potentially conflictive dynamics of groups where greater motivations necessitate that they maintain some form of group membership. Some of these people who are blanked by particular groups hold their heads up high and continue to frequent Veracruz's danzón events, either participating independently or joining new groups.

By meeting Marianita in a group setting, rather than independently, Ramiro could justify dancing with Marianita publicly (in the Port's main square, no less) by simply stating that she was another group member; he did not go to meet Marianita per se but went to fulfill his obligations as a member of the group, particularly when he was secretary of the Rojo group. For Ramiro and Marianita, being in a group was key to enabling Ramiro to conceal his romantic relationship with Marianita from his wife, family, and others (theoretically, at least). Reputation relates to both group membership and amorous encounters, and particularly where these intertwine, blanking has different impacts on different people, depending on what else is at stake. Ramiro's reputation beyond the danzón scene outweighed the unpleasantness of being ostracized by a former group, and as soon as they left one group, he and Marianita joined another so they could be together. Marianita had told her children that she was with Ramiro, but some women I knew withheld such information from their families.

We must remember that danzón and son cubano events take place in prominent public spaces, making people's relationships there public, yet there are rarely public displays of affection (unlike the occasional kissing in Mexico City's semi-public dance halls). Many women (and some men) told me that they take care with whom they dance with and how, so that other people do not think they might be with someone. A woman dancing with a younger man will often detract gossip, given a presumption that younger men are not interested in older women. However, the converse is the case only when the age gap is much greater (and it is usually only extremely "good" male dancers who dance with much younger women). Women in groups dance (in theory, rather than practice) with all the men in their group (justifying their dancing with any man) and vice versa, whereas non-group women tend to dance with one or several regular dancing partners. The distinction between dancing partners and lovers is often unclear and the subject of speculation and gossip. Men will ask the permission of a woman's regular dancing partner before asking her to dance, often unaware whether they are lovers. Once rejected, a man will rarely ask the same woman to dance again, so a woman has to judge carefully whether to accept. Even if she wants to dance with this man, she may decide it is not worth it in terms of the presentation of her self and having to negotiate gossip.

Taking a married man as a lover is a precarious act, for a woman risks tainting her reputation if the man appears to be cheating on his wife and family, acting as a *cabrón* (as Dolores intimated was the case with Marianita and Ramiro). Moreover, the Catholic Church prohibits (what it views as) adultery, and some priests forbid "adulterers" from taking Holy Communion, both a spiritual and a public act. It is women who bear the spiritual well-being of most families and who visit church most, so it is women who are more likely to make their adultery public through not taking communion (and lying to God was not an option for the Catholic women I knew). One woman told me that she was thinking about leaving her sentimental partner but was afraid it would mean she could no longer dance. She did not want to subject herself to (potential) gossip and be left without a dance partner. To appear "decent," she told me that she did not want to be seen moving from man to man and dancing with someone who was not her long-term sentimental partner.

Although some people gossiped, most were generally accepting and convivial with others, despite their affairs, that is, unless they were more intimately involved. It was not always clear what was going on, and whether people were or had been sentimentally and/or sexually entwined. The intimacies that some dance partners share, the knowledge of each other's dancing bodies, remain on the dance floor, while others also know each other as lovers, friends, acquaintances, or otherwise. Sexual and sentimental relationships, past and present, were often veiled in silence. Several (older and very few younger) women confided in me that they had had amorous encounters with male dancers, that these had ended, and that the men now frequented danzón events with other women. Many people enjoyed recounting the well-known saying "*lo bailado, nadie te lo quita*," (what you have danced, no one will take away from you): while you might repent, what is done is done, and already danced. Moreover, people will generally "forgive but not forget," I was told: after "falling out," people slowly begin to talk to each other again and sometimes regroup with the very people who blanked them. However, it remains striking how many people in Veracruz danzón circles do not talk to each other, given initial impressions of conviviality, impressions exploited in tourist and municipal propaganda of the Port. Several people enjoyed telling me that they were "*unidos en un nido de víboras*," united in a vipers' nest ("united" punning ironically with "a nest"). Most people, including musicians, dancers, regular onlookers, and me, were entangled in this nest, entangled in the animosities and rivalries, the blanking and politeness that combined with the joyousness and conviviality of Veracruz's daily danzón events. Although there was gossip, there was also a considerable amount of discretion (or what might be considered collusion) and plenty of ambivalence, for many people had histories of their own—histories that they preferred to remain quiet about.

Romance, Danzón, and Older Age

Given interest in sexuality in Latin America (e.g., Balderston and Guy 1997; Hirsch 2003; French and Bliss 2007; Wade 2009), it is striking how little attention has been paid to older people's romantic lives beyond marriage, to how older Latin American women and men create new ways of being, new identities, and new sexual selves. Where older people have been foregrounded, the focus has largely been on heterosexual women's romantic and sexual lives when young (and procreation was an issue), courtship, the onset of marriage and child-rearing, or older people's attitudes to contemporary young people's lives, rather than heterosexual and LGBTQ+ older people's current sexual practices, their affective attachments, women's apparent independence, and the desire of some adult children to regulate their aging parents' lives. An exception is Emily Wentzell's ethnographic study of erectile dysfunction in a urology department of a hospital in Cuernavaca, Mexico, which provides deep insights into shifting masculinities, aging, and illness, and is complemented by this analysis of the negotiations around older men and women's sexual lives in the danzón sphere. Here, I touch on issues of sexuality and widowhood, men's potency, and the power of children in regulating their parents' lives, areas that require further investigation, together with the other issues I raise.

Analyses of relationships between aging, music, and dance are creeping onto the academic agenda. For example, Schwaiger (2012) and Martin (2017) address this in relation to ballet and contemporary dancers who are usually expected to retire in their thirties; Bennett (2013), Hodkinson, Bennett et al. (2013), and Jennings, Gardner et al. (2016) analyze the shifting lifestyles and values of aging hippies, rockers, punks, and clubbers; Fairley explores music and aging in relation to the Buena Vista Social Club (2009). The few investigations there have been of older people and dance (Cooper and Thomas 2002; Paulson 2005; Thomas 2004; Amans 2013; Skinner 2013) neglect sexuality and intimacies, however, and in other dance scholarship, older women are mostly de-sexualized. In her study of Greek dance, Cowan describes an older woman as "a large ship," dancing with "the qualities of gravity, grace, and a controlled yet undeniable sensual power" (1990, 195), implying that unlike younger women, older Greek women do not have to grapple with balancing the choreographic demands of moving sensually and potential accusations of flirtatiousness. And Savigliano (1995) implies that older Argentinian tango dancers are only desirable as dancers, rather than sexual partners. Savigliano denies the sexual desire of older women and relates older men's desire for older women as homosocial (displaying their competence to other men rather than women), leaving little space for sexual relationships involving older people. Sugarman (2003) discusses shifts in what is acceptable for Prespa Albanian women to do—instead of being objects of men's desire, women become subjects of their own sexuality and sensuality—but implies that different standards apply to different age groups. She focuses on women nearer the beginning of their sexual lives (where virginity and legitimate reproduction are concerns), rather than shifting mores over the life course *and* distinct standards being applied to older women. The scenarios above are strikingly different from what is happening in Veracruz. The sexuality of grandparents and great-grandparents has mostly been elided in the literature, but notable exceptions include Bosse's (2015) ethnography of ballroom dancing in Illinois, in the United States, which addresses older women's sexuality positively, and Hutchinson's (2016) analysis of Dominican merengue típico. Hutchinson argues that, particularly in her older age (seventy-plus), famed merengue típico accordionist and singer Fefita La

Grande challenges hegemonic gender stereotypes by wearing tight clothes, singing with a raspy voice (considered masculine), and assuming a sexual, assertive stage persona. Fefita has paved the way, Hutchinson propounds, for more subversive gender performances among merengue típico performers. Older women's sexuality in danzón practice is not as transgressive or public as Fefita's.

While the publicness of danzón events participates in (re)creating a local "tradition," the question of the opportunities they may offer for newfound romance and sex is rarely raised. Beyond danzón and son cubano events, few opportunities exist for fifty-plus-year-olds to find new partners outside of their existing networks. That danzón spaces are sexual arenas was effaced by the tourists I spoke to who watched them, and even by some academics. Such notions reinforce ideas of the longevity of relationships, together with stereotypes that older people do not have sex lives or embark on new romances (especially post-menopausal women and impotent men). In her article, "The Mexican Danzón: Restrained Sensuality," Cashion states that "What is missing, however, is the romantic fire of the younger dancers [...] danzón seems to attract married couples enjoying a night out with the added benefit of cardiovascular exercise. Although seniors' bodies are no longer supple and their hand gestures are arthritic, there is a smile on their lips and joy in their movement" (2009, 250). Yet of the only three actually married couples I knew who had been together for many years (rather than pretending to be so), two told me how danzón had reignited their sex lives, while another pointed to how it had prompted their separation (as the woman left for another man). Had Cashion interrogated the "restrained sensuality" in the title of her essay further, she might have gleaned that the dancers were not married to each other, and the "smile on their lips" required investigation.

Madrid and Moore propose that "Mexican danzoneros refer to their enjoyment of the dance as *cachondería*: an experience of subdued lust" (2013, 19), yet this was not a term that I heard danzón practitioners in Veracruz employ. Madrid and Moore state that *cachondo* "is an elusive term [...] and is about subdued lust" (2013, 192), yet it may also be translated as "horny." When I quizzed Ciro Carlos Mizuno Guzmán (a danzón aficionado-investigator who has spent many years in Mexico City's dance halls) about this in 2018, he responded:

> *La palabra cachondo es un especie de grosería. Y él que empezó a decir esto fue Jesús Flores y Escalante en sus libros que publicó. Pero el danzón no es un baile cachondo: quiere decir erótico, ¿no?, que de acoso sexual vaya, y eso es mentira. El danzón se baila con respeto a la mujer, pero no es un*

> *baile cachondo, ni erótico para producir una relación sexual porque se baila pegado. Pero esta mal conceptuado lo del cachondo.*
>
> The word *cachondo* is kind of rude. And the person who started saying this was [another danzón aficionado investigator] Jesús Flores y Escalante in his books that he published. But danzón is not a *cachondo* dance: it [*cachondo*] means erotic, right, sexual harassment, and that's a lie. Danzón is danced with respect for women, but it is not a *cachondo* dance, nor erotic leading to a sexual relationship because it is danced close together. But it's misconceived the *cachondo* thing.

Mizuno Guzmán had a somewhat competitive relationship with Jesús Flores y Escalante (as I discuss elsewhere; Malcomson 2014a), yet it is noteworthy that he rejects the idea that danzón is cachondo. I also asked another danzón practitioner, a woman in her seventies, about the term, and she responded:

> *El danzón puede ser sensual, pero no es cachondo. Cachondo es mas como alegre o placentero, algo agradable. Cachondo no lo asocio con lo sexual.... Para mi, el danzón es un baile elegante, sensual. El danzón no genera mas que el gusto de baile, no la pasión. Y el montuno es mas cadencioso, pero no es sexual.*
>
> Danzón may be sensual, but it's not *cachondo*. *Cachondo* is more like happy or pleasant, something nice. I don't associate *cachondo* with the sexual.... For me, danzón is an elegant, sensual dance. Danzón does not generate more than an enjoyment of dancing, not passion. And the montuno is more cadenced/rhythmic, but not sexual.

Here, she rejects that danzón is cachondo and downplays the idea that danzón might be sexual, but in this instance, the term *cachondo* is associated with "something nice," rather than the sensual. The jury is thus out on whether danzón is cachondo (Madrid and Moore, 2013, claim that it is, while the danzón practitioners I consulted suggested it is not). But in the last instance, what I want to highlight here is that, regardless of whether danzón is conceived as sensual, erotic, or respectable, danzón events are places where older people (spanning ages from late-forties to mid-eighties) often find sentimental and sexual partners.

Notions that older people are "past it" circulate not only in academia but also in Veracruz's danzón circles. Carolina, a seventy-eight-year-old great-grandmother who lives on her widow's pension, met Pablo, 84, a retired builder, ten years ago and became sentimental partners shortly afterward. She told me that she lost seven years of her life after her husband died, for she did not realize that she could have a sentimental partner again. Several women commented that the majority of the men were sexually "useless" because of their age, but that did not seem a deterrent (regardless of whether they used drugs such as Viagra). One man joked that he was a member of the Club de los Pájaros Caídos (the "Fallen Cock's Club"), which issued certificates to members and had its own *décima* (verse of ten octosyllabic lines), composed by Félix Martinez González (see Figure 6.1): this was his way of informing men and women of his situation and former sexual prowess, suggesting he had already had more than his fill of sex and used up all his potency. It was his way of encouraging women to approach him should they be interested, and they did.

Although (widowed and divorced) men were often open about seeking sexual and/or sentimental partners, women were generally more discreet, as women's reputations could be more easily sullied, and women had more to lose if they appeared promiscuous. One woman told me: "*Te buscan más (los hombres) siendo mujer que señorita, porque saben que te pueden chingar. [...] Cuando eres viuda, todos se te acercan*" (Men look for you more once you've been married, as they know they can "fuck you over." [...] When you're a widow, all the men approach you). Virginity and reproduction are no longer an issue for (most of) these women, and although attitudes toward intimacy and sexual partners have shifted dramatically over the life course of these people (particularly after the 1960s and 1970s), notions of decency continue to regulate behavior, and maintaining a man's fidelity can be vital to a woman's reputation. At first sight, it seems that as a woman, once you are a widow or divorced, you have more freedom than younger or married women, sexually and otherwise, particularly if you are financially independent (for example, with a widow's pension).

Ideas of freedom and the ability to choose one's partner at will were central to the discourses of many of the widowed and divorced women I spoke to, but not all adhered to notions of gender equality. Moreover, potential social mobility was a consideration for some. For example, Carmen, a widow in her mid-seventies, told me that she had done the right thing: had a husband and children and always done her duty; after her husband died, she was free and did as she chose. Carmen met her sentimental partner, Ernesto (a former builder and widower), at a danzón event, and when I met them, they had been together for a couple of years. Ernesto prefers to dance the (non-group) freer lírico style of danzón, so Carmen left her group to be with him. She was a much stronger dancer than him but was willing to dance a more awkward dance to be with him. Moreover, unlike Ramiro and Marianita, they have nothing to hide, for their reputations were not tarnished by being together, at first sight at least. They were both widowed, and there was no need to marry to be together (few danzón practitioners had re-married). Carmen was much wealthier than most danzoneros (her late husband having been a manager of a large local business), and Ernesto was much poorer than her, but she refused to heed criticism (so she said) or ask permission of her children about this relationship (instead, she told them it was happening). Yet, like other women in the Port, Carmen still refers to her children for permission to act in relation to other parts of her life. For example, she goes only to places they approve of as "safe" when she visits Mexico City.

One octogenarian woman I knew allowed her (adult) children to control most aspects of her life, but many older women, at least those who were still active and danced danzón, like Carmen, had more choice about how to manage the knots of emancipation and dependency relating to older age. Carmen no longer had to fulfill social mores to marry a wealthy man, having done this once, although pressures remained. Soon after they met, she bought Ernesto new, smarter clothes so that they could look more elegant together at danzón events (see Vignette 6). However, she did not take him to many other social events and limited how often he could come to her house (and rarely visited his). Three years later, she told me that Ernesto had started drinking heavily again, and she was becoming increasingly embarrassed about going to danzón events with him, so they went less regularly. But she did not end the relationship, for she feared she would have to give up dancing altogether and damage her reputation, and that she would not find another sentimental partner. Her supposed newfound freedom was thus heavily compromised and bound by social mores that kept her in a relationship that became violent.

Another woman I knew, forty-eight-year-old María Luisa, had survived a violent relationship with her ex-husband and wept as she told me that she never wanted to be with another man. She attended danzón events with the Verde group and danced with various men in her group, but she would not even take a regular dance partner from among them. Danzón events are also spaces where women can dance with men and not become emotionally or sexually involved. And another widowed woman I knew cooked for her danzón partner and lover every day, as she had for her husband, choosing to reproduce many of the facets of her married life. She cooked in the hope that he would turn up, yet she was often pained that he did not even phone to let her know when he was not coming. Cooked food piled up in her fridge, evidencing his lack of concern. Other men were more considerate, but unequal power dynamics between women and men were generally reproduced.

It is enlightening to consider Veracruz's danzón scene in relation to María Novaro's film *Danzón*, released in 1991. This film brims with sexual tension: the protagonist Julia (played by María Rojo), a single mother, leaves her job and teenage daughter to travel to Veracruz in search of her danzón partner,

Carmelo (played by former docker Daniel "El Catrín" Rergis, discussed in Chapter 2). In Veracruz, Julia encounters trans women, sex workers, and sailors, and she takes a young lover but does not track down Carmelo. Only once she is back in Mexico City does she find Carmelo, and the film ends with their eyes interlocked, dancing a danzón. This film has prompted substantial scholarly attention (e.g., Arredondo 1999; Nahoum-Grappe 2001; Foster 2002; Mora 2006), particularly in relation to gender mores and feminism. Iglesias Prieto (2004) explores gendered, sexualized readings of the film; and López comments that "the danzón is a 'cage', a social grid, but it is *her* [Julia's] grid and she can transform its pleasures and risk breaking its rules" (1997, 339). When I interviewed the film's director, María Novaro, she told me:

> *Soy feminista, o sea estoy en otro mundo, pero me fascinó justo que en el mundo del danzón me decían los danzoneros, mis amigos, me decían que "en el danzón, como en la vida, el hombre manda y la mujer obedece" ¿no? Entonces me encantó porque dije, "yo voy a hacer una película en que pues no, ¿no? pero en el baile sí."*

> I am a feminist, that is, I am in another world, but I loved that precisely in the world of danzón, the danzoneros, my friends, would say to me that "in danzón, as in life, the man leads and the woman obeys." I loved it, and I said, "I am going to make a film in which it's not like that, but it is still in the dance."

Novaro, a trained sociologist, spent a year researching Mexico City's danzón scene before making this film. She implies here that she is challenging notions that "in danzón, as in life, the man leads and the woman obeys," breaking down homologies between everyday coupledom and danzón dancing. However, some women, such as Raquel, the maestra of the Amarillo group, lead the dance while appearing to be led (subverting and reproducing conventional power relations). Moreover, the routines that groups learn consist of prescribed steps that can be anticipated by both dancers in a couple, thereby shifting the relationship between the leader and led in the dance. Some women prefer to dance routines, for they dislike being led, and group routines allow both men and women to dance a non-led dance (again appearing to reproduce conventional power relations, but in a way that suits these women). Men largely lead in the dance, and patriarchal mores are commonplace in danzoneros' discourse and practice. Yet Novaro's film is a much more nuanced portrayal of gender and danzoneros than a mere feminist critique (despite Schaefer's claims to the contrary, 1999), for, like Julia in the film, surprisingly few danzoneros, in Veracruz at least, actually live together. Most of the older women who participate in Veracruz's danzón events are freer and more financially independent (if not wealthier) than many married women, at least of their generation. In their new sentimental partnerships, some of these women choose to what extent they want to take on the gendered roles that they might have when married, but such so-called freedom is still heavily constrained by social mores where women are disadvantaged. There is a shifting sense of older womanhood, distinct from the feminist aims of being beyond men's control and hegemonic gendered regulation, but nevertheless generally more independent than the marital roles associated with married women of a similar age.

The arena that these women enter, once they are widowed, separated, or divorced, remains one where men have most power. Not only do men lead in the dance (and even where they do not, they appear to) and get to ask women to dance (whether the invitation is accepted or not), but they also dominate the economic, sentimental, and sexual fields. Many men have more money and status than women through work, although this may diminish after retirement, and widows get only half of their husbands' pensions, which become devalued the longer the women live. As Eva Illouz (2012) argues, the ideal of romantic love sustains gender inequalities such as access to finances, sexual partners (since men determine the aesthetics of love, set the rules, and dominate the field), and self worth beyond the home (which men mostly gain through economic and job status, while women rely more on emotional attachment, on the gaze of intimate others for recognizing and reaffirming the self). "Men have far more sexual and emotional choice than women," Illouz argues, "and it is this imbalance that creates emotional domination" (2012, 240–41). Illouz's work focuses on younger heterosexual men and women (in France, Germany, Israel, and the United States). In the context of older people in Veracruz's danzón arena, the inequalities are exacerbated: women far outnumber men, partly because, like other popular dance forms, danzón tends to attract more women than men, but also (for those at the upper end of this age range) because women tend to outlive men. Moreover, it is acceptable (if frowned upon) for men to have a wife and a lover, their reputation being tarnished slightly, but little in comparison to the impact on a woman behaving similarly. This further enhances men's domination of the romantic and sexual fields. While men can be womanizers, it is much harder for women to go from man to man. Even where women dominate men economically, as we saw with Carmen and Ernesto, social mores dictated that women's reputations remained fragile and women could not easily move from man to man. The ambivalences of the failure to achieve the utopian promises of love intersect in this instance with ambivalences about the presentation of the self, the normative disciplining of women, and the horrors of domestic violence. And even where there is no such violence, love is far from a force to overcome gender inequalities here. In this context, romantic love is often portrayed as Janus-faced: looking forward to utopian futures, or back to pre-reproductive moments, to courting, weddings, and honeymoons. A fear of physical decline, dependency, and death can intensify and disturb the promises of love and life—and the dancing possibilities for older people.

Conclusion

In this chapter, I explored how ideas about age are represented and negotiated in Veracruz's danzón arena. I suggested that ideas that danzón was an older people's dance were denied for three reasons. First, people of various ages have performed danzón throughout its history in Mexico, and it was not a genre linked to notions of youth. Second, danzón is a tourist attraction in the Port and is promoted as a local "tradition" (rather than as a resource for older people). And third, age is contextual and relative. "Decline narratives" (Gullette 2004, 13) and agism pertain in Veracruz (as they do in the United Kingdom and the United States), and few people wanted to be "old" or identified as such.

I argued in Chapter 4 that the older age of many danzón practitioners was promoted to authenticate this local "heritage," but older people were not sought out as "authentic" practitioners of this "tradition" (unlike another local music-dance form, son jarocho). And we saw how the popularity of danzón mushroomed from the 1980s, groups formed, and modes of transmission changed, attracting thousands of fifty-plus-year-olds to join the dance. In this chapter, I examined how an aesthetic of disciplined danzón was valued and promoted, particularly by empire builders, where younger dancers flourished with their "sponge-like," "elegant" bodies. Most younger people lack the sexual experience and *cadencia* of older dancers, however, and I argued that two representations of the Port's danzón have emerged: one pertaining to the highly valued, disciplined form of danzón where younger dancers, and especially *Tres Generaciones*, excelled and were promoted on the national danzón scene; and another, promoted by Veracruz's tourist industry, where older people danced danzón académico in groups and independent couples performed in the freer lírico style.

I also interrogated how the *flexibility* of danzón dance groups contributed to the danzón revival, since danzón dance groups simultaneously facilitate the dance's codification and encompass the multiple motivations of practitioners (akin to the amateur naturalists analyzed by Star and Griesemer 1989). Dance group leaders often strive to create groups of "good" dancers to compete with other groups (as we saw in Chapter 5), yet some group dancers are less interested in competition. While many dancers, young and old, seek conviviality in groups, others have more compelling reasons to belong to groups. Not only do groups provide legitimate structures, supported by government institutions, in which to perform, but they also afford formal settings in which romantically entwined couples can be together without too much explanation.

Most studies of popular music and dance have dismissed older people's, and particularly older women's, sexuality. In this chapter, I also proposed that danzón is not accessible to most married women in the Port, attracting women before or after this stage of their lives. I explored how women negotiate romance within the danzón sphere; how some men indulge in a form of serial monogamy involving both their wives and lovers; how decency must be constantly (re)created and gossip negotiated; and how widowed women enact independent forms of womanhood, distinct from feminist ideals. I contended that the utopian ambivalences of love are complicated by the dialectic ambivalences of aging, but not entirely disturbed. Gender inequalities are shifted by some women, but men's power is dislodged by few.

Figure 6.1. Diploma issued by Veracruz's Club de los Pájaros Caídos, with artwork and décima by Félix Martinez González. It translates as: Club of the fallen cocks / which no longer inspire love, / they lived a better time / today they are saddened. / All floppy, done in, / they only serve to pee, / they should be put into retirement, / enough of messing around / with these bloody saggy skins, / tired of fornicating! // Only if you die early / as Don Ambrosio said / will you not achieve membership / of this Veracruzano Club. / Since your worldly life, / will wear out your little cock, / and you will see it getting smaller / as time goes by, / and you will live sighing / about when you were young. (Photograph by the author of a diploma belonging to a member of the club.)

VIGNETTE SEVEN

Diana

(fiction)

Carefully drawing her eyebrows with a pencil, Diana stared into the mirror. Now that Juana had died, who would look after Tito? Diana didn't know how long she could go on.

Diana. Big-boned. Long, red viscose dress and matching top, embossed with pineapples. Swollen feet crammed into black leather sandals: a bit clompy. Large, off-gold, hooped earrings. Foundation-covered, pale brown skin, softened with age. Wide, thin red lips outlining veneered teeth. Short, wiry brown hair. Wispy fringe.

Diana lost her husband in the car crash that left Tito, her youngest, brain damaged. Then Diana's eldest son killed himself. In her devastation, she focused on Tito. Diana again taught him to eat, to speak, to read and write, forty-one years after the first time. Despite what the doctors said, he improved. Slowly. Her solace was writing plays and singing: when Tito was well enough, they dressed up and put on shows for Juana, Diana's daughter, during her visits from Merida. That was a joy. Then they learned to dance danzón.

Tito. Shorter than his mother by a couple of centimeters. Bald head. Large, wire-framed glasses that sloped slightly to the left, obscuring light-brown eyes. Broad, stubby nose. Protruding ears. Proud belly projecting from loose, white guayabera shirt. Diana inspected him: top button firmly fastened, white leather shoes polished, fingernails clean.

As their taxi pulled up, danzón was squealing from the main plaza. Chairs allocated to their dance group awaited them. Diana yearned for Javier, the group leader, to invite her to dance: she loved being led, showing off her turns. But there were never enough men, and she mostly danced with Tito. With her eighty-six years and his lumbering fifty-nine, they danced awkwardly: her limbs did not do as she wanted, and it was hard to dictate his. Yet dancing let her forget, for a bit; float. Sometimes, she told Tito to dance with other women. But he'd hold their hands too long: however gracefully they rejected him, she felt embarrassed.

After a year, Javier, the dance group leader, started coming to lunch. For eight months, he ate but brought nothing. She couldn't afford it but didn't say. At least she got to dance with him a little more. Then he shouted at her. Petrifyingly. She never knew why. Her daughter, Juana, pleaded with her to stand up to him, to dance independently of the group, anything. Diana didn't have the strength. She stopped dancing.

Four years later, Juana died. Cancer. They hadn't seen it coming.

After the funeral, Diana and Tito stayed home, apart from their fast-paced 5 a.m. walks. That was before the intense violence came. Before Covid. Then they just stayed home. Waiting.

Notes

Introduction

1. The Port of Veracruz is situated in the State of Veracruz, Mexico. I follow local practice in referring to the city as Veracruz or the Port (and I capitalize the "P" of the Port to distinguish the city from the harbor/port).

2. Numerous musicians and dancers wished to be named. I use pseudonyms where there is reason to protect people.

3. Rather confusingly, the term *timbales* is used in Mexico to refer to both these small timpani (often 50 and 55 cm in diameter) and the more portable *tarolas* that are sometimes used as substitutes. The term "tarolas" is used in Veracruz to refer to the two single-headed cylindrical metal drums mounted on a stand, struck with two wooden sticks, and famously played by Tito Puente (which are called timbales in Puerto Rico and New York).

4. To ease reading, I refrain from using scare quotes around words such as "race," "Afro," "black," and "white." Here I want to reiterate how problematic such terms are: "race" is a classificatory system demarcating phenotypical difference; and notions of people being black, white, Afro, or otherwise are socially constructed markers of difference that have served to legitimate oppression, inequality, and exclusion. Please note that in this book, I distinguish between "black" and "indigenous" as non-identity markers (with a lowercase "b" and "i"), and "Black" and "Indigenous" as politicized identities (with a capital "B" and "I").

5. Such a call for multiple theoretical orientations chimes with Yael Navaro-Yashin's (2009) proposal that paradigms such as object-oriented analysis (e.g., Latour 2005) and linguistic approaches should be combined. Rather than merely linguistic approaches, I would broaden this to include all interpretive approaches that build on such influential thinkers as Plato (1908), Kant (1998), and Hegel (1994), where there is a notion that truth lies beyond experience (see Sontag 1964).

6. See also the Special Issue of *Feminist Theory* edited by Robyn Wiegman (2014).

7. Bauman (1991) argues that the modern post-Enlightenment imperative to rationalize, to classify and create order, simultaneously draws attention to and produces further chaos. Eli Zaretsky (1992) critiques Bauman, arguing instead that rather than rationalization, the post-Enlightenment era is characterized by individual and collective self-critique, together with a greater tolerance for otherness. Other analyses of modernity and ambivalence from various perspectives include Andrew Weigert (1991), Barry Smart (1998), and Nadia Lie (2017).

8. Parts of Chapter 1 appeared in Malcomson (2010), Malcomson (2011), and Malcomson (2016). Parts of the second half of Chapter 6 appeared in Malcomson (2012).

9. I consulted numerous archives and libraries, including the Archivo General del Estado de Veracruz, Archivo Histórico de Veracruz, Biblioteca de la Artes, Centro Nacional de las Artes, CONACULTA, Biblioteca Gener y del Monte, Matanzas, Biblioteca Nacional "José Martí" La Habana, Centro de Investigación y Desarrollo de la Música Cubana, La Habana, CIESAS-GOLFO (Centro de Investiagaciones y Estudios Superiores de Antropologia Social), Fototeca del Instituto Veracruzano de Cultura, Instituto de Investigaciones Histórico-Sociales de la Universidad Veracruzana, Instituto Nacional de Antropologia e Historia (INAH), Instituto Nacional de Estadística Geografía e Informática (INEGI), Universidad Cristóbal Colón, Universidad Nacional Autónoma de México (UNAM), and the Universidad Veracruzana.

10. For much of the twentieth century, the Municipal Band uniform included white military-style peaked hats and white shirts and trousers, and it was often confused with the very similar Naval Band uniform, which was demarcated by black and yellow hat and shoulder adornments. The Naval Band rarely play in the Zócalo, however. From the 2000s, the Municipal Band uniform was changed as, with increased narco-state violence, it was safer for these musicians to be distinguished from military personnel. Other workers in the Port who also changed their sartorial behavior include medical staff who stopped wearing their uniforms in public for personal safety reasons: they did not want to be kidnapped so that they could attend (organized) criminals.

Chapter One. Racial Ambivalence

1. Madrid and Moore (2013), Manuel (2009), and Miller (2014) provide detailed analyses of histories of danzón and related genres.

2. See Moore (1997) and Madrid and Moore (2013) regarding the history of danzón in Cuba.

3. Note that within the State of Veracruz, there is regional variation and, Jones (2013) proposes, a rural-urban divide in relationships to blackness.

4. For further understanding of mestizaje in Mexico, see, for example, Gall (2013), Moreno Figueroa (2010), Moreno Figueroa and Saldívar Tanaka (2016), and Ortega Domínguez (2022).

5. All translations of interviews and Spanish-language texts are my own, unless otherwise stated.

6. See videos of Silverio López Contreras (*Alma de Veracruz*, Veracruz) and Hipólito "Polo" González Peña (*Danzonera Acerina*, Mexico City) performing on the the Danzón Days playlist: https://www.youtube.com/playlist?list=PLqlxu0QXGsBCvfLIzSKjwmRDgSJzusE5r.

And also: *Danzonera Alma de Veracruz* "Danzón en el Zócalo de Veracruz" (Nereidas) https://youtu.be/SulRISwtEDY?t=59 (August 12, 2012); *Danzonera Acerina* "Nereidas" https://www.youtube.com/watch?v=MD-gqwNODow (April 13, 2017).

7. Mexico City's *Danzonera Acerina*, for example, consists of two alto, two tenor, and one baritone saxophone; two trumpets; trombone; violin; keyboard; electric bass; timbales; and a güiro/claves player. Veracruz's *Alma de Veracruz* aimed to include two clarinets, tenor saxophone, three trumpets, trombone, keyboard, electric bass, congas, timbales, and a güiro/claves player.

8. *Jarocha/o* is often employed to denote people from the Port of Veracruz, or the Veracruz coast, but it is sometimes used by Porteña/os to describe people from the Papaloapan valley just south of the Port, the Sotavento region and the Tuxtlas. The term *Porteña/o* designates people specifically from the Port of Veracruz, while *Veracruzana/o* is used to refer to people from the Port and/or the State of Veracruz. All three terms are commonly employed interchangeably.

9. In Veracruz, *morena/o, prieta/o,* and *güera/o* are commonly used, relative terms denoting skin color. Morena/o (darker than or brownness) and prieta/o (dark) are used to describe people with darker skin (relative to others); while güera/o implies lighter, whiter, blonder coloring. While prieta/o can have pejorative overtones, güera/o is employed extensively in the Port of Veracruz as a compliment, famously by ice-cream sellers in the Calle Manuel Gutiérrez Zamora, to refer to people regardless of their coloring, but emphasizing their privileged position as potential consumers. Here privilege is equated with "race" in a particularly striking manner. Note that in other parts of Mexico, such as the Costa Chica, the term *morena/o* is employed to denote people with indigenous/black ancestry (see Lewis 2012).

10. In Mexico, the term *chino* is multivalent and includes reference to China and a specific form of hair, and it was employed as a racial category in colonial times. In colonial *casta* paintings, such as those of the *Colección del Museo Nacional de México*, "chino/a" refers to the offspring of a Spaniard with a *morisca/o* (morisca/o being the offspring of a *mulata/o* with Spaniard) (Aguirre Beltrán 1972, 176–77).

11. See Lewis (2012), Hoffmann and Rinaudo (2014), and Vaughn (2013) for analyses of understandings of blackness in various areas of Mexico.

12. See Martínez Novo (2006) and Saldívar Tanaka (2008) for an exploration of the relationship of indigenous peoples to the Mexican nation over this period.

13. The difficulties of recognizing racial identities in Mexico are interrogated by Moreno Figueroa (2011) and Moreno Figueroa and Saldívar Tanaka (2016).

Chapter Two. Ambivalent Nostalgia

1. Spot Enrique Peña Nieto Veracruz by Aristegui Noticias http://www.youtube.com/watch?v=lIzjsNb7au4&list=PLDCB20C9498D0E40E (April 8, 2012).

2. Agustín Lara's song *Veracruz* (1936) begins: "Yo nací, con la luna de plata, / y nací, con alma de pirata. / He nacido rumbero y jarocho, trovador de veras. / Y me fui, lejos de Veracruz. / Veracruz: rinconcito donde hacen su nido las olas del mar. / Veracruz: pedacito de patria que sabe sufrir y cantar. / Veracruz: son tus noches diluvio de estrellas, palmera y mujer. / Veracruz: vibra en mi ser; / algún día hasta tus playas lejanas / tendré que volver." (I was born with the silver moon, / and I was born with a pirate's soul. / I was born a rumbero [party animal] and jarocho, a real troubadour; / and I went, far from Veracruz. / Veracruz, little corner where the waves of the sea make their nest. / Veracruz, a little piece of mother-country that knows how to suffer and to sing. / Veracruz, your nights are flooded with stars, palm trees and woman. / Veracruz, vibrate in my being; / some day I will have to return to your distant beaches). Transcribed from: Lara, Agustín. "15 Inolvidables en la voz de Agustín Lara. Versiones Originales." RCA Victor-2381. LP. 1984: Mexico.

3. Madrid and Moore argue that "danzón enthusiasts attempt to recreate a time in which the danzón and associated practices enjoyed an exalted position within the national imaginary" (2013, 19). They link pachucos' chauvinist values to the "paternalistic and domineering single-party [PRI] government" (2013, 187) that held office from 1929 until 2000, arguing that chauvinism and paternalism are compromised by calls for gender equality and democracy, but that the fragility of the contemporary Mexican state creates a space where "nostalgia offers the promise of a return to familiar categories […] for the reimagination of the past in the present" (2013, 187). Pachucos are not associated with the Port of Veracruz, where distinct logics of attachment to danzón and nostalgia operate.

4. Sir Weetman Dickinson Pearson's English company played a major role in modernizing the city, being contracted to oversee not only the harbor and port expansion but also the sanitation work, electricity, trams, and trains. The company also won other large concessions from the Mexican government, including the Isthmus of Tehuantepec railway. By the early twenty-first century, the company was known as Pearson plc and had worldwide media and publishing interests (Connolly 1999).

5. The lineup of Severiano Pacheco and Albertico Gómez's danzoneras, for example, consisted of two clarinets, cornet, timbales, güiro, trombone, euphonium, and bass in one incarnation of the group, although this changed over time. And Francisco "Tiburón" González García (n.d.) states that the *Danzonera de los Chinos Ramírez* included two clarinets, trumpet, trombone, ophicleide, bass, timbales, and güiro.

6. Moore and Madrid (2013) date Tiburcio Hernández's coining of the term *danzonera* later (in the 1910s), and Simón Jara Gámez et al. (1994) suggest that it occurred around 1920. Hernández later moved to Mexico City and performed at the inauguration of the *Salón México* dance hall in 1920.

7. See Spottswood (2004) and Madrid and Moore (2013) regarding early danzón

recordings. Flores y Escalante (1993) provides a list of danzones recorded on major labels from 1904.

8. It should be noted that the Mexican Revolution is best understood as a civil war rather than a socialist revolution: while certain factions were socialist, properly understood, others were not, including the majority of PRI governments that ruled thereafter.

9. The *Orquesta de Chato Rojas y sus Lobos Marinos*, which mostly played jazz, usually consisted of three trumpets (one played by Bernardo García, who would later lead the *Danzonera Alma de Veracruz*), trombone, two clarinets (doubling alto sax), tenor sax, drums, maracas, piano/guitar, and bass.

10. Francisco de Goya's painting "The Burial of the Sardine" (ca. 1792/3) depicts such a carnival ritual in Madrid.

11. Víctor Manuel "'Manolo" Sánchez Marín was also a founding member of Gaby Moreno's well-known local ensemble, *Orquesta de Veracruz*.

12. In Mexico, as in much of Latin America, the fifteenth birthday (*quinceañera*) is an important celebration for young girls, who often don beautiful dresses and, finances permitting, host parties (where often a highlight is the dancing of a waltz).

13. My reference to dialectic ambivalence here might be clearer if we consider Bakhtin's notion of the grotesque: "a phenomenon in transformation, an as yet unfinished metamorphosis, of death and birth, growth and becoming. The relation to time is one determining trait of the grotesque image. The other indispensable trait is ambivalence. For in this image we find both poles of transformation, the old and the new, the dying and the procreating, the beginning and the end of the metamorphosis" (Bakhtin 1984, 24). Dialectic ambivalence is clearly at play in Bakhtin's grotesque as it concerns becoming and transformation rather than static polarized opposites.

14. Note that Herzfeld's "*structural nostalgia*—the longing for an age before the state" (2005, 22) is not applicable in the case of Veracruz.

Chapter Three. Elegant Moves

1. See videos of académico and lírico dancing in Veracruz on the *Danzón Days* playlist: https://www.youtube.com/playlist?list=PLqlxu0QXGsBCvfLIzSKjwmRDgSJzusE5r.

2. See video of Carlos Mizuno dancing to the Danzón Mizuno with Silvia in the Salón Los Ángeles, Mexico City, on the Danzón Days playlist:
https://www.youtube.com/playlist?list=PLqlxu0QXGsBCvfLIzSKjwmRDgSJzusE5r.

3. See video of Tomás and Amanda showing off their own brand of danzón de fantasía in the Zócalo, Veracruz, on the *Danzón Days* playlist: https://www.youtube.com/playlist?list=PLqlxu0QXGsBCvfLIzSKjwmRDgSJzusE5r.

4. Apart from *Hoy y Siempre* (Veracruz's first danzón group) and *Tres Generaciones* (Veracruz's only group of young dancers), I have changed the names of groups to colors.

5. A güiro is a serrated gourd scraped with a small stick. Claves are round wooden sticks, often around 15 cm long and 2.5 cm in diameter, played by striking one against the other, held in a cupped hand.

6. See videos of danzón in Veracruz's Zócalo on a Saturday on the *Danzón Days* playlist: https://www.youtube.com/playlist?list=PLq1xu0QXGsBCvfLIzSKjwmRDgSJzusE5r.

7. See video of Armando Valdés Abreu and Adolfina de Valdés dancing danzón at the monthly Círculo Amigos del Danzón peña del danzón, La Víbora, La Habana, Cuba, on the *Danzón Days* playlist: https://www.youtube.com/playlist?list=PLq1xu0QXGsBCvfLIzSKjwmRDgSJzusE5r.

8. See video of Tomás and Amanda dancing danzón de fantasia in the Zócalo, Veracruz, on the *Danzón Days* playlist: https://www.youtube.com/playlist?list=PLq1xu0QXGsBCvfLIzSKjwmRDgSJzusE5r.

9. Indigenismo was the political and cultural project that glorified the pre-Hispanic indigenous past while advocating the integration of contemporary indigenous peoples into mestizo (culturally and racially mixed) national life (via education and the establishment of indigenous music, dance, and ritual as "folklore") (Knight 1990b).

10. Moreno Figueroa (2010) analyzes how forms of whiteness are entangled with the Mexican racial project of mestizaje more broadly.

Chapter Four. Moves to Rescue

1. For further information about danzón in Mexico City, see books by danzón aficionados Ángel Trejo (1992), Simón Jara Gámez et al., (1994), and Jesús Flores y Escalante (1993, 1994); the ethnography of the capital's dance halls in the 1990s, together with social history, by anthropologist Amparo Sevilla (1996, 2003); the two short essays on the dance halls by Carlos Monsiváis (1981); cultural historian Robert Buffington's (2005) structuralist reading of danzón and shifts in gender relations in the post-revolutionary period; Mark Pedelty's broad historical overview of *Musical Ritual in Mexico City: From the Aztec to NAFTA* (2004); Madrid and Moore's (2013) exploration of the flows of danzón around the circum-Caribbean; and Tamariz Estrada's (2014) ethnography of a dance group led by Fredy Salazar and Maru Mosqueda in Coyoacán in the early 2010s (in the south of the city), which focuses on aging.

2. See García (2006b) for an analysis of the reception of mambo in mid-twentieth-century Mexico City, Havana, and New York City.

3. Jara Gámez et al., (1994) date this at 1957, but Monsiváis (1997) and Zolov (1999) concur that it was 1959.

4. Ciro Carlos Mizuno Guzmán told me that there were four power groups in the danzón scene consisting of the following men: (1) 1930s-1950s: "El Maestro" Balderas, Ventura Miranda* (died 1963), "El Maestro" Romero. (2) 1950s and 1960s: "El Bucles" (Ringlets), Carlos "El Calcetín" (the Sock) Berriel, Vicente "El Alegría" (Happiness) Hernández (b. 1910), Pascual "El Pato" (the Duck) Ramírez, Jesús "Chucho/El Muerto" (the Dead Man) Ramírez* (1913–92), Enrique Tapia. (3) 1970s and 1980s: Antonio

"El Mirruñas" (the Small Insignificant Thing) Arellano, Miguel Ángel "El Lagañoso" (With Lots of Sleep in His Eyes) Cisneros, Roberto "El Chale" Salazar* (chale is an inoffensive expression of surprise), Arturo "El Capullo" (the Cocoon/Wonderful One) Sánchez Rivera, Pedro "El Abuelo" (the Grandfather) Velázquez, Víctor "El Toby" Escobar Bautista, Pedro Scott. (4) 1990s to 2010s: Miguel Ángel Zamudio Abdala, Fredy Salazar*, Miguel Ángel Vázquez. Membership of these groups overlaps, and the asterisk indicates the dancer that Mizuno thought was "considered the best danzón dancer in this period." Notable is that the men in Groups 1–3 were all based in Mexico City, while from the 1990s (Group 4), power becomes spread more widely: Miguel Ángel Zamudio Abdala is based in the Port of Veracruz, Fredy Salazar in Mexico City, and Miguel Ángel Vázquez in Mexico State. And crucially, note the absence of women, such as Maru Mosqueda, who jointly ran a group with Fredy Salazar.

5. Mizuno Guzmán told me that the members of *Club Inspiración* included Jesús "Chucho/El Muerto" Ramírez, Vicente "'El Alegría" Hernández, Ventura Miranda and his wife Ema (Manuela) "La Negra Palomares," Carlos "El Calcetín" Berriel, Carlos "El Manotas" (the Big Hands), Isabel y María Eugenia "Las Cuatas" (the Mates), Pepe "La Burra" (the Donkey), El Bucles (the Ringlets), Fernando "El Patrullero" (the Patrolman), and "El Fotografo" (the Photographer).

6. Acta (1983) Notaria Publica No. 32, Lic. Evangelina Baca de Montiel, H. Veracruz, Ver: 27 de Marzo 1992. Testimonio de la Escritura No. 2825, Volumen XLV. Constitucion de Asociación Civil Denominada: "Club de Bailadores de Danzón de Hoy y Siempre del Puerto de Veracruz, Asociacion Civil" (November 5, 1983). Members of *Hoy y Siempre* named in this document include Eutiquio Madrigal Hernández, Benito Torres Díaz, Francisco "El Tiburón" (the Shark) González García, Joaquín Ortiz Absalón, Ernesto Espinosa Ortiz, Profesora Isis de Jesús Grijalva, Mario Escalante Flores, and Guillermina de Bandala. The first president was Eutiquio Madrigal Hernández, followed by Efraín Sierra Hernández (from 1985), Natalia Pineda Burgos, and then Margarita Castro Olvera from 1991 to the 2010s.

7. Members of *Pro-Rescate* included men listed in the third group of Footnote 6: Roberto "El Chale" Salazar, Miguel Ángel "El Lagañoso" Cisneros, Arturo "El Capullo" Sánchez Rivera, Antonio "El Mirruñas" Arellano, and Pedro "El Abuelo" Velázquez.

8. Members of the *Fraternidad* included Roberto "El Chale" Salazar, Miguel Ángel "El Lagañoso" Cisneros, Arturo "El Capullo" Sánchez Rivera, Pepe Durán, Carmen Estévez, and Víctor "El Toby" Escobar Bautista.

9. These included the National Institute of Anthropology and History (INAH), the National Institute of Fine Arts (INBA), and the Mexican Institute of Cinematography (IMCINE).

10. Founding members of *Tres Generaciones* included Rosa Abdala Gómez, Efraín Sierra Hernández, Gloria Vázquez Ravelo, Modesto Morales Rodríguez, Gerardo Castro Pacheco, and his mother, Carolina Pacheco Chávez.

11. Members of *La Academia Nacional de Danzón A.C.* included Antonio "El Mirruñas" Arellano, Miguel Ángel Cisneros, Félix Renteria, Arturo "El Capullo"

Sánchez Rivera, Roberto "El Chale" Salazar, Pedro Scott, Pablo Tapia Vargas (who later formed the *Danzonera Yucatán*), and Pedro "El Abuelo" Velázquez.

12. See video of the Bello Veracruz group performing an académico routine at a danzón festival in Veracruz on the Danzón Days playlist:

https://www.youtube.com/playlist?list=PLq1xu0QXGsBCvfLIzSKjwmRDgSJzusE5r.

13. The three groups in Veracruz were *Hoy y Siempre*, led by Margarita Castro de Juárez, *Tres Generaciones*, led by Rosa Abdala Gómez, and the *Club Círculo Amigos del Danzón Miguel Faílde Pérez*, led by Natalia Pineda Burgos (set up in the late 1980s and named after a similarly named association Pineda Burgos met when visiting Cuba). Thirty-one Mexico City groups are listed in the program for the 1994 Encuentro Internacional de Danzón.

14. Danzones titles commonly refer to women's names (*Cecilia, Fefita*), beautiful women (*Almendra, La Mora*), places (*Acayucan, Mocambo*), dance halls (*Salón México, Nereidas*), famous people (*Ninón Sevilla, Kid Azteca*), love stories (*Mi Consuelo es Amarte, Amor Perdido*). Yet even if they have lyrics when played with another rhythm (such as a bolero), rarely are danzones sung. (There are exceptions, such as the short unison choruses sung by the musicians in the *montuno* sections of *La Mora, Champotón,* and *Pulque Para Dos.*) I have not heard performances of the sung danzonete form in Veracruz.

15. Carlos Campos y su Orquesta, "Nereidas" https://www.youtube.com/watch?v=cWNXm80KTgw (August 11, 2017).

Chapter Five. United in a Vipers' Nest

1. Acta (1983) Notaria Publica No. 32, Lic. Evangelina Baca de Montiel, H. Veracruz, Ver: 27 de Marzo 1992. Testimonio de la Escritura No. 2825, Volumen XLV. Constitucion de Asociación Civil Denominada: "Club de Bailadores de Danzón de Hoy y Siempre del Puerto de Veracruz, Asociacion Civil" (5 November 1983).

2. Acta (1983) Notaria Publica No. 32, Lic. Evangelina Baca de Montiel, H. Veracruz, Ver: 27 de Marzo 1992. Testimonio de la Escritura No. 2825, Volumen XLV. Constitucion de Asociación Civil Denominada: "Club de Bailadores de Danzón de Hoy y Siempre del Puerto de Veracruz, Asociacion Civil" (5 November 1983).

Chapter Six. Loving Ambivalence

1. *Zapatear* is a form of percussive footwork widespread in Spain (such as flamenco) and throughout Latin America (see Stobart 2006 for an example of Andean zapateo). It is characteristic of the *baile de artesa* of Mexico's Costa Chica and of Veracruz's son jarocho (see Sheehy 1979; Ruiz Rodríguez 2005). It was not unusual for danzoneros to have learned son jarocho dancing before learning danzón.

2. Few of the people I knew in Veracruz admitted to me that they had had same-gender relationships, but this was not the focus of my research. From what I did glean,

Veracruz's scenario differs from UK or US conceptualizations of men who have sex with men (who may be considered gay, bisexual, or queer). Many of the ideas put forward in Lancaster's analysis of men's homosexual relationships in Nicaragua back in 1992 held in Veracruz into the 2010s (see also Gutmann 1996; Prieur 1996; Carillo 2004): it is *chotos* (literally, "young goats") who are, in the collective imaginary at least, the men who are anally penetrated in man-man sexual practices (further investigation is required into the etymological links between *chotos* and *cabrones* "he-goats"). For moralists, *chotos* carry the stigma of being homosexual, rather than the men who penetrate or engage in other sexual practices with men. Men who identify as "gay" or "homosexual" are usually described by others as *chotos* (regardless of their sexual practices). Veracruz is renowned for its large population of homosexual men and trans women (discussed briefly in Flores Martos 2004). Building on the work of Ponce (2006), which analyzes sexualities in a village outside the Port, and Córdova Plaza (2011), which explores men's and trans women's sex work in the Port of Veracruz and the state capital, Xalapa, further research is needed on gender and sexuality in the Port itself, as well as (understandings of) homophobia in this context.

Glossary

Baile de salón   Dance hall (ballroom) dance.

Cadencia   Rhythmic cadence, articulated through subtle hip movement when dancing.

Cha-cha-chá   Often performed by *charangas*, the cha-cha-chá combines elements of the *danzonete*, the *ritmo nuevo*, and Pérez Prado's *mambo*. It emerged at the end of the 1940s and is considered a *baile de salón*.

Charanga (also known as Charanga Francesa)   An ensemble that emerged from the *orquesta típica* in Cuba around the beginning of the twentieth century. They often consist of flutes (usually five-key), one to three violins, (electric) bass, (electric) keyboard, *congas*, *güiro* and claves, *tarolas*, and one to three vocalists. Their repertoire is usually centered around *danzones*, *danzonetes*, and cha-cha-chás.

Cinquillo   Meaning quintuplet. Usually performed in danzones in the two-bar unit: ♫♫♫ (in 3–2 *clave*), this rhythm occurs throughout the circum-Caribbean in son cubano, Haitian vodou, and Dominican merengue. As well as being played as ♫♫♫, variations occur, such as evenly spacing the notes into quintuplets.

Clave   The two-bar repeated rhythmic figures that underpin most Cuban genres (such as danzón and son cubano). For example, the (3–2) son clave is ♫♫♫. I find it helpful to conceptualize the clave as metric and to conduct it as: 3+3+2 /8 then 2+2+2+2 /8.

Claves   Two round wooden sticks, often around 15 cm long and 2.5 cm in diameter, played by striking one against the other, held in a cupped hand. In danzones, the claves often play the son clave pattern.

Comparsa   A comparsa is a group of people who form part of a carnival parade, usually wearing specially created outfits, playing music, and dancing together.

Conga   A multivalent term referring to a comparsa (or its music); a woman or thing from the Congo; or more commonly in Veracruz, a large single-headed hand drum, also known as a tumbadora. Usually two or three conga drums of different sizes are played together.

Contradanza   See *Contredanse*.

Contradanza cubana   The characteristic marker of the Cuban contradanza is the tango isorhythm. The contradanza cubana began to include closed-position dancing.

Contredanse   A series of seventeenth-century French dances (that were derived from English country dances after being notated by dance master André Lorin, see Guilcher 1969). Contredanses tended to be written in 2/4 or 6/8, with two repeated eight-bar sections (AABB), like the subsequent Cuban contradanzas. They were generally danced lengthways by two lines of dancers in open position, with variations incorporated. *Contradanza* is the Spanish for *contredanse*, and both incorporate a shifting set of music-dance forms (see Malcomson 2011).

Criolla/o   Person born in the circum-Caribbean, especially of European descent.

Danza   A term sometimes used synonymously with *contradanza (cubana)*, or to refer to a later form of this music-dance form.

Danzón   Danzón is characterized by its rondo form (ABACAD), and its two-bar *cinquillo* pattern (in 3-2 *clave*). The rondo form was to have a profound impact on the choreography of danzón, which is characterized by its A sections being "non-danceable": the *descansos* (rests).

Danzonera   Female danzón performer or danzón ensemble including clarinets and/or saxophones, trumpets, trombone, keyboard, electric bass, timbales, and güiro/claves player, and congas in Veracruz and Cuba.

Danzonera/o   Female or male danzón performer. The plural *danzoneros/danzonerxs* includes both women and men.

Danzonete   Danzón that includes extensive vocal texts (akin to those of *son cubano*). The first danzonete was (probably) Aniceto Díaz's *Rompiendo la Rutina* (1929).

Décima   Verse of ten octosyllabic lines, sometimes sung.

Descanso   Meaning "rest." In danzón dancing, the descanso is the rest in the non-danceable A sections of danzón's rondo form (ABACAD).

English Country Dance   A series of dances (round, longways, jig), such as those published by Playford from 1650 (e.g., 1698).

Güiro   A serrated gourd scraped with a small stick.

IVEC   Instituto Veracruzano de la Cultura (Veracruz Culture Institute)

Jarocha/o   The term *Porteña/o* designates people specifically from the Port of Veracruz, while *Veracruzana/o* is used to refer to people from the Port and/or the State of Veracruz. *Jarocha/o* is often employed to denote people from the Port of Veracruz, or the Veracruz coast, but is sometimes used by Porteña/os to describe people from the Papaloapan valley just south of the Port, the Sotavento region and the Tuxtlas. All three terms are commonly employed interchangeably.

Mambo   This multivalent term is generally used to denote a (usually final) section of a piece, characterized by repeated syncopated (often sax or brass) patterns, as well as a genre, epitomized by Pérez Prado, incorporating a big-band sound. The term is sometimes used synonymously with *ritmo nuevo*.

Marimba   Marimba ensembles in Veracruz usually consist of one to three players on the marimba (using rubber mallets), drum kit, and *güiro*. Such ensembles are widespread in Oaxaca, Chiapas, and Guatemala.

Mestiza/o / Mestizaje   Mestizaje refers to "racial" or cultural intermixture brought about by both sexual and social relations. Mestiza/o refers to the person.

Montuno   Literally, "from the mountains or countryside." Used to refer to the final section *of son cubano* (and also integrated into danzones), characterized by rhythmic and harmonic *ostinati* (repeated riffs), call and response, and improvisation.

Mulata/o   Mulata/o refers to people of Afro-Caribbean/"African" and Spanish/European parentage (both "racially" and culturally).

Municipal band   Mexico's municipal bands often combine flutes, clarinets, saxophones, trumpets, trombones, sousaphone, *güiro*, clash cymbals, bass drums, and *timbales*.

Música tropical   "Tropical Music." An umbrella term encompassing Cuban music, such as son cubano, guaracha, and cumbia. See *Rumba*.

Orquesta de baile (often shortened to orquesta)   Dance orchestra.

Orquesta típica   The ensembles that most commonly played danzones in the late nineteenth and early twentieth centuries. They often consisted of two clarinets, a cornet, ophicleide (*figle*), trombone, euphonium (*bombardino*), *timbales, güiro*, two violins, and bass.

Pachuco/a   A pachuco is a male zoot-suit-clad dandy. Pachuco counterculture is key to understanding mid-twentieth-century Chicano cultures, and the look was made famous in Mexico by the actor Johnny Weissmuller (renowned for playing Tarzan), and then by film star Germán "Tin Tan" Valdés. While there is a female Pachuca look, I have not seen danzoneras in Mexico assume this.

Porteña/o   Person (or thing) from the Port. See *Jarocha/o*.

Ritmo nuevo   "New rhythm." A form of danzón that emerged in the early 1940s, with Orestes and *Cachao* López and *Arcaño y sus Maravillas*, featuring syncopated melodies and riffs, particularly in the final section. The term is often used synonymously with *mambo*.

Rumba   The multivalent term *rumba* refers both to the polyrhythmic Cuban music-dance forms *guaguancó, yambú*, and *columbia*, sung and played on a variety of percussion instruments; and the commercial forms of *rumba* popular in the Americas and Europe from the 1930s. The term *rumba* was used in Mexico until around the 1970s to denote Cuban music (such as son cubano and guaracha), which was later referred to as *música tropical*, and *salsa*. Usually, danzón was not included under these umbrella terms and was identified separately. The term *rumba* also evokes Mexico's "rumberas" (often scantily clad rumba dancers) of 1940s and 1950s film fame, such as Ninón Sevilla, Meche Barba, and Rosa Carmina.

Salsa   Literally, "sauce." An umbrella term (like *rumba* and *música tropical*) used to refer to several genres performed and promoted commercially by Latinxs (particularly Cubans, Puerto Ricans, Colombians, Nuyoricans) since the 1970s.

Son cubano (also refered to as son montuno) An Afro-Cuban genre that became popular in the 1920s, often performed by ensembles including a vocalist, *tres* player, and percussionist.

Son jarocho A music-dance genre particularly associated with the Sotavento region, south of Veracruz. Son jarocho ensembles often include one or more *jaranas* (small guitars of various sizes with eight single and paired strings tuned to five pitches), a *requinto* (another small guitar with four strings), and a single-strung, diatonic harp (without pedals). It is danced with *zapateo* (stamping) on a *tarima* (percussion platform).

Sonora Ensemble playing primarily *son cubano*. Sonoras vary considerably in terms of instrumentation, but in Veracruz today, they often consist of *tres*, one or two guitars, bass, *bongos*, *congas*, *tarolas* (with cymbal and cowbells), one to three vocalists (often playing hand-held percussion: maracas, *cencerro* (cowbells: metal and plastic), *güiro* (metal and plastic), *claves*, tambourine, one to three trumpets, and sometimes a saxophone, clarinet, trombone, and electric keyboard.

Tango As well as referring to the rhythm , the term *tango* was used to denote enslaved people dancing in the streets in the mid-nineteenth century (Carpentier 1946), and the dance that became popular in Argentina around the 1880s.

Timbales Two small timpani (usually 50 and 55 cm in diameter).

Tres A small Cuban guitar with three pairs of metal strings, usually tuned G, C, E. In Veracruz, it is often called a *tresillo* (a term also meaning "triplet").

Select Discography

Acerina y su Danzonera. *30 Exitos 30. Album de Oro con sus 30 Grandes Exitos*. Orfeon JM-07. 1985. LP.
Alberto Corrales y su Orquesta Panorama. *La Flauta en el Danzón Vol. 1*. Areito-LD-4399. 1988. LP.
Carlos Campos. *Danzones Melódicos*. Musart D-121P. 1956. LP.
Danzonera Alma de Sotavento. *De la Habana a Veracruz con la Danzonera Alma de Sotavento*. Promex PRO-LP-505. No date. LP.
Danzonera La Playa. *55 Años en el Danzón*. Ediciones Pentagrama APCD459. 2001. CD.
Lara, Agustín. *15 Inolvidables en la Voz de Agustín Lara. Versiones Originales*. RCA Victor MKS-2381. 1984. LP.
Rotterdam Conservatory Orquesta Típica. *Cuba: Contradanza & Danzones*. Nimbus NI5502. 1996. CD.
Various artists. *Centenario del Danzón*. Orfeon JM-315. No date. LP.
Various artists. *Cuban Danzón: Before There Was Jazz: 1906–1929*. Arhoolie CD-7032. 1999. CD.
Various artists. *Cuban Danzoneras 1932–1946*. Harlequin Records HQCD 65. 1998. CD.
Various artists. *Danzones del Porfiriato y la Revolución*. BMG Entertainment Mexico. AMEF T-44-03, RCA—PECD-367. 1994. CD.
Various artists. *De Cuba con Amor. Una Historia del Danzón en México*. Discos Pentagrama DCD-260. 2006. CD.
Various artists. *Early Cuban Danzón Orchestras 1916–1920*. Harlequin Records HQ CD131. 1999. CD.

Select Filmography

Bustillo Oro, Juan, dir. *Solo Veracruz es Bello.* México: Producciónes Grovas, 1949.
Fernández, Emilio, dir. *Salón México,* México: Clasa Films Mundiales, 1949.
García Agraz, José Luis, dir. *Salón México.* México: Televicine, 1994.
Gout, Alberto, dir. *Aventurera.* México: Cinematográfica Calderón, 1949.
Novaro, María, dir. *Danzón.* México/Spain: IMCINE, 1991.

Bibliography

Abu-Lughod, Lila. 1986. *Veiled Sentiments: Honor and Poetry in a Bedouin Society*. Berkeley: University of California Press.
Acosta, Leonardo. 2004. *Otra Visión de la Música Popular Cubana*. La Habana: Editorial Letras Cubana.
Aguirre Aguilar, Genaro. 2008. "Texturas del Amor Contemporáneo. Imaginarios Juveniles y Prácticas Amorosas Urbanas." PhD, Department of Social Anthropology, University of Granada.
Aguirre Beltrán, Gonzalo. 1972. *La Población Negra de México. Estudio Etnohistórico*. 2nd ed. (México D.F.: Fondo de Cultura Económica. Original edition, 1946.
Aguirre Cristiani, Gabriela. 1994. "The Ballet and Its Founder." In *Amalia Hernández' Folkloric Ballet of Mexico*, edited by Gabriela Aguirre Cristiani and Felipe Segura Escalona. México D.F.: Fomento Cultural Banamex.
Alonso, Ana María. 2004. "Conforming Disconformity: 'Mestizaje,' Hybridity, and the Aesthetics of Mexican Nationalism." *Cultural Anthropology* 19, no. 4: 459–90.
Amans, Diane. 2013. *Age and Dancing: Older People and Community Dance Practice*. New York: Palgrave Macmillan.
Améry, Jean. 1994. *On Aging: Revolt and Resignation*. Translated by John D. Barlow. Bloomington: Indiana University Press. 1968.
Anzaldúa, Gloria. 1987. *Borderlands / La Frontera: The New Mestiza*. San Francisco: Aunt Lute.
Aparicio, Frances R., and Susana Chávez-Silverman. 1997. "Introduction." In *Tropicalizations: Transcultural Representations of Latinidad*, edited by Frances R. Aparicio and Susana Chávez-Silverman, 1–17. Hanover: University Press of New England.
Archetti, Eduardo P. 1999. *Masculinities: Football, Polo and the Tango in Argentina*. Oxford: Berg.
Argyriadis, Kali. 2013. "Santeros, Brujos, Artistas y Militantes: Redes Transnacionales y Usos de Signos 'Afro' entre Cuba y Veracruz." *Ollin: Revista del Centro INAH de Veracruz* 12: 7–20.

Arredondo, Isabel. 1999. "By Popular Demand: I Will See *Danzón* until I Can't Stand It Anymore." *Journal of Communication Inquiry* 23, no.2: 183–96.

Astorga, Luis. 2005. *El Siglo de las Drogas: El Narcotráfico, del Porfiriato al Nuevo Milenio*. México: Plaza y Janés.

Avila, Jaqueline. 2019. *Cinesonidos: Film Music and National Identity during Mexico's Época de Oro*. New York: Oxford University Press.

Back, Les. 2007. *The Art of Listening*. Oxford: Berg.

Back, Les. 2014. "Journeying through Words: Les Back Reflects on Writing with Thomas Yarrow." *Journal of the Royal Anthropological Institute* 20, no. 4: 766–70.

Báez-Jorge, Félix. 2007. "Contrapuntos de una Identidad Festiva." In *Jarochilandia*, edited by Anselmo Mancisidor Ortiz, 9–20. Veracruz: Gobierno del Estado de Veracruz de Ignacio de la Llave.

Bakhtin, Mikhail. 1984. *Rabelais and His World*. Translated by Hélène Iswolsky. Bloomington: Indiana University Press. 1965.

Balderston, Daniel, and Donna J. Guy, eds. 1997. *Sex and Sexuality in Latin America*. New York: New York University Press.

Bauman, Zygmunt. 1991. *Modernity and Ambivalence*. Ithaca: Cornell University Press.

Bennett, Andy. 2013. *Music, Style, and Aging: Growing Old Disgracefully?* Philadelphia: Temple University Press.

Berlanga Gayón, Mariana. 2015. "El Espectaculo de la Violencia en el Mexico Actual: Del Feminicidio al Juvenicidio." *Athenea Digital* 15, no. 4: 105–28.

Berlant, Lauren. 1998. "Intimacy: A Special Issue." *Critical Inquiry* 24, no. 2: 281–88.

Berlant, Lauren. 2001. "Love, a Queer Feeling." In *Homosexuality and Psychoanalysis*, edited by Tim Dean and Christopher Lane, 432–51. University of Chicago Press.

Berlant, Lauren. 2006. "Cruel Optimism." *Differences: A Journal of Feminist Cultural Studies* 17, no. 3: 20–36.

Berlant, Lauren. 2011. "A Properly Political Concept of Love: Three Approaches in Ten Pages." *Cultural Anthropology* 26, no.4: 683–91.

Bion, Wilfred. 1961. *Experiences in Groups and Other Papers*. London: Tavistock.

Bithell, Caroline, and Juniper Hill, eds. 2014. *The Oxford Handbook of Music Revival*. New York: Oxford University Press.

Bleuler, Eugen. 1911. "Vortrag über Ambivalenz." *Zentralblatt für Psychoanalyse* 1: 266–68.

Born, Georgina. 1995. *Rationalizing Culture: IRCAM, Boulez, and the Institutionalisation of the Musical Avant-Garde*. Berkeley: University of California Press.

Bosse, Joanna. 2007. "Whiteness and the Performance of Race in American Ballroom Dance." *The Journal of American Folklore* 120, no. 475: 19–47.

Bosse, Joanna. 2015. *Becoming Beautiful: Ballroom Dance in the American Heartland*. Urbana: University of Illinois Press.

Bourdieu, Pierre. 1977. *Outline of a Theory of Practice*. Translated by Richard Nice. Cambridge: Cambridge University Press. 1972.

Bourdieu, Pierre. 1984. *Distinction: A Social Critique of the Judgement of Taste*. Translated by Richard Nice. New York: Routledge. 1979.

Bourdieu, Pierre. 1993. *The Field of Cultural Production: Essays on Art and Literature.* Translated by Richard Nice. Edited by Randal Johnson. Cambridge: Polity.

Boym, Svetlana. 2001. *The Future of Nostalgia.* New York: Basic Books.

Browning, Barbara. 1995. *Samba: Resistance in Motion.* Bloomington: Indiana University Press.

Buechler, Hans. 1989. "Apprenticeship and Transmission of Knowledge in La Paz, Bolivia." In *Apprenticeship: From Theory to Method and Back Again,* edited by Michael William Coy, 31–50. Albany: State University of New York Press.

Buffington, Robert. 2005. "La 'Dancing' Mexicana: Danzón and the Transformation of Intimacy in Post-Revolutionary Mexico City." *Journal of Latin American Cultural Studies* 14, no. 1: 87–108.

Bull, Anna. 2019. *Class, Control, and Classical Music.* New York: Oxford University Press.

Butler, Judith. 1993. *Bodies That Matter: On the Discursive Limits of 'Sex.'* New York: Routledge.

Cahn, Peter S. 2008. "Consuming Class: Multilevel Marketers in Neoliberal Mexico." *Cultural Anthropology* 23, no. 3: 429–52.

Carillo, Héctor. 2004. "Neither *Machos* nor *Maricones*: Masculinity and Emerging Male Homosexual Identities in Mexico." In *Changing Men and Masculinities in Latin America,* edited by Matthew C. Gutmann, 351–69. Durham: Duke University Press.

Carpentier, Alejo. 1946. *La Música en Cuba.* 2nd ed. *Colección Popular.* México D.F.: Fondo de Cultura Económica.

Carroll, Patrick J. 2001. *Blacks in Colonial Veracruz: Race, Ethnicity, and Regional Development.* Austin: University of Texas Press.

Cashion, Susan. 2009. "The Mexican Danzón: Restrained Sensuality." In *Dancing across Borders. Danzas y Bailes Mexicanos,* edited by Olga Nájera-Ramírez, Norma E. Cantú, and Brenda M. Romero, 237–55. Urbana: University of Illinois Press.

Castillo Faílde, Osvaldo. 1964. *Miguel Faílde, Creador Musical del Danzón.* La Habana: Editorial Consejo Nacional de Cultura.

Castillo, Gustavo, and Eduardo Murillo. 2020. "Se Dispara el Tráfico de Drogas en Barcos." *La Jornada* (9 Abril 2020). https://www.jornada.com.mx/ultimas/politica/2020/04/09/se-dispara-el trafico-de-drogas-en-barcos-9691.html.

Chasteen, John Charles. 2004. *National Rhythms, African Roots: The Deep History of Latin American Popular Dance.* Albuquerque: University of New Mexico Press.

Civeira Taboada, Miguel. 1978. *Sensibilidad Yucateca en la Canción Romántica Vol I.* México D.F.: FONAPAS. 1880.

Clifford, James, and George E. Marcus, eds. 1986. *Writing Culture: The Poetics and Politics of Ethnography.* Berkeley: University of California Press.

Cole, Ross. 2019. "On the Politics of Folk Song Theory in Edwardian England." *Ethnomusicology* 63, no. 1: 19–42.

Connidis, Ingrid Arnet, Klas Borell, and Sofie Ghazanfareeon Karlsson. 2017. "Ambivalence and Living Apart Together in Later Life: A Critical Research Proposal." *Journal of Marriage and Family* 79, no. 5: 1404–18.

Connolly, Priscilla. 1999. "Pearson and Public Works Construction in Mexico, 1890–1910." *Business History* 41, no. 4: 48–71.

Cook, Matt. 2020. "Portable Closets: Secrets and Lives in Queer Britain since Gay Liberation." Abstract for talk at the University of Lincoln, February 13, 2020. https://lgbtplushistorymonth.co.uk/events/portable-closets-secrets-and-lives-in-queer-britain-since-gay-liberation.

Cooper, Lesley, and Helen Thomas. 2002. "Growing Old Gracefully: Social Dance in the Third Age." *Ageing and Society* 22, no. 6: 689–708.

Córdova Plaza, Rosío. 2011. "Sexualidades Disidentes: Entre Cuerpos Normatizados y Cuerpos Lábiles." *La Ventana. Revista de Estudios de Género* 4, no. 33: 42–72.

Cortés Rodríguez, Martha Inés. 2000. *Los Carnavales de Veracruz*. Veracruz: Instituto Veracruzano de Cultura.

Covarrubias, Miguel. 1947. *Mexico South: The Isthmus of Tehuantepec*. London: Cassell and Co.

Cowan, Jane K. 1990. *Dance and the Body Politic in Northern Greece*. Princeton: Princeton University Press.

Coy, Michael William, ed. 1989a. *Apprenticeship: From Theory to Method and Back Again*. Albany: State University of New York Press.

Coy, Michael William. 1989b. "From Theory." In *Apprenticeship: From Theory to Method and Back Again*, edited by Michael William Coy, 1–12. Albany: State University of New York Press.

Dar, Sadhvi. 2018. "De-Colonizing the Boundary-Object." *Organization Studies* 39, no.4: 565–84.

Davis, Kathy. 2015. "Should a Feminist Dance Tango? Some Reflections on the Experience and Politics of Passion1." *Feminist Theory* 16, no. 1: 3–21.

Daynes, Sarah. 2004. "The Musical Construction of the Diaspora: The Case of Reggae and Rastafari." In *Music, Space and Place: Popular Music and Cultural Identity*, edited by Sheila Whiteley, Andy Bennett, and Stan Hawkins, 25–41. Aldershot: Ashgate.

Degnen, Cathrine. 2007. "Minding the Gap: The Construction of Old Age and Oldness amongst Peers." *Journal of Aging Studies* 21: 69–80.

Derrida, Jacques. 2001. "From Restricted to General Economy: A Hegelianism without Reserve." In *Writing and Difference*, 317–50. London: Routledge. Original edition, 1967.

Domínguez Pérez, Olivia, and Sergio López Galván. 1994. "La Requisa y Privatización de Servicios Portuarios de Veracruz." *Anuario IX, Centro de Investigaciones Históricas, Instituto de Investigaciones Historicos Sociales, Universidad Veracruzana*: 277–89.

Du Bois, W. E. B. 1897. "Strivings of the Negro People." *Atlantic Monthly Company* 80 (August): 194–98.

Du Bois, W. E. B. 1994. *The Souls of Black Folk*. London: Dover Publications. 1903.

El Dictamen. 1983. "Banda de Música del Hospicio 'Manuel Gutiérrez Zamora.'" *El Dictamen*, February 27, 1983, Magazine Dominical.

El Dictamen. 1986. "Se Instituyó 'La Noche del Danzón.'" *El Dictamen*, July 17, 1986, 2.

Esposito, Joseph L. 1987. *The Obsolete Self: Philosophical Dimensions of Aging*. Berkeley: University of California Press.

Feldman, Heidi Carolyn. 2006. *Black Rhythms of Peru: Reviving African Musical Heritage in the Black Pacific*. Middletown: Wesleyan University Press.

Ferber, Abby L. 2007. "Whiteness Studies and the Erasure of Gender." *Sociology Compass* 1, no. 1: 265–82.

Figueroa Hernández, Rafael. 2007. *Tres Generaciones del Danzón Veracruzano*. Xalapa: published by author.

Finnegan, Ruth. 1989. *The Hidden Musicians: Music-Making in an English Town*. Cambridge: Cambridge University Press.

Flores Martos, Juan Antonio. 1996. "Una Mitología Urbana: Las Historias de 'Locos' y 'Personajes' en Veracruz." *La Palabra y el Hombre* 99: 133–48.

Flores Martos, Juan Antonio. 2000. "Viajes Espirituales en el Puerto de Veracruz (México)." *Cuadernos Hispanoamericanos* Dossier "Religiones Populares Iberoamericanas" (597): 43–53.

Flores Martos, Juan Antonio. 2004. *Portales de Múcara. Una Etnografía del Puerto de Veracruz*. Xalapa: Universidad Veracruzana.

Flores y Escalante, Jesús. 1993. *Salón México: Historia Documental y Gráfica del Danzón en México*. 2nd ed. México D.F.: Asociación Mexicana de Estudios Fonográficos.

Flores y Escalante, Jesús. 1994. *Imagenes del Danzón: Iconografia del Danzón en México*. 2nd ed. México D.F.: Asociación Mexicana de Estudios Fonográficos.

Foster, David William. 2002. *Mexico City in Contemporary Mexican Cinema*. Austin: University of Texas Press.

Foucault, Michel. 1977. *Discipline and Punish: The Birth of the Prison*. Translated by Alan Sheridan. New York: Vintage Books, Random House. 1975.

Foucault, Michel. 1986. "Of Other Spaces." *Diacritics*: 22–27. Translated by Jay Miskowiec.

Franco, Jean. 1999. "La Malinche: From Gift to Sexual Contract." In *Critical Passions: Selected Essays*, edited by Jean Franco, Mary Louise Pratt, and Kathleen Newman, 66–82. Durham: Duke University Press. Original edition, 1992.

Frankenberg, Ruth. 1993. *White Women, Race Matters: The Social Construction of Whiteness*. Minneapolis: University of Minnesota Press.

French, William E., and Katherine Elaine Bliss, eds. 2007. *Gender, Sexuality, and Power in Latin America since Independence*. Lanham: Rowman and Littlefield.

Galán, Natalio. 1983. *Cuba y Sus Sones*. Madrid: Pre-Textos.

Galindo Valencia, Miguel A. 1988. "La Cultura y Las Casas de Cultura en el Estado de Veracruz." In *Jornadas de Homenaje a Gonzalo Aguirre Beltrán*, 61–65. Veracruz: IVEC.

Gall, Olivia. 2013. "Mexican Long-Living Mestizophilia Versus a Democracy Open to Diversity." *Latin American and Caribbean Ethnic Studies* 8, no. 3: 280–303.

García, David F. 2006a. *Arsenio Rodríguez and the Transnational Flows of Latin Popular Music*. Philadelphia: Temple University Press.

García, David F. 2006b. "Going Primitive to the Movements and Sounds of Mambo." *The Musical Quarterly* 89 (4): 505–23.

García, David F. 2017. *Listening for Africa: Freedom, Modernity, and the Logic of Black Music's African Origins.* Durham: Duke University Press.

García, David F. 2018. "The Afro-Cuban Soundscape of Mexico City: Authenticating Spaces of Violence and Immorality in Salón México and Víctimas del Pecado." In *Screening Songs in Hispanic and Lusophone Cinema,* edited by Lisa Shaw and Rob Stone, 167–88. Manchester: Manchester University Press.

García de León Griego, Antonio. 1996. "Con la Vida de Un Danzón: Notas Sobre el Movimiento Inquilinario de Veracruz en 1922." In *Actores Sociales en Un Proceso de Transformación: Veracruz en Los Años Veinte,* edited by Manuel Reyna Muñoz, 33–53. Xalapa: Universidad Veracruzana.

García Díaz, Bernardo. 1992. *Puerto de Veracruz: Imágenes de Su Historia.* Xalapa: Archivo General del Estado de Veracruz.

García Díaz, Bernardo. 1999. "Dinámica y Porvenir del Puerto de Veracruz: Crecimiento y Transformaciones en el Siglo XX." In *Veracruz: Primer Puerto del Continente,* 218–53. México D.F.: Espejo de Obsidiana. Original edition, 1996.

García Díaz, Bernardo. 2002. "Danzón y Son: Desde Cuba a Veracruz (1880–1930)." In *México y el Caribe: Vínculos, Intereses, Region,* edited by Laura Muñoz, 266–81. México D.F.: Instituto Mora.

García Díaz, Bernardo, and Horacio Guadarrama Olivera. 2004. *Breve Historia del Instituto Veracruzano de la Cultura. Tomo I: Los Primeros XV Años.* Veracruz: Gobierno del Estado de Veracruz-Llave.

Gilroy, Paul. 1991. "Sounds Authentic: Black Music, Ethnicity, and the Challenge of a 'Changing' Same." *Black Music Research Journal* 11, no. 2: 111–36.

Gilroy, Paul. 1993. *The Black Atlantic: Double Consciousness and Modernity.* Cambridge: Harvard University Press.

Gilroy, Paul. 2004. *After Empire: Melancholia or Convivial Culture?* London: Routledge.

Goffman, Erving. 1959. *The Presentation of the Self in Everyday Life.* Garden City: Doubleday.

González, Anita. 2010. *Afro-Mexico: Dancing between Myth and Reality.* Austin: University of Texas Press.

González García, Francisco "Tiburón." n.d. *Casos y Cosas de mi Veracruz.* Veracruz: Published by author. ca. 1989.

Goody, Esther N. 1989. "Learning, Apprenticeship and the Division of Labor." In *Apprenticeship: From Theory to Method and Back Again,* edited by Michael William Coy, 233–57. Albany: State University of New York Press.

Greene, Graham. 1993. *The Lawless Roads.* Harmondsworth: Penguin. 1939.

Griffiths, Hugh, and Michael Jenks. 2012. "Maritime Transport and Destabilizing Commodity Flows." *SIPRI Policy Paper* Stockholm International Peace Research Institute (No. 32).

Guadarrama Olivera, Horacio. 2002. "Los Carnavales del Puerto de Veracruz." In

La Habana / Veracruz, Veracruz / La Habana. Las Dos Orillas, edited by Bernardo García Díaz and Sergio Guerra Vilaboy, 468–93. México D.F.: Universidad Veracruzana.

Guerrero C., Alejandro, and César Rivera, T. 2009. "México: Cambio en la Productividad Total de Los Principales Puertos de Contenedores." *Revista Cepal* 99: 175–87.

Guilcher, Jean-Michel. 1969. *La Contredanse et les Renouvellements de la Danse Française.* Paris: Mouton.

Gullette, Margaret Morganroth. 2004. *Aged by Culture.* Chicago: University of Chicago Press.

Gutiérrez, Laura G. 2019. "Afrodiasporic Visual and Sonic Assemblages: Racialized Anxieties and the Disruption of Mexicanidad in *Cine de Rumberas.*" In *Decentering the Nation: Music, Mexicanidad, and Globalization,* edited by Jesús A. Ramos-Kittrell, 1–22. Lanham: Lexington Books.

Gutiérrez, María Elisa Velázquez. 2018. "Calidades, Castas y Razas en el México Virreinal. El Uso de Categorías y Clasificaciones de las Poblaciones de Origen Africano." *Estudios Ibero-Americanos* 44, no. 3: 435–46.

Gutmann, Matthew C. 1996. *The Meanings of Macho: Being a Man in Mexico City.* Berkeley: University of California Press.

Gutmann, Matthew C. 2002. *The Romance of Democracy: Compliant Defiance in Contemporary Mexico.* Berkeley: University of California Press.

Hahn, Tomie. 2007. *Sensational Knowledge. Embodying Culture through Japanese Dance.* Middletown: Wesleyan University Press.

Hajda, Jan. 1968. "Ambivalence and Social Relations." *Sociological Focus* 2, no. 2: 21–28.

Hale, Charles R. 2006. *Más que un Indio = More Than an Indian: Racial Ambivalence and Neoliberal Multiculturalism in Guatemala.* 1st ed. Santa Fe: School of American Research Press.

Hegel, Georg Wilhelm Friedrich. 1874. *The Logic of Hegel. Translated from the Encyclopaedia of the Philosophical Sciences, with Prolegomena by William Wallace.* Oxford: Clarendon Press.

Hegel, Georg Wilhelm Friedrich. 1994. *Hegel's Phenomenology of Spirit.* Translated by Howard P. Kainz. University Park: Pennsylvania State University Press. Original edition, 1807.

Hertzman, Marc A. 2013. *Making Samba: A New History of Race and Music in Brazil.* Durham: Duke University Press.

Herzfeld, Michael. 1987. *Anthropology through the Looking-Glass: Critical Ethnography in the Margins of Europe.* Cambridge: Cambridge University Press.

Herzfeld, Michael. 2004. *The Body Impolitic: Artisans and Artifice in the Global Hierarchy of Value.* Chicago: University of Chicago Press.

Herzfeld, Michael. 2005. *Cultural Intimacy: Social Poetics in the Nation-State,* 2nd ed. New York: Routledge.

Hilder, Thomas R. 2012. "Repatriation, Revival and Transmission: The Politics of Sámi Musical Heritage." *Ethnomusicology Forum* 21, no. 2: 161–79.

Hill, Juniper, and Caroline Bithell. 2014. "An Introduction to Music Revival as Concept, Cultural Process, and Medium of Change." In *The Oxford Handbook of Music Revival*, edited by Caroline Bithell and Juniper Hill, 3–42. New York: Oxford University Press.

Hillcoat-Nallétamby, Sarah, and Judith E Phillips. 2011. "Sociological Ambivalence Revisited." *Sociology* 45, no. 2: 202–17.

Hinshelwood, R. D. 1989. *A Dictionary of Kleinian Thought*. 2nd ed. London: Free Association Books.

Hirsch, Jennifer S. 2003. *A Courtship after Marriage: Sexuality and Love in Mexican Transnational Families*. Berkeley: University of California Press.

Hobsbawm, Eric. 1983. "Introduction: Inventing Traditions." In *The Invention of Tradition*, edited by Eric Hobsbawm and Terence Ranger, 1–14. Cambridge: Cambridge University Press.

Hobsbawm, Eric, and Terence Ranger, eds. 1983. *The Invention of Tradition*. Cambridge: Cambridge University Press.

Hochschild, Arlie Russell. 2003. *The Managed Heart: Commercialization of Human Feeling*. Berkeley: University of California Press. 1983.

Hodkinson, Paul, and Andy Bennett. 2012. *Ageing and Youth Cultures: Music, Style and Identity*. Oxford and New York: Berg.

Hoffmann, Odile, and Christian Rinaudo. 2014. "The Issue of Blackness and Mestizaje in Two Distinct Mexican Contexts: Veracruz and Costa Chica." *Latin American and Caribbean Ethnic Studies*: 1–18.

Hurston, Zora Neale. 1935. *Mules and Men*. New York: Harper Perennial.

Hutcheon, Linda, and Mario J. Valdés. 2000. "Irony, Nostalgia, and the Postmodern: A Dialogue." *Poligrafías. Revista de Literatura Comparada* 3 (1998–2000): 18–41.

Hutchinson, Sydney. 2009. "The Ballet Folklórico de México and the Construction of the Mexican Nation through Dance." In *Dancing across Borders. Danzas y Bailes Mexicanos*, edited by Olga Nájera-Ramírez, Norma E. Cantú, and Brenda M. Romero, 206–25. Urbana: University of Illinois Press.

Hutchinson, Sydney. 2016. *Tigers of a Different Stripe: Performing Gender in Dominican Music*. Chicago: University of Chicago Press.

Iannaccone, Laurence R. 1998. "Introduction to the Economics of Religion." *Journal of Economic Literature* 36, no. 3: 1465–95.

Iglesias Prieto, Norma. 2004. "Gazes and Cinematic Readings of Gender: Danzón and Its Relationship to Its Audience." *Discourse* 26, no. 1–2: 173–93.

Illouz, Eva. 2012. *Why Love Hurts: A Sociological Explanation*. Cambridge: Polity Press.

INEGI. 2020. "Instituto Nacional de Estadística Geografía e Informatica: Censo de Población y Vivienda 2010." Accessed April 22, 2020. https://www.inegi.org.mx/app/biblioteca/ficha.html?upc=702825002042.

INEGI. 2021. "Defunciones por Homicidios." Accessed December 22, 2021. https://www.inegi.org.mx/sistemas/olap/proyectos/bd/continuas/mortalidad/defuncioneshom.asp?s=est.

Jara Gámez, Simón, Aurelio Yeyo Rodriguez, and Antonio Zedillo Castillo. 1994.

De Cuba con Amor: El Danzón en México. México D.F.: Consejo Nacional para la Cultura y las Artes.

Jiménez, Lucina. 2006. *Políticas Culturales en Transición. Retos y Escenarios de la Gestión Cultural en México.* México D.F.: Colección Intersecciones, Consejo Nacional para la Cultura y las Artes, Fondo Regional para la Cultura y las Artes de la Zona Sur.

Jones, Jennifer Anne Meri. 2013. "'Mexicans Will Take the Jobs That Even Blacks Won't Do': An Analysis of Blackness, Regionalism and Invisibility in Contemporary Mexico." *Ethnic and Racial Studies* 36, no. 10: 1564–81.

Kant, Immanuel. 1998. *Critique of Pure Reason.* Translated by Paul Guyer and Allen W. Wood. Cambridge: Cambridge University Press. Original edition, 1781.

Kaufman, Sharon R. 1986. *The Ageless Self: Sources of Meaning in Late Life.* Madison: University of Wisconsin Press.

Kingsbury, Henry. 1988. *Music, Talent and Performance: A Conservatory Cultural System.* Philadelphia: Temple University Press.

Klein, Melanie. 1975. *Envy and Gratitude and Other Works 1946–1963.* London: Hogarth Press.

Knight, Alan. 1990a. *The Mexican Revolution: Counter-Revolution and Reconstruction.* Vol. 2. Lincoln: University of Nebraska Press. 1986.

Knight, Alan. 1990b. "Racism, Revolution, and Indigenismo: Mexico, 1910–1940." In *The Idea of Race in Latin America, 1870–1940*, edited by Richard Graham, 71–114. Austin: University of Texas Press.

Knight, Alan. 2002. *Mexico: The Colonial Era.* Cambridge: Cambridge University Press.

Kracauer, Siegfried. 1995a. "The Group as a Bearer of Ideas." In *The Mass Ornament: Weimar Essays (translated and edited by T. Y. Levin)*, 143–70. Cambridge: Harvard University Press. Original edition, 1922.

Kracauer, Siegfried. 1995b. "The Mass Ornament." In *The Mass Ornament: Weimar Essays (translated and edited by T. Y. Levin)*, 75–86. Cambridge: Harvard University Press. Original edition, 1927.

Kun, Josh. 2005. *Audiotopia: Music, Race, and America.* Vol. 18. Berkeley: University of California Press.

Lacan, Jacques. 1990. "The Mirror Stage as Formative of the Function of the I as Revealed in Psychoanalytic Experience." In *Écrits: A Selection*, 1–7. London: Routledge. Original edition, 1949.

Lancaster, Roger. 1992. *Life Is Hard: Machismo, Danger and the Intimacy of Power in Nicaragua.* Berkeley: University of California Press.

Lancaster, Roger N. 2003. "Skin Color, Race, and Racism in Nicaragua." In *Race and Ethnicity. Comparative and Theoretical Approaches*, edited by John Stone and Rutledge Dennis, 99–113. Chichester: Blackwell.

Latour, Bruno. 1987. *Science in Action: How to Follow Scientists and Engineers through Society.* Milton Keynes: Open University Press.

Latour, Bruno. 2005. *Reassembling the Social: An Introduction to Actor-Network-Theory*. Oxford: Oxford University Press.

Le Clercq Ortega, Juan Antonio, and Gerardo Rodríguez Sánchez Lara, eds. 2018. *La Impunidad Subnacional en México y sus Dimensiones. Índice Global de Impunidad México. IGI-Mex 2018*. Puebla: Fundación Universidad de las Américas, Puebla.

Lehmann, David. 2010. "Rational Choice and the Sociology of Religion." In *The New Blackwell Companion to the Sociology of Religion*, edited by Bryan S. Turner, 181–200. Chichester: Wiley.

León, Argeliers. 1991. "Notes toward a Panorama of Popular and Folk Music." In *Essays on Cuban Music: North American and Cuban Perspectives*, edited by Peter Manuel, 3–23. Lanham: University Press of America.

Lewis, Laura A. 2012. *Chocolate and Corn Flour: History, Race, and Place in the Making of "Black" Mexico*. Durham: Duke University Press.

Lewis, Oscar. 1961. *The Children of Sánchez: Autobiography of a Mexican Family*. New York: Vintage.

Lie, Nadia. 2017. *The Latin American (Counter-) Road Movie and Ambivalent Modernity*. Cham: Palgrave Macmillan.

Lindsay, Shawn. 1996. "Hand Drumming: An Essay in Practical Knowledge." In *Things as They Are: New Directions in Phenomenological Anthropology*, edited by Michael Jackson, 196–212. Bloomington: Indiana University Press.

Livingston, Tamara E. 1999. "Music Revivals: Towards a General Theory." *Ethnomusicology* 43, no. 1: 66–85.

Lock, Graham. 1999. *Blutopia: Visions of the Future and Revisions of the Past in the Work of Sun Ra, Duke Ellington, and Anthony Braxton*. Durham: Duke University Press.

López, Ana M. 1997. "Of Rhythms and Borders." In *Everynight Life: Culture and Dance in Latin/o America*, edited by Celeste Fraser Delgado and José Esteban Muñoz, 310–44. Durham: Duke University Press.

López Beltrán, Carlos. 2007. "Hippocratic Bodies. Temperament and Castas in Spanish America (1570–1820)." *Journal of Spanish Cultural Studies* 8. No. 2: 253–89.

Lortat-Jacob, Bernard. 1995. *Sardinian Chronicles*. Chicago: University of Chicago Press.

Luker, Morgan James. 2016. "Tango as Intangible Cultural Heritage: Development, Diversity, and the Values of Music in Buenos Aires." In *Audible Empire: Music, Global Politics, Critique*, edited by Ronald Radano and Tejumola Olaniyan, 225–45. Durham: Duke University Press.

Madrid, Alejandro L., and Robin D. Moore. 2013. *Danzón: Circum-Caribbean Dialogues in Music and Dance*. Oxford: Oxford University Press.

Malcomson, Hettie. 2010. "La Configuración Racial del Danzón: Los Imaginarios Raciales del Puerto de Veracruz." In *Mestizaje, Diferencia y Nación: Lo "Negro" en América Central y el Caribe*, edited by Elisabeth Cunin, 267–298. México D.F.: INAH, UNAM, CEMCA, IRD.

Malcomson, Hettie. 2011. "The 'Routes' and 'Roots' of Danzón: A Critique of the History of a Genre." *Popular Music* 30, no. 2: 263–78.

Malcomson, Hettie. 2012. "New Generations, Older Bodies: Danzón, Age and 'Cultural Rescue' in the Port of Veracruz, Mexico." *Popular Music* 31, no. 2: 217–230.

Malcomson, Hettie. 2013. "Composing Individuals: Ethnographic Reflections on Success and Prestige in the British New Music Network." *Twentieth-Century Music* 10, no. 1: 115–36.

Malcomson, Hettie. 2014a. "Aficionados, Academics, and Danzón Expertise: Exploring Hierarchies in Popular Music Knowledge Production." *Ethnomusicology* 58, no. 2: 222–53.

Malcomson, Hettie. 2014b. "Contradanza Cubana." In *The Bloomsbury Encyclopedia of Popular Music of the World, Volume 9. Genres: Caribbean and Latin America*, edited by David Horn, Mona-Lynn Courteau, Heidi Feldman, Pamela Narbona Jerez, and Hettie Malcomson, 218–23. London: Bloomsbury.

Malcomson, Hettie. 2016. "The Expediency of Blackness: Racial Logics and Danzón in the Port of Veracruz, Mexico." In *Afro-Latin@s in Movement: Critical Approaches to Blackness and Transnationalism in the Americas*, edited by Petra Rivera-Rideau, Jennifer A. Jones, and Tianna Paschel, 35–59. New York: Palgrave Macmillan.

Malnig, Julie. 2006. *Dancing till Dawn: A Century of Exhibition Dance*. New York: State University of New York Press.

Malnig, Julie, ed. 2009. *Ballroom, Boogie, Shimmy Sham, Shake: A Social and Popular Dance Reader*. Urbana: University of Illinois Press.

Mancisidor Ortiz, Anselmo. 2007. *Jarochilandia*. Veracruz: Gobierno del Estado de Veracruz de Ignacio de la Llave. Original edition, 1971.

Manuel, Peter, ed. 2009. *Creolizing Contradance in the Caribbean*. Philadelphia: Temple University Press.

Marchand, Trevor Hugh James. 2001. *Minaret Building and Apprenticeship in Yemen*. Richmond: Curzon Press.

Martin, Susanne. 2017. *Dancing Age(ing): Rethinking Age(ing) in and through Improvisation Practice and Performance*. Vol. 122. Bielefeld: transcript Verlag.

Martínez Furé, Rogelio. 1991. "Tambor (Drum)." In *Essays on Cuban Music: North American and Cuban Perspectives*, edited by Peter Manuel, 27–50. Lanham: University Press of America.

Martínez Montiel, Luz María. 1988. *La Gota de Oro*. Veracruz: IVEC.

Martínez Novo, Carmen. 2006. *Who Defines Indigenous?: Identities, Development, Intellectuals, and the State in Northern Mexico*. New Brunswick: Rutgers University Press.

Matory, J. Lorand. 1999. "Afro-Atlantic Culture: On the Live Dialogue between Africa and the Americas." In *Africana: The Encyclopedia of the African and African American Experience*, edited by K. A. Appiah and H. L Gates Jr. New York: Basic Civitas Books.

McMains, Juliet E. 2006. *Glamour Addiction: Inside the American Ballroom Dance Industry*. Middletown: Wesleyan University Press.

Merton, Robert K. (with Elinor Barber). 1976. "Sociological Ambivalence." In *Sociological Ambivalence and Other Essays*, 3–31. New York: The Free Press.

Miller, Sue. 2014. *Cuban Flute Style: Interpretation and Improvisation.* Lanham: Scarecrow Press.
Miller, Sue. 2021. *Improvising Sabor: Cuban Dance Music in New York.* Jackson: University Press of Mississippi.
Miranda, Francisco J. 1900. *Monografía Descriptiva de la Ciudad de Veracruz.* México D.F.: Talleres de la Tipografía Artística.
Moehn, Frederick. 2007. "Music, Citizenship, and Violence in Postdictatorship Brazil." *Latin American Music Review* 28, no, 2: 181–219.
Monsiváis, Carlos. 1981. *Escenas de Pudor y Liviandad.* México D.F.: Grijalbo.
Monsiváis, Carlos. 1997. *Mexican Postcards.* Translated by John Kraniauskas. London: Verso.
Moore, Robin D. 1997. *Nationalizing Blackness: Afrocubanismo and Artistic Revolution in Havana, 1920–1940.* Pittsburgh: University of Pittsburgh Press.
Mora, Sergio de la. 2006. *Cinemachismo: Masculinities and Sexuality in Mexican Film.* Austin: University of Texas Press.
Moreno Figueroa, Mónica G. 2008. "Historically Rooted Transnationalism: Slightedness and the Experience of Racism in Mexican Families." *Journal of Intercultural Studies* 29, no. 3: 283–97.
Moreno Figueroa, Mónica G. 2010. "Distributed Intensities: Whiteness, Mestizaje and the Logics of Mexican Racism." *Ethnicities* 10, no. 3: 1–15.
Moreno Figueroa, Mónica G. 2011. "Naming Ourselves: Recognising Racism and Mestizaje in Mexico." In *Contesting Recognition: Culture, Identity and Citizenship,* edited by Janice McLaughlin, Peter Phillimore, and Diane Richardson, 122–43. Basingstoke: Palgrave Macmillan.
Moreno Figueroa, Mónica G. 2012. "'Linda Morenita': Skin Colour, Beauty and the Politics of Mestizaje in Mexico." In *Cultures of Colour: Visual, Material, Textual,* edited by Chris Horrocks, 167–80. Oxford: Berghahn Books.
Moreno Figueroa, Mónica G. 2022. "Entre Confusiones y Distracciones: Mestizaje y Racismo Anti-Negro en México." *Estudios Sociológicos* 40: 31–60.
Moreno Figueroa, Mónica G., and Emiko Saldívar Tanaka. 2016. "'We Are Not Racists, We Are Mexicans': Privilege, Nationalism and Post-Race Ideology in Mexico." *Critical Sociology* 42, no. 4–5: 515–33.
Moreno Guerrero, Armando. 1992. "México, País de Leyendas." In *Cien Viajeros en Veracruz, Crónicas y Relatos (Tomo IX),* edited by Martha Poblett Miranda, 260–69. Veracruz: Gobierno del Estado de Veracruz. Original edition, 1945.
Nahoum-Grappe, Véronique. 2001. "La Cambrure sur l'Eau." *Autrement: Serie Mutations:* 56–71.
Navaro-Yashin, Yael. 2009. "Affective Spaces, Melancholic Objects: Ruination and the Production of Anthropological Knowledge." *Journal of the Royal Anthropological Institute* 15: 1–18.
Nayak, Anoop. 2007. "Critical Whiteness Studies." *Sociology Compass* 1, no, 2: 737–55.
Nettl, Bruno. 1983. *The Study of Ethnomusicology: Twenty-Nine Issues and Concepts.* Urbana: University of Illinois Press.

Nettl, Bruno. 1995. *Heartland Excursions: Ethnomusicological Reflections on Schools of Music.* Urbana: University of Illinois Press.

Neuman, Daniel M. 1990. *The Life of Music in North India: The Organization of an Artistic Tradition.* Chicago: University of Chicago Press. Original edition, 1980.

Ngai, Sianne. 2005. *Ugly Feelings.* Cambridge: Harvard University Press.

Nooshin, Laudan. 2015. *Iranian Classical Music: The Discourses and Practice of Creativity.* Farnham: Ashgate.

Ochoa Gautier, Ana María. 2006. "Sonic Transculturation, Epistemologies of Purification and the Aural Public Sphere in Latin America." *Social Identities* 12, no. 6: 803–25.

Okely, Judith. 1990. "Clubs por *le Troisième Âge:* Communitas or Conflict." In *Anthropology and the Riddle of the Sphinx: Paradoxes of Change in the Life,* edited by Paul Spencer, 194–212. London: Routledge.

Ortega Domínguez, Abeyamí. 2022. "The Mestizo Gaze: Visualizing Racism, Citizenship, and Rights in Neoliberal Mexico." *Ethnic and Racial Studies:* 1–22.

Orwell, George. 2009. *Nineteen Eighty-Four.* London: Penguin. Original edition, 1949.

Overing, Joanna, and Alan Passes, eds. 2000a. *The Anthropology of Love and Anger: The Aesthetics of Conviviality in Native Amazonia.* London: Routledge.

Overing, Joanna, and Alan Passes. 2000b. "Introduction: Conviviality and the Opening up of Amazonian Anthropology." In *The Anthropology of Love and Anger: The Aesthetics of Conviviality in Native Amazonia,* edited by Joanna Overing and Alan Passes, 1–30. London: Routledge.

Page, Tiffany. 2017. "Vulnerable Writing as a Feminist Methodological Practice." *Feminist Review* 115, no. 1: 13–29.

Pandian, Anand, and Stuart McLean. 2017. *Crumpled Paper Boat: Experiments in Ethnographic Writing.* Durham: Duke University Press.

Paschel, Tianna S. 2016. *Becoming Black Political Subjects.* Princeton: Princeton University Press.

Pasquel, Leonardo. 1969. *Biografía Integral de la Ciudad de Veracruz 1519–1969.* México D.F.: Editorial Citlaltepetl.

Paulson, Susan. 2005. "The Social Benefits of Belonging to a 'Dance Exercise' Group for Older People." *Generations Review* 15, no. 4: 37–41.

Paz, Octavio. 1963. *El Laberinto de la Soledad.* 3rd ed. México D.F.: Fondo de Cultura Económica. Original edition, 1950.

Pedelty, Mark. 1999. "The Bolero: The Birth, Life, and Decline of Mexican Modernity." *Latin American Music Review [Revista de Música Latinoamericana]* 20, no. 1: 30–58.

Pedelty, Mark. 2004. *Musical Ritual in Mexico City from the Aztec to Nafta.* Austin: University of Texas Press.

Pedwell, Carolyn. 2014. "Cultural Theory as Mood Work." *New Formations* 82: 47–63.

Pérez Montfort, Ricardo. 1999. "Expresión y Colorido de la Cultura Popular en el Puerto de Veracruz." In *Veracruz: Primer Puerto del Continente,* 186–217. México D.F.: Fundación Miguel Alemán, ICA. Original edition, 1996.

Peristiany, John George, ed. 1966. *Honour and Shame: The Values of Mediterranean Society*. London: Weidenfeld and Nicolson.

Phelan, Peggy. 1996. *Unmarked: The Politics of Performance*. London: Routledge.

Piedras Feria, Ernesto. 2006. "Crecimiento y Desarollo Económicos Basados en la Cultura." In *Las Industrias Culturales y el Desarollo de México*, edited by Néstor García Canclini and Ernesto Piedras Feria, 45–86. México D.F.: Siglo XXI Editores.

Plato. 1908. *The Republic of Plato*. Translated into English by Benjamin Jowett. Third Edition. Oxford: Clarendon Press. ca. 380 bc.

Playford, John. 1698. *The Dancing Master; or, Directions for Dancing Country Dances, with the Tunes to Each Dance, for the Treble-Violin. The Tenth Edition Corrected; with the Addition of Several New Dances and Tunes Never before Printed*. London: Printed by J. Heptinstall, for H. Playford. Original edition, 1651.

Ponce, Patricia. 2006. *Sexualidades Costeñas. Un Pueblo Veracruzano entre el Río y la Mar*. México D.F.: CIESAS, Casa Chata.

Prampolini, Ida Rodríguez. 2017. *La Crítica del Arte en el Siglo XX*. México: UNAM, Fondo de Cultura Económica.

Prieur, Annick. 1996. "Domination and Desire: Male Homosexuality and the Construction of Masculinity in Mexico." In *Machos, Mistresses, Madonnas: Contesting the Power of Latin American Gender Imagery*, edited by Marit Melhuus and Kristi Anne Stølen, 56–107. London: Verso.

Pulido Llano, Gabriela. 2017. "Claves de la Música Afrocubana en México. Entre Músicos y Musicólogos, 1920–1950." *Desacatos* (53): 56–73.

Pyke, Karen, and Tran Dang. 2003. "'Fob' and 'Whitewashed': Identity and Internalized Racism among Second Generation Asian Americans." *Qualitative Sociology* 26, no. 2: 147–72.

Quirk, Robert E. 1962. *An Affair of Honor: Woodrow Wilson and the Occupation of Veracruz*. New York: Norton.

Redacción Animal Político. 2011. "Revelan que en el Asesinato de los 35 Muertos de Boca del Río Se Usaron Técnicas Castrenses." *Animal Político* (September 30, 2011). https://www.animalpolitico.com/2011/09/revelan-en-el-asesinato-de-los-35-muertos-de-boca-del-rio-se-usaron-tecnicas-castrenses/.

Richardson, Philip John Sampey. 1946. *A History of English Ballroom Dancing, 1910–45. The Story of the Development of the Modern English Style*. London: Herbert Jenkins.

Rinaudo, Christian. 2010. "Más Allá de la 'Identidad Negra': Mestizaje y Dinámicas Raciales en la Ciudad de Veracruz." In *Mestizaje, Diferencia y Nación: Lo "Negro" en América Central y el Caribe*, edited by Elisabeth Cunin, 225–66. México D.F.: INAH, UNAM, CEMCA, IRD.

Rinaudo, Christian. 2012. *Afromestizaje y Fronteras Étnicas: Una Mirada desde el Puerto de Veracruz*. Translated by Lorraine Karnoouh. Veracruz: Universidad Veracruzana.

Rivera Ávila, Francisco. 1992. *Algo sobre el Danzón*. Veracruz: Comisión V Centenario Ciudad de Veracruz, Ayuntamiento de Veracruz. Original edition, 1971.

Rowe, William, and Vivian Schelling. 1991. *Memory and Modernity: Popular Culture in Latin America*. London: Verso.

Ruiz Rodríguez, Carlos. 2005. *Versos, Música y Baile de Artesa de la Costa Chica. San Nicolás, Guerrero, y El Ciruelo, Oaxaca*. México: El Colegio de México.

Ruiz Rodríguez, Carlos. 2019. "Del 'Rescate' al 'Emblema': El Resurgimiento del Baile de Artesa y sus Desafíos como Patrimonio." *TRANS: Revista Transcultural de Música, Transcultural Music Review* 21–22. http://www.sibetrans.com/trans/articulo/546/del-ldquo-rescate-rdquo-al-ldquo-emblema-rdquo-el-resurgimiento-del-baile-de-artesa-y-sus-desafios-como-patrimonio.

Saldívar Tanaka, Emiko. 2008. *Prácticas Cotidianas del Estado: Una Etnografía del Indigenismo*. México D.F.: Plaza y Valdés.

Sánchez de Fuentes, Eduardo. 1928. *Folklorismo*. La Habana: Molina.

Sandoval, Víctor. 2003. "Casas de Cultura y Centros Culturales." In *Atlas de Infraestructura Cultural de México*, 131. México D.F.: CONACULTA.

Santos-Granero, Fernando. 2000. "The Sisyphus Syndrome, or the Struggle for Conviviality in Native Amazonia." In *The Anthropology of Love and Anger: The Aesthetics of Conviviality in Native Amazonia*, edited by Joanna Overing and Alan Passes, 268–87. London: Routledge.

Savigliano, Marta E. 1995. *Tango and the Political Economy of Passion*. Boulder: Westview Press.

Savigliano, Marta E. 1998. "From Wallflowers to Femmes Fatales." In *The Passion of Music and Dance: Body, Gender, and Sexuality*, edited by William Washabaugh, 103–10. Oxford: Berg.

Savigliano, Marta E. 2003. *Angora Matta: Fatal Acts of North-South Translation*. Middletown: Wesleyan University Press.

Schaefer, Claudia. 1999. "Framing the Feminine: From Frida to Danzón." *Revista Canadiense de Estudios Hispánicos* 23, no. 2: 289–310.

Scruggs, T. M. 1998. "Cultural Capital, Appropriate Transformations, and Transfer by Appropriation in Western Nicaragua: 'El Baile de la Marimba.'" *Latin American Music Review/Revista de Música Latinoamericana* 19, no. 1: 1–30.

Sefchovich, Sara, Dolores Pla Brugat, Bernardo García Díaz, Carlos Martínez Assad, Martha Díaz de Kuri, Alicia Gojman de Backal, Ricardo Pérez Montfort, José Benigno Zilli Manica, Jorge Gómez Izquierdo, and David Skerrit Gardner. 2000. *Veracruz: Puerto de Llegada*. Veracruz: H. Ayuntamiento de Veracruz.

Segura Escalona, Felipe. 1994. "The Work of Amalia Hernández." In *Amalia Hernández' Folkloric Ballet of Mexico*, edited by Gabriela Aguirre Cristiani and Felipe Segura Escalona. México D.F.: Fomento Cultural Banamex.

Sennett, Richard. 2003. *Respect: The Formation of Character in a World of Inequality*. London: Allen Lane.

Sevilla, Amparo. 1996. "Aquí Se Siente Uno como en su Casa: Los Salones de Baile Popular de la Ciudad de México." *Alteridades* 6, no. 11: 33–41.

Sevilla, Amparo. 2003. *Los Templos del Buen Bailar*. México D.F.: Consejo Nacional para la Cultura y las Artes.

Shay, Anthony. 2002. *Choreographic Politics: State Folk Dance Companies, Representation and Power.* Middleton: Wesleyan University Press.

Sheehy, Daniel Edward. 1979. "The Son Jarocho: Style and Repertory of a Mexican Musical Tradition." PhD, Ethnomusicology, University of California.

Skinner, Jonathan. 2013. "Social Dance for Successful Aging: The Practice of Health, Happiness, and Social Inclusion Amongst Senior Citizens." *Anthropology and Aging Quarterly* 34, no. 1: 18–29.

Smart, Barry. 1998. *Facing Modernity: Ambivalence, Reflexivity and Morality.* London: Sage.

Sontag, Susan. 2001. "Against Interpretation." In *Against Interpretation and Other Essays,* 3–14. New York: Picador. Original edition, 1964.

Spivak, Gayatri Chakravorty. 1987. *In Other Worlds: Essays in Cultural Politics.* New York: Methuen.

Spottswood, Dick. 2004. "Appendix: Caribbean and South American Recordings." In *Lost Sounds: Blacks and the Birth of the Recording Industry, 1890–1919,* edited by Tim Brooks and Richard Keith Spottswood, 523–30. Urbana: University of Illinois Press.

Star, Susan Leigh, and James R. Griesemer. 1989. "Institutional Ecology, 'Translations' and Boundary Objects: Amateurs and Professionals in Berkeley's Museum of Vertebrate Zoology, 1907–39." *Social Studies of Science* 19, no. 3: 387–420.

Starobinski, Jean. 1966. "The Idea of Nostalgia" (translated by William S. Kemp). *Diogenes* 14, no. 54: 81–103.

Stepputat, Kendra, and Elina Djebbari. 2020. "The Separation of Music and Dance in Translocal Contexts." *the world of music* 9, no. 2: 5–30.

Stewart, Kathleen. 2007. *Ordinary Affects.* Durham: Duke University Press.

Stigberg, David Kenneth. 1980. "Urban Musical Culture in Mexico: Professional Musicianship and Media in the Musical Life of Contemporary Veracruz." PhD, Musicology, University of Illinois at Urbana. http://wwwlib.umi.com/dissertations/fullcit/8026603.

Stobart, Henry. 2006. *Music and the Poetics of Production in the Bolivian Andes.* Aldershot: Ashgate.

Sue, Christina A. 2009. "The Dynamics of Color: *Mestizaje,* Racism, and Blackness in Veracruz, Mexico." In *Shades of Difference: Why Skin Color Matters,* edited by Evelyn Nakano Glenn, 114–28. Palo Alto: Stanford University Press.

Sue, Christina A. 2013. *Land of the Cosmic Race: Race Mixture, Racism, and the Blackness in Mexico.* Oxford: Oxford University Press.

Sugarman, Jane C. 1997. *Engendering Song: Singing and Subjectivity at Prespa Albanian Weddings.* Chicago: University of Chicago Press.

Sugarman, Jane C. 2003. "Those "Other Women": Dance and Femininity among Prespa Albanians." In *Music and Gender: Perspectives from the Mediterranean,* edited by Tullia Magrini, 87–118. Chicago: University of Chicago Press.

Tagg, Philip. 1989. "Open Letter: 'Black Music,' 'Afro-American Music' and 'European Music.'" *Popular Music* 8, no. 3: 285–98.

Tamariz Estrada, María Cristina. 2014. "Ageing Culture, el Surgimiento de Una Edad Social. Danzoneros en la Ciudad de México." PhD, Centro de Estudios Sociológicos, El Colegio de México.

Taruskin, Richard. 1995. *Text and Act: Essays on Music and Performance*. New York: Oxford University Press.

Taylor, Julie. 1998. *Paper Tangos*. Durham: Duke University Press.

Thomas, Helen. 2004. "Mimesis and Alterity in the African Caribbean Quadrille: Ethnography Meets History." *Cultural and Social History* 1, no. 3: 280–301.

Thompson, Paul Richard, Catherine Itzin, and Michele Abendstern. 1990. *I Don't Feel Old: The Experience of Later Life*. Oxford: Oxford University Press.

Timmermans, Stefan, and Marc Berg. 1997. "Standardization in Action: Achieving Local Universality through Medical Protocols." *Social Studies of Science* 27, no. 2: 273–305.

Titon, Jeff Todd. 1978. "Every Day I Have the Blues: Improvisation and Daily Life." *Southern Folklore Quarterly* 42: 85–98.

Toral, Esperanza, ed. 2012. *Ciudad y Puerto, Veracruz Ayer y Hoy*. Xalapa: Editorial las Ánimas.

Torres, Dora Ileana. 1995. "Del Danzón Cantado al Chachachá." In *Panorama de la Música Popular Cubana*, edited by Radamés Giro, 171–97. La Habana: Editorial Letras Cubanas.

Trejo, Ángel. 1992. *Hey, Familia, Danzón Dedicado a . . . !* México D.F.: Plaza y Valdés.

Turino, Thomas. 1989. "The Coherence of Social Style and Musical Creation among the Aymara in Southern Peru." *Ethnomusicology* 33, no. 1: 1–30.

Turino, Thomas. 2000. *Nationalists, Cosmopolitans, and Popular Music in Zimbabwe*. Chicago: University of Chicago Press.

Turino, Thomas. 2003. "Nationalism and Latin American Music: Selected Case Studies and Theoretical Considerations." *Latin American Music Review/Revista de Música Latinoamericana* 24, no. 2: 169–209.

Ulloa Anasco, Francisco Salvador. 1992. "El Danzón Baile Nacional." *Perfil de Santiago (Suplemento del Periódico Sierra Maestra, Santiago de Cuba)*, 152.

Ulloa, Bertha. 1986. *Veracruz, Capital de la Nación, 1914–1915*. México D.F.: El Colegio de México, Gobierno del Estado de Veracruz.

Ureste, Manu. 2017. "Ellos Son los 17 Periodistas Asesinados durante el Gobierno de Duarte." *Animal Político* (April 19, 2020). https://www.animalpolitico.com/2017/04/periodistas-asesinados-veracruz-duarte/.

Valencia, Sayak. 2018. *Gore Capitalism*. Translated by John Pluecker. Semiotext(e): South Pasadena. 2010.

Valenzuela Arce, José Manuel. 2014. "Juvenicidio y Necropolítica." In *Jovens Latino-Americanos. Necropolíticas, Culturas Políticas e Urbanidades*, edited by Silvia H. S. Borelli and José Manuel Valenzuela Arce, 15–37. Buenos Aires: CLACSO, COLEF.

Van Sertima, Ivan. 1977. *They Came before Columbus: The African Presence in Ancient America*. New York: Random House.

Vasconcelos, José. 1948. *La Raza Cósmica. Colección Austral.* México D.F.: Editorial Planeta. 1925.

Vaughn, Bobby. 2013. "Mexico Negro: From the Shadows of Nationalist Mestizaje to New Possibilities in Afro-Mexican Identity." *The Journal of Pan African Studies* 6, no. 1: 227–40.

Vianna, Hermano. 1999. *The Mystery of Samba: Popular Music and National Identity in Brazil.* Translated by John Charles Chasteen. Chapel Hill: University of North Carolina Press. 1995.

Wade, Peter. 1997. *Race and Ethnicity in Latin America.* London: Pluto Press.

Wade, Peter. 2000. *Music, Race and Nation: Música Tropical in Colombia.* Chicago: University of Chicago Press.

Wade, Peter. 2001. "Racial Identity and Nationalism: A Theoretical View from Latin America." *Ethnic and Racial Studies* 24, no. 5: 845–65.

Wade, Peter. 2009. *Race and Sex in Latin America.* London: Pluto Press.

Wainwright, Steven P., and Bryan S. Turner. 2006. "'Just Crumbling to Bits'? An Exploration of the Body, Ageing, Injury and Career in Classical Ballet Dancers." *Sociology* 40, no. 2: 237–55.

Wainwright, Steven P., Clare Williams, and Bryan S. Turner. 2006. "Varieties of Habitus and the Embodiment of Ballet." *Qualitative Research* 6, no. 4: 535–58.

Wallace, William. 1874. "Prolegomena." In *The Logic of Hegel. Translated from the Encyclopaedia of the Philosophical Sciences, with Prolegomena by W. Wallace,* xiii-clxxxiv. Oxford: Clarendon Press.

Waxer, Lise A. 2002. *The City of Musical Memory: Salsa, Record Grooves, and Popular Culture in Cali, Colombia.* Middletown: Wesleyan University Press.

Weigert, Andrew J. 1991. *Mixed Emotions: Certain Steps toward Understanding Ambivalence.* Albany: State University of New York Press.

Wiegman, Robyn. 2014. "The Times We're In: Queer Feminist Criticism and the Reparative 'Turn.'" *Feminist Theory* 15, no. 1: 4–25.

Willson, Andrea E., Kim M. Shuey, Glen H. Elder, and K. A. Wickrama. 2006. "Ambivalence in Mother-Adult Child Relations: A Dyadic Analysis." *Social Psychology Quarterly* 69, no. 3: 235–52.

Wood, Andrew Grant. 2001. *Revolution in the Street: Women, Workers, and Urban Protest in Veracruz, 1870–1927.* Wilmington: Scholarly Resources.

Wood, Andrew Grant. 2003. "Introducing la Reina del Carnaval: Public Celebration and Postrevolutionary Discourse in Veracruz, Mexico." *The Americas* 60, no. 1: 87–107.

Wood, Andrew Grant. 2010. "On the Selling of Rey Momo: Early Tourism and the Marketing of Carnival in Veracruz." In *Holiday in Mexico: Critical Reflections on Tourism and Tourist Encounters,* edited by Dina Berger and Andrew Grant Wood, 77–106. Durham: Duke University Press.

Wood, Andrew Grant. 2014. *Agustín Lara: A Cultural Biography.* New York: Oxford University Press.

Yúdice, George. 2003. *The Expediency of Culture.* Durham: Duke University Press.

Zadeh, Chloë. 2012. "Formulas and the Building Blocks of ṭhumrī Style-a Study in "Improvised" Music." *Analytical Approaches to World Music* 2, no. 1. http://aawmjournal.com/articles/2012a/Zadeh_AAWM_Vol_2_1.pdf.
Zaretsky, Eli. 1992. "Review of 'Modernity and Ambivalence' by Zygmunt Bauman." *American Journal of Sociology* 97, no. 5: 1519–21.
Zolov, Eric. 1997. "Rebeldismo in the Revolutionary Family: Rock 'N' Roll's Early Challenges to State and Society in Mexico." *Journal of Latin American Cultural Studies* 6, no. 2: 201–16.
Zolov, Eric. 1999. *Refried Elvis: The Rise of the Mexican Counterculture*. Berkeley: University of California Press.

Index

Abdala Gómez, Rosa, 126, 145, 146, 168, 171
Abu-Lughod, Lila, 179
Academia Nacional de Danzón, La, 145, 148
Acerina. See *Acerina y su Danzonera; Danzonera Acerina*; Valiente Robert, Consejo "Acerina"
Acerina y su Danzonera, 135. See also *Danzonera Acerina*
aesthetics, dance, and colonialism, 118, 119, 120, 122
African subcontinent, 32, 43–44
Afrocaribeño festival, 48, 52, 140
Afrocubanismo, 32
aging. See older dancers
Aguirre Beltrán, Gonzalo, 50, 140
Agustín Lara Museum (*La Casita Blanca*), 81, 150–51
Alcántara, Sigfrido, 71–72, 132–34, 135–36, 163, 190
alienation, ambivalence, and racialization processes, 50–51
Alma de Sotavento. See *Danzonera Alma de Sotavento*
Alma de Veracruz. See *Danzonera Alma de Veracruz*
Almendra, 156
ambivalence: affective ambivalence, 9; aging, gender, love and, 187, 203–4, 205; anxiety and, 11; audiotopia and, 14–15; biological ambivalence, 9; conviviality and, 175; cross dressing and, 85; cultural ambivalence, 9; cultural intimacy and, 87; danzón groups and, 169, 177–78, 181; danzón, Veracruz and, 7–8, 16; dialectic ambivalence, theorization of, 8, 12–13, 15, 213n13; dualisms and, 8, 9, 10–11, 12, 85; embodied ambivalence, 9–10; envy, arrogance and, 171, 180; honor, shame and, 180; intellectual ambivalence, 9; intersecting intensities of, 11–12; love and, 14; manifestations of ambivalences, 8–16; nostalgia and, 16–17, 59–62, 83–88; political democracy and, 15; psychological ambivalence, 9; racialization processes and, 15, 16, 29–56, 118, 187; social ambivalence, 9; static ambivalence, theorization of, 8, 12–15, 16–17, 87–88; structural ambivalence, 9, 11; theoretical explorations of, 8–13; utopian ambivalence, theorization of, 8, 13–18; voluntary, 9. See also nostalgia; racialization processes
Améry, Jean, 188
amorous encounters, 5, 19, 130, 196; age and, 186, 196–204; dance groups and, 190–91; morality, gender, age and, 19, 86, 180, 192–94; volatility of, 13–14, 193. See also marriage and post-marriage; sexuality and romance
Anzaldúa, Gloria, 11
Aparicio, Francis, 48
apprenticeships, 168–71
Argumedo, Luis, 76
Arredondo, Juan "Cumbá," 63

Arthur Murray Dance Party, 153
audiotopia, ambivalence and, 14–15
authenticity narratives, and danzón: dance and, 18, 32, 48, 61, 71; dance revival and, 127, 137–38, 141, 153, 158–59; music and, 157; older dancers and, 204
Aventurera (film), 125

Babuca, La, 71–72
Back, Les, 25
Báez-Jorge, Félix, 87
Bailadores de Danzón del INSEN de Veracruz, 145
baile de marimba (Nicaragua), 155, 156, 157
Bakhtin, Mikhail, 84–85, 213n13
Ballet Folklórico de México, 17, 115; modernist aesthetics, danzón and, 119–20, 121, 122
baqueteo, 36, 38
Barber, Elinor, 10–12, 13
Barcelata Trujillo, Genaro, 80, 142
Bauman, Zygmunt, 11, 210n7
Bellas Artes, Palacio de, 119
Benítez, Laureano, 130
Berlanga Gayón, Mariana, 99
Berlant, Lauren, 13–14, 62
Berriel, Carlos "El Calcetín," 129, 214n4, 215n5
Bion, Wilfred, 178
blackness. *See* racialization processes
Blanco Cancino, Manuel, 67
Bleuler, Eugen, 8–9, 10–11, 13
blues, 15, 112, 113, 129
bolero, 91, 129, 216; *bolero español*, 106
Born, Georgina, 178
Bosse, Joanna, 115–18, 122, 197
boundary objects, 193–94
Bourdieu, Pierre, 110, 117, 125–26, 181, 189–90
Boym, Svetlana: danzón, ambivalence, nostalgia and, 16–17, 60–62, 83, 139, 158–59; poverty, nostalgia and, 87
Brito, Alfredo, 156
Buechler, Hans, 170
Buena Vista Social Club, 197
Bueno, Roberto, 142–43
bufos (Cuban blackface), 128

cabarets, 129, 151; danzón, decency and morality, and, 151–52; *El Quinto Patio*, 74
cachondería, 198–99

cadencia, 105, 107, 141–42, 190, 204
Calderón, Felipe, 22
California Dancing Club (Mexico City dance hall), 76, 129, 130, 135
Camerero, Cipriano, 74
Camerero, Moisés, 74
Campos, Carlos, 128, 156, 216n15
Cárdenas, Lázaro, 70
Cardona, Alejandro, 76, 128
Caribbean. *See* circum-Caribbean
carnival: carnival, history of in Veracruz, 17, 68–73, 75–77, 80, 82–87; class and, 62, 64, 68–73; colonialism and, 68, 69; colonialism and, 68, 69; cross-dressing and, 84–85; danzón and, 125, 149, 170; tourism and, 75–77, 80–82; unions and, 69, 71, 77, 85; Veracruz's party atmosphere and, 21, 68–69, 83–86, 92
Carpentier, Alejo, 31, 33
Carranza, Venustiano, 64, 100
casas de cultura, 139–40, 145–46, 152
cascara (shell of timbal), 39, 41
Cashion, Susan, 198
Casino Español, 69
Casino Veracruzano, 64–65
Casita Blanca. *See* Agustin Lara Museum
Casquera, José, 76
Castillo Faílde, Osvaldo, 31
Castro, Pepe, 71–72
Castro Olvera, Margarita, 4–7
Catholicism: Cristero War, 66; divorce and, 192; healing and, 172; sexuality and, 7, 19, 192, 195. *See also* decency and morality; marriage and post-marriage
Cazas, Andrés, 132
Ceballos, Gamboa, 76
Cecilia, 113, 156
centenary of danzón, 134–35
Centro Convenciones Tlatelolco, 129
cha-cha-chá, 30, 128, 129, 219
charanga: *charanga francesa*, 36–38, 41–42, 219; *La Charanga del Puerto*, 149–50
Charecua, El, 71–72
Charleston, 129
Chavela "La Cuata," 131
Chávez-Silverman, Susana, 48
children: dance groups and, 140–41, 143–47, 151; dancers, as, 96, 119, 144; danzón maestros, transmission and, 168; older dancers and, 6–7, 78, 144, 191; regulating their older parents' lives, 196, 201

248   Index

Chinos Ramírez, Los, 67
Chinto Ramos y su Orquesta, 67
choreographic composition of danzón routines, 113–15
choreographic knowledge, transmission and restriction of, 168–71
cinquillo rhythms, 30–32, 38–40, 42, 102, 219; popular histories of danzón and, 43, 46, 53, 55
circum-Caribbean, 34, 42–45, 54, 59, 190; music, dance and, 30–31, 42, 54, 141–42
Cisneros, Miguel Ángel, 137, 215n4, 215n7, 215n8, 215n11
class: ambivalence and, 8–11; carnival and, 69, 75; clothing and, 111; creativity and Veracruz's lower classes, 60, 80–83; danzón dancers and, 5–6, 146, 150; danzón groups and, 181; danzón musicians and, 101; decency, morality and, 10; elegance, Veracruz, racism and, 117–18; history of danzón and, 17, 128, 130; history of Veracruz and, 60, 63, 66, 139, 146; nostalgia, Veracruz and, 83–88; post-cosmopolitanism and, 75; racialization processes, racism and, 16, 33, 45, 48–51, 55; sexuality and, 68; tourism to Veracruz and, 92; Veracruz's upper classes, 55–56, 68, 83; vignettes and, 9–10, 183–84 ; *Villa del Mar* and, 66–68; women and, 67, 68, 82–83, 128; youth cultures and, 186. *See also* clothing, elegance, modernist aesthetics, nostalgia
clave instrument, 20, 38, 100–101, 132, 219
clave rhythms, 36, 41, 219; clave changing within pieces, 36; confusion of, 42
clothing, danzón and, 109–12, 111, 114
Club de Bailadores de Danzón de Hoy y Siempre del Puerto de Veracruz. *See* Hoy y Siempre
Club de los Pájaros Caídos, 200, 206
Club Inspiración, 131
CNIDDAC (*Centro Nacional de Investigación y Difusión del Danzón A. C.*), 149–50, 151, 152–53, 167
Cole, Ross, 121
colonialism: aesthetics, dance and, 118, 119, 120, 122; auto-exoticization and, 48; carnival and, 68, 69; colonial violence, 17, 45, 122; cosmopolitanism and, 115; racial logics and, 46, 52, 211n10; tropicalization and, 48

Comisión Nacional Coordinadora de Puertos, 77
competition: dance competitions, 129, 130–31; dance routines and, 145, 146–47; dancers, competitiveness and, 125–26, 158; danzón aficionados and, 199; danzón empires and, 148–49, 152–54, 158, 194; danzoneras and, 73, 76, 80, 132, 155; group dynamics, competitiveness and, 175, 179, 181–82, 205; nicknames and, 72; revival and, 134, 149; rules for, 133–34
CONACULTA (*Consejo Nacional para la Cultura y las Artes*), 126, 140, 146, 148, 149–50
CONADE (*Comisión Nacional de Cultura Física y Deporte*), 149, 158
Confesión, 130
conga drums, 20, 38–39, 42, 101, 219–20; *son cubano* pattern on, 41
contradanza cubana, 30–32, 100, 220
contredanse, 30–32, 100, 220
Contreras Fernández, Silvio, 156
conviviality, 163–64, 173–80
Cook, Matt, 21
Copland, Aaron, 128
Cortés, Hernán, 53, 100, 173
cosmopolitanism, modernist aesthetic and, 115–16; post-cosmopolitanism, 75; Veracruz, nostalgia and, 62–63, 74–75. *See also* modernist aesthetic
Covarrubias, Miguel, 66–67
cowbell, 38–39, 41–42, 71, 222
creativity: danzón and, 112–15; Veracruz and working class, 60, 80–83
cross-dressing, 84–85
Cuba, 3, 4, 7, 16, 20, 29, 30; *cinquillo* and, 31, 40, 43; Cuban women, racialization of, 49; danzón as "National Dance of," 33; influences on danzoneras in Veracruz and Mexico City, 38–42; musicians from, migration to Veracruz, 63. *See also* circum-Caribbean; *son cubano*
cultural institutions, decentralization of, 126
cumbia, 33, 74, 129, 143, 221

dance groups: amorous encounters, dance groups and, 190–96; apprenticeships, 169–70, 170–71; "blanking," ostracism and, 177–78; "boundary object," group as, 194; *cachondería*, 198–99; choreographic knowledge, management of, 168–69; competitiveness and, 175, 179, 181–82, 205; conviviality, 174–80; danzón, older dancers and, 185–88; *danzón académico* and, 188–89, 190, 194, 204; discord, conviviality and, 173–74; envy, power and, 171–74; flexibility of dance and, 18–19, 185–205; group dynamics, 18, 163–82; group rules, ambiguity of, 164–65, 167–68; group structures, 164–65; honor and shame, tensions between, 179–80; hostilities, 172–73, 174–75, 177–78; intimacy and, 18, 174–81; knowledge, transmission and restriction of, 168–71; legitimation, desire for, 167–68, 172, 178–79, 180, 181; multiplication of groups, 165–68; music, hierarchy of generations and, 186; officially sanctioned dance groups, 134–39; older dancers and, 185–91, 194–99, 201, 202–4, 205; oldness, understandings of, 186–87; ostracism, 175–78, 179, 181–82; power and envy, 171–74 ; power relations, patriarchy and, 202–4; regeneration, new generations and, 188–90; reputation and, 195–96, 200; romance, danzón, older age and, 196–204; standardization, production of, 193–94; state sponsorship and, 145–47; youth cultures, danzón and, 186. *See also*, amorous encounters; children; decency and morality; gossip; *Hoy y Siempre*; older dancers; racialization processes; revival of danzón; sexuality and romance; *Tres Generaciones del Danzón*; women; vignettes

danza, 30–32, 63, 220

danzón: dance moves in relation to structure of, 101–8; emergence in Cuba of, 4; institutional support, space and, 92–97; leader-follower dynamics and, 102–8, 111–12, 113, 202; Mexican nation and, 52–56; migratory flows and, 30–32; newcomers to, age of, 127; older dancers and, 187–90; Veracruz and adoption of, 33–35, 42–45. *See also* competition; Cuba; dance groups; *danzón académico*; *danzón lírico*; decency and morality; gender; histories of danzón; modernist aesthetics; older dancers; racialization processes; revival; women

Danzón (film), 60, 101, 132; Daniel Rergis and, 79, 146; danzón revival and, 4–5, 126, 146; gender and, 201–2

danzón abierto (open position danzón), 92, 104, 128–29, 137

danzón académico, authenticity narratives, notions of tradition and, 138; children and, 141; clothing, uniforms and, 95–96, 103, 110, 113–14, 117; codified steps in, 93, 94, 95; creativity and, 112–15, 178–79; Cuba, in, 34; dance groups and, 95, 126, 188–90, 194, 204; dance routines and, 93, 106–8, 112–13, 121, 145–47; danzón dancing aesthetics, and, 152–54; danzón empire builders and, 147–49, 152; danzón habitus, as, 189; *danzón lírico*, Veracruz and, 93–97, 104–8, 115–22, 169, 181–82; exemplary dancers and, 152–53; *Forum Danzones en el Puerto* and, 5, 150–51; funding of, 96, 126, 145–46; leader-follower dynamics and, 102–8, 111–12, 113, 202; modernist aesthetic, elegance, whiteness and, 17, 92, 115–22, 178–79, 190; music-dance relationship and, 155–56; older and younger bodies, aesthetics and, 188–90; revival of danzón and, 127, 139–43, 149; transmission of, 168–71; *Tres Generaciones* and, 189–90, 204. *See also* dance groups; *danzón lírico*; gender; modernist aesthetics; older dancers; racialization processes; revival; women

danzón acrobático, 92

danzón cerrado (closed position danzón), 92

danzón de fantasía, 114

Danzonera Acerina, 37–38, 156, 221n6, 221n7

Danzonera Alma de Sotavento, 76, 80, 132, 142, 146. *See also Danzonera Alma de Veracruz*

Danzonera Alma de Veracruz: danzón, economic boom and, 73–78; municipalization and, 142–43, 155; master of ceremonies of, 100–101; musicians in, 101, 138; nostalgia and, 71, 73–74, 76, 80, 102; repertoire, 113; and Veracruz 59–60

Danzonera de Camerino Vázquez, 71

Danzonera de Cipriano Camerero, 74

Danzonera de los Chinos Ramírez, 63, 71

Danzonera La Playa, 155–56, 185

Danzonera Manzanita y su son, 4, 5, 132, 135, 146, 155

Danzonera México, 76
Danzonera Modelo, 76
Danzonera Veracruz, 76
Danzonera Veracruzana "Pazos," 73
Danzonera Yucatán, 157
danzonete, 30, 216n14, 219, 220
danzón lírico: authenticity narratives, notions of tradition and, 125, 137–38, 154, 156; clothing and, 110; dance groups and, 103, 113–14, 181–82, 200, 204; *danzón académico*, Veracruz and, 93–97, 104–8, 115–22, 169, 181–82; older dancers and, 188–190. *See also* dance groups; *danzón académico*; gender; modernist aesthetics; older dancers; racialization processes; revival; women
danzón musicians, class and, 101; competition and, danzoneras and, 73, 76, 80, 132, 155; Cuban musicians and Veracruz, 63; generation and, 186; revival of danzón and, 155–57; vignettes and, 24, 57; women, 6, 73, 82. *See also* Cuba; *Danzonera Alma de Veracruz*
Daynes, Sarah, 45
decency and morality: cabarets, danzón and, 151–52; dance groups and, 190–96; dancers, danzón and, 10, 104, 133–34, 152, 165; danzón champions and, 131; gender, age and, 7, 19, 20, 200, 205–6; honor, shame, gender and, 179–80; racialized notions of music genres and, 31, 54–55; sexuality and gendered, racialized notions of, 86, 109, 190–96; Veracruz, the Caribbean and gendered, racialized notions of, 45, 47, 49, 55–56. *See also* Catholicism; class; sexuality and romance
Delgado Rannauro, Dante, 142
descansos, choreomusical practice and, 5, 94, 104–8, 133, 220; clothes, flirting and, 108–9
Desterrado, El, 65
dialectics, 8, 12–13, 61. *See also* ambivalence
Díaz, Aniceto, 132, 156, 220
Díaz, Porfirio, 62, 64
Díaz Andrade, Miguel "El Venado," 71–72, 132, 135
Díaz Vázquez, Eliseo, 100–102
Dictamen, El, 77, 136
Diez, Paco, 135
Djebbari, Elina, 155

dockers and danzón in Veracruz, 69–73
dualisms, ambivalence and, 8, 9, 10–11, 12, 85
Duarte, Javier, 23
Du Bois, W. E. B., 10, 11, 14, 15, 51

Early Music (European). *See* modernist aesthetics
Echeverría, Luis, 77
economic boom in Veracruz, 74
economic bust and danzón boom, 64–70, 78–80
Egües, Richard, 36
elegance, 106–7, 110–11, 115–19, 122. *See also* class; clothing; gender; modernist aesthetics; older dancers; racialization processes; women
El Paso del Elefante, 101
empire builders, revival of danzón and, 147–51
Encuentro Internacional de Danzón, 146, 216n13
English Country Dance, 30, 100
envy, power and, 171–74
Escalona, Segura, 120
Escobar Bautista, Víctor "El Toby," 136–37, 145–49, 152, 154, 158
Escuela de Bellas Artes, 157
Escuela de la Fraternidad del Danzón, 136–37
Espíndola Jiménez, Quinto Longino, 145
Espinoza, Firpo, 132
Esposito, Joseph, 187
Estrada, Tamariz, 111, 214n1
experimental ethnographic writing. *See* writing, experimental ethnography

Faílde Pérez, Miguel, 30, 135
Federación Mexicana de Baile y Danza Deportiva, 149, 152, 158
Fefita La Grande, 197–98
Feldman, Heidi, 146–47
feminism, 9, 202–3, 205
Figueroa, Moreno, 46, 47
Figueroa Hernández, Rafael, 157, 171
Finnegan, Ruth, 148
Flamers, Los, 143
Flauta Mágica, 156
Flores, Chino, 76
Flores Martos, Juan Antonio, 45–46, 48, 72–73, 83–85, 172

Flores y Escalante, Jesús, 43, 63, 145, 151–52, 199
Fonseca, Fernando, 74
Foucault, Michel, 15, 189
foxtrot, 112, 129, 130
Frade Álvarez, José "Pepe," 69, 80
Frankenberg, Ruth, 117
Fraternidad del Danzón Clásico, 136–37, 145
Freud, Sigmund, 9

Gamio, Manuel, 119
García, Bernardo (trumpeter), 72, 73, 143, 213n9
García, David, 45
García de León Griego, Antonio, 65
García Díaz, Bernardo, 34, 43, 62–63, 69, 74, 87
gender: dancing danzón and, 102–8, 114–15, 128–29, 133–34, 202–3. *See also* amorous encounters; Catholicism; class; clothing; cross-dressing; decency and morality; feminism; patriarchy; LGBTQ+; marriage and post-marriage; sexuality and romance; Veracruz; widow- and widowerhood; women
gharana (India), 168
Gilroy, Paul, 30, 43, 174
Goffman, Erving, 17, 174, 176, 180–81
González, Anita, 120–21, 122
González Mendoza, Rosario "Doña Charito," 100–101
González Peña, Hipólito "Polo," 37, 39, 42
Goody, Esther, 170
Gordillo, Dellanira, 131
gossip: bellicose violence and, 99; dance, envy and, 172; dance invitations, gender and, 103, 195–96; danzón spaces and, 7, 97, 101, 195–96, 205; gender, sexuality, morality and, 7, 19, 97, 99, 195; minimization of, 180, 195; patios de vecindad and, 64. *See also* decency and morality; group dynamics; sexuality and romance; tensions within danzón spheres; *unidos en un nido de víboras*
Gran Café de la Parroquia, 59, 82, 83
Gran Café del Portal, 82, 114
Greene, Graham, 66
groups. *See* dance groups
Guadarrama Olivera, Horacio, 84
guaracha, 63, 74, 129, 221
güiro, 38, 42, 100–102, 214n5

Gutmann, Matthew, 81, 173, 192, 217
Guzmán Concha, Gilberto, 156

Haiti, 30, 100, 219
Hajda, Jan, 9, 10–11, 13
Hale, Charles, 15, 51
Havana, 4, 34, 43–44, 84
Hegel, Georg, 12–13, 15
Hernández, Amalia, 17, 115, 119–21, 122
Hernández, Tiburcio "El Babuco," 63
Herzfeld, Michael, 87–88, 168–69, 170, 179–80
hip hop, 4, 110
histories of danzón and racialization processes, 30–33, 55
Hobsbawm, Eric, 137–38, 151
Hochschild, Arlie, 10
Hofer, Johannes, 60
honor and shame, 179–80
Hospicio Manuel Gutiérrez Zamora, 73, 143
Hoy y Siempre (dance group), history of, 4–5, 135–37, 140–41, 146–47; formation of danzón groups in Veracruz and, 163–64, 167, 174, 178
Huerta, Victoriano, 64
Hurston, Zora Neale, 24
Hutchinson, Sydney, 119–20, 122, 197–98

Iannaccone, Laurence, 18, 175–76
Illouz, Eva, 203
IMSS (*Instituto Mexicano del Seguro Social*), 140
INAPAM (*Instituto Nacional de las Personas Adultas Mayores*), 144–45
INBA (*Instituto Nacional de Bellas Artes y Literatura*), 139, 151
Indigeneity, 11, 50–51, 120, 173, 209n4. *See also* mestizaje; racialization processes
Indigenismo, 119–20, 214n9
INEGI (*Instituto Nacional de Estadística Geografía e Informatica*), 22, 35
inequalities, nostalgia and reproduction of, 86–88
Inés "La Rompecuero," 71–72
INSEN (*Instituto Nacional de la Senectud*), 145
institutional support: danzón spaces and, 92–97
instrumentation, danzón: in Cuba, 31; Cuba and Mexico, 33; differences between México City and Veracruz, 35–42; impact of swing bands on, 37–38; in Ve-

racruz, 101. *See also* danzonera; orquesta típica; timbales
International DanceSport Federation, 149
invented tradition, danzón as, 137–39
Isora Club, 156
ISTD (Imperial Society of Teachers of Dancing), 153
IVEC (*Instituto Veracruzano de la Cultura*), 75, 83, 87, 166–67, 190; Afro-Caribbean festival and, 52; Miguel Zamudio and, 190; music transmission and, 157; revival of danzón and, 140, 143, 148–50

jarabe tapatío, 33
jazz, 32, 67, 213n9; *Jazz Montezuma*, 67; *Jazz Nacional*, 67
Jiménez, Lucina, 140, 151
Jones, Leroi (Amiri Baraka), 30
Juárez, Benito, 53–54, 100

Klein, Melanie, 10, 178
Knight, Alan, 64
knowledge, transmission and restriction of choreographic and musical, 168–71
Kracauer, Siegfried, 18, 163–64, 166, 178, 181
Kun, Josh, 14–15

ladino (Guatemala), 15, 51
La Huaca, 45, 63–64, 75
La Maraka, 129
Lara, Agustín, 59, 70, 100
Las Alturas de Simpson, 30, 134–35
Las Delicias, 70
Latour, Bruno, 154, 209
legitimation, desire for, 167–68, 172, 178–79, 180, 181
Lewis, Oscar, 191–92
LGBTQ+, 21, 196; trans women, 85, 92, 202, 217n2
Lindsay, Shawn, 188
Livingston, Tamara, 127, 134, 138, 147, 149
Lock, Graham, 15
Lonja Mercantil, 68, 69
López, Bernardo, 59, 143
López, Coralia, 156
López, Marga, 125
López Contreras, Silverio, 37, 101–2
Lorenzo Camacho, Bernardo "Nayo," 82
Los Matecocos, 143
love: ambivalence and, 13–14. *See also* amorous encounters; marriage and post-marriage; sexuality

Madero, Francisco, 64
Madrid, Alejandro, and Robin Moore, 19–20, 61–62, 128, 151, 198–99
malandro, 131
Malinche, La, 173
mambo, 220; dance moves, 112, 130, 188; histories of danzón and, 30, 76, 128, 156; Mexico City's dance halls and, 128–29; Pérez Prado and, 42
Mancisidor Ortiz, Anselmo, 69, 84, 85, 87
Marchand, Trevor, 170
marches, danzon performance and, 157
mariachi, 33, 91
Marimba Orquesta La Costeñita, 114
Marine Band, 58, 142
marriage and post-marriage: absence of married women danzón dancers, 7, 19, 143–44, 189, 191, 205; ambivalence and, 12; Catholicism, divorce and, 192; men and post-marriage women, 7, 191–96; misplaced assumption danzón couples are married, 3, 19, 198; sexuality and gender post-marriage, 200–203; women, post-marriage, 7, 14, 191–96. *See also* sexuality and romance
Martínez, Elvira "La Boogie," 131
Martínez Furé, Rogelio, 32
Martínez González, Félix, 81, 82–83, 200, 206
Martínez Montiel, Luz María, 50
Masacre, 156
Mata Majá, 113, 145
Matus Meléndez, Eliseo "Manzanita" (Little Apple), 76, 132–33
Media Hora del Danzón, La, 73–74
merengue, 62, 197–98, 219
Merton, Robert, 10–12, 13
mestizaje, 29, 33–34, 46, 48, 50–54. *See also* racialization processes
methodological strategies, 16, 20–23, 29, 194; vignettes and, 24–25. *See also* writing experimental ethnography
Mexican Revolution, 53, 62, 64–65, 128, 213n8
Mexico City: dance halls in, 128–30; danzón champions in, 130–31; danzón dancing aesthetic in, 128–29; differences in instrumentation between México City and Veracruz, 35–42; performance of

Index 253

danzón, continuity in, 125–26; timbaleros in, 38–41. *See also* Cuba, racialization processes
Mi Consuelo es Amarte, 41–42, 156
migratory flows and racialization of danzón, 30–32
Miller, Sue, 36, 37, 38
Miranda, Francisco, 67
Mizuno Guzmán, Ciro Carlos, 130, 198–99
Mocambo, 156
modernist aesthetics, danzón and, 17–19; age and, 190, 204; Amalia Hernández's Ballet Folklórico de México and, 119–22; ballet and, 115, 116, 119–21, 168, 189; ballroom and, 108, 115–18, 122; beauty and, 117; cosmopolitanism, and, 115–16, 122; *danzón académico*, modernist aesthetic of, 115–22; danzón "habitus," 189; development of, 125–36, 204; European Early Music and, 115–17, 122; fascist cultural ideology and, 121; festivals and, 152–53; institutional support, dancing spaces and, 92–97; Moiseyev Dance Company and, 119–20; nationalism and, 17, 92, 115, 119–22; social policing and, 179; son jarocho, folkloric dance and, 120, 122; whiteness, elegance and, 117–18. *See also* class; clothing; dance groups; *danzón académico*; elegance; gender; older dancers; revival of danzón; state sponsorship of danzón
modernization of Veracruz port and danzón, 62–70
Moehn, Frederick, 15
Moiseyev, Igor, 120
Moiseyev Dance Company, 115, 119–20
montuno (section), *cadencia*, dancing and, 199; dancing and, 104–5, 108, 133, 137, 141; music performance and, 30, 36, 39–42, 128, 221; older dancers and, 188; vignettes and, 124
Moore, Robin, 210n2. *See also* Madrid, Alejandro, and Robin Moore
Mora, Pablo, 110
morality. *See* decency and morality
Moreno, Armando, 66
Moreno, Gustavo, 156
Moreno Figueroa, Mónica, 45, 47, 51, 53, 187
Mosqueda, María Eugenia "Maru," 148, 214n1, 215n4

movement aesthetic, discipline in, 126–27. *See* modernist aesthetics
Muestra Nacional de Danzón, 149–50
Municipal Band, 5, 23, 132, 139, 142; carnival and, 69–70
música tropical, 33, 74, 221

national belonging and racialization processes in Veracruz, 29, 50–51
national imaginaries of Veracruz and nostalgia, 59–60
Negra Palomares, La, 129, 131
Nereidas, 36–37, 156
Nettl, Bruno, 113
New Year and *El Viejo*, 71
Ngai, Sianne, 171
Nieto, Miguel, 146
norteño trios, 91
nortes winds in Veracruz, 68
nostalgia: ambivalence and, 60–62; ambivalence in Veracruz and, 83–86; carnival, Veracruz and, 68–69, 83–86; "cosmopolitan air" of Veracruz and, 62–63, 74–75; cross-dressing in Veracruz and, 84–85; danzón, *Alma de Veracruz*, economic boom and, 73–78; dockers and danzón in Veracruz, 69–73; economic boom in Veracruz and, 74; economic bust and danzón boom, 64–70, 78–80; gendered representations of Veracruz, 59; modernization of Veracruz port and danzón, 62–70; national imaginaries of Veracruz and, 59–60; reflective nostalgia (Boym) and ambivalence, 60, 61, 85–86; reproduction of inequalities and, 86–88; restorative nostalgia (Boym) and ambivalence, 60–62; tourism, carnival and, 75–76; *Villa del Mar* and, 66–9, 70, 74, 76, 80–81; working class creativity and, 80–83
Novaro, María. *See Danzón* (film)
Nuñez, Arturo, 76, 128, 142

older dancers: aging, music, and dance, 197; agism, 187; amorous encounters and, 190–96, 196–206; "cultural rescue" of danzón and, 143–45; dance, sexuality and older age, 196–98; dancing aesthetics and, 189–90; newcomers to danzón and age, 127; oldness, understandings, 186–87; portrayal of danzón and age,

185–88. *See also* amorous encounters; dance groups; decency and morality; gossip; marriage and post-marriage; revival of danzón; sexuality and romance; vignettes; widow- and widowerhood; women
Olivares, Leopoldo, 41–42, 156
ophicleide (*figle*), 38, 63, 67, 212n5, 221
Orozco, José Clemente, 119
Orquesta Aragón, 37
Orquesta Danzonera Tres Generaciones, 149–50, 157
Orquesta de Chato Rojas y sus Lobos Marinos, 67–68, 143, 213n9
orquesta típica, 37–38, 41, 221
Orquesta Universitaria de Pepe Luis, 129
Orquesta Villa del Mar, 67
Orwell, George, 9, 88
ostracism. *See* blanking

Pacheco, Gerardo, 132, 141
Pacheco, Severiano, 69
pachuco, 17, 61, 110, 212n3, 221
Page, Tiffany, 25
Parque Zamora, Veracruz, 4–5, 6, 94–95, 101, 135
paso doble, 92, 112, 129
Pasteur, Louis, 154
patios de vecindad in Veracruz, 63–64; Patio San Carlos, 71
patriarchy, 130, 134, 202–4
Paz, Octavio, 173
Pazos, Luis, 64
Pazos Sosa, Fernando, 74
Pedwell, Carolyn, 10
PEMEX (*Petróleos Mexicanos*), 70, 78
Peña Nieto, Enrique, 59
percussion in danzón performance. *See cinquillo* rhythms; *clave* instrument; *clave* rhythms; congas; cowbell; *güiro*; racialization processes; *son Cubano*; timbales
Pérez, Estela, 129
Pérez, Pachito, 76
Pérez, René, 129
Pérez de León, José "El Popocha," 81
Pérez Montfort, Ricardo, 64
Pérez Prado, Dámaso, 42, 219, 221
Pérez Torres, Amador "Dimas," 36–37, 156
Pineda Burgos, Natalia, 35, 44, 71, 81
Plato, 12

Plaza de Armas. *See Zócalo*
Plazuela de la Campana, 1, 94–95, 174
political democracy and ambivalence, 15
Ponce Reyes, Tomás, 63
Poo Ulibarri, Gerardo, 136
post-cosmopolitanism, 75
PRD (*Partido de la Revolución Democrática*), 79
Premio Estatal a la Preservación de las Tradiciones Veracruzanas, 149
Prespa Albanians, 180, 197
PRI (*Partido Revolucionario Institucional*), 22
Prieto, Iglesias, 202
Proal, Herón, 65
Pro-Rescate y Difusión de Danzón Clásico, 136, 145
Pulque para Dos, 156

Quinta Corona (dance hall), 128

racial ambivalence, 15, 16, 29–56, 187. *See also* racialization processes and racism
racialization processes and racism: alienation, ambivalence and, 15–16, 50–51; ambivalence and, 15, 16, 29–56, 187; class and, 16, 45, 48–51, 55; colonialism and, 46, 52, 211n10; danzón, Mexican nation and, 52–56; danzón, Veracruz and, 20, 29, 33–35, 42–45; danzón music performance in Veracruz, Mexico City, Cuba and blackness, 35–42; elegance, racism and, 118; expedient blackness, racism and, 45–51; migratory flows, danzón and, 30–32; music, racialization of, 30–33; national belonging and, 29, 50–51; popular histories of danzón and, 30–33, 55; racism 29, 45–47, 50–51, 54–56, 187; temperament and, 45; tropicalization and, 48; Veracruz and, 45–48, 54–56, vignettes and, 24, 27. *See also* class; decency and morality; sexuality and romance
Ramos, Jacinto "Chinto," 67
Ranger, Terence, 137–38, 151
recordings of danzón, circulation of, 63, 74; danzoneras and, 76; danzón groups and, 150; dislike of dancing danzón to, 6, 80, 135; modernist aesthetic and, 115, 122; revival, relationship of music to dance and, 155–57

Index 255

Recreo Veracruzano, 63
reflective nostalgia (Boym): ambivalence and, 60, 61, 85–86; in revival of danzón, 158–59
Regata Club, Veracruz, 64–65
reggae, 45
reggaeton, 33, 186
Renté, Emilio, 156
repertoire: charanga repertoire, 36, 219; danzón repertoire, 101, 113, 130, 156–57
Rergis Aguiler, Daniel "El Catrín," 60; *Danzón* (film) and , 79, 146, 202; history of, 70–73, 77–79, 84–85
restorative nostalgia (Boym) and ambivalence, 60–62
revival of danzón, 17–18, 125–59; competition, 134, 149; creativity and, 112–15; cultural institutions, decentralization of, 126; empire builders, 147–51; fascist cultural ideology and revival movements, 121; festivals, tourism and, 139–43; "invented tradition" and, 137–39; movement aesthetic, discipline in, 126–27; music and musicians in revival, 155–57; music revivals, Hill and Bithell on, 126–27; new generations and age, 127, 188–90; non-heritage revival, 127–28; older dancers and, 127, 143–45; "reflective nostalgia" and revival, 158–59; rivalry and rescue in, 134–39; standardization, attempts at consensus and, 151–55; state involvement in, 139–43, 145–47; tourism, promotion of and, 144–45. *See also* authenticity narratives; competition; dance groups; *danzón académico*; *danzón lírico*; *Hoy y Siempre*; IVEC; modernist aesthetics; older dancers; *Tres Generaciones del Danzón*; women
Rincón Brujo, 74
River, Antonio, 135
Rivera, Diego, 119
Rivera Ávila, Francisco "Paco Píldora," 82, 134–35
rock and roll, 128, 186
Rodríguez Prampolini, Ida, 75, 83, 140
Rojas, Chato, 67
Rojo, María, 78–79, 148, 201–2
Romeu, Antonio María, 156
rondo form of danzones, 5, 24, 104, 133, 156. See also *descansos*
Rosa Abdala Gómez Prize, 148–49

Ruiz Rodríguez, Carlos, 152, 216n1
rumba, 32, 221

Saint Domingue, 30, 31
Salamanca, Guillermo "Memo," 128
Salazar, Fredy, 148, 214n1, 215n4
Salinas de Gortari, Carlos, 78, 79
Salón Atzin (Mexico City dance hall), 129
Salón Bahia (dance venue), 74
Salón Colonia (Mexico City dance hall), 76, 130, 132
Salón Copacabana (Mexico City dance hall), 135
Salón Los Ángeles (Mexico City dance hall), 76, 129, 130, 146
Salón México (film), 125, 146
Salón México (Mexico City dance hall), 128, 130
Salón Riviera (Mexico City dance hall), 130
Salón Zaragoza (dance venue), 74
salsa, 62, 221–22; salsa dancing, 75, 129, 148, 191; salsa music, 57–58, 101, 169
samba, 33, 75
Sánchez de Fuentes, Eduardo, 32
Sánchez García, Víctor Manuel, 73–74
Sánchez Marín, Víctor Manuel "Manolo," 60, 73–74, 76, 79–80
Sánchez Rivera, Arturo "El Capullo," 129, 137, 215n4-11
San Juan de Ulúa, 100, 133
Santos-Granero, Fernando, 18, 175, 178
Savigliano, Marta, 24, 33, 48, 103, 197
scores: history of danzón and, 63; leading danzoneras and, 80, 143, 157
Scott, Pedro, 215n4, 216n11
Scruggs, T. M., 155, 156, 157
SEC (*Secretaría de Educación y Cultura*), 140
Sedgwick, Eve Kosofsky, 10
Sennett, Richard, 81–82
SEP (*Secretaría de Educación Pública*), 140
SERPOVER (*Sociedad Mercantil de Servicios Portuarios de Veracruz*), 77, 78
Sevilla, Ninón, 125
sexuality and romance: age, freedom of choice and, 200–201; aging, gender and, 7, 18–19, 186, 190–206; aging, music and dance, analysis of, 197; ambivalences and, 10–11, 12, 13–14, 15; *cachonderia* and, 198–99; Catholicism and, 7, 192, 195; cross-dressing and, 85; dance

groups and, 190–94; dancing, age and, 190; dancing and, 107–8, 118; danzón spaces and, 5, 130, 145, 186, 196–204; decency and, 7, 134; extramarital relationships and, 7, 97, 190–96; flirting and, 67, 101, 104, 108–9, 197; honor, shame and, 179; LGBTQ+, 20–21, 196; marriage, 191; menopause, 7, 198; men's potency and the "Fallen Cocks Club" and, 199, 206; morality, gender, age and, 19, 86, 180, 194; older people and, 7, 9, 190–206; racialization of in Veracruz, 45, 48–49, 56, 109, 190; racialization of, 11, 118; temperament and, 45; Viagra, 7, 200; vignettes engaging with, 1, 24, 89, 123, 183. *See also* amorous encounters; decency and morality; gender; LGBTQ+; marriage and post-marriage; vignettes
sex work, 92, 131, 133, 151, 202
Sharp, Cecil, 121
Sindicato de Empleados de Comercio, 74
Siqueiros, David Alfaro, 119
Smyrna Club, 131
Solo Veracruz es Bello (film), 21–22
Son Cuba de Marianao, 70
son cubano, 21, 33, 39, 41–42
son jarocho, 33, 120, 122, 152, 204
Spivak, Gayatri Chakravorty, 48
SRE (*Secretaria de Relaciones Exteriores*), 135
standardization: attempts at consensus in, 151–55; production of, 193–94
state sponsorship: of danzón, 94–95, 139–43; rise of danzón groups and, 145–47
Stepputat, Kendra, 155
Sternhell, Zeev, 121
Sue, Christina, 43, 46–47
Sueños de Oro, 65
Sugarman, Jane, 179–80, 197
swing (music/dance), 37, 67, 112, 128, 129

Taboada, Civeira, 34
Tagg, Philip, 31
Tampico Affair, 64
TAMSA (*Tubos de Acero de México*), 6, 74, 81, 100
tango (Argentinian), 9, 33, 48, 131, 197; competitions, 130; heritage status of, 152; tango steps and danzón, 92, 112, 114, 129
tango rhythm, 30, 220, 222
Tapia, Enrique, 129

Tapia, Pablo, 157
Taruskin, Richard, 116, 122
Teléfono a Larga Distancia, 132, 156
tensions within danzón spheres, 21, 24, 89, 161, 177; *unidos en un nido de víboras* (united in a vipers' nest), 6, 196. *See also* gossip; vignettes
timbales: Danzonera Alma de Veracruz, Alma de Sotavento and, 76, 101; danzón performance, in, 37–42, 101–2; history of danzoneras in Veracruz and, 63, 67, 71, 74, 132; setting up a danzonera and, 157; *tarolas* and, 209n3, 222
timpani. See *timbales*
Toña La Negra, 45, 70, 100
tourism: carnival and, 69, 75–76, 87; Daniel Rergis and, 79; danzón and, 5, 18, 35, 126, 143–45, 153; danzón dancers and, 3, 95, 97, 103, 170; expediency of culture and, 139, 143; history of tourism in Veracruz, 48, 66, 75, 80, 92, 142; municipal provision of danzón events and, 94, 126, 142–43, 158; nostalgia, Veracruz and, 85, 86
Trejo, Ángel, 133, 135, 142, 190
Tres Generaciones del Danzón Veracruzano (dance group), age and, 187, 189–90; dance aesthetics and, 118, 141–42, 145–47, 189–90, 204; danzón revival and, 126, 145–51, 152–53, 154; group dynamics and, 167, 171; transmission and, 168
tresillo, 30, 222
tropicalization, 48
tuning: lack of tuning up of danzonera instruments, 58, 184; timbales and, 40
Turino, Thomas, 112, 115–16, 120, 169, 173

Ulloa, Bertha, 64–65
Ulloa Anasco, Francisco, 33
UNESCO intangible cultural heritage recognition, 152
unidos en un nido de víboras (united in a vipers' nest), 6, 196. *See also* gossip; tensions within danzón spheres; vignettes
unions (workers'): AUVER (Astilleros Unidos de Veracruz), 76–77, 78; carnival and, 69, 71, 77, 85; clientelism and, 77; Confederación de Trabajadores Mexicanos, 66; Confederación General de Trabajadores, 66; Confederación Regional Obrera Mexicana, 65–66; Fed-

eración Local de Trabajadores del Puerto de Veracruz, 66; history of in Veracruz, 65–66, 80; *Liga de Trabajadores de la Zona Marítima*, 66; nostalgia and, 17, 83; political power and, 77, 80; requisition port of Veracruz, containerization and, 78–79, 86; Unión de Estibadores, 66; unionization, 62

Universidad Veracruzana, 155

Urbán, Felipe, 76

Uruchurtu, Ernesto, 129

Valdés, Abelardo, 156

Valencia, Sayak, 88

Valenzuela Arce, José Manuel, 22

Valiente Robert, Consejo "Acerina," 39, 42, 63

Varela, Gonzalo, 155

Vasconcelos, José, 119

Vázquez, Camerino, 71, 142

Vázquez, Miguel Ángel, 148, 214n1

Velasco, Abraham, 65

Velázquez, Pedro "El Abuelo," 137

Veracruz, 7–8, 9–11, 13, 16–23; Afro-Caribbean heritage of, 42–56, 101, 140–42; ambivalence, danzón and, 7–8, 16, 83–86; bellicose violence in, 21–23, 83–84, 88, 208, 210n10; carnival 68–69, 75–76, 83–86; "cosmopolitan air" of, 62–63, 74–75; cross-dressing, nostalgia, and, 84–85; danzón, *Alma de Veracruz*, economic boom and, 73–78; danzón champions in, 132–34; dockers and danzón in, 69–73; economic bust and danzón boom in, 64–70, 78–80; gendered representations of, 59; modernization of the port and danzón in, 62–70; national imaginaries of, 59–60; nostalgia, economic boom, and, 74; *Operation Veracruz Seguro*, 23; *portales*, Veracruz, 74, 91–92, 100; post-cosmopolitanism of, 75; *Que bello es Veracruz* ("how beautiful is Veracruz"), 84; racialization processes in, 45–56; Teatro Reforma in, 150–51; timbaleros in, 38–41; tourism and danzón, 5, 48, 66, 143–45; working class creativity in, 80–83. *See also* carnival; circum-Caribbean; class; dance groups; danzón; danzón festivals; decency and morality; gender; gossip; nostalgia; *patios de vecindad*; racialization processes;

revival of danzón; *son jarocho*; *timbales*; unions; women

Veracruz (song), 59

Veracruz Siempre Mexicana, 64

vignettes: dance groups, 24, 123, 161, 207; danzonera musicians, 24, 57; ethnographic challenges, 6, 21, 24, 161–62, 177; experimental writing and ethnography, 24–25; older dancers, 24–25, 207–8; racism, 24, 27; sexuality and romance, 1, 24, 89, 123, 183; tensions within danzón spheres, 89, 161. *See also* writing experimental ethnography

Villa, Francisco "Pancho," 64

Villa del Mar (dance hall), 100, 144; nostalgia and, 66–69, 70, 74, 76, 80–81

Vuelta y Flores, José "Joseíto Vueltiflor," 63

Wade, Peter, 11, 46, 51, 68, 196

Wallace, William, 12–13

waltz, 31, 92, 112, 128, 213n12

Wentzell, Emily, 196–97

whiteness, modernist aesthetic and, 117–18

widow- and widowerhood: pension and, 5, 6; post-marriage dancers, and, 7, 19, 97, 111, 143, 191; sexuality and, 14, 108, 200–206. *See also* amorous encounters; marriage and post-marriage; sexuality and romance; women

Wilson, Woodrow, 64

women: aging and, 6, 19, 187; alcohol consumption and, 165–66; bellicose violence and, 22–23; class and, 67, 68, 82–83, 128; clothing, danzón and, 109–12, 114; dancing danzón and, 102–8, 114–15, 128–29, 133–34, 202–3; danzón champions, as, 129, 131, 214–15n4; domestic violence and, 25, 201, 203–4; feminism, 9, 202–3, 205; flirtatiousness, and, 108–9, 197; group leaders, as, 103, 147; groups and, 6, 112, 180; history of danzón and, 86; leading the dance, 107; livelihood of, 6, 64, 202–3; marriage status and, 6–7, 19; menopause, 7, 198; musicians, 6, 73, 82; naming of danzones and, 216n14; older people's spaces, danzón and, 145; outnumbering men at danzón events, 6, 203; participation in danzón, 7; public spaces and, 97, 111; racialized, sexualized stereotypes of, 49, 53, 55–56; tourists in Veracruz and danzón, 142; trans women,

85, 92, 202, 217n2; Veracruz and, 59, 60, 81–82; Veracruz personalities and, 82. *See also* amorous encounters; class; decency and morality; elegance; gossip; LGBTQ+; marriage and post-marriage; patriarchy; racialization processes; sexuality and romance; widow- and widowerhood

writing, experimental ethnography and, 24–25; ethics of, 25. *See also* vignettes

XEU (radio station, Veracruz), 73–74, 80, 142
XEW (radio station, Mexico City), 74

Yanesha communities, 175, 178
Yesterday, 157
youth cultures, danzón and, 186

Zamudio Abdala, Miguel: danzón and tourism in Veracruz, 158; danzón empire, and, 5, 126, 148–54, 215n4; danzón music ensembles formed by, 157; danzón transmission and, 168; local dancers and, 167, 193; *Tres Generaciones*, age and dance aesthetics, 189–90
Zapata, Emiliano, 64
Zedillo Ponce de León, Ernesto, 79
Zócalo (Veracruz), 34, 67, 165, 176–79, 193; chairs, positioning and colors of, 91; danzón dance styles and, 91–92, 94–96, 97–108; *Noche de Danzón* in, 136; *portales*, Veracruz, 74, 91–92, 100; Saturday, danzón event in, 97–108
Zolov, Eric, 128, 186

HETTIE MALCOMSON is an associate professor of ethnomusicology and social anthropology at the University of Southampton.

Music in American Life

William Sidney Mount and the Creolization of American Culture
   Christopher J. Smith
Bird: The Life and Music of Charlie Parker   Chuck Haddix
Making the March King: John Philip Sousa's Washington Years, 1854–1893
   Patrick Warfield
In It for the Long Run   Jim Rooney
Pioneers of the Blues Revival   Steve Cushing
Roots of the Revival: American and British Folk Music in the 1950s
   Ronald D. Cohen and Rachel Clare Donaldson
Blues All Day Long: The Jimmy Rogers Story   Wayne Everett Goins
Yankee Twang: Country and Western Music in New England   Clifford R. Murphy
The Music of the Stanley Brothers   Gary B. Reid
Hawaiian Music in Motion: Mariners, Missionaries, and Minstrels
   James Revell Carr
Sounds of the New Deal: The Federal Music Project in the West   Peter Gough
The Mormon Tabernacle Choir: A Biography   Michael Hicks
The Man That Got Away: The Life and Songs of Harold Arlen   Walter Rimler
A City Called Heaven: Chicago and the Birth of Gospel Music
   Robert M. Marovich
Blues Unlimited: Essential Interviews from the Original Blues Magazine
   Edited by Bill Greensmith, Mike Rowe, and Mark Camarigg
Hoedowns, Reels, and Frolics: Roots and Branches of Southern Appalachian
   Dance   Phil Jamison
Fannie Bloomfield-Zeisler: The Life and Times of a Piano Virtuoso
   Beth Abelson Macleod
Cybersonic Arts: Adventures in American New Music   Gordon Mumma,
   edited with commentary by Michelle Fillion
The Magic of Beverly Sills   Nancy Guy
Waiting for Buddy Guy   Alan Harper
Harry T. Burleigh: From the Spiritual to the Harlem Renaissance   Jean E. Snyder
Music in the Age of Anxiety: American Music in the Fifties   James Wierzbicki
Jazzing: New York City's Unseen Scene   Thomas H. Greenland
A Cole Porter Companion   Edited by Don M. Randel, Matthew Shaftel,
   and Susan Forscher Weiss
Foggy Mountain Troubadour: The Life and Music of Curly Seckler
   Penny Parsons
Blue Rhythm Fantasy: Big Band Jazz Arranging in the Swing Era   John Wriggle
Bill Clifton: America's Bluegrass Ambassador to the World   Bill C. Malone
Chinatown Opera Theater in North America   Nancy Yunhwa Rao
The Elocutionists: Women, Music, and the Spoken Word   Marian Wilson Kimber
May Irwin: Singing, Shouting, and the Shadow of Minstrelsy   Sharon Ammen

Peggy Seeger: A Life of Music, Love, and Politics   *Jean R. Freedman*
Charles Ives's *Concord*: Essays after a Sonata   *Kyle Gann*
Don't Give Your Heart to a Rambler: My Life with Jimmy Martin, the King
    of Bluegrass   *Barbara Martin Stephens*
Libby Larsen: Composing an American Life   *Denise Von Glahn*
George Szell's Reign: Behind the Scenes with the Cleveland Orchestra
    Marcia Hansen Kraus
Just One of the Boys: Female-to-Male Cross-Dressing on the American
    Variety Stage   *Gillian M. Rodger*
Spirituals and the Birth of a Black Entertainment Industry   *Sandra Jean Graham*
Right to the Juke Joint: A Personal History of American Music   *Patrick B. Mullen*
Bluegrass Generation: A Memoir   *Neil V. Rosenberg*
Pioneers of the Blues Revival, Expanded Second Edition   *Steve Cushing*
Banjo Roots and Branches   *Edited by Robert Winans*
Bill Monroe: The Life and Music of the Blue Grass Man   *Tom Ewing*
Dixie Dewdrop: The Uncle Dave Macon Story   *Michael D. Doubler*
Los Romeros: Royal Family of the Spanish Guitar   *Walter Aaron Clark*
Transforming Women's Education: Liberal Arts and Music in
    Female Seminaries   *Jewel A. Smith*
Rethinking American Music   *Edited by Tara Browner and Thomas L. Riis*
Leonard Bernstein and the Language of Jazz   *Katherine Baber*
Dancing Revolution: Bodies, Space, and Sound in American Cultural History
    Christopher J. Smith
Peggy Glanville-Hicks: Composer and Critic   *Suzanne Robinson*
Mormons, Musical Theater, and Belonging in America   *Jake Johnson*
Blues Legacy: Tradition and Innovation in Chicago   *David Whiteis*
Blues Before Sunrise 2: Interviews from the Chicago Scene   *Steve Cushing*
The Cashaway Psalmody: Transatlantic Religion and Music in Colonial Carolina
    Stephen A. Marini
Earl Scruggs and Foggy Mountain Breakdown: The Making of an
    American Classic   *Thomas Goldsmith*
A Guru's Journey: Pandit Chitresh Das and Indian Classical Dance in Diaspora
    Sarah Morelli
Unsettled Scores: Politics, Hollywood, and the Film Music of Aaron Copland
    and Hanns Eisler   *Sally Bick*
Hillbilly Maidens, Okies, and Cowgirls: Women's Country Music, 1930–1960
    Stephanie Vander Wel
Always the Queen: The Denise LaSalle Story   *Denise LaSalle with David Whiteis*
Artful Noise: Percussion Literature in the Twentieth Century   *Thomas Siwe*
The Heart of a Woman: The Life and Music of Florence B. Price
    Rae Linda Brown, edited by Guthrie P. Ramsey Jr.
When Sunday Comes: Gospel Music in the Soul and Hip-Hop Eras
    Claudrena N. Harold

The Lady Swings: Memoirs of a Jazz Drummer   *Dottie Dodgion and Wayne Enstice*
Industrial Strength Bluegrass: Southwestern Ohio's Musical Legacy   *Edited by Fred Bartenstein and Curtis W. Ellison*
Soul on Soul: The Life and Music of Mary Lou Williams   *Tammy L. Kernodle*
Unbinding Gentility: Women Making Music in the Nineteenth-Century South   *Candace Bailey*
Punks in Peoria: Making a Scene in the American Heartland   *Jonathan Wright and Dawson Barrett*
Homer Rodeheaver and the Rise of the Gospel Music Industry   *Kevin Mungons and Douglas Yeo*
Americanaland: Where Country & Western Met Rock 'n' Roll   *John Milward, with Portraits by Margie Greve*
Listening to Bob Dylan   *Larry Starr*
Lying in the Middle: Musical Theater and Belief at the Heart of America   *Jake Johnson*
The Sounds of Place: Music and the American Cultural Landscape   *Denise Von Glahn*
Peace Be Still: How James Cleveland and the Angelic Choir Created a Gospel Classic   *Robert M. Marovich*
Politics as Sound: The Washington, DC, Hardcore Scene, 1978–1983   *Shayna L. Maskell*
Tania León's Stride: A Polyrhythmic Life   *Alejandro L. Madrid*
Elliott Carter Speaks: Unpublished Lectures   *Edited by Laura Emmery*
Interviews with American Composers: Barney Childs in Conversation   *Edited by Virginia Anderson*
Queer Country   *Shana Goldin-Perschbacher*
On the Bus with Bill Monroe: My Five-Year Ride with the Father of Blue Grass   *Mark Hembree*
Mandolin Man: The Bluegrass Life of Roland White   *Bob Black*
Music and Mystique in Muscle Shoals   *Christopher M. Reali*
Buddy Emmons: Steel Guitar Icon   *Steve Fishell*
Music in Black American Life, 1600–1945: A University of Illinois Press Anthology   *Compiled by Laurie Matheson*
Music in Black American Life, 1945–2020: A University of Illinois Press Anthology   *Compiled by Laurie Matheson*
Ballad Hunting with Max Hunter: Stories of an Ozark Folksong Collector   *Sarah Jane Nelson*
Play Like a Man: My Life in Poster Children   *Rose Marshack*
Samuel Barber: His Life and Legacy   *Howard Pollack*
Aaron Copland in Latin America: Music and Cultural Politics   *Carol A. Hess*
Stringbean: The Life and Murder of a Country Music Legend   *Taylor Hagood*
Danzón Days: Age, Race, and Romance in Mexico   *Hettie Malcomson*

The University of Illinois Press
is a founding member of the
Association of University Presses.

University of Illinois Press
1325 South Oak Street
Champaign, IL 61820-6903
www.press.uillinois.edu